KNOWLEDGE SOCIETIES

NICO STEHR

SAGE Publications
London • Thousand Oaks • New Delhi

First published 1994

 SAGE Publications Ltd
6 Bonhill Street
London EC2A 4PU

SAGE Publications Inc
2455 Teller Road
Thousand Oaks, California 91320

SAGE Publications India Pvt Ltd
32, M-Block Market
Greater Kailash – I
New Delhi 110 048

British Library Cataloguing in Publication data

A catalogue record for this book is available from the
British Library.

ISBN 0 8039 7891 X 18792189
ISBN 0 8039 7892 8 pbk

Library of Congress catalog card number 94–68279

Typeset by Photoprint, Torquay, Devon
Printed in Great Britain by The Cromwell Press Ltd,
Broughton Gifford, Melksham, Wiltshire

Contents

Acknowledgments

Some formulations used in this volume are idiosyncratic adaptations and extensions of ideas found in an essay first written in collaboration with Gernot Böhme and published as a contribution to our collection, *The Knowledge Society* (1986). I am grateful to Gernot Böhme for his kind permission for me to do so. My debt for the generous support of the University of Alberta, and the excellent working conditions I enjoyed at the university while working on this study, is considerable. I am also grateful to the Rockefeller Foundation for an intellectually challenging stay at the Rockefeller Study Center in Bellagio, Italy. Central parts of this study were completed while in residence at the Center. Work on this project was facilitated by research funds from the Social Sciences and Humanities Research Council, Ottawa, Canada.

I am grateful for critical and encouraging comments on different chapters and aspects of this study by Zygmunt Bauman, Paul Bernard, David Bloor, Gernot Böhme, S.N. Eisenstadt, Richard V. Ericson, Eliot Freidson, Karol J. Krotki, Donald N. Levine, Robert K. Merton, Raymond Morrow and Hermann Strasser. It is perhaps needless to mention that they do not necessarily always agree with the thrust of my formulations and the underlying interpretations of contemporary social reality. I am grateful to Dennis Bray and Guy C. Germain for the search and acquisition of materials often very difficult to locate and assemble.

Preface

There should be a new agenda for social science today because the age of labor and property is at an end. None the less, modern society is still widely conceived in terms of property and labor. Labor and property have an extended and close association in social, political and economic theory and reality. In practice, individuals are forced to define their identities on the basis of their relation to these factors. However, as labor and property (capital) gradually give way to a new constitutive factor, namely knowledge, older struggles and contests, centered for instance on ownership of the means of production, also make room for rising sentiments of disaffection with beliefs and values once firmly associated with labor and property and ultimately result in very different moral, political and economic debates and conflicts. These realities require, I believe, a fresh examination of the agenda of social theory designed to shed light on modern society.

This book is written in response to the fundamental observation that contemporary science is not merely, as was once widely thought, the key and solution to the mysteries and miseries of the world, but is the becoming of a world. Science has converted an apocalyptic nightmare into a concrete possibility: the destruction of mankind through war or environmental disaster is quite real. Yet scientists are the dominant, though not unchallenged, cognitive authorities on these and other nightmares. Our world is increasingly produced by science and our understanding of these transformations increasingly relies on ideas generated in science.

Evidently, science and technology are remaking our basic social institutions, for example, in such areas as work, education, physical reproduction, culture, the economy, and the political system. The hope that scientific knowledge will open up many, if not all, secrets of nature and the heavens and that such insights will prove to be instrumental in building a better world, based on nature's design but for the benefit of mankind, is a dream long associated with the legitimation of scientific activity. In this sense, therefore, the idea that science represents the becoming of a world could in fact mean that much of the dream is about to be realized. Depending on what one may have in mind, this may be true, but the dream may not come true in quite the exceptional manner envisioned. Paradoxically, therefore, as general belief in the benefits of science weakens, and weakens not least because of scientific reflections on science,[1] the impact of scientific knowledge on the life-world continues to increase.

But this does not mean that there are no limits to the power of scientific knowledge. Despite the hopes or fears widely expressed during the past century that scientific knowledge would soon eliminate traditional 'knowledge' and beliefs, the evident persistence and function of non-scientific forms of knowledge in modern society at least suggest certain limits to the cognitive authority of science. Thus, any analysis of the social basis and impact of science has also to examine its evident limits.[2] Nevertheless, in most instances, the 'solutions' to the risks and disjunctures generated by science and the implementation of scientific knowledge, for example, in the form of technological artifacts, despite the increasingly pervasive skepticism about the social and cultural benefits of science and technology, require answers and solutions which must emanate from science and technology. Most strategic social, political and economic action cannot really afford to bypass science. In the public discourse of advanced societies, scientific knowledge has almost a monopoly as a source of legitimation. This monopoly is not fundamentally undermined, presently, by cognitive dissensus in science and among scientists as experts.

Contrary to the very image science and technology still has, at least until very recently, among many social scientists and scientists, the transformations brought about by the 'scientification' of human life are not always clear cut and linear, or viewed as largely beneficial and as the outcome of preconceived plans. Nor are they, to highlight the other extreme, mainly repressive outcomes, that is, instruments which enhance the domination of those who always dominated in society. Paradoxically perhaps, although impulses and the nature of relevant outcomes of change may be traced to, and are often generated in, science, the patterns of change and the structures produced are less and less subject to rational planning, predetermination or concentrated control. Knowledge actually undermines order. Power is not always enhanced by knowledge. On the contrary, power is often rendered obsolete by knowledge. Knowledge may empower the powerless by upsetting existing balances of power. I would

---

[1] The critique of first technology and later science by philosophers, theologians, intellectuals and scientists has, however, a considerable and, as some would see it, an honorable tradition, at least in some societies. In Germany, for example, skepticism about the material fruits of science were voiced widely among intellectuals during one of the first economic depressions of the modern era (1873–1896). Considerable misgivings about the moral and cultural impact of science, however, are raised in the process (cf. Köhnke, 1986; Dahme, 1988). A history of the utopian designs involving technological developments and the critique which almost invariably accompanied such blueprints over the centuries can be found in Sibley (1973).

[2] There is also a related terminological problem because the term 'knowledge', at least its usage in the English language, often resonates closely with the meaning of 'truth' (cf. Boulding, 1966:1). The closeness exists for good reasons. In the course of evolution of the legitimation of modern science such a link proved useful as a cultural device justifying the claims of scientific knowledge to be both different from other forms of 'knowing' and particularly efficacious in practice.

argue that at present and even more so in the future, fortuitous circumstances and events take on greater importance both in reality and in
theoretical accounts of shifting fluctuations around broader secular trends,
and this despite the 'growing' knowledge about nature and society. And
since knowledge is never absolute, fragility and ambivalence remain
endemic to social life. Whether these in fact increase with increasing
knowledge is one of the puzzles of modern society, and this is what I plan
to address in this study.

In addition to the central theme of this study, namely the need for a
theory of society that resonates with the new social realities, there are a
number of additional important issues and approaches that I would like to
mention at least briefly at this point. As my comment on the limits of the
power of scientific knowledge has already indicated, this study seeks to
complicate matters which have often been rendered increasingly simple in
the history of sociological thought. Discourse on science, technology,
culture and society still tends to be dominated by reflections among the
overcommitted. For example, proponents and opponents of modern
science alike agree that scientific knowledge transcends traditional knowledge and, in modern society, will take its place. Social scientists favor this
assertion, despite the growing strength and acceptance of the philosophical
thesis that common-sense concepts about things, persons, agency or
intention may have an immovable character. However, I agree with the
methodological and theoretical strategy for science which Clifford Geertz
(1973:33) succinctly states: 'Scientific advancement commonly consists in a
progressive complication of what once seemed a beautifully simple set of
notions but now seems an unbearably simplistic one.' Consensus in the
social sciences is usually based on traditional conjecture and at times even
thoughtless repetition of particular knowledge claims.

In addition, our knowledge about knowledge remains unsophisticated
and incomprehensive despite, and for a time, because of the efforts of the
sociology of knowledge. Scientific discourse developed a kind of natural
attitude toward its own knowledge. And for this reason, but not merely for
this reason, the number of well-explicated categories of knowledge has
been fairly limited in sociology. We really have not moved much beyond
the proposals about different forms of knowledge found in Max Scheler's
early contributions to the sociology of knowledge. Often knowledge is
treated as a black box. Thus, it seems to be important to explicate a
sociological concept of knowledge and its role in modern social relations.

Furthermore, there are a number of important reasons for closely
addressing the nature of the changing economic structure in modern
society. The development of knowledge societies is connected to basic
transformations in the structure of economic activities. Paradoxically
perhaps, the self-transformation of the economy diminishes, though does
not eliminate, the importance of the economy. My interest in the changing
economic structure of modern societies is not based on a functionalist
perspective which primarily exhibits an interest in the social and political

effects of a diminishing marginal utility of economic determinism in advanced industrial society (cf. Inglehart, 1987:1289). On the contrary, my concern is also with the conditions that give rise to and constitute the motor of change in modern economic activities. As far as some of the consequences are concerned and from the point of view of the individual, for example, central life interests drift away from purely economic ones, or from the perspective of social conflicts, a shift toward generalized struggles can be expected to dominate political agendas in knowledge societies. The conditions which allow for such displacements are last but not least economic transformations. However, it cannot suffice to merely state that in highly developed societies scarcity, for instance, has declined significantly in comparison.[3]

The volume and nature of work, as well as its social organization, are transformed in knowledge societies. I will discuss these changes in the context of the changing economic structure, but I will also try to outline the theoretical significance and practical importance of the growing stratum of experts, counselors and advisers, or of knowledge-based occupations in contemporary society. The basic claim will be that this stratum of occupations is the fastest growing segment of the labor force in modern society. Interest will center on the peculiar place of experts in knowledge societies, the reasons for the demand for expert knowledge, the nature of expertise, the unusual attributes of knowledge-bearing occupations and, generally, the culture and power of knowledge in contemporary society as it is mediated and represented by knowledge-based occupations. Thus, despite evidence of considerable disenchantment with the merits of expertise, even fear about a 'tyranny of the experts' and the loss of citizenship in modern societies, everyone must (still) defer and, under some circumstances, is forced to defer to the authority of experts today, not only in matters of grave and far-reaching consequence, but also in many of the most mundane routines of everyday life. For example, we all express our doubts about the validity of weather forecasts, yet the planning of daily activities and routines are to a considerable extent affected by such forecasts. Although there is, on the surface at least, nothing novel about the influence of experts, the role of knowledge and the occupations which mediate access to knowledge take on rather different qualities in advanced societies than heretofore, even in what are known as industrial societies.

---

[3] One of the most impressive contemporary sociological theories that is firmly anchored in an elaboration of classic sociological discourse is Jürgen Habermas' theory of communicative action. In his theory, Habermas removes the conventional notions of labor and economic production from the center of theoretical concern and therefore relativizes their role as the motor of societal change. The vacated center is filled by the antagonisms and contradictions between the life-world and the societal subsystems of rational conduct (the state and the economy). But it is not my intention in this study to engage Habermas' theory in any detail by, for example, discussing the differentiation between labor and interaction, since his reflections are strongly linked to what is a scientific conception of scientific knowledge; cf. Habermas' (1982:274–278) self-critical remarks on this issue.

In terms of space/time co-ordinates, my inquiry primarily attempts to address the realities of societies with so-called 'high-income economies'[4] from the year 1960 to the present and of course the foreseeable future, as far as this is possible. The justification for starting my inquiry into modern society with the 1960s has a lot to do with the fact that the decade of the 1960s signaled not so much a discrediting of Keynesian demand stimulation policy, as some would argue, but the end to its efficacy and the signaling of an entirely new era in economic life for modern society.

But a note of caution is also in order. This is not a futuristic study. I will try my best to stay close to the ground. Goethe's observation that there is no standpoint within an epoch to view an epoch has a distinct ring of truth to it, and my claim is not that we are either in an age of post-modernity nor that we are in the midst of the epoch of the knowledge society. At most, there are signs and indications that we are moving in important and relevant ways into a form of society which differs markedly from what we have been accustomed to for most of the century.

---

[4] More precisely, my focus for the most part will be on the member countries of the Organization for Economic Cooperation and Development. If one uses the definition of 'high income economies' developed by the World Bank (e.g. 1992), then a number of other countries such as Singapore, Hong Kong and United Arab Emirates are classified as high-income economies. Within the group of OECD countries, my focus will be, especially in the case of providing illustrative comparative empirical macro-economic information on a handful of these countries, the major industrial countries of Canada, the United States, Germany, United Kingdom, Japan, France and Italy. These countries combined represent close to 90 percent of the gross domestic product of the entire OECD. It is important to note that the relative economic weight of OECD countries and regions continues to shift in significant ways. Broadly speaking, between 1960 and 1990, and especially during the decade of the 1960s and 1970s, the gross domestic product of the United States as a percentage of the world's market economies declined significantly, while the share of the market economies of (Western) Europe and Japan increased substantially.

Introduction:
Knowledge and Social Action

> After the catastrophes that have happened, and in view of the catastrophes
> to come, it would be cynical to say that a plan for a better world is
> manifested in history and unites it.
>
> (Theodor W. Adorno, *Negative Dialectics*)

In *Negative Dialectics*, Theodor Adorno's ([1966] 1973) sober diagnosis
and insistent warning that universal history must at once be imagined and
denied, captures well the inherent dilemma of the modern intellectual and
practical encounter with the promise and reality of science and technology.
The wisdom embodied in science cannot be separated any more from its
practical denial, at least in part and in a part which threatens the whole.
The danger is that the promise of science is turned into its opposite by
science.

But despite many insightful, sophisticated and engaged inquiries into the
interrelation of science and society, particularly in the 1920s and early
1930s, and again in the 1960s and early 1970s, a theory of society capturing
the dynamics of science and technology remains to a significant extent
lacking. The fundamental issue of 'the modes of interplay between society,
culture and science are with us still' (Merton, 1973:175). The difficulty, of
course, is to uncover the immediate and mediated impact of the material
and intellectual forces issuing from science and technology, and the social
relations which become and serve as the fabric within which these artifacts
and ideas come to live. Of course, we cannot hope to erase fully the need
for such a theory here; however, we are convinced that a fresh and
comprehensive attempt to formulate and ultimately test such a theory is
required. Generally speaking, such a theory of society is based, as were its
more distant as well as recent predecessors, on the assumption that many
of the major, especially economic, transformations in industrial society are
tied to 'advances' in scientific knowledge and technology. And, further, the
terms 'science' and 'scientific' have to include not only the natural but also
the social sciences and humanities. The term 'science' is always employed
here in its broadest sense, as signified in *Wissenschaft*, for example.

A new effort designed to capture the growing and contradictory societal
consequence of science and technology is made all the more urgent
because contemporary social and economic conditions require a theory of
society attentive to the forceful and epochal impact of science and
technology on the nature of its change. It is also necessary to assign a much

more salient role to science and technology since the very nature of advanced society is fatefully shaped by artifacts and ideas emanating from science. But this means also, to put it into Marxian terminology, that more attention is required toward the development of a theory of the super-structure. However, the divisions between the material and intellectual are not fixed; they diminish in knowledge societies. Increasingly, history is etched into nature (cf. Godelier, 1984).

That the immense impact of science and technology on society has become, and therefore must be analyzed as, one of the defining character-istics of modern society is, so it seems, a widely shared assumption among contemporary social theorists. However, there are notable dissenters. Niklas Luhmann (1981:118), for example, is very much opposed to viewing modern society, in the first instance, as defined and formed by the successes of science and technology and its varied consequences for society. From the point of view of his theory of social systems, modern society is first and foremost defined by its historically unique functional differentiation; all else follows from this fact. In fact, the relative importance of science to modern society warrants, as I would like to argue, the term 'knowledge society' for its now evolving structure and culture.

In order to avoid any misunderstandings from the outset, it is important to stress that the theory of society I would like to develop is not in any direct way related, unlike most of its prominent predecessors, to those theories of society which also emphasize the crucial function of science and technology, based on the premise of the omnipresence of scientific knowledge, or on hopeful promises or more distant utopian expectations that society will surely become a more rational and manageable entity. Further, the theory to be developed here will not stress that scientific knowledge or reasoning will displace most if not all other forms of knowledge. That society will definitely take on, because of the inevitable victory of science, a much more human face and lead to a better, more equitable and just form of life cannot be assumed to be a given. Such hopes are not warranted, though not precluded, but mainly, for the purposes of our considerations, not built into the 'scientification' of social life itself.

For example, in the political realm, the almost pervasive hope as expressed by Lane (1966:657–658) is that

> if one thinks of a domain of 'pure politics' where decisions are determined by calculations of influence, power, or electoral advantage, and a domain of 'pure knowledge' where decisions are determined by calculations of how to implement agreed-upon values with rationality and efficiency, it appears to me that the political domain is shrinking and the knowledge domain is growing, in terms of criteria for deciding, kinds of counsel sought, evidence adduced, and the nature of the 'rationality' employed.

Lane is clearly mistaken, for there is simply no such linear trade-off between the increase in knowledge and the territory of 'irrational' politics. On the contrary, the growth of knowledge does not necessarily go hand in hand with an increase in the inability to plan, control or predict. In short, to perform all those activities well, which generations of social and natural scientists have believed and promised to be an almost inevitable outcome of science, cannot be expected from science. The growth of knowledge may well foster an increase in opposite outcomes, namely, a rising fragility of nature and society. In brief, I agree with the assessment by Jean-Jacques Salomon (1973:60) that, paradoxically perhaps, the 'myths of human "progress" have been killed by the progress of science itself; the "scientistic illusion" regards technology as a substitute for social and political choices.'

Equally, many who express fears that science and technology reduce and impoverish the possibilities of human action (e.g. Arendt, 1958) are, for the most part, underestimating the extent to which the penetration of scientific knowledge allows for the opposite, namely, the extension of the potential and range of social action, including, of course, resistance to the application of scientific knowledge and the introduction of technical artifacts themselves. Further, the profound effect science has on all of social life does not imply that all actors will adopt a scientific outlook on their lives, that the output of science is, directly or indirectly, merely technical in nature,[1] that everyday thinking becomes identical with scientific reasoning, that political rule becomes more centralized and even authoritarian,[2] that there are no systemic limits[3] and serious constraints on the use of scientific knowledge, that the use of scientific knowledge does not fail, that material production (for example, in the sense of the manufacturing sector of the economy) is no longer important,[4] or that there are but a few or even manageable dangers associated with 'scientification'.[5] It implies that science and technology play an increasingly important role in

[1] And that science also barely affects the different functions that subsystems in modern society perform, as Luhmann (1981:117) for example states, is an observation about the nature of contemporary science. Yet, Luhmann also considers functional differentiation as a precondition for the unimpeded growth of science.

[2] Compare, for example, the fears associated with discussions concerning technocratic rule or the alarm expressed by McDermott (1969) during the height of the Vietnam War, and in light of predictions that knowledge will be an increasingly important societal force, that the concentration of practical knowledge about American society in several large organizations can lead to no other result than a substantial decline in the capacity of ordinary Americans to control their society and those organizations.

[3] As Rouse (1987:230), for example, stresses and explicates, 'there may even be systematic constraints that the remaking of the world to resemble laboratory micro worlds may impose upon us.'

[4] The assertion that material production almost disappears or at least no longer constitutes a central activity in society indeed is a pivotal part of prominent perspectives on modern society and is, at the same time, an equally strong point of departure for a vigorous defense of the opposite thesis, namely that a epochal break cannot really be detected in modern society because material production (and its peculiar organization) remains constitutive for contemporary society (e.g. Calhoun, 1993). The result of such jealous possessiveness of perspectives is that observers fail to inquire into the transformation rather than the abolition of material production.

[5] Cf. Charles Perrow's (1984) notion of 'normal accidents' of certain high-risk technological systems as a consequence of the 'tight coupling' and interactive complexity between technical systems and social organization.

most spheres of life and that our dependence on knowledge-based occupations is growing considerably (cf. Böhme, 1988:36). And it implies that the remaining disjuncture, distance, relation or even opposition between scientific knowledge and other forms of knowledge acquires particular importance. Knowledge societies open social action to transformation and constraint by the ideas and artifacts emanating from science and technology and, at the same time, shield and protect it, allowing for the emancipation of action from science and technology and offering means of resistance to the transformation of social action by science.

Paradoxically perhaps, at least if one employs the more conventional view of the consequences of science and technology on society, the dominance of scientific knowledge goes hand in hand with an increasing contingency of social action. Both developments are part of the same process. Knowledge societies, therefore, are far from being identical with the image of the technical state or civilization found in recent, prescriptive theories of the impact of technology and science on society, for example, in the works of Ellul (1954), Mumford (1962, 1970) or Schelsky ([1961] 1965).

1

The Concept of Knowledge Societies

> The difficulty lies, not in the ideas, but in escaping from the old ones, which ramify, for those brought up as most of us have been, into every corner of our minds.

> (J.M. Keynes, *The General Theory of Employment, Interest and Money*)

One of the first authors to employ the term 'knowledgeable society' is Robert E. Lane (1966:650). He justifies the use of this concept by pointing to the growing societal relevance of scientific knowledge and defines a knowledgeable society, in a 'first approximation', as one in which its members

> (a) inquire into the basis of their beliefs about man, nature, and society; (b) are guided (perhaps unconsciously) by objective standards of veridical truth, and, at the upper levels of education, follow scientific rules of evidence and inference in inquiry; (c) devote considerable resources to this inquiry and thus have a large store of knowledge; (d) collect, organize, and interpret their knowledge in a constant effort to extract further meaning from it for the purposes at hand; (e) employ this knowledge to illuminate (and perhaps modify) their values and goals as well as to advance them. Just as the 'democratic' society has a foundation in governmental and interpersonal relations, and the 'affluent society' a foundation in economics, so the knowledgeable society has its roots in epistemology and the logic of inquiry.

In other words, Lane's conception of a knowledgeable society is tied rather closely to the promise of a particular theory of science and reflects, also, the great optimism of the early 1960s which suggested that science would somehow allow for the possibility of a society in which common sense would be replaced by scientific reasoning. That is, as Lane stresses in his definition, members of the knowledgeable society are guided in their conduct, if only subconsciously, by the standards of 'veridical truth'.

In *The Age of Discontinuity*, Peter Drucker (1969) also employs the term knowledge society. The general thesis presented in his book places knowledge 'as central to our society and as the foundation of economy and social action', and is, in this most general sense, close to the idea of a knowledge society as explicated here. Although Drucker's emphasis of knowledge is, in many ways, pioneering, it is not evident, however, whether he attributes to the knowledge principle, in the late 1960s at least, the same centrality for society as does, for example and at about the same time, Daniel Bell. None the less, Drucker goes to considerable and informative lengths to describe some of the novel features and attributes of contemporary knowledge. Bell also employs the term 'knowledge society' in the context of his discussion of the emergence of *post-industrial society*, a designation he prefers. Bell at times uses the concept knowledge society interchangeably with the notion of 'post-industrial society'. For example, he exclaims at one point in his discussion that 'the post-industrial society, it is clear, is a knowledge society' (Bell, 1973a:212). The basic justification for such an equivalence is, of course, that 'knowledge is a fundamental resource' of post-industrial society. As a matter of fact, Bell (1973a:37) indicates that he could have substituted 'knowledge society'[1] for 'post-industrial society' because either term, and others, for example 'intellectual society' (Bell, 1964:49), might be just as apt in describing at least some salient aspects of the emerging structure of society that he proposes to examine in his study of the structure and culture of modern society.

Past theories of society, and I will have occasion to critically expand on some of their constitutive theoretical features, choose to designate, quite properly, those attributes of social relations which are constitutive of the specific nature of that society as identifying labels. Thus, such names as 'capitalist' society or 'industrial' society were created. For the same reasons, I choose to label the now emerging form of society as a 'knowledge' society because the constitutive mechanism or the identity of modern society is increasingly driven by 'knowledge'.

The appearance of 'knowledge societies' does not occur suddenly; it represents not a revolutionary development, but rather a gradual process during which the defining characteristic of society changes and a new one emerges. Even today, the demise of societies is often as slow as is their beginning. Social transformations rarely occur in spectacular leaps. None the less, proximity to significant social, economic and cultural changes seems to assure that what comes into view appears to be particularly significant and exceptional. The disruption of routines displaces orientations but it remains 'difficult to pinpoint the actual crystallization of a new state of affairs so as to identify, both clearly and unequivocally, the emergence of a new society and its new modes of behavior' (Narr, [1979] 1985:32).

Knowledge societies do not come about as the result of a simple uni-modal unfolding and in an unambiguous fashion. Knowledge societies do not turn into some kind of one-dimensional social configurations. Knowledge societies become similar by remaining or even becoming dissimilar. New technological modes of communication and transportation break down the distance between groups and individuals but the isolation between regions, cities and villages remains. The world opens up and creeds, styles and commodities mingle, yet the walls between convictions

---

[1] Bell (1968:198) uses the term in an earlier context and indicates that post-industrial society is clearly 'a knowledge society in a double sense: first, the sources of innovation are increasingly derivative from research and development (and more directly, there is a new relation between science and technology because of the centrality of *theoretical* knowledge); and second, the "weight" of the society – measured by a larger proportion of the Gross National Product and a larger share of employment – is increasingly in the knowledge field.'

of what is sacred do not come tumbling down. The meaning of time and place erodes while boundaries are celebrated.

Modern society was, until recently, conceived primarily in terms of property and labor. Labor and property (capital)[2] have had a long association in social, economic and political theory.[3] Work is seen as property and as a source of emerging property. In the Marxist tradition, capital is objectified, encapsulated labor. On the basis of these attributes, individuals and groups were able or constrained to define their membership in society. In the wake of their declining importance in the productive process, especially in the sense of their conventional economic attributes and manifestations, for example as 'corporeal' property such as land and manual work, the social constructs of labor and property themselves are changing. My focus, therefore, is primarily on the role of labor and property in generating added economic value and is less concerned with exclusivity as the distinguishing attribute of property (Durkheim, [1950] 1957), or with the extent to which only labor may be viewed as a source of value.[4]

While these features of labor and property certainly have not disappeared entirely, a new principle, 'knowledge', has been added which, to an extent, challenges as well as transforms property and labor as the constitutive mechanisms of society.[5] As Rueschemeyer (1986:139–140), for example, underlines and cautions at the same time,

> taken together, the power sharing of the different knowledge-bearing occupations

[2] As Albert Borgmann (1992:61) notes and as every (small) bank customer also knows well, 'Capital is less real than land; it is relatively mobile and, as financial capital, quite intangible. But the latter is always within hailing distance on being properly balanced with material goods.'

[3] Nineteenth-century social theory, for example, paid close attention to property and labor and was convinced that we would enter an era in which property would become obsolescent and in which labor would take on a very different social, political and economic status. My immediate focus, however, is not on the nature of the totality of changes in these social constructs, conceived as independent entities nor on the ways in which labor and property can be used to identify major social formations in modern society. I will be more concerned with the reduced economic and therefore societal relevance of these constructs as forces of production. It is, of course, likely that the social, legal and political conception and the predominant symbolic function of these phenomena will be transformed *in response* to their lesser status in production (cf. also Luhmann's, 1988:151–176 discussion of the cognitive significance and decline of capital and work as salient categories of social theory).

[4] In his examination of the *Economy of Society* (*Die Wirtschaft der Gesellschaft*), Niklas Luhmann (1988:164–166) attributes the decline of the theoretical and practical relevance of capital and labor to their neglect of the demand and consumption side of modern economic activity. Patterns of social inequality of workers (*Lebenslagen*), for example, are much more driven by consumption activities than by wages (see also Chapter 6).

[5] In the course of past waves of economic development and failure, the transformation of nature by man during, for example, the past two centuries of modern societies, has resulted in a predominantly man-made environment. From an economic point of view therefore, it has become almost impossible to distinguish between the rent which may accrue to property due to its natural advantage and the quasi-rent of the same property due to man's transformation.

has probably diluted the concentrations of power based on property, coercion and popular appeal; but that is a far cry from saying that the power of partial interests and the conflicts between them have become irrelevant or even muted.

The types of societies, based on these core principles, reflect, of course, these constitutive mechanisms and their replacement. Bourgeois society was originally a society of owners. Later it became a 'laboring society' (*Arbeitsgesellschaft*), and now is transforming into a knowledge society. The decline of the societal importance of labor and property is associated with rising *sentiments of disaffinity* (Borgmann, 1992:20) toward those beliefs and convictions that center around the once dominant forces of production of industrial society. There is a growing feeling and need among individuals and groups to reinterpret the leading sentiments of the age.

Radovan Richta and his colleagues (1969:276) date the beginning of the profound transformation of modern society, through the scientific and technological revolution, from the 1950s. Daniel Bell (1973a:346) argues, even though he points out that really it is foolhardy to give precise dates to social processes, that the 'symbolic' onset of the post-industrial society can be traced to the period from the end of the Second World War, for it was during this era that a new consciousness about time and social change began to emerge. In contrast, Block and Hirschhorn (1979:368), who ask about the beginning of the emergence of the new productive forces typical of post-industrial society, namely knowledge, science and technology, and in particular the period when they began to make a decisive difference in production, reach the conclusion that the 1920s already saw such a qualitative shift occurring. In the 1920s, at least in the United States, the input of labor, time and capital were constant or had begun to decrease, while output had begun to rise. In economic terms, therefore, knowledge has become the crucial source of (added) value.

The increased social significance of science in *modern* society is the reason for analyzing its knowledge structure. The purpose of such a theoretical focus, therefore is, as Offe (1984:39) has described it in his discussion of the transformation of the 'laboring society', to examine for what reasons 'the sphere of work and production evidently loses its capacity to structure and organize society and in the wake of the "implosion" of its ability to determine social action sets free new patterns of action with new actors and rationalities.'

Of course, knowledge has always had a function in social life; one can justifiably speak of an anthropological constant: human action is knowledge based. Social *groups* and social roles[6] of all types depend on, and are mediated by, knowledge. Relations among *individuals* are based on

---

[6] Florian Znaniecki (1940:23), for example, emphasizes that 'every individual who performs any social role is supposed by his social circle to possess and believes himself to possess the knowledge indispensable for its normal performance.'

knowledge of each other.[7] Similarly, power has frequently been based on advantages in knowledge, not only on physical strength. And, last but not least, societal reproduction is not merely physical reproduction but, in the case of humans, always cultural, i.e. the reproduction of knowledge.

In retrospect, one is able to describe a variety of ancient societies as knowledge societies; for example, ancient Israel, which was a society structured by its religious law-like Tora-knowledge. Ancient Egypt was a society in which religious, astronomical and agrarian knowledge served as the organizing principle and the basis of authority.

Contemporary society may be described as a knowledge society based on the penetration of all its spheres of life by scientific knowledge. Marxist theories of society have always assigned decisive importance to the forces or means of production for societal development since 'man's understanding of nature and his mastery over it by virtue of his presence as a social body . . . appears as the great foundation-stone (*Grundpfeiler*) of production and of wealth', so that general knowledge becomes a direct force of production (Marx, [1939–1941] 1973:705). Contemporary Marxist theories, especially through the notion of the scientific-technological revolution developed by Radovan Richta and others, have analyzed scientific and technical knowledge as the principal motor of change. Max Weber's seminal inquiry into the unique features of Western civilization stresses the pervasive use of reason to secure the methodical efficiency of social action. The source of rational action and, therefore, of rationalization is found in particular intellectual devices. The theory of industrial society, as developed by Raymond Aron ([1966] 1968), which encompasses both socialist and capitalist forms of economic organization, stresses first and foremost the extent to which science and technology shape the social organization of productive activities and, therefore, other forms of life in society. More recent theories of post-industrial society and similar efforts at forecasting the course of social evolution of industrial society, in particular those of Daniel Bell, have elevated theoretical knowledge as the axial principle of society.

The knowledge referred to in these theories, and the groups of individuals which acquire influence and control with it, tends to be conceptualized rather narrowly. Paradoxically perhaps, there is a tendency to overestimate the efficacy of 'objective' technical-scientific or formal knowledge. Theories of modern society lack sufficient detail and scope in their conceptualization of the 'knowledge' supplied, the reasons for the demand of more and more knowledge, the ways in which knowledge travels, the rapidly expanding groups of individuals in society who, in one of many ways, live off knowledge, the many forms of knowledge which are considered as pragmatically useful, and the various effects which knowledge may have on social relations.

---

[7] Compare Georg Simmel's ([1908] 1992:383–455) analysis of 'The secret and the secret society' in his *Soziologie*.

The emergence of knowledge societies signals first and foremost a radical transformation in the *structure of the economy*. Productive processes in *industrial society* are governed by a number of factors, which appear to be on the decline in their significance as conditions for the possibility of a changing, particularly growing economy: the dynamics of the supply and demand for primary products or raw materials; the dependence of employment on production; the importance of the manufacturing sector which processes primary products; the role of labor (in the sense of manual labor) and the social organization of work; the role of international trade in goods and services; the function of time and place in production and of the nature of the limits to economic growth. The most common denominator of the changes in the structure of the economy seems to be a shift from an economy driven and governed, in large measure, by 'material' inputs into the productive process and its organization to an economy in which transformations in productive and distributive processes are determined much more by 'symbolic' or knowledge-based inputs.

The economy of industrial society is, in short, initially and primarily a *material economy* and then changes gradually to a *monetary economy*; for example, Keynes' economic theory, particularly his *General Theory* (1936), reflects this transformation of the economy of industrial society into an economy affected to a considerable extent by monetary matters. But, as more recent evidence indicates, the economy Keynes described now becomes a (non-monetary) *symbolic economy*. The changes in the structure of the economy and its dynamics are increasingly a reflection of the fact that knowledge becomes the leading dimension in the productive process, the primary condition for its expansion and for a change in the limits to economic growth in the developed world. In the knowledge society, most of the wealth of a company is increasingly embodied in its creativity and information. In short, the point is that for the production of goods and services, with the exception of the most standardized commodities and services, factors other than 'the amount of labor time or the amount of physical capital become increasingly central' (Block, 1985:95) to the economy of advanced societies.[8] Central attention of any sociological analysis of modern society, therefore, has to focus on the peculiar nature and function of knowledge in social relations and, of course, on the main carriers of such knowledge.

More concretely, the advance of science into the life-world and economic production may be described in various terms:

- as the penetration of most spheres of social action, including production, by scientific knowledge ('scientization');
- as the displacement, although by no means the elimination, of other forms of knowledge by scientific knowledge, mediated by the growing

[8] See especially Drucker (1986) and Lipsey (1992).

stratum of and dependence on experts, advisers and counselors, and the corresponding institutions based on the deployment of specialized knowledge;

- as the emergence of science as an immediately productive force;
- as the differentiation of new forms of political action (e.g. science and educational policy);
- as the development of a new sector of production (the production of knowledge);
- as the change of power structures (technocracy debate);
- as the emergence of knowledge as the basis for social inequality[9] and social solidarity;
- as the trend to base authority on expertise;[10]
- as the shift in the nature of societal conflict from struggles about the allocation of income and divisions in property relations to claims and conflicts about generalized human needs.[11]

What justifies the designation of the emerging society as a knowledge society rather than, as is at times the case, a science society (e.g. Kreibich, 1986), an information society (e.g. Nora and Minc, 1980), a post-industrial society or a technological civilization? Several reasons are relevant for the

[9] Somewhat more narrowly, the emergence of intellectuals as a new social class has been identified as the characteristic feature of advanced societies in which science and technology assume a powerful role (cf. Gouldner, 1979; Konrád and Szelényi, 1979). Whether this 'class' constitutes a power elite or not depends on more detailed theoretical reflections and is by no means uncontroversial, as remarks by Daniel Bell (1979a:204), addressing this question, for example, indicate, 'such an elite has power within intellectual institutions . . . but only influence in the larger world in which policy is made.' But possible limits to the power of this new class have not discouraged others from sketching the dawning of a new age as a result of the development of 'political knowledge': 'As engagement in the world is encouraging the appearance of a new breed of politicians–intellectuals, men who make it a point to mobilize and draw on the most expert, scientific, and academic advice in the development of political programs . . . [so] the largely humanistic-oriented, occasionally ideologically-minded intellectual–dissenter, who saw his role largely in terms of proffering social critiques, is rapidly being displaced by experts and specialists, who become involved in special government undertakings, or by generalist-integrators, who become in effect house-ideologues for those in power, providing overall intellectual integration for disparate action' (Brzezinski, 1968:22).

[10] The shift of authority toward expertise is, at the same time, accompanied by disputes about the legitimacy and basis for expertise. Expertise becomes therefore an essentially contested attribute and the self-evident quality of expert knowledge is not always easily established and maintained (e.g. Smith, 1986).

[11] Alain Touraine ([1984] 1988:111) captures the change I have in mind well. He states that in mercantile societies, the 'central locus of protest was called *liberty* since it was a matter of defending oneself against the legal and political power of the merchants and, at the same time, of counterposing to their power an order defined in legal terms. In the industrial epoch, this central locus was called *justice* since it was a question of returning to the workers the fruit of their labor and of industrialization. In programmed [or, post-industrial] society, the central place of protest and claims is *happiness*, that is, the global image of the organization of social life on the basis of the needs expressed by the most diverse individuals and groups.' Touraine ([1969] 1971:30) employs the term 'programmed' society for the new, emerging type of society in order to refer to the 'nature of their production methods and economic organization'.

choice of term. Much of the discussion about the information society[12] is animated by a concern with the 'production, processing, and transmission of a very large amount of data about all sorts of matter – individual and national, social and commercial, economic and military' (Schiller, 1981:25). But every society has to transmit information. Less, or very little, is said about the genesis of the substance of information, the media of communication, especially human ones, or the reasons for the demand for, and changes brought about by, the content of the information which is communicated. Nor are discussions about the information society usually concerned with questions of solidarity or domination in modern society and whether any economic effects of this spread of information and communication technologies cannot just as well be accommodated within more conventional economic discourse, namely 'as phenomena best understandable in terms of long-established and familiar market-based criteria' (Schiller, 1981:xii).

The notion of post-industrial society will play a significant role in my considerations if only because the most comprehensive theoretical model of the developments at issue here have, to date, been examined under the heading of that particular label. Briefly, the category 'post-industrial society' is not quite suited, and is, to a degree, misleading because 'industry' or manufacturing does not vanish. True, industry is transformed, as will be described, but it is misleading to think that it will essentially disappear. Moreover, one cannot really live without 'industry', just as one cannot exist through leisure (*société des loisirs*) only (cf. König, 1979). The kinds of changes I will attempt to analyze here are the developments which occur with respect to the forms and dominance of knowledge itself. My focus is not merely on science, but on the relationships between scientific knowledge and everyday knowledge, declarative and procedural knowledge, knowledge and non-knowledge, and on knowledge as a capacity for social action.

In various discussions of the impact of science on society, including recent theoretical efforts, for example as part of an attempt to devise an accounting scheme for the social impact of science (cf. Holzner et al., 1987), the nature of the impact of science on social relations tends to be conceptualized more restrictively than will be the case here. In most conventional accounts, science is said to generate, first and foremost, if not exclusively, new types of possibilities for, or constraints on, practical action. The notion discussed in this context is much broader; science and technology not only allow for the possibility of new forms of action, but eliminate others and have an impact on the experience of action, while also assuring the 'survival' (in the sense of continued relevance) of existing

---

[12] Wiio (1985) claims that the term can first be found in a report submitted to the government of Japan in 1972. Frequently, discussions invoking the term 'information society' fall back, in the end, on the language of the theory of post-industrial society (cf. Lyon, 1986).

forms of action and, in some sense, even generating occasions which affirm traditional action.

The concept of scientific knowledge to be elaborated here is therefore quite distant from any notion associated with technological or scientific determinism, especially the one-sided or uni-directional forms of determinism. The constraining features of science and technology are, however, by no means underestimated. But in contradistinction to most arguments in favor of technological and scientific determinism, and the theories of society associated with such views, the crucial point about knowledge societies is that science and technology have simultaneously strong features which allow for resistance to homogeneous transformation. That is, science and technology have important enabling features which increase the number of available strategies, heighten flexibility or affect the ability of the powerful to exercise control and constraining forces which limit choices, reduce options and impose penalties and risks. It is therefore by no means contradictory to maintain that knowledge societies can simultaneously become more standardized and more fragile.

Generally, it is important to avoid overstating the extent to which science and technology are forces which are merely means of control and regulation and therefore constrain human agency and limit social action. They do, but that is only part of their consequences. The other part is represented by the 'opposite' because science and technology enter relational fields of social action and can assume quite different values or outcomes especially for opposing social forces and purposes. This means, at the same time, that the thesis advanced here does not imply that knowledge societies become uniform social and intellectual entities. It allows, for example, for the co-existence, even interdependence, of historically distinct forms of social organization and thought. Knowledge societies do not spell the end of ideology or irrationality. Nor is scientific knowledge, as a cultural ensemble, merely a way of deciphering the world; it is also a model for the world.

However, in order to demonstrate and appreciate fully the significance of knowledge for societies and social action generally, and for advanced societies in particular, one first has to formulate a sociological concept of knowledge. One must be able to differentiate between what is known, the content of knowledge, and knowing itself. What is it, then, that we know? Some examples taken from the *Oxford Dictionary of Current English* indicate the following instances: 'Every child knows that two and two make four. He knows a lot of English. Do you know how to play chess? I don't know whether he is here or not.' These examples show that knowing is a relation to things and facts, but also to laws and rules. In any case, knowing is some sort of participation: knowing things, facts, rules, is 'appropriating' them in some manner, including them into our field of orientation and competence. A very important point, however, is that knowledge can be objectified, that is, the intellectual appropriation of things, facts and rules can be established symbolically, so that in the future in order to know, it is no longer necessary to get into contact with the things themselves but only with their symbolic representations. This is the social significance of language, writing, printing and data storage. Modern societies have made dramatic advances in the intellectual appropriation of nature and society. There is an immense stock of objectified knowledge which mediates our relation to nature and to ourselves. In a general sense, this advancement has been called, in other contexts, modernization or rationalization. This secondary nature is overgrowing the primary nature of humans. The real and the fictional merge and become indistinguishable; theories become facts and not vice versa, that is, facts do not police theories.

It is only after one acquires a sense of the societal significance of such opposites and oppositions that the full sociological significance of knowledge begins to emerge. Such a perspective assures that one realizes the extent to which knowledge can form the basis for authority, that access to knowledge becomes a major societal resource and the occasion for political and social struggles.

Although knowledge has always had a social function, it is only recently that scholars have begun to examine the structure of society and its development from the point of view of the production, distribution and reproduction of knowledge.[13] Applied to contemporary society, the question becomes whether knowledge can provide the principle for social hierarchies and stratification, for the formation of class structure, for the distribution of chances of social and political influence and for the nature of personal life and, finally, whether knowledge may also prove to be a normative principle of social cohesion and integration even though the variations and alterations in the reproduction of knowledge appear to be enormous. Paradoxically, efforts to entrench necessity in history or eliminate chance from history has produced, at least at the collective level, it seems, its opposite. The role of chance at the collective level continues to be part of the way society comes to be organized.

As indicated, one of the first comprehensive sociological analyses of societies in which the knowledge-producing sector attains decisive importance for the dynamics of social relations is Daniel Bell's *The Coming of Post-industrial Society* (1973a). Radovan Richta's theory of the scientific-technical revolution constitutes the socialist counterpart to Bell's theory of society. Bell (1973a:212) argues that post-industrial society is a knowledge society for two major reasons: (1) 'the sources of innovation are increasingly derivative from research and development (and more directly, there is a new relation between science and technology because of the centrality of theoretical knowledge)', and (2) 'the weight of the society – measured by a larger proportion of Gross National Product and a larger share of employment – is increasingly in the knowledge field.' The pace and scale of the translation of knowledge into technology provides the basis for the

---

[13] For example, Malinowski (1955) and Machlup (1962).

possibility of modernity. Thus, if there is a 'radical gap between the present and the past, it lies in the nature of technology and the ways it has transformed social relations and our ways of looking at the world' (Bell, 1968:174).

The recognition by social scientists of the social and political importance of knowledge is perhaps but another important instance and self-exemplification of the general impact of knowledge on the development of contemporary society and of society's consciousness of this increased influence (cf. Richta et al., 1969:216). As I will have occasion to observe, with respect to a number of features of the theories of society which assign 'objective knowledge' such a central position, these theoretical perspectives are in important and relevant ways self-exemplifying. Since all tend to stress the tempo of social and intellectual change, it is perhaps no surprise that these theories of contemporary, and in some instances even future, society are themselves promptly superseded by events. But that they are often replaced so rapidly or become irrelevant has also to do with the logic of their theoretical basis. It is not unusual to find that these theories, including Daniel Bell's theory of post-industrial society, Radovan Richta's theory of scientific-technological revolution, Helmut Schelsky's (1961) theory of scientific civilization, or John K. Galbraith's (1967) theory of the new industrial state, adopt quite readily those principles of theory construction characteristic of classic (sociological) theories of society. Among such principles is not merely a considerable aura of optimism about the future, and the conviction that there is a radical, even revolutionary, break in social relations but often also rather deterministic, law-like assumptions about the tempo, the course and the direction of social transformations. It is doubtful, as I will try to indicate, that these almost invariant features of classic theories of society are of much help in a stringent analysis of advanced societies. The rapid obsolescence of many theories of contemporary society is linked much more to the elusive character of contemporary social forms and configurations. Classic theories of society looked to principles of theory building which attempted to capture social formations much more permanently.

I will not attempt primarily to document, let alone provide an up-to-date and detailed empirical account of, trends in various societal sectors which emphasize that knowledge plays an increasingly important role in modern societies. Moreover, the precision with which the contribution of scientific and technical knowledge can be factored out is far from certain in most instances. For example, as the economist Heertje (1977:203) concludes,

> empirical analyses of the quantitative contribution of technical change to [economic] growth are indeterminate, partly because of the diversity of technical development and the difficulty of separating the development of technical possibilities from the expansion of technical knowledge . . . Empirical observations in this field form a complex that cannot be unraveled without introducing arbitrary assumptions.

A typical example of the few existing contributions to the discussion of the nature and emergence of a 'knowledge society' two decades ago may be in the work of Fritz Machlup. His analysis is constituted by an elaborate apparatus of empirical, often census-type information about observable shifts and trends, such as in the occupational structure, intended to show that a knowledge society is indeed emerging and can therefore be documented in its own self-exemplifying terms, that is, in a quantitative (rational) manner. Today, we are able, in some sense at least, to take some of this documentary work for granted and can concentrate on what is, in my view, largely undocumented and unanalyzed in the same theoretical approaches.

Nor am I able here to attend to many important theoretical issues which are clearly associated with any theory of society in general and of contemporary society in particular. But in as much as the knowledge society can be expected to restructure many existing societal configurations and to produce new social forms, all of social science is challenged to advance theoretical and empirical inquiry into knowledge societies.

I have to limit myself. My focus cannot directly be on such otherwise important questions as the issue of political or moral bases of authority in knowledge societies (cf. Basiuk, 1977:266–274),[14] how the development of science and technology can be controlled (cf. Küng, 1976; Richta, 1977:27), the difficult measurement issues involved in attempts to estimate the changing size and contribution to the gross national product of what Fritz Machlup (1962) called the 'knowledge industry' (also Machlup, 1981, 1984; Rubin and Huber, 1986), the range of national and especially international policy questions raised in and by knowledge societies (cf. Bell, 1979a:193–207), or whether a knowledge society must be a democratic society (cf. Bernal, 1954; Polanyi, 1962; Lane, 1966:650; Richta et al., 1969; Merton, 1973).

Most importantly, I am impressed by the degree to which modern society is becoming an 'indeterminate' social configuration. The indeterminacy of modern society is the direct outcome of the growing importance of a highly differentiated societal institution, namely the scientific and the impact of its products on society. Knowledge societies are (to adopt a phrase by Adam Ferguson) the result of human action but not of deliberate human design. Knowledge societies emerge as adaptations to persistent but evolving needs and changing circumstances of human conduct. Among the most

---

[14] Such a restriction in foci extends to the questions of the range of rights and duties of individuals and corporate actors concerning the management and diffusion of knowledge. This implies, more concretely, deferring discussion of questions pertaining to 'informed consent', confidentiality or publicity of information, the obligation to transmit or prevent the transmission of knowledge, and the problem of secrecy in exchange processes of information in knowledge societies. In Chapter 9, however, I will examine, in quite a general manner, the social control of knowledge in modern societies.

significant transformations in circumstances that face human conduct is the continuous 'enlargement' of human action. This observation leads me to make certain brief critical methodological and theoretical comments on some general problematic features of orthodox classic and contemporary theories of society in the next chapter.

2

Theories of Society

What classical sociology calls society is nothing but the confusion of a
social activity – which can be defined in broad terms as industrial
production or the market-place – with a national state. Its boundaries are
not theoretical but real: they are marked by its border customs offices.
Society is a pseudonym for fatherland.

(Alain Touraine, *Return of the Actor*)

Following Alain Touraine (1977), one is able to identify two contradictory
conceptions of the texture of society in contemporary discussions of the
role of science and technology in modern society. According to one
conception, the logic of science and technology (or scientific rationality)
allows increasingly for the creation of a rationally organized and planned
society which will displace and replace all irrational and particularistic
forms of social power. I will discuss a strong version of this thesis in
Chapter 8 under the heading 'The technical state'. According to the second
view, scientific and technical knowledge provides economic, political and
military organizations with a new, secure power base, and these apparatuses
impose their technocratic interests against the will of those who oppose
them. In other words, one is forced to ask whether moral, political and
economic authority and social relations generally are mainly the apex of
scientific rationality, or whether science and technology will be dominated
more than ever by politics and by the economy.

Both images are likely overdrawn and indicate that they are still strongly
linked to certain attributes of classic social theory, namely its deterministic
currents and undercurrents and a specific image of the nature and future of
science and technology. Despite these persistent features, the history of
theories of society, at least since the eighteenth century, demonstrates also
that these theories have progressively lost their characteristic utopian
blueprints of society. Gradually and perhaps reluctantly, more modern
theories of society have acknowledged the overwhelming contingency of
social reality and have abstained increasingly from the production of
designs for an uncertain future of society because they are, for one thing,
almost assuredly to be disappointed by socio-historical developments.
Thus, the growing contingency of social events becomes a characteristic
feature of theories of society itself. As a result, such theories are, if they
are compared with their predecessors from Comte to Marx, and even
Durkheim, much more ambivalent, open-ended and themselves con-

tingent. However, a more systematic exposition of some of the salient attributes of classic discourse on modern society and how its assumptions may be transcended is still lacking. I will attempt to provide a first sketch of a perspective more in tune with contemporary social, economic and political realities.

Daniel Bell's (1973a:373) theory of post-industrial society, to be discussed here in some detail, exemplifies the more recent systemic features of theories of society, perhaps not in every detail but to a significant degree. Part of the ambiguity of Bell's theory of post-industrial society is linked, no doubt, to the fact that he wrote about and explicated its central features for more than a decade from the mid-1960s to the mid-1970s. It is unavoidable (and the present study is by no means immune either) that theoretical efforts resonate with the political issues of their day. Differences in emphases, for example, often easily spotted, may be attributed to efforts to respond to the problems of the time. But some modern theories of society, in addition, have a built-in element of ambiguity which is less transitory but likely present by design.[1]

Contemporary social theories are much more bound to the present and abstain from both extensive historical reflection and discussion of what might be termed utopia. Classic discourse, in contrast, took for granted that it was simultaneously concerned with history and with designs for the future. The restriction of contemporary social theory has a number of causes, chief among them being an increasingly rigid division of intellectual labor in social science. Also, the widespread credence of methodological prescriptions proclaims that 'positive' discourse is best served through a 'proper' delimitation of theoretical reasoning to 'genuine' disciplinary issues.

The texture of modern society in classic discourse

Our theoretical understanding of modern society in terms of the master paradigms and master concepts of the social sciences, which by now effectively shape and even govern everyday perspectives of social reality, continues to be an intellectual descendant of nineteenth-century thought, or a derivative of classic discourse on society. There are dominant spatial as well as processual and substantive references. The prevalent spatial referent of most modern theories of society is the nation-state whose sovereignty happens to be under increasing threat, while the master movement is social differentiation and its inevitable accompaniment of the

---

[1] One of Bell's (1973a:374) self-exemplifying assertions reads for example: 'The decisive social change taking place in our time – because of the interdependence of man and the aggregate character of economic actions, the rise of externalities and social costs, and the need to control the effects of technical change – is the subordination of the economic function to the political order.' But the question of exactly who and how the political order is managed remains open.

growing rationalization of social relations.[2] Taken together, the sum total of orthodox assumptions inadequately deals with the authentic variety of paramount worlds in the midst of what is claimed to be a world dominated by uniform process and culture. I will first critically outline the logic of the orthodox perspective and then attempt to offer an alternative theoretical perspective of long-term social development which is both non-teleological and non-evolutionary.

The logic of orthodox perspectives

Despite the cognitive diversity of contemporary social science discourse, it is perhaps somewhat surprising to conclude that there are dominant intellectual orthodoxies and the appearance of 'premature closure' among reigning theories of society. These attributes then transcend otherwise firmly entrenched strategic and substantive disagreements among social scientists about what problems need what attention, namely urgent researchable issues, proper theoretical strategies, fruitful methods and interpretation of findings variously generated. In spite of vigorous cognitive dissent, there are a few common as well as core thematic features of theories of contemporary society, mostly derivative of classic discourse, which inform much of the theoretical and empirical work in social science today.

Among the important common features of contemporary social scientific theories of society are:

1 The tendency to fix boundaries of societal systems as identical with those of nation-states; as a result, for most perspectives, 'causality' is intrasocietial.
2 The conviction that the key to the distinctiveness of modern society is primarily related to the persistent functional differentiation of societal subsystems and greater specialization of social institutions.
3 The widespread confidence that traditional or irrational beliefs are transcended by rational knowledge resulting in a greater rationalization of social activities.
4 The virtual certainty that societal formations of one historical stage or type are ultimately replaced by entirely different, new social arrangements.

---

[2] Consistent with this characterization of the master concepts of sociological discourse, Jeffrey C. Alexander (1992a:179; also 1990:11) underlines that 'differentiation comes closer than any other contemporary conception to identifying the over all contours of civilizational change and the texture, immanent dangers, and real promises of modern life.' However important the notion of differentiation may in fact be, it really cannot be severed from its cognitive twin, namely rationalization. And, differentiation theory, it seems, does not provide the theorist with any practical or predictive frame to forecast the course of societal development, for example, in the case of state socialist societies (see Alexander, 1990:13).

Society as nation-state

The unit of (macro)-social scientific analysis tends to be society in the sense of the *nation-state*. Society, for all intents and purposes, becomes indistinguishable from the nation-state.[3] Social transformations primarily occur as the result of mechanisms that are part of and built into the structure of a given society. The conflation of modern society with the nation-state is a legacy of the nineteenth-century origins of social science discourse. Obviously, there may have been and perhaps still are some good reasons for the identification of the boundaries of the social system with those of the nation-state.[4] For example, the formation of social science discourse to some extent coincides with the constitution of the identity of the modern nation-state and violent struggles among nation-states. Yet, it is quite inadequate to retain the restrictive framework of the territorial state today. The major institutions of modern society, the market economy, the state, education, religion, science, everyday life and also the ecology of a society are all profoundly affected by a progressive 'globalization' of human affairs or by circumstances in which 'disembedded institutions, linking local practices with globalised social relations, organize major aspects of day-to-day life' (Giddens, 1990c:79). The eclipse of time and distance in economic activities, environmental changes which recognize no boundaries, the global connectedness of the electronic media, the progressive internationality of the scientific community, growing transnational cultural activities and the dynamics of multinational corporate activity and political institutions all represent persuasive evidence for re-constituting the focus of social science discourse away from society and the nation-state toward groups of national societies, networks of transnational political and economic power and divisions not only within the world, but also the global society (cf. Giddens, 1990c; Bauman, 1992).

But to question the adequacy of such an emphasis does not necessarily imply embracing uncritically the notion of 'global society' or a global economic and cultural unity and uniformity of man. Nor does a shift in the primary theoretical referent toward a transnational focus already imply a definitive response to the question of whether the project of modernity simply continues to unfold, though under new circumstances and at a new level, or alternatively signals the emergence of a new historical epoch. However, to deny that the sole and dominant focus has to be society is to acknowledge the existence of systemic relations and trends which both divide and unite, which reduce the range of the sovereignty, power and autonomy of the nation-state in important respects (cf. Giddens, [1973]

[3] For a discussion of the traditional centrality of the nation-state and its sovereignty within political theory, especially theories and critiques of liberal democracy, see Held, 1991.

[4] However, for a number of anthropologists, historians and archeologists intrasocietal frames are generally inadequate points of reference; as a result, their research and theorizing pushes the concept of a world-system back several thousand years (cf. Friedman, 1992:335–372).

1980:265) and which assure that local, regional and national identities and social action are intermeshed with various cultural and economic forces which reside at a distance and transcend national boundaries. At issue are not absolute similarities in development, but relational convergences and the assimilation of strange worlds into local contexts. Concretely, the question is not whether interest rates are identical in all nation-states but whether their differences and their movement relative to each other tends to converge and how economic actors cope or construct adjustments through local practices to fluctuations induced elsewhere. Social science discourse is recognizing these new realities, although it often remains entangled in perspectives which deny the need to re-assess the notion of society as a nation-state. Paradoxically, the dissolution of the nation-state also pushes to the forefront forces which would appear to raise anew the plausibility and viability of local and regional identities. In other words, globalization cannot only mean processes which originate somewhere in the world and affect everyone in the same, almost submissive and passive fashion, but must also be seen as active responses, in specific communities, to developments which may not be controlled locally but which have local adaptive repercussions. Disembedding forces have to be combined, as Giddens (1990c:79–80) also stresses, with 're-embedding' activities that result in the 'reappropriation or recasting of disembedded social relations so as to pin them down (however partially and transitory) to local conditions of time and place.'

Differentiation

The pivotal and apparently irreplaceable (socio-evolutionary) master mechanism or (desirable) trend which represents, at least in some instances, *both* the conditions for the possibility, that is, the motor for social change, as well as the primary outcome of social change in modern society is the notion of functional *differentiation*. But in the majority of the theoretical accounts of functional differentiation, it serves as an *explanans* and not as an *explanandum*, leaving the question of the reasons for an apparently perpetual social differentiation unanswered (cf. Schimank, 1985). Similarly, questions of agency and the agents of differentiation, if any, often remain obscured.

However, before I discuss the concept of functional differentiation in greater detail, it should be pointed out that there appears to be a close bond between the thesis of the centrality of functional differentiation and a frequent spatial focus of theories of society on intra-state processes. The notion of functional differentiation appears to be closely coupled to the nation-state as a frame of reference since the kind of social differentiation which serves as the paradigm for the separation and demarcation among social institutions makes sense only within the framework of a territorial state with a closed population, although the boundaries are more typically described as those of a society (cf. Bogner, 1992:41).

The idea of functional differentiation generally is that modern social reality, as it replaces traditional forms of life, is subjected to progressive specialization and that clusters of social activity, in relation to each other, for example, in the organization of production, education and government, become more and more self-contained, self-centered and self-propelled sub-systems of society.[5] Society potentially loses, assuming it ever possessed it, its center. An implied consequence of functional differentiation, therefore, is the absence of an integrating system which serves to check the perpetual or insatiable (as Marx observes it in the case of capital) realization of self-centered, that is, specialized goals, such as profit. The consensus in social science I have in mind primarily refers to the process of functional differentiation as such. It does not necessarily extend to the repercussions of functional differentiation and it most definitely does not extend to the question of the reasons for differentiation (and its reproduction), assuming that the process is not from the beginning seen as one which is largely self-propelled and therefore virtually beyond the control of individuals and groups.

Differentiation for some is a process set in motion as the result of population pressures and therefore of efforts to adapt in a more efficient manner via greater specialization to increased density. For others, it is the historical emergence of certain ideas and social groups which promote and assure the gradual transformation of society. Still other theorists see the main cause of differentiation as the product of contradictions between the forces and the relations of production or as the result of complicated networks of actors, groups, social movements, institutions, states and civilizations. Also contentious is the assumption of a governing or constitutive mechanism of some sort within modern society, such as a shift from the pre-eminence of the substructure to the superstructure. Is such a supposition in accord with the assertion about functional differentiation? As a matter of fact, functional differentiation is seen by some to be totally incompatible with such possibilities (e.g. Luhmann, 1988:11). My interest, however, is not with the theoretical admissibility of trans-institutional mechanisms ('disembeddedness') in modern society, the possible 'causes' for or effects of functional differentiation.[6] It centers more on the question of the nature and importance of the logic or the master process of functional differentiation itself.

Nineteenth-century observers of social and political developments in general and the emergent social sciences in Europe in particular dealt with

---

[5] Max Weber ([1920] 1978:571) describes the consequence of the differentiation and the gain in the autonomy of different spheres of social action as the 'construction of the specific nature of each special sphere existing in this world.'

[6] Cf. the general critique of the variety of theories of functional differentiation in Joas (1992:326–336), where he also formulates an alternative theory to functional differentiation that omits reference to transhistorical trends of social development and stresses instead the intentionality of social action, particularly the need to trace action, in order to make it comprehensible, to the intentionalities of specific actors.

very real changes in their respective societies. In addition, the discovery of traditional or undifferentiated 'primitive' society at the same time provided a further substantiation and legitimation of the logic of specialization. Although the master concept of differentiation was not uncontested in the nineteenth century, it has assumed the unrivaled status of cognitive authority in social science proclaiming that first, 'increasing differentiation was the dominant, nearly inexorable logic of large-scale change; [and] second, that over the long run differentiation leads to advancement' (Tilly, 1984:44).

Differentiation generally is thought to improve the functional capacity (efficacy) of emerging smaller social units. The problem of integrating or co-ordinating a much more differentiated social context is, in some ways, also 'solved' by further differentiation, namely new organizations, positions and roles. More recently, since the Second World War, these core assumptions have crystallized into theories of modernization and development. Structural differentiation all too easily became identified with a certain Western developmental path and fell short of the require-ments of analyzing the experience of societal change in non-Western societies (cf. Nettl and Robertson, 1968:49–57). But these perspectives have now been challenged by dependency theories and the world-system approach (cf. So, 1990).

But instead of emphasizing the logic of differentiation as the principal concept and key for the analysis of social change, it is perhaps more sensible and closer to the historical evidence to be skeptical toward theoretical notions which excessively simplify what are not necessarily extremely complex processes, but rather social transformations which are extremely variable and contingent. Such variability includes the possibility not merely of repeating history but also of reversing it. Integration, homogenization, de-differentiation (cf. Nettl and Robertson, 1968:45–49) or concentration may, depending on the circumstances, for example, the resolve of individual and corporate actors, displace differentiation. In addition, if the transformations themselves are seen as contributing toward further variability, fragility, contingency and volatility, then justification for a directional master concept becomes even more dubious. I believe Charles Tilly (1984:48) is correct when he stresses:

> Not that differentiation is an unimportant feature of social processes. Many significant social processes do involve differentiation. But many social processes also involve dedifferentiation: linguistic standardization, the development of mass communication, and the agglomeration of petty sovereignties into national states provide clear examples. Furthermore, differentiation matters little to other important social processes such as capital concentration and the diffusion of world religions. Indeed, we have no warrant for thinking of differentiation in itself as a coherent, general, lawlike social process.

Moreover, most theories of society which operate with the assumption of the salience of functional differentiation have difficulties, it seems to me, coping with cultural and cognitive entities in the schemes of their designs.

Parsons' treatment of the cultural system as both at the apex of regulative hierarchies and as somehow situated in a no man's land is only one indication. Cultural and cognitive factors, especially their boundaries, are conflated with the limits of subsystems in society, underestimating the ease with which they travel, without too many impediments, across alleged check-points. In other words, what is at times much more important is the failure of boundaries to do their job, the number of unobserved spots on the frontiers and the speed with which borders are penetrated.

Paradoxically perhaps, the general point about the master concept of differentiation therefore is that no *single* process is always basic to social transformations.[7] In addition, as Anthony Giddens (1990c:21) has stressed, the notion of functional differentiation is not well equipped to handle the phenomenon of 'the bracketing of time and space by social systems'. For Giddens, the image invoked by the idea of 'disembedding', that is, the lifting out of 'social relations from local contexts of interaction and their restructuring across indefinite spans of time-space', is better suited to capture social mechanisms designed to transcend boundaries between contexts. The specific modes or media of bracketing Giddens discusses are expert systems (that is, knowledge) and symbolic tokens (for example, money) designed to bridge time and space. I would agree with Giddens that these media of interchange undercut the differentiation and specialization of institutions and that the process of disembedding is important. None the less, the bracketing of time and space *within* specialized institutions, for example, the economy as the result of new products, production methods and modes of organizing production, or in the national political systems as the result of integration, is equally or perhaps more important. At the same time, money and knowledge have very different properties and it is perhaps somewhat misleading to conflate their qualities and overemphasize the extent to which the 'application' of knowledge can emancipate itself and oneself from local constraints.

Rationalization

Also associated with the social, political and economic developments of the nineteenth century is thought to be a specific cultural transformation, namely the loss of *traditional certainties*, beliefs and expectations. As Kurt Hübner ([1978] 1983:214), reflecting the widespread agreement among social scientists now and in prior decades, observed, 'the way in which

---

[7] Several social theorists have recently set out to extend and revise the functional theory of differentiation (cf. Alexander and Colomy, 1990). They understand their work on such extensions, as Colomy (1990:465) for example underlines, 'as responses to several previous critiques leveled against the functionalist approach to change, and represent efforts to revise the theory in order to save it.'

present-day human society, as an industrialized society, understands itself rests, to a very great extent, on genuine technological-scientific forms and ideas.' Earlier generations of social scientists shared this conviction. Max Scheler ([1926] 1980:207), for example, asserts essentially the same fateful development because of the three ideal types of knowledge (knowledge of salvation, cultural knowledge and knowledge of domination) he identifies; only the last type of knowledge, the ability to control and produce effects, has ever more exclusively been cultivated for the purpose of 'changing the world' in the West while knowledge of culture and knowledge of salvation have been successively relegated to the background (cf. also Scheler, [1925] 1960:43).

Max Weber's views about the vital omnipotence of modern science, quite similar to but better known than Scheler's, can be found in the 'Zwischenbetrachtung' in his *Gesammelte Aufsätze zur Religionssoziologie* (Weber, [1920] 1978:564). For Parsons (1937:752), Weber's work culminates precisely in his 'conception of a law of increasing rationality as a fundamental generalization about systems of action'. This law constitutes the most fundamental generalization that emerges from Weber's work. Emile Durkheim's discussion, in *Elementary Forms of Religious Life*, of the conflict or reciprocal relations between science and religion also proceeds from the premise that science will displace religion, although Durkheim ([1912] 1965:477–480) is prepared to grant a continual though limited role to religious knowledge in modern society.

Of course, not all sociological classics assign science such an uncontested function in the structure and culture of modern society. Vilfredo Pareto celebrates and justifies the societal function of illogicality (as a capacity for action), though he attempts to do so on the basis of strictly logical reasoning. In spite of such exceptions, an overwhelming majority of social scientists anticipates either with fear or in disillusionment, an 'age of science and technology', and an increasing rationalization of irrational forces. In the end, however, all sides of the debate on the social and cultural capacity of modern science and technology in nineteenth-century sociological discourse and contemporary theoretical perspectives share a naive faith in the intellectual ability of science and scientific institutions to (re)shape the attitudes and beliefs of the individual mind.

The 'troubling' persistence of traditional beliefs or even a 'de-rationalization' process in some spheres of society give one good reason to doubt the general assertion of the universal efficacy of scientific knowledge and the incessant and irresistible drive toward greater rationalization of all realms of life. Modernization and rationalization may not necessarily converge. Thus, recognition of the mutual importance of rationalization and counter-rationalization processes and the persistence of traditional beliefs is required. A more balanced perspective would be aware of the limits of the power of scientific knowledge in modern society and would not commit the fallacy of an over-reliance on rationalization or tradition.

Societal development

The interest in and search for more or less exact boundaries between stages of social, economic, political and cultural development of societal formations is also a legacy of nineteenth-century thought. Teleological, evolutionary, dualistic and linear approaches prevailed. But the asymmetric dichotomy which above all preoccupied all of these theoretical endeavors was the search for indicators which separated *modern* from *traditional* society. Classic nineteenth-century theories of society were persuaded that there are ways, or even that there is a singular method, in which different types of society can be clearly distinguished from each other. Thus, the theoretical perspectives which were developed presumed to be operative at the level of society or the territorial state. The model of Western society, of course, served as the exemplary path societal transformation was bound to follow. The most 'advanced' or developed society shows to others the image of their unavoidable future. One therefore finds, superimposed on the continuum of historical change, a bipolar conception of progressive versus regressive social developments. In addition, 'various forms of belief in monolithic inevitability fell in with the misleading analogy between societal development and the stages through which an individual organism must pass' (Riesman, 1953/1954:141).

In general, however, the attempt of classic sociological discourse from Auguste Comte to Talcott Parsons to press societal transformations into an iron dichotomy of traditional and modern has been discredited by history itself. Societies that appeared and claimed for themselves to have reached a higher evolutionary stage reached back into barbarism; also, the alleged medieval curses of miracle, magic, superstition, mystery and false authority are still very much alive. Civilization has not passed successively and successfully in stages from the theological, to the metaphysical and the positive. At the same time, the actual path of social, political and economic development of different societies is less than one-dimensional. None the less, the purposes and the language of social theory require ways of differentiating forms of societies and attention to the question of the kinds of developmental patterns that characterize societies (cf. Touraine, 1986:15–16).

As a matter of fact, the social sciences, depending on their knowledge-guiding interests and the boundaries of their subject matter, employ a great variety of points of empirical and normative reference indicating different stages of societal development. Within classic sociological discourse, the specific empirical referent or process introduced for the purpose of capturing the iron pattern of social development may, on the one hand, refer to a fundamental mechanism such as the notion of contradiction (cf. Eder, 1992) which consistently initiates basic social changes or, on the other hand, fundamental attributes of social life, such as the dissolution of a certain form of social solidarity, which spell and signal the end of the identity of a particular type of society and simultaneously transcend in its consequences any single, historically concrete society. Within the Marxist theory of society, contradictions between corporate actors are the moving force of history. Auguste Comte's or Emile Durkheim's differentiation of societies is based on distinctions in the nature of the moral, legal, intellectual and political relations and therefore the basis of social solidarity which may prevail in different societies. But types of societies may also be differentiated on the basis of the ways in which human needs, understood as anthropological constants and therefore as needs which transcend specific concrete societies, are fulfilled. In general, however, it is evident that typologies of societies rest on certain fundamental anthropological considerations about the nature of society and human individuals. Ultimately, there are quite a few contenders claiming to have discovered the master key to social evolution. It is not uncommon that theories of society are convinced that the master process of social evolution is one which operates in an almost self-propelled fashion which cannot be arrested or altered in any fundamental sense. Once set in motion, social evolution is bound to run its predetermined and often linear course.

It is much easier to express credible doubt and creative skepticism toward these received notions of nineteenth-century social thought and therefore to break down the often binary classificatory schemes found in the work of Malthus and Spencer, Comte and Durkheim, Pareto and Veblen or Saint-Simon and Marx, than it is to imagine and develop potential alternative approaches. As briefly indicated, the understanding of the development of human societies *does* require theoretical models in social science which aim to comprehend long-term transformations of social structure and culture. However, such theories do not have to be built on nineteenth-century assumptions about either the direction of long-term social processes nor on what are essentially holistic notions about the inescapable systemic identity of social order. It is questionable whether society, its institutions and everyday life indeed derive from an overall, definitive character of an assemblage of social patterns that give definition to virtually all its parts and unity to their interrelations. It is prudent, I believe, to proceed without rigid preconceptions about evolutionary stages and types of society.

For illustrative purposes at least, I will attempt to make a case for viewing modernization as not conforming to strict historical stages and schemes of society but as a much more moderate and open, even reversible, process, namely as movement toward an *enlargement of social action*. That is, in contrast to classic or orthodox assumptions, I propose to advance a conception of embedded social change which focuses on 'marginal' or incremental change and therefore social development which consists of 'additions', both forward and backward in time, as a more appropriate image both for the kinds of society described by classic social science discourse and even more so contemporary society. I propose to conceptionalize the modernization process as a process of 'extension'. The enormous growth of the modern communication system, for example, the 'invisible' telephone system, first and foremost represents an enlargement of communication opportunities rather than a functional differentiation of communication. Or, even while it is true that the functions of cities vary widely and that cities have taken more and different functions in the course of history, one of the most salient changes that affect cities and towns around the world is their persistent and tremendous increase in size.

More recently, social science discourse has lost much of its pre-occupation with the search for evolutionary stages in the course of the social transformation of societies and the identification of distinctive societal formations. Some observers, most notably Norbert Elias (1987), have even detected a more radical conversion and re-orientation in social science discourse, namely a shift away from describing history as structured toward a view of social change as essentially without any structure whatsoever or, as he diagnoses it, a 'retreat of sociologists into the present'. Despite Elias' observations that an abundance of contemporary empirical research in sociology is carried out without reference to theory or to long-term historical development and his plea that the understanding of human society requires a comprehension of long-term processes as well as attention to certain universal properties found in all human societies, work in sociology and in the other social sciences which has a macro-orientation continues to involve, to some degree at least, attention to longer-term social transformations. Discussion of the end of industrial society is a prominent example.

Modernization as extension and enlargement

Instead of suggesting that the 'modernization' process is driven by a kind of definitive and unavoidable master process (such as functional differen-tiation, rationalization or conflict and contradiction which, moreover, is virtually unintentional as well as of recent origin and therefore manifests itself almost exclusively in contemporary societies), I would like to contend that modernization essentially involves multiple and not necessarily uni-linear processes of 'extension' or 'enlargement' and commences earlier in human history.

Extension refers, on the one hand, to the enlargement, expansion or 'growth' of sentiments, social connections or exchanges and their progressive multiplication, their increasing density and liberation from barriers – for example, those of time (e.g. life expectancy) and place (the environment) taken for granted in some ages – in the course of human history and, on the other hand, to the dissolution or retrenchment, but not always in the sense of elimination,[8] of cultural practices and structural figurations which come

---

[8] As Alain Touraine ([1984] 1988:104), for example, observes with respect to the historic transformation of economic structures, 'an industrial society does not give up the benefits acquired through commerce; a postindustrial society does not give up the organization of labor.'

into conflict with novel expectations and forms of conduct generated and supported by extension. Extension and enlargement of social conduct involves both intentional (purposive) action and non-intentional strategies and consequences (cf. Merton, 1936). Life once meant social encounters virtually confined to familiar acquaintances; now everyday life for many means living with growing numbers of strangers daily. However, 'the loss of insulating space' or eclipse of distance for example 'is not only the foreshortening of time and space in flying across continents, or in being in instant communication with any part of the globe by television or radio, it also is, as regards the *experienced* time of the person, an eclipse of social, esthetic and psychic distance as well' (Bell, 1973a:314).

Extension of time and distance cannot be viewed as a simple linear or additive process whereby equal increments are added in equal installments to all existing aggregate structures and practices. Extension is a process embedded in local circumstances that produces an authentic variety of forms.[9] Colonization not only transforms the colonies but also those who colonize. Extension is a stratified process. In fact, stratification itself is not immune to extension. Gradients and patterns of social inequality today are both much steeper and much more varied than they have ever been. Increments of extension are unevenly distributed and do not necessarily promote greater equality. Moreover, the speed of extension (and dissolution) is not constant or evenly distributed, nor are reversals in the density of social links impossible. The extension and expansion of cultural practices, production, trade, of media of exchange, communication and of social reproduction generally do not always follow the same pattern, especially patterns established in the past. What appears to be a contraction of social density or a decline in a certain attribute of social existence may in fact be a case of expansion. For example, the collapse of an empire actually constitutes a form of expansion in the conditions for identity formation, the basis of social inequality, the ethos of social conduct and acceptable beliefs, etc. The decline of infant mortality actually represents, at the individual level, an extension in life expectancy and, at the aggregate level, one of the bases for the population explosion. The decline in the use of manual labor constitutes an enlargement of physical power and productivity.

At times extension may only constitute an enlargement of cognitive *possibilities*, that is, of what is now imaginable conduct, for example, as the result of the production of new forms of art or access to new fiction. The separation of the private from the public spheres constitutes a form of extension and not merely obliteration of sanctioned forms of conduct. Criteria and units constitutive of social order may be enlarged. Ascriptive criteria such as birth, color, race, religious or social class decline but the dissolution is based on the emergence of more achievement-oriented standards and therefore an extension in the relevant criteria for an

---

[9] Cf. Stewart Clegg's (1992) analysis of the embeddedness of enlarged economic action in the case of the production of French bread, Italian fashion and Asian business.

accumulation of status attributes but not necessarily the complete elimination of ascriptive features of social conduct. Of course, some forms of inequality may be marginalized in the process of expanding the basis of inequality. Emerging standards and criteria of inequality often even have a common hostility to past standards but they rarely succeed in canceling these social constraints.

The process of extension generally also involves the absorption of novel connections into existing configurations and their transformation, representing yet another means of extension. Enlargement and extension, in contrast to the prevailing sense and direction of movement and time in most orthodox modernization theories, do not necessarily have to occur in but one direction, namely forward. On the contrary, extension can also involve enlargement directed 'backwards' or toward our past, as contemporary archeologists and others for example begin to expand our understanding of the Maya civilization, as archives of totalitarian regimes are opened, or as modernist elites reactivate traditional values (e.g. Zghal, 1973) to bolster the legitimacy of their power. Extension in one sphere may result in a concomitant enlargement in another; as some observers for instance are quick to note, any extension of knowledge may be accompanied by an enlargement of the area of ignorance.

Since the extension of social connections or the enlargement of production and commodities accumulated has a rather close affinity to the notion of *growth*, also in the sense of a growth in knowledge or consumption patterns, it is important to stress that the concept of growth does not quite do justice to the dynamic under consideration or fully express the transformations which result from an expanded social, cognitive or material density. With Norbert Elias ([1987] 1991:99–100), I would want to emphasize that enlargement and accumulation result in a change of the *level* of activity, consciousness or standards. The special advantage (or difficulty, as it may be) with the notion of a change in level is, as Elias also stresses, that new viewpoints for instance do not simply abolish perspectives from other levels of consciousness. In the course of the successive extension of human consciousness, it becomes a multi-layered consciousness enabling us to discover perspectives which rise above the horizon of past societies forming the foundation of new forms of self-consciousness. Enlargement and extension of the capacity to act also transforms the *kind* of consciousness that prevails in social relations; for example, as the capacity to act is enlarged, interest in and, as some might argue, an excessive concern with the conviction that the status quo has to be transgressed becomes prevalent as a motive force.

As a matter of fact, as the extension of social connections accelerates, the retrieval or number and reliability of depositories of past standards of conduct and patterns of consciousness increase as well, reducing the probability that social structures which have undergone massive change and the cultural practices which appear to have been abandoned actually vanish without a trace. Memory expands as well. Protests mount and stronger and stronger feelings of misgiving against extension appear. Opposition to the extension of social connections is fostered not only by the sense of conserving the status quo or even past conditions imagined to be less troubling, but also by the realization that extension does not always heal past and present plights and without fail offers a therapeutic solution to perceived existential dilemmas.

Space and time are widened and lengthened in both directions, that is, forward and backward, as the result of modernization through extension. Space once confined to the boundaries of a village has exploded to include, for some but certainly not for all, much of the globe. Time has accelerated and become more varied both 'backwards' into historical realms as well as 'forward'.

Extension may be based on imitation, violence, curiosity, disintegration, conquest, a premium placed on novelty, multiplication of options, diffusion, a desire to achieve recognition, the attempt to overcome embeddedness in conventional relations, the basic need for physical reproduction, etc. The mere enumeration of multiple and often interconnected ways in which extension may be set in motion and sustained already indicates that the process of extension may be quite deliberate or often driven by fortuitous circumstances.

Extension is facilitated by expanding the media of exchange but the enlargement of social action generally results in a decreasing degree of social integration. And knowledge societies, to use a metaphor Alain Touraine ([1984] 1988:109) employs, do not refer their actors back to 'one central point but rather to separate centers of decision that form a mosaic rather than a pyramid'.

In view of these considerations, therefore, it can be stated that the modernization process *commences* once social conduct is no longer a zero-sum game. Once the production of intellectual and material resources exceeds immediate needs and results in a surplus, modernization becomes a process of enlarging means and ends of conduct. Though initially, modernization may have been limited to some spheres of social life, it is subsequently evident and manifests itself in every social institution.

3

The Constitution of Modern Societies

Constitutive of *classic* sociological discourse and therefore of the concerted effort to reflect on the emergence of modern society out of the womb of 'traditional' society is, in the work of Ferdinand Tönnies, Karl Marx, Herbert Spencer, Emile Durkheim, Georg Simmel, Max Weber and, perhaps the last classic social theorist, Talcott Parsons (e.g. Bottomore, 1960; cf. Meja and Stehr, 1988), the strong conviction that the modern and traditional are worlds apart.[1] Identity, communality, conformity, consensus and the like, but not inequality, as basic social features of a disappearing form of life, give way to social differences in and conflicts about identities, structures and opinions. Homogeneity is replaced by heterogeneity. The growing lack of uniformity is, one could also summarize, the operative principle and direction of social change. In many instances, the changes described are viewed as distinctively progressive forces or, at least, as the conditions for the possibility of a progressive transformation of society located in the not too distant future, despite evident but temporary tensions, struggles and suffering. For many early social theorists, the exact nature of the emerging social order is not quite evident. The foundations of the society on the horizon are based on what are precarious and fragile but also transitory conditions. Once the process of 'functional differentiation' is fully operational and well understood as the main theoretical principle governing theories of modern society, the notion of modernity is firmly installed and accepted.

Modern society as industrial society

It was a considerable time before sociological discourse began to sketch in firmer terms the contours of modern society. It is only since the Second World War that social theorists, based on the particulars of historical

---

[1] The same, implicit, point of reference is evident from Alexander's (1992a:187) description of what recommends Parsons' analytical apparatus more highly than Durkheim's theoretical treatment of modern society and what therefore constitutes theoretical progress in social science discourse: 'Parsons is able to provide a much more intuitively compelling reconstruction of the modern world than Durkheim was able to provide himself. He can succeed in demonstrating what Durkheim merely suggested, namely, the extraordinary distance that has been traveled from band societies to the societies of the present day. In doing so, Parsons succeeds in legitimating the meaningful foundations of modern life.'

experience, especially the rapid and sustained economic expansion,[2] and the exemplars of classic discourse, have developed the outlines of theories of society which take contemporary social, political and economic conditions as their core explanatory problematic.

Despite even more recent and extensive reflections about its demise as a promising ideal type for the analysis of modern society, the most important sociological reconstruction of contemporary society in the post-war era is still the notion of modern society as an *industrial society*. The theory of industrial society, moreover, is linked quite closely to the intellectual history of sociology itself because it is only with the emergence of 'scientific' sociology at the turn of this century that the term industrial society came to be employed with increasing frequency. Thus, as Ralf Dahrendorf ([1967] 1974:65) has observed: 'Sociology is, on the one hand, an offspring of industrial society; it appears and gains in significance in the course of industrialization. On the other hand, "industrial society" itself is the favorite child of sociology; its concept can be understood as the product of modern social science.'

Origins of the theory of industrial society

Although the term 'industrial society' goes back to the nineteenth century, its full recognition and wide application only occurred during the past few decades: 'The political economists and social scientists of the 18th century did not have a name for the change taking place in front of their own eyes. In the 19th century sociologists polemically viewed their society mainly as a capitalist society, as a society of alienation, injustice, poverty and subjugation' (Dahrendorf, [1967] 1974:67). It is evident, moreover, that the theory of industrial society continues to display the same primarily optimistic vision of classic sociological theory, for example in terms of the hopeful conviction and anticipation of a better world in which the gradients of social inequality would be less pronounced.

In as much as the theory of modern society as an industrial society is the outcome of classic sociological discourse, it may be seen to represent the result of a complicated convergence of themes found in the writings of Weber, Durkheim, Spencer and Comte, a convergence of classic sociological ideas in the sense in which Parsons, for example, postulated it for his theory of action in *Structure of Social Action* (1937).

More specifically, the theory of industrial society, as developed during the post-war era, can be traced to the intellectual traditions and developments associated with the work of Henri Saint-Simon and Auguste Comte. According to Saint-Simon and his disciples, the new society that originated

---

[2] The role and possible responsibility of Keynesian economic policy in the unprecedented economic expansion up to the middle of the 1970s is discussed in Stehr, 1992.

with the French Revolution was characterized by a specific system of production, namely industrialism. For Comte, this type of society was destined to become universal. But Marxists have always been skeptical toward any theory of society proclaiming to formulate a theory of industrial civilization since the notion of capitalism has a much more central theoretical function within Marxism. Marxists, therefore, interpret attempts to formulate a theory of industrial society, which makes the case for the existence of a single industrial civilization, as an apologetic effort designed to hide the real nature of capitalism by talking about a societal formation incorporating both socialist and capitalist relations and conditions of production. Whatever their objections may be, a political economy of industrial civilization would certainly represent a much broader and more powerful explanatory theory of society than a theory of the historically specific form of either socialist or capitalist society. None the less, one cannot totally overlook the fact that the theory of industrial society evolved, in the minds of some, into a serious intellectual competitor and rival of Marxist theories of modern society (see Goldthorpe, 1971:265). Social theorists in the former socialist societies surely viewed the theory of industrial society as a rival theoretical (and political) program which had to be exposed for what is really was, namely an attempt to devise an apologetic perspective of capitalism under the guise of a social scientific analysis of modern society.[3]

Until recently, the conceptual attribute valued in Western societies was usually 'industrial' and not 'capitalist', while in socialist countries the latter attribute was preferred over 'totalitarian'. This indicates, of course, that the notion of industrial society as well as capitalism became part of a polemical political discourse and continues to be employed as a linguistic weapon. The concept 'industrial society' has a multiple career, by no means confined to the social sciences alone. But unless one is prepared to forgo completely the use of the concept in social science, one has to be aware of its varied and, at times, pejorative functions in different intellectual and political settings.

---

[3] The 1969 edition of the *Philosophische Wörterbuch* (see also Rose, 1971) published in the German Democratic Republic refers, in the context of its entry 'industrial society', explicitly to this difference and observes that the concept of industrial society is 'a central notion of contemporary *bourgeoisie philosophy and sociology* and which is employed instead of the class-based concept of capitalist and socialist society as defined by Marxism-Leninism . . . The concept of industrial society is a notion of society void of its *social content*. It lacks reference to any of the essential social differences between capitalism and socialism and treats the decisive socio-structural issues of the societal formations of our age as a merely technical-organization problem' (Heyden, 1969:520). Since the theory of industrial society emphasizes, moreover, certain similarities in these societal formations, the author of the entry feels, convinced that socialism is the correct doctrine, literally put down (*diffamiert*) by the theory of industrial society. At most, the author of this entry concludes, 'the concept of industrial society . . . is without scientific merit and does not lead to insights of any value but performs a purely apologetic function' (Heyden, 1969:520).

Raymond Aron's theory of modern industrial society

Raymond Aron, the French sociologist cum intellectual who died in 1983, is undoubtedly the most important social theorist of industrial society and the originator of the present-day account of industrial civilization in social science. His influential conception can be traced to a series of lectures he offered at the Sorbonne during the mid-1950s devoted to an analysis of the unique features of modern society and its future (Aron, 1964b).[4] In his lectures in 1955–56, Aron attempted to discern, in a critical spirit and in a conscious attempt to distance himself from Marxism, a number of common structural and cultural features of developed societies.[5] His intellectual and political opposition to Marxism perhaps culminates in the thesis that one cannot discern a pattern of uni-linear historical development which is, moreover, determined by changes in the socio-economic base of society. Comparable economic developments are, on the contrary, compatible with different paths of social and political development. Societies organized according to capitalist and socialist economic principles are not merely examples of societies which have certain features in common but are also distinct societal formations. The common feature of industrial society Aron postulates is a restricted unity, which does not obliterate all manifestations of different social, political and cultural developments among societies.

For Aron, there were at least two relevant intellectual precursors which prompted him to explicate the notion of industrial society. First, in the 1940s, Aron devoted considerable energy to an exegesis of classic sociological discourse. A direct confrontation of the ideas of Karl Marx with those of Vilfredo Pareto prompted Aron to try a comparative analysis of the modern political revolutions initiated by communists and fascists. The outcome of his efforts is only available in manuscript form. Secondly, Aron was fascinated by the ideas of the economist Colin Clark in *The Conditions of Economic Progress*, first published in 1940. Clark, and later his French student Jean Fourastié ([1951] 1960), made the point that one is able to compare, using data about increases in the gross national product, the economic growth patterns of capitalist and communist societies. Both types of societies have, despite basic differences in their political structure and culture, certain common macro-economic features. Moreover, in both systems, the conditions for economic growth are similar since they may be seen to be linked to the shift of the relative importance and performance of the different sectors of economic activity. Clark and Fourastié argue that in

---

[4] Cf. also Aron's ([1983] 1990:265–285) autobiographical recollections of the reasons for the importance of this subject to him in the mid-1950s in his *Memoirs*.

[5] Not surprisingly, Aron's, and related hypotheses by other observers at the time, gave rise, in East and West, to a heated discussion of the likely 'convergence' of socialist and capitalist societies (e.g. Rose, 1971). It is obvious that this discussion has been superseded by history, for it has been shown that 'socialism is not the other industrial society, but a political method of promoting development. It is a developing-country phenomenon' (Dahrendorf, 1988:104).

each of these societies, the relative growth of the tertiary sector is of crucial importance as a condition for economic growth, as is the accumulation of capital and the growing productivity of labor. Both societal formations are dependent, moreover, for their economic expansion on rising productivity. These common features suggested to Aron that it would be sensible to propose the term 'industrial society' as a category which extends to and covers both socio-economic systems.

Aron's intellectual convictions were reinforced both by the politics of the day and by a process of cognitive distancing from Europe. The latter strengthened his belief, as he relates it, that the central concept of the age ought to be 'industrial society' because 'Europe, as seen from Asia, does not consist of two fundamentally different worlds . . . It is one single reality: industrial civilization. Soviet and capitalist societies are only two species of the same genus, or two versions of the same social type, progressive industrial society' (Aron, [1966] 1968:41; see also Adorno, 1969). Politically, the fierce cold-war competition between East and West about rates of growth in the 1950s also explains Aron's preoccupation with a conception which joins different political systems in a common societal frame of reference (cf. Aron, [1983] 1990:276).

But how does Aron define 'industrial society'? Assuming that all economic systems, especially large-scale ones, have to fulfill certain functions, the constitutive attribute of industrial society is the extensive employment of technical means in addition to the utilization of the methods of science, for example, quantification, prediction and, in an even more general sense, the rationalization of the means of social action which effect the organization of collective projects.[6] A minimal definition of industrial society refers, therefore, to a social system 'in which the industry, in particular, large scale industry, constitutes the characteristic mode of production' (Aron, 1964b:69). Aron employs the term 'industrial society', following the usage established by Saint-Simon and Comte, in such a general sense that not only economies based on private ownership of the means of production and the regulation of the relations among its units based on the market, but also economies organized according to socialist principles and the regulation of its relations according to a plan, become

[6] In a skeptical re-examination and refreshing re-evaluation of Aron's perspective, Ralf Dahrendorf (1988:99) argues that he cannot quite agree with Aron and others who have repeatedly stressed the decisive role of technical and scientific changes as the motor of modern societal change. More specifically, he misses in these observations the realization that such developments are not self-propelling processes and that therefore technical changes and innovations are not isolated events but matters which have to be realized under actual circumstances. More specifically, Dahrendorf wishes to see reference to concrete social forces and actors, for example innovative entrepreneurs, responsible for employing, in an instrumental sense, science and technology toward certain ends. Although Dahrendorf emphasizes the role of those who chose to employ the instruments of science and technology, his entirely justified skepticism toward the use of an optimistic, even technocratic, concept of science and technology by Aron and others ultimately remains imprisoned in the same unexplicated use of these terms.

examples of industrial societies.[7] But it is also true that capitalist society requires a high degree of industrialization as one of its important preconditions, while industrialization does not presume capitalism. Based on this consideration, Giddens ([1973] 1980:141), for example, defines 'industrialization' as the 'transfer of inanimate energy sources to production through the agency of factory organization'. This implies that an economic system may be industrialized within the context of rather distinct political organizations and cultural institutions. And capitalism, in the sense of a private organization of the conditions and relations of production, historically precedes the industrialization of the organization of production.

Basic to the emergence of industrial society is, as I have indicated, the widespread application and use of science and technology for the purpose of organizing collective activities. What is decisive, however, is the quantity of the scientific and technological means which are employed since the use of technical means *per se* is, of course, much older; only a rapid increase in the availability of new means of production results in a qualitative change of society. Because of the extensive use of science and technology, economic expansion no longer has to rely on the 'rationality' of the conquest of colonies or military victories. Industrial societies do not pursue unique goals or purposes but are compatible with a multitude of political and social motives, for example, with a state-planned economy or one based on the promotion and exigencies of competition among privately owned businesses.

Yet Aron's definition as well as Giddens' conception of industrial society are largely silent about the precise nature and origin of the technology and the knowledge which allowed both of them to link in large-scale production units as the characteristic transformative force and framework of labor in industrial society. As a result, neither Aron's conception, nor its elaboration by Giddens, is capable, or considers it relevant, to date the historical origin of industrial society using the nature of its technical artifacts and knowledge as an indicator. It may be quite significant, therefore, to observe that most of the technologies which shape production in industrial society were invented and utilized for the first time in the half-century which preceded the beginning of the First World War. Nor can it be entirely irrelevant that most of these technologies were experience based. Thus, an industry, a manufacturing sector and, even more generally, labor, in which technology is, in a decisive contrast, knowledge based, must, almost by definition, represent a fundamental transformation of the nature of the productive process and of the relations of production. And the evolution of modern technology alters the nature of the social relations in society. Under these conditions, it is quite possible that the social relations, as Adorno (1969:12), for instance, observes in his essay on 'Late

---

[7] Daniel Bell (1968:155) concurs fully with this conception of industrial societies: 'Industrial society is the organization of machines for the production of goods, and in this respect capitalism and socialism are two variants of industrial society. They differ in the relationship to property and the decision centers of investment, they are both technical civilizations.'

capitalism or industrial society', which once defined capitalism, namely the transformation of human labor into commodities and therefore class antagonism, could lose their relevance and deteriorate to superstition.

But Raymond Aron is still primarily concerned with industrial societies and not their transcendence. Industrial societies represent, despite their differences in political organization and regulation of economic relations, a common societal formation. Adorno (1969:18) recognizes the political critique implicit in such a position, but he agrees with Aron that contemporary society is an industrial society because if one considers the state of the forces of production in present-day society, industrial forms of work have become the typical pattern of labor in all societies independent of their political structure. And these forms of production threaten to become universal as these methods are extended to all spheres of material production, to administration, distribution and even culture. At the same time, Adorno maintains that the nature of the relations of production continues to determine why some industrial societies are capitalist societies. However, Adorno's emphasis on what amounts to an almost static conception of the relations of production in modern society hints perhaps that he is prepared to revise Marx's thesis about the dominance of the forces of production for historical development. As a matter of fact, Adorno (1969:20) stresses that Marx's expectation that the forces of production have historical priority and that their development alters the relations of production is too optimistic. Though Marx is a foe of German idealism, in this respect at least, he remains a proponent of its affirmative historical vision. The relations of production have taken a subsidiary role to the forces of production and have remained much the same, while the methods of production are relentlessly transformed.

None the less, Aron enumerates a number of socio-economic patterns as well as socio-structural features which have implications for the life-world in these societies, common to state socialist and capitalist systems which warrant the observer to conceptualize both types of society as industrial societies. He indicates that capital accumulation, which for Marx represented a characteristic feature of capitalist societies, is a necessity in all industrial societies in order to assure the extension of production and the realization of productivity gains, recognized as goals in both forms of societies. Both socialist and capitalist economies generate surplus value which is not distributed to the workers but retained by the firm or the production unit. In both systems, the wages of the workers do not correspond fully to the value of the commodities and services they produce since a portion of the surplus has to be re-invested.

The notion of a progressive, growing economy cannot be separated, therefore, from the idea of industrial society. In both systems, some form of rational economic calculation is required (Aron, 1964b:70). A more extensive technical division of labor is superimposed on more traditional forms of labor division. In all industrial societies, one can observe a separation of places of work or business and family as well as a geographical concentration of the labor force at the place of work and with it the development of tensions between employer and worker. Finally, in both systems, structures of social inequality and privilege persist (Aron, 1964a:23–24).[8]

In its most general terms, Raymond Aron's concept of industrial society points to the existence of an economic system which delivers and is characterized by almost perpetual economic expansion and growth.[9] Such a feature of industrial society – easily seen as a reflection of the immense growth and sustained expansion of the economy of the post-war era – none the less invites the question of the possible source of its continued economic expansion. As can be seen, Aron's response is indebted to Max Weber and Joseph Schumpeter. In a first approach, Aron (1964b:146) refers to patterns of expectation and attitudes of the relevant economic subjects. More specifically, it is a certain 'scientific-technical' spirit, the spirit of rational calculation and the propensity to innovation. Supportive institutional conditions are also necessary in order to effectively encourage these attitudes toward economic processes, for example, a relatively rational public administration and legal system. The second set of reasons for any sustained economic expansion, according to Aron, has to be found in the presence of certain incentives, for instance, the existence of a specific relation between costs and benefits associated with work, especially one which is perceived as equitable. The third and somewhat less subjective factor pertains to the presence of capital and population. Finally, all factors stand in a certain interdependent relationship. In any event, it becomes evident that Aron considers science and technology and attitudes of economic subjects affected by scientific reasoning to be among the decisive sources for economic growth in industrial society.

Aron's theory of industrial society is certainly characterized by, as Ralf Dahrendorf ([1967] 1974:71) puts it, a not entirely unpleasant degree of over-generalization.[10] But all the unique features of English, Canadian, French, German and Russian society blend into each other and for Aron represent but so many exemplars of the same type of society.

[8] Equally remarkable are those features of industrial society Aron does not enumerate; for example, the almost universal high literacy of its population and extensive occupational training of its workforce as well as the propensity of individuals to be mobile and willing to shift from place to place, or from function to function, in the labor force (cf. Gellner, 1983:35).

[9] Ernest Gellner (1983:22), in a brief discussion of industrial society, accepts these observations and therefore points out that 'industrial society is the only society ever to live by and rely on sustained and perpetual growth, on an expected and continuous improvement' (also Dahrendorf, 1988:99). Such a form of society tends to buy off social aggression 'with material enhancement'; by the same token, industrial society experiences its greatest weakness and crises once it is unable to provide 'social bribery' (Gellner, 1983:22).

[10] After almost two more decades of observing the pace and consequences of economic expansion in the developed world, Dahrendorf's (1988:100) overall judgment about Aron's theory of industrial society is clearly less favorable because the 'idyllic picture of an industrial society proceeding peacefully to more wealth and welfare for all is misleading for several reasons.'

The transformation of industrial society

The theory of industrial society, it seems, does not anticipate or contemplate its own transcendence and therefore spend any time and effort on the possibility that it may give way to another type of society, as other social theorists were quick to suggest just a few years later. Major changes underway in employment patterns or the kinds of work typically performed actually constitute evidence for the continuity of industrial society as the dominant modern social formation. For example, despite further shifts of employment toward the tertiary sector, the foundation of economic activities remains agriculture and manufacturing (Aron, [1966] 1968:104).

In an autobiographical reflection on the origins and nature of his influential conception of industrial society, Aron, however, reiterates his conviction that the idea of industrial society remains a valid theoretical model, though he does express doubt that the Soviet system as a distinctive political system is capable of surviving or, for that matter, will be able to generate economic wealth in step with capitalist societies. Aron underestimated the inefficiencies of the political organization for the economy. But Saint-Simon and Comte were correct when they foresaw the almost universal spread of industrialism. Aron ([1983] 1990:277) affirms that the 'Saint-Simonians saw clearly' while Marx 'distorted their philosophy by substituting capital (or capitalism) for industrialism'. But Aron ([1983] 1990:277) also believes that what is now called post-industrial society 'should be interpreted as an original phase in the application of science to production and more broadly to the very life of man'.

One of the theoretical foci that has animated discussion among social scientists about the special qualities of developed societies is the characterization of contemporary societies as examplars of 'post-modern' societies. In the context of the assertion that we are in the midst of the transformation of modern society into a post-modern societal formation, one might for example ask whether, as Aron already asserts in the context of his conception of post-industrial society, such a society is constituted as the result of a new phase in the application of science and technology, or whether the qualities of post-modernity, as might be suspected, are primarily seen as the outcome of symbolic and cultural changes in modern society. The latter indeed appears to be the case for central contributions to the discourse on post-modernity.

4
The Design of Post-industrial Societies

Our age gives the impression of an intermediate condition; the old ways of regarding the world, the old cultures still partially exist, the new are not yet sure and customary and hence are without decision and consistency. It appears as if everything would become chaotic, as if the old were being lost, the new worthless and ever becoming weaker.

(Friedrich Nietzsche, *Menschliches, Allzumenschliches*)

Although the term 'post-modern' is now the favorite expression that professional observers invoke to symbolize and signal the boundary of an epoch as well as the transition to a new era, just twenty-five years ago a very different term, but one with a virtually identical message, rapidly gained ascendancy and made a lasting impact on social science discourse, namely the observation that we are living in a 'post-industrial society' and therefore also in an interstitial time.

In describing and discussing the design of post-industrial societies, I will primarily make reference to Daniel Bell's theoretical conception. However, Bell's proposals for a theory of society, cognizant of the dramatic changes which bring about the demise of industrial society and signal the emergence of a type of society which retains some of the crucial features of its predecessor, for example, rapid economic expansion, was, at the time, by no means the only theoretical perspective developed to stress the pending transformation of modern society into post-industrial society.[1] Perhaps most notable is the family resemblance between Bell's notion and the concurrent conception of a scientific-technological revolution explicated by Radovan Richta and his research team which first appeared in 1967. In his own analysis of the transition to post-industrial society, Daniel Bell (1973a:105–112) favorably summarizes Richta's views concerning the crucial role of science and technology in production and the extent to

---

[1] Daniel Bell is responsible for the contemporary meaning of the term 'post-industrial society' and the prominence on the agenda of social science discourse of discussions about the possible demise of industrial society, but he did not coin the term. Bell began using the term, first in oral communication only, in 1959 (cf. also Bell, 1973a:36–40). The concept may be found in earlier writings of social scientists, for example, in David Riesman's ([1958] 1964) analysis of leisure patterns in modern society and, much earlier, as Bell (1973a:37n) also notes, in a now forgotten work of Penty (e.g. 1917), who was concerned about the negative effects of industrialism. Similar considerations, in a way, affected Riesman's observations since his concern with the increasing importance of leisure time in modern society was predicated on the belief that technological progress in the form of automating production would make work even less meaningful and challenging; hence, workers would try to seek and realize the meaning of life increasingly outside of work in leisure activities.

which these developments force corrections upon accepted Marxist positions. I will also refer to Richta's ideas since they illustrate well the fact that the conception of a post-industrial society cannot be seen to represent an isolated (American) intellectual innovation. The theory of post-industrial (and what was, at the time, construed to be post-socialist) society[2] resonates with and refers to specific intellectual and historical developments in a number of societies.[3] Daniel Bell and Radovan Richta endorse, with respect to this 'new' level of societal development, Raymond Aron's views about the universality of industrial organization, independent of the political and cultural peculiarities of different states.

The power of Daniel Bell's (1973a) theory of post-industrial society, its many notable merits and the challenging problems posed by his work should not obscure crucial difficulties associated with his theory. Although in subsequent pages I will stress the challenges posed by his approach, I also intend to refer to notable and attractive features of Bell's theory, for example, the lack of theoretical closure, the indeterminateness and deliberate openness of his conceptual apparatus, inviting constructive developments which are a constitutive part of his perspective (cf. Bell, 1973a:xxv; Brick, 1986). One of the particular merits of his theory is, in my view, that he tries to engage with classic sociological discourse and its designs, on the one hand, and that he attempts to contrast quite explicitly, on the other hand, the period in history transformed and dominated by industrial society with that which appears to emerge, as the result of its peculiar modern economic dynamic, from its womb. At the same time, Bell's theory of post-industrial society is one of the most enduring as well as controversial theoretical designs and, at least in that important sense, successful theories of contemporary society.[4]

The theory of post-industrial society[5] recognizes a particular central

[2] The collapse of state socialism in Eastern European countries is not, however, the result of a transformation of their economies by science and technology and therefore a consequence of a growing contradiction between economy, culture and politics but is, contrary to the at least implicit expectations of Bell and Richta, the outcome of a vastly insufficient transformation of the productive systems in these states by modern science and technology. But the historical changes in Eastern Europe are not the reason for or the subject of this chapter.

[3] My subsequent discussion of Helmut Schelsky's theory of modern society as a scientific-technical civilization, or of Herbert Marcuse's critique of the emergence of one-dimensional individuals will show further substantive resemblances between contemporary theoretical designs.

[4] Vogel (1980:9) and Feigenbaum and McCorduck (1983:22) refer to the tremendous reception and interest Bell's theory of post-industrial society found among Japanese engineers and intellectuals in the mid-1970s. In addition, at this time, Bell's theory was quite influential in shaping Japanese science and technology policies.

[5] This is an idea which from an epistemological point of view, as Bell (e.g. 1973a:14) at times stresses, constitutes and acquires meaning as a *conceptual scheme* (or possibly as an ideal type) *only*. I am not sure what intentions Bell precisely attempts to pursue on the basis of what he obviously considers a restrictive principle, or what kind of criticism he may care to pre-empt by invoking the notion of an ideal type. Anyhow, the theorizing he in fact pursues has few formal resemblances to Weber's methodological notion.

principle, viewed as a kind of dominant logic, which allows the observer to impose a specific conceptual order on vast societal developments of modern (Western) society. Bell describes his theory as concerned primarily with changes in the social framework of 'society', that is, its *social structure* which analytically, along with the *polity* and *culture*, comprises society. The social structure of a society refers, more specifically, to its 'economy, technology and the occupational system' (Bell, 1973a:12) and the structure of social roles. The kind of changes in the social structure Bell attempts to chart primarily are those induced by the 'axial principle' of his theory of society, namely 'the centrality of theoretical knowledge as the source of innovation and of policy formulation for the society' (Bell, 1973a:14). For Bell (1979a:164) the axial principle is likened to 'director of social change' in and for post-industrial society. However, he does not claim, and in that sense the axial principle lacks deterministic centrality, that the changing social structure invariably produces corresponding transformations in the polity or the culture of society.

But this cautionary methodological principle does not deter Bell from advancing a number of intriguing general assertions or projections about the nature of social life in post-industrial society. For example, 'if the struggle between capitalist and worker, in the locus of the factory, was the hallmark of industrial society; the class between the professional and the populace, in the organization and in the community, is the hallmark of conflict in post-industrial society' (Bell, 1972:167). If I correctly interpret these remarks, the well-established trend toward greater individualism in modern society will be replaced, in post-industrial society, by a greater degree of communalism; that is, the dominant reference point for decisions are social units rather than individual actors. Public choice rather than individual demands become the mechanism for the allocation of goods (cf. Bell, 1972:166–167).[6] None the less, Bell repeatedly endorses the virtues of what might be called theoretical ambivalence, of conditional conclusions and an explicit rejection of promises to be able to locate the master key to (an explanation of) social transitions in all sectors of modern society.[7] However, these cautionary appeals which I believe are fully justified still introduce a peculiar tension into his analysis of the centrality of 'theoretical knowledge' as the determining property of changing social structures in modern society. This is because one is confronted, on the one hand, with

[6] And as Bell (1973a:481) stresses elsewhere, 'the political ethos of an emerging post-industrial society is communal . . . It is sociologizing rather than economic . . . as the criteria of individual utility and profit maximization become subordinated to broader conceptions of social welfare and community interest.'

[7] In the context of his summary of Radovan Richta's conception of a scientific-technological revolution, Bell (1973a:112) endorses a retreat from theory 'if by theory one means a model of social structure that specifies the determinate interaction of the crucial variables of a system, establishes empirical regularities that predict future states of relation, and provides an explanatory principle of its history and operation'.

what is a much less rigorous, logically tight and demanding form of 'knowledge' about what, on the other hand, is represented as a rather concise, even scientistic exemplar of 'theoretical knowledge' and its productive and almost surgical-like impact on social structural processes.

In the post-industrial society, production and business *decisions* will be subject to or will be determined by other sectors in society. More specifically, 'the crucial decisions regarding the growth of the economy and its balance will come from government, but they will be based on the government's sponsorship of research and development, of cost-effectiveness and cost-benefit analysis.' At the same time, it is important to note that decision-making 'because of the intricately linked nature of their consequences, will have an increasingly technical character' (Bell, 1973a:344).[8] The image of the centrality and independence of the role of science and technology in political decision-making, in this instance it seems, is somewhat tempered compared to the 'end of ideology' debate of the 1950s and early 1960s (cf. Bell, 1960; Lipset, 1960), where the idea that 'political criteria decline in importance relative to more universalistic scientific criteria' (Lane, 1966:659; cf. also Vidich and Lyman, 1985:289–294) was a much more prominent expectation or projection about the state of politics in modern society.

The effort to restrict any built-in determinism is further underscored by Bell's (e.g. 1973a:14) insistence that he merely refers to certain *tendencies* in social transformations which, in the end, may or may not work themselves out to their full logical potential. And as Bell (1987:1), obviously in a deliberately ambivalent fashion, has stressed, the three 'levels of analysis' are not assumed to be 'strongly linked, for society is not a "system" wherein a set of changes in one sector has determinate consequences in all others. Yet they are interdependent in strong or loose fashion.' We are expressly cautioned that

> there is no specific determinism between a 'base' and a 'superstructure'; on the contrary, the initiative in organizing a society these days comes largely from the political system. Just as various industrial societies – the United States, Great Britain, Nazi Germany, the Soviet Union, post-World-War II Japan – have distinctly different political and cultural configurations (Bell, 1973a:119).

And in that sense, Bell's conceptual scheme certainly constitutes a more open and flexible view of society than most competing contemporary theories of society, including neo-Marxist or structural-functionalist schemes. The openness in the degree of integration among sectors of society allows for a theoretical focus on incompatible, even contradictory, conflictual and divergent developments among these spheres of society.

One of Bell's (1973a:114) major theoretical preoccupations and contributions, then, is concerned with the tension and the 'disjunction, in Western society, between the culture and the social structure, the one

---

[8] Compare the section on the discovery of the modern 'technical state' by Helmut Schelsky and Herbert Marcuse in Chapter 8.

becoming increasingly anti-institutional and antinomian, the other oriented to functional rationality and meritocracy'. This research interest culminated in the 1976 publication of Bell's analysis of *The Cultural Contradictions of Capitalism*. In the context of this study, Bell advances the argument that a *modernist, secular culture*, especially the hedonistic principles of unlimited self-fulfillment and enjoyment, increasingly contributes to the destruction of the moral prerequisites of a *rationalized society*; as a result, contradictions between the motivational principles which drive the economy and the administration of society embodied in the old values of the Protestant ethic and those of cultural activities afflict society. Capitalism loses, as Max Weber had anticipated, its original sacred legitimation.

The looseness of fit and multiple patterns of relationships among sectors of capitalist society signal the conditions for the possibility of a development of separate moral qualities or functions and therefore tensions between social and cultural modernity.[9] Bell (1973c:402) describes the distinct identities (or different axial principles) of each social sphere and the contingent interrelations of spheres as follows:

> Culture embraces the areas of expressive symbolism (painting, poetry, fiction) which seek to explore these meanings in imaginative form; the codes of guidance for behavior which spell out the limits, prescriptive and prohibitive or moral conduct; and the character structures of individuals as they integrate these dimensions in their daily lives. But the themes of culture are the existential questions that face all human beings at all times in the consciousness of history – how one meets death, the nature of loyalty and obligation, the character of tragedy, the definition of heroism, the redemptiveness of love – and there is a principle of limited possibilities in the modes of response. The principle of culture is a ricorso, returning, not in its forms but in its concerns, to the same essential modalities that represent the finitude of human existence.
>
> The polity, which is the regulation of conflict under the constitutive principle of justice, involves the different forms of authority by which men seek to rule themselves: oligarchy and democracy, elite and mass, centralization and decentralization, rule and consent. The polity is *mimesis*, in which the forms are known and men choose those appropriate to their times.
>
> The social structure – the realm of the economy, technology and occupational system – is *epigenetic*. It is linear, cumulative and quantitative, for there are specific rules for the process of growth and differentiation.

The nature of the disjuncture of sectors of society, especially between social structure and culture, therefore reflects a sharp *gradient in the rationality* of activities in the sphere of social structure and culture. Such an assumption is quite common in sociological discourse and resonates quite well with many classic theories of society. However, one of the distinct 'advances' of Bell's perspective is the absence of the assumption, still a central component of many classic theories, that the resolution of the disjuncture in rationalities is imminent and occurs with almost iron necessity in favor of the rationalization of those sectors of society which are

---

[9] An affirmative stance toward those forces which sustain the social modernity of society and a denigration of the sources of cultural modernity characterize, according to Habermas ([1980] 1981a:7–8; [1982] 1983:78), all neo-conservative diagnoses of contemporary society.

still organized according to more traditional principles. None the less, the remaining deficiency of this assumption constitutes one of the primary challenges posed by the theory of post-industrial society.

Post-industrial society is no longer organized around the co-ordination of individuals and machines for the production of commodities, but around knowledge. It is a game between persons. Post-industrial society witnesses a shift from the commodity-producing to the tertiary or service sector and a corresponding decline in the pre-eminence of the occupations of the manufacturing sector of society. One important contrast, therefore, is that a desirable standard of life in post-industrial society is no longer defined by the quantity of goods but by the quality of life as reflected in ready access to services and amenities such as health, education, leisure and the arts (cf. Bell, 1972:166).

The occupational distribution shifts toward the 'professional and technical class'. By the end of the century, this group, instead of the industrial worker, will be the largest occupational group (Bell, 1972:165). And the kind of work individuals increasingly perform requires theoretical knowledge. The chief 'resource of the post-industrial society is its scientific personnel' (Bell, 1973a:221). The importance of the 'new class' of scientists, engineers and professionals,[10] to which at this point in my discussion mere reference is made,[11] also has the result that the normative center of society shifts toward the ethos of science (Bell, 1973a:386; cf. also Whitehead, 1926; Lane, 1966; Gouldner, 1976). But despite these hints about a new normative centering in modern society, Bell's discussion of the possible basis for social solidarity and social integration of post-industrial society remains tentative and weak. It is clearly not among his central theoretical interests. By way of what Bell (1973a:26; see also Holzner and Marx, 1979:31–32) optimistically describes as 'new modes of technological forecasting', post-industrial societies may be able to plan and direct technological growth.[12] Modern (Western) society creates for its benefit a new kind of 'intellectual technology' in order to cope with the organized

[10] Radovan Richta's (1977:54) response to this kind of analysis is to argue that Bell's contentions about the rise of a 'new class' is in essence designed to contend 'with the Marxist findings concerning the crucial role of the working class in our epoch'. Moreover, as the size of the scientific and technical class increases under capitalism, it will, in some ways at least, move closer to the working class and its interests and hence contribute to conditions which may lead to its own abolition. In short, the conditions of the scientific and technological revolution have not, at least according to Richta (1977:57–59), diminished the leading role of the working class. See also Chapter 7 on the role of experts, counselors and advisers.

[11] I will discuss Bell's claim about the progressive upgrading of work, and its direct challenge, the claim by Marxist authors of the opposite long-term trend in advanced societies, namely a systematic degrading of skill levels or de-skilling of work – also linked to the technical transformation of the production process and services – later in this study in the context of the economic transformation of modern society (Chapter 6) and the role of the fastest growing component of the labor force – experts, advisers and counselors (Chapter 7).

[12] Radovan Richta (1977:26) anticipates, perhaps even more optimistically than Bell, 'a science-based revolutionary reconstruction of society'.

complexity of modern society, its varied forms of interdependence and multiplication of interaction. Such an intellectual technology represents a response to this challenge, specifically, an attempt to replace intuitive judgments with algorithms or problem-solving rules (Bell, 1973a:29). And, to the extent to which such a technology becomes 'predominant in the management of organizations and enterprises, one can say that it is as central a feature of postindustrial society as machine technology is in industrial society' (Bell, 1979a:167). In other words, the centrality of theoretical knowledge at least has a dual function. It is both the source of innovation and a foundation for policy formation in society. The extent to which and how intellectual technologies in the form of planning, for example, may also form the condition for the possibility of social solidarity and integration, however, is largely left aside by Bell as a topic of explicit consideration. The significance of any 'intellectual technology' is made all the more important in post-industrial society because Bell (1968:239) still anticipates, in addition to a general increase in the size of government, that we should expect the 'increasing substitution of political for market decisions'.

The axial structures of the emerging society are the universities and research institutions in which intellectuals work, and where 'theoretical knowledge is codified and enriched' (Bell, 1973a:26). Despite many persisting political and cultural differences among post-industrial societies, a common core of problems related largely to the management of the relations between science and public policy emerges in all of these societies (Bell, 1973a:119; also Dahrendorf, 1977:79–82).

The vision of the world in theories of post-industrial society

Daniel Bell's theory of post-industrial society[13] as the dominant socio-structural formation of the twenty-first century of the United States, Japan, the Soviet Union, and Western Europe,[14] is for the most part an up-beat, perhaps even optimistic and in many ways hopeful image of the future trends of the social structure of Western society.[15] In this respect too,

[13] Bell's theory developed over a period of some twenty years between the 1950s and the early 1970s, but mainly during the 1960s (Bell, 1973a:33–40); prior to the publication of *The Coming of Post-industrial Society* in 1973, articles in *The Public Interest* (Bell, 1967a, b) provided an initial outline of this thesis. On the whole, his approach remained remarkably consistent and underwent just minor adjustments or changes over this period. It is, therefore, possible to analyze Bell's theory of post-industrial society as being quite homogeneous; it is unnecessary to refer to stages of its development and exposition.

[14] As far as the historical origin of the new social order 'post-industrial society' is concerned, Bell (1973a:380) notes that its birth years date to the period immediately following the Second World War.

[15] It must be noted, however, that Bell (1974:24) does not agree with such a reading of his theory of post-industrial society. He does not claim to have and does not intend to convey an optimistic view of future states of society. On the contrary, he indicates emphatically, 'my view is deeply pessimistic on sociological and cultural grounds'. Post-industrial society has a

Bell's theory of society has not divorced itself from most of its classic counterparts in sociology. Some of humanity's age-old dreams, Bell insists, are about to be realized, and social change in particular will become an almost manageable process because technological development, the motor of change and growth, may be subject to rational planning and effective control.[16] With the growing sophistication of simulation procedures, Bell confidently anticipates that it will be possible to chart future alternative courses of social action, thus 'greatly increasing the extent to which we can choose and control matters that affect our lives' (Bell, 1967a:30; 1971:5). For the most part, Bell's observations then display, as was the case for sociology's theories of industrial society, an unbroken faith in the authority and power of rationality and science. Industry and science become almost indistinguishable. Science provides the cognitive basis for industry and industry the ecological underpinning of science (cf. also Gellner, 1964).

Bell's message represents an extension of the narrative of progress and its conviction of beneficial outcomes everywhere in society as the result of the increasing unlocking of the secrets of nature and society by science first expressed in the eighteenth century and then more fully developed in the nineteenth. More specifically, Bell's theory of post-industrial society also constitutes a continuation of classic sociological discourse and its stress on the cumulative possibilities and the penetration of social and political conduct by reason. Of course, Bell's promise in this respect is somewhat tempered because he restricts effective rationalization primarily to the sphere of those activities located in the social structure of modern society. None the less, Bell (1971:2) echoes Talcott Parsons' (1937:752) sentiment that 'rationality occupies a logical position in respect to action systems analogous to that of entropy in physical systems.' As rationality assumes its

---

metaphysical deficit because it lacks a transcendental ethic and political decision-making. And post-industrial society produces another vacuum since it displaces the market and is bound to generate more conflicts among groups with divergent interests. Post-industrial society therefore faces the very problems Durkheim identified as threats to social solidarity in modern society in his *Division of Labour in Society* ([1893] 1964). The solution for the missing cement that will hold society together which Bell offers does not rely on Durkheim's civic morals. Instead, Bell (1979a:169) refers us to religious answers. However, the interpretation of Bell's perspective rests to a large extent with the relative importance one is prepared to assign to structural as against cultural forces in modern society. None the less, there are other hints in Bell's multitude of observations about post-industrial society, especially of course with respect to the socio-structural transformations and their origins, that allow quite another reading of hidden sentiments of the theory and enable one to point to continuities with leading assumptions of classic social science discourse.

[16] As far as I can see, Bell (1973a:26–27) does not mean to suggest that the process of inventing technological artifacts or the development of scientific knowledge may be subjected to rigorous planning and control and that one therefore might even be able to say that history has reached its end (cf. Bell, 1971:8); however, the process of implementing 'technological advance' is increasingly subject to conscious control as his reference to technology assessment and the reduction of deleterious effects in the use of technologies in this context would appear to imply. At the same time, the quality of technological and scientific advance is transformed as well. Tinkering or trial and error gives way to a theory-driven development.

progressively dominant and enabling role in modern social affairs, the reproduction and construction of society may increasingly be predetermined and planned. These achievements, in turn, are not least the result of the growing rationalization of social science discourse and the corresponding usefulness of such discourse in society (cf. Stehr, 1992). Daniel Bell also hints strongly, in a pattern first observed for industrial society, that the economic implications of the new role of theoretical knowledge assure an almost uninterrupted expansion of capitalist and socialist economies.

While the *enabling* consequences clearly predominate in Bell's theoretical design, he identifies, both within sectors of society and as the result of the interrelation among sectors, a number of possible constraints, risks and sources of conflict related to the new quality of social relations. For example, in a thesis somewhat reminiscent of Georg Simmel's notion of a 'cultural tragedy', or Ogburn's theory of 'cultural lag', Bell (1973a:114) anticipates a major normative disjunction between culture and social structure because of the 'one becoming increasingly anti-institutional and antinomian, the other oriented to functional rationality and meritocracy'.

The same pronounced confidence and expectancy is evident in the description of the origin and consequences of massive social changes brought about by the scientific and technological revolution under state socialism,[17] as sketched by Radovan Richta and his colleagues of the Czechoslovak Academy of Sciences in the 1960s.[18] While the extensive and even dramatic social transformation of our age is triggered by science, especially in the productive sector of society, Richta also expresses his secure conviction that science and technology will be capable of controlling and checking their own consequences.[19]

For example, Richta (1977:26) stresses:

it would be difficult today to find an area of social life that remains neutral

[17] Or as Bell (1979a:112) characterizes it, 'post-socialist society'.

[18] Not suprisingly, perhaps, there are remarkable differences in certain crucial aspects of the political message between the so-called Richta Report (1969) and post-1968 statements on the same set of issues (e.g. Richta, 1977). However, the general expectations of the impact of the scientific and technological revolution does not change dramatically. Yet, the stress on democratic preconditions for a most effective implementation of the scientific and technological revolution, in particular in socialist countries (e.g. Richta et al., 1969:220, 229), is less evident later.

[19] There is a considerable, perhaps deliberate, degree of ambivalence in Richta's confidence to devise plans and programs to render the future of society transparent, or 'to steer the totality of society's growth' (Richta et al., 1969:271) since one of the constitutive attributes of the emerging society is that 'the historical process ceases to bear the stamp of an inexorable course of civilization' and that the predictability of the future is therefore diminishing (Richta et al., 1969:269). Perhaps it should be said that the pre-1968 statements, on balance, signal the conviction that any planning under the conditions of scientific and technological revolution is a precarious instrument. For example, one encounters the observation that the 'more we advance on to the actual ground of the scientific and technological revolution, the more diverse will be the ends to which its process leads, and the more unknown variants it will reveal' (Richta et al., 1969:277). The same deliberate ambivalence applies to Daniel Bell's conception of a post-industrial society.

towards and unaffected by the scope and the frequency of the sweeping changes currently under way in the fields of natural science and technology. At the same time, the wide-ranging and most significant social consequences ensuing from the application of science today relate to the tasks of a science-based control of social development, a science-based revolutionary reconstruction of society.

While Richta claims that science and technology are capable of controlling their own consequences and development, he does suggest nevertheless that 'society cannot control the scientific and technological revolution until such social relations are introduced that allow for an adequate development of man and society' (Richta, 1977:44). He therefore agrees with those critics of technology and science in *capitalist* countries who argue that the course of scientific and technological development in their societies is in danger of getting out of control.[20]

As a matter of fact, Richta describes pessimistic assessments of the growing role of science and technology as directly linked to the 'conflict-ridden development of productive forces under capitalism' which frequently generates conceptions of social development in which technology is seen as the ultimate author of all ills of society (Richta, 1977:37).[21] For Richta the problem (1977:40) may be located exactly in the opposite direction, namely in an inadequate utilization of the potential of science and technology. Thus, the limited use of the potential of science and technology in capitalist countries is itself a matter of the restricted 'rationality' of capitalist society:

> In a bourgeois society, technological progress and subsequently science . . . adhere to their own rational principles only in so far as, in these principles, the restricted 'rationality' is *a priori* incorporated. As a result, the development of science and technology follows a restricted one-sided course, offering neither the feasible nor the optimal alternative of the scientific and technological revolution (Richta, 1977: 42).

Under re-made relations of production, the scientific and technological revolution does not continually promote and suffer from structural deformities of society but contributes to the 'general development of human potentialities'. Richta affirms his belief that human beings are quite malleable because 'through its practical application, science releases the potential for an all-round development of the abilities and creative activities of the working people' (Richta, 1977:47).[22]

Moreover, the community on which the achievements of the scientific and technological revolution depend is a collectivity in the shape of a

---

[20] See also Richta et al. (1969:271–273) and Wolkow (1969:709–720).

[21] Richta (1977:38) reports on the extensive disillusionment and critical assessment of social change induced by technological inventions but describes such an evaluation of technology as a dangerous development because it tends to follow its own logic as the necessary outcome of the 'blatant absence of the human aspect in specific types of technological progress in capitalist countries' which presumably is absent from or repaired in socialist societies.

[22] Science may also, Richta (1977:47) claims, prevent 'wastage of this potential in fruitless and even harmful activities'.

'community of developing individuals' (Richta et al., 1969:266). The scientific community therefore exemplifies, as a number of social theorists anticipated, future social relations. A kind of new 'free individuality' (Karl Marx) ought to develop in society generally, minimizing our dependence on collectivities of all kinds; at a certain point individualization will, therefore, dominate as the collective social force.

Given the general spirit and world-view of the theory of post-industrial society and its Marxist inclination, it would not be too far-fetched to suggest that it may possibly represent the last serious example of such a species, that is, a sophisticated and much more subtle successor to the intellectual lineage of nineteenth-century evolutionism that located particular socio-economic and, to a lesser degree because they are dependent on the former, cultural developments at the apex of social evolution. Unfortunately, the fate of such ambiguous theoretical designs, especially the early versions of the tradition, has been to serve as a convenient ideology to legitimize the exploitation, subordination, destruction of and contempt for entire cultures.

Bell calls his theory an 'essay in sociological forecasting'. Richta's own conception is even more exacting since it is intended to (or had to) function as a socio-political program. After more than thirty years of experience with the post-industrial society and the scientific-technological revolution, however, we have become much more skeptical and careful. Neither the technocratic predictions nor the humanistic hopes have been fulfilled, yet the penetration of society by scientific knowledge appears to have continued unabated. Thus, we need to examine in greater detail why this is the case, what both authors mean when they refer to the growing 'scientification' of modern society and how they conceive of the social and economic transformations brought about by science and technology. Since these questions address, at the same time, the central problematic of this investigation, a complete answer is not possible. I will have to return to these issues repeatedly. However, some illustrative answers found in Bell and Richta are possible, answers about the role of science and technology which further testify to some of the underlying assumptions of these theoretical perspectives.

Critique of theories of post-industrial society

Theories of post-industrial and post-socialist societies have found many critics. The critical reflections, the most substantive and challenging of which I will try to discuss below, resonate with the variety and range of theoretical positions in contemporary social science and issues of the day. The alternative theory of modern society as a knowledge society developed here is part of the same critical work and further substantiates the suggestive nature of Daniel Bell's theory of post-industrial society which is a mark of all good theories.

Agreement among social scientists (and politicians) on the kinds of change which prompt speculation about an end to industrial society is fairly widespread. Virtually all theorists and most policy-makers who have posed the question of a transformation of contemporary into a post-industrial society identify social and economic developments which are broadly related, for example, the change from a goods-producing to a service economy[23] accompanied by a decline in the number and importance of blue-collar workers in the labor force, or the change in the kind of technology which drives production.[24] Thus, 'the progression of an economy such as America's from agriculture to manufacturing to services is a *natural* change' (emphasis added).[25] Perhaps the rather obvious and, in some sense at least, indisputable nature of these changes in industrial society, often made even more 'compelling' by using mainly quantified representations of these trends (e.g. Bell, 1968:154; and Table 4.1, which extends the information Bell used up to the present), forces observers to base their theoretical reflections and then interpretations, first and foremost, on these aggregate developments in the labor force of modern society.[26]

But whether these and related changes are compelling enough and

---

[23] Among the significant broad changes would be the fact that, from 1940 to 1983, in the United States, for example, employment in the manufacturing sector dropped from a quarter to a fifth of total employment. However, these broad figures representing the shrinkage of the manufacturing sector as a source of employment are by no means uncontested. Compare, for example, the assertion Heilbroner (1973:165) advances about the myth of a decline ('massive emigration from') in employment in the industrial sector, or a 'real' increase in employment in the service economy: 'if post-industrial society in fact represents a new stage of socioeconomic relationships, the cause must be sought elsewhere than in the disappearance of the industrial sector as a milieu of work.' Note also the equally definitive statements of Cohen and Zysman (1987:4) about the 'relentless decline in manufacturing employment [in the US], from about 50 percent of all jobs in 1950 down to about 20 percent now, and an irresistible increase in service jobs, up to about 70 percent of all jobs'.

[24] And as Jonathan Gershuny (1988:4–5) suggests, 'we *have to* conceptualise socio-economic change in terms of the changing balance of consumption and output and employment amongst primary and manufacturing and services, because this is the *only vocabulary that is available to use*. And of course, the only statistical accounting for employment and consumption and output is organised in terms of this vocabulary, which serves to confirm and reinforce our inability to describe the world in any other terms.'

[25] US President Ronald Reagan in a report to Congress on trade agreements in 1984/85 (cf. Office of the US Trade Representative, *Annual Report of the President of the United States on Trade Agreements Program*, 1984–1985:43).

[26] As prescribed by the premises of the logic of orthodox social science, the unit of analysis for the enumeration of the labor force is of course the *nation-state*. In addition, the classification originates with census-like data in the sphere of *production* of the national economy. As a result, information about labor force trends from within a nation as the preferred unit of analysis and uncoupled from consumption patterns within that nation may lead to information that tends to strengthen the argument about a shift toward a service economy. In an age of growing international trade, certain jobs and demand for specific commodities do not disappear altogether but are 'exported' (compare also the discussion of the decline of the use of raw materials and the changing patterns of consumption of major commodities in different regions of the world in Chapter 6).

Table 4.1 *Employment activity by sector in the United States, 1940–1988 (percentage of the workforce)[1]*

Employment sector	1940	1970	1983	1988
Agriculture, forestry, fisheries	18.3	4.5	3.5	2.6
Mining	2.2	0.6	0.9	0.6
Construction	7.0	6.1	6.1	6.6
Manufacturing	23.9	26.4	19.8	18.5
Transport, communication, utilities	8.3	6.8	6.9	6.9
Wholesale and retail trade	14.4	19.1	19.8	20.3
Finance, insurance, real estate	3.1	5.0	6.5	6.8
Professional and related services	8.0	16.4	20.5	20.6
Other services	11.4	9.4	10.1	11.5
Public administration[2]	3.4	5.7	4.7	4.6
Total	100.0	100.0	100.0	100.0
(*N* in millions)	(50)	(79)	(101)	(115)

[1] 1940: percentage of employed persons 16 and over.

[2] The employment sector 'public administration' does not appear in the 1940 data; instead the more inclusive 'government' is used.

Source: US Bureau of the Census, I (1940:180; 1975:138; 1985:404) and US Bureau of the Census, *Statistical Abstracts of the United States*, 1990

therefore add up to a kind of *break* in societal formations which justify the term 'post-industrial society' (and its functional equivalents) gains less assent among observers of the same trends. It is perhaps not surprising to find that the initial consensus among theoreticians of modern society begins to disintegrate early. It is a simple truth that cognitive agreement on relevant conventions and premises in social science on what constitutes sufficient evidence for a 'break' in social formations is lacking, and only such a consensus would allow for broader agreement. Thus, one can at best discern degrees of agreement and disagreement in social science discourse.

At times, though, there is a peculiar form of agreement among originators and critics of the theory of post-industrial society alike, namely the absence of any discussion of issues which appear to be both central to the original formulation and crucial to any critical assessment of the theoretical and empirical merits of the approach. A number of these themes will be enumerated and discussed in some detail later. At this juncture, it might be sufficient to point to a sustained lack of discussion of the preconditions for the possibility of these fundamental changes in the nature of contemporary society. For example, the decisive element repeatedly designated as the motor of change, namely scientific and technical knowledge, is habitually taken for granted. Neither is the exact (sociological) nature of this dimension examined, nor are the ways in which profound changes in society and especially the economy occur in the first place. The kinds of consequences scientific knowledge appears to have for social relations generally, and for major societal institutions and individual forms of life, remain elusive. But the critics of the theory of post-industrial society at least began work on these matters.

While the critical response to the theory of post-industrial society has been quite extensive, discussion of the notion of a post-industrial society has abated somewhat in recent years; and at least one sympathetic observer has concluded that the theory of post-industrial society has been marginalized.[27]Some critics, of course, have assailed the very notion of a post-industrial society as simply mistaken, or worse, as a conspicuous and flawed ideological effort to disguise persisting contradictions in industrial society and hide the real interests of those who benefit from such a state of affairs. Thus, the most radical critique, not only based on neo-Marxist premises, argues, while accepting that science and technology have assumed a much more significant societal function, that the 'spread of technical rationality into organizational and economic life and, hence, into social life' is more aptly 'described as a second and much more intensive phase of the industrial revolution' (McDermott, 1969:34). The shape of social conflicts and of major political and economic contradictions in contemporary society therefore is but an extension of those already in clear evidence in industrial society (e.g. Walker, 1985). The radical critique of the theory of post-industrial society affirms the continuity of the modern world while post-industrial theorists assert that modern life is a world of change.

But the fixation of the more radical critique of the theory of post-industrial society on features of industrial society which are more or less persistent, if not permanent, attributes of modern society, namely the existence of power elites, social inequality, unemployment, poverty, a concentration of control in the economy, societal antagonisms and contradictions, social control and constraints, can, in my view, only distract from gaining insights into the *dynamic* character of modern society. That is, the radical critique is long on constant, static and fixed ills and somewhat short on dynamic and evolving configurations of socio-economic and political realities in modern society. Without question, there are many enduring social attributes, but the dynamic features may well be the key for the very persistence of inequality and conflict. It is also true that theorists of post-industrial and post-socialist society display a misplaced optimism that an analysis of these features can be discarded because they are bound to evaporate before long. At the same time, the radical critique of theories of post-industrial society is often as repetitive as are alleged permanent features of modern society. But the radical critique rarely manages to advance our understanding of modern, changing societies aside, of course, from warning us about and alerting us to certain enduring social structures.

My review of the critiques which, with the theorists of post-industrial society, shares the assumption that modern society is undergoing funda-

---

[27] One prominent work of American social scientists devoted to the state of American life and entitled *America at Century's End* (Wolfe, 1991), for example, does not once mention Daniel Bell and his theory of post-industrial society (see also Block, 1990:5). On the other hand, in the context of lively debate and dispute about modernity and post-modernity, the same theoretical project is often taken into consideration (cf. Turner, 1990).

mental transformations requiring a new theoretical perspective, has to be selective. Some of the issues pursued by the critics are raised more properly elsewhere in the analysis, or are pervasive themes of this analysis generally. Among these issues are, for instance: the question of the nature of power relations or the authority of the state; the pertinence of a reversal of the relation between 'base' and 'superstructure' and the importance to the service sector of the economy of cultural and socio-structural relations. Still other matters raised at length years ago by a range of critics are evidently dated by events.[28] As a result, they do not warrant further and serious discussion except as indications of the fragility of theoretical programs in the face of pressing issues of the day. Theoretical programs are often rapidly reduced to rhetorical resources in intellectual and political disputes. However, their career as such rhetorical devices indicates, at the same time, that they have achieved a measure of practical influence. But such immediate practical success is limited to a smaller range of theoretical ideas in social science.

Daniel Bell's theory of post-industrial society was first proposed in a historical context where intellectual energies were challenged and then preoccupied by the student movement, its prospect and the role of social aggregates other than the working class as decisive historical forces in capitalist societies. Such points of reference inevitably affected the design and message of the theory of post-industrial society as did, for other reasons, the particulars of the then widely discussed conditions for limits to economic growth, or even more obviously, the lengthy comments by Bell on current political events found in sections of *The Coming of Post-industrial Society* (1973a). Similarly, every critique and adaptation of Bell's theory has its own agenda and peculiar points of reference. The same applies to my review of these comments; they, too, are grounded in specific theoretical concerns.

A good example of the genre of the liberal adaptation of a concept and the rapid obsolescence of the transformation is Christopher Lasch's discussion of post-industrial society in the early 1970s. He uses the term to connect a range of manifold observations about American political and social issues of the day. However, these statements are advanced as profound claims about apparently irreversible socio-historical trends rather than as casual opinions and comments on socio-political and intellectual struggles of the day.

---

[28] Among the issues raised and then projected into the future in Bell's observations are some which prove to be, after almost thirty years, close to accurate. For example, Bell (1964:50) discussed the effects of the growing importance of education for patterns of inequality in general and advancement and mobility in particular and anticipates that in the United States, in the next twenty or thirty years, the 'economic position of the Negro may become relatively worse'. Indeed, recent studies have shown, contrary to the expectations of many programs and policy intentions in those decades, that this is the case (e.g. Jaynes and Williams, 1989; Hacker, 1991).

To list but a few of the more obvious cases, one might refer to his assertions that post-industrial society 'demands a continual state of military emergency and a global crusade against an enemy, the "international communist conspiracy", with which there can be no compromise', or 'it is apparent that higher education is extended to women not because their skills are needed in production but because they are consumers *par excellence*' and that in post-industrial society 'poverty is found isolated in "pockets" or "islands" and tends to become "invisible"' (Lasch, 1972:42,43,37). Virtually every single claim, as events since have shown, is of dubious merit. But Lasch (1972:48) advances one observation, though it is twinned with an assertion which further illustrates the general point, which is worth taking seriously, namely that post-industrial society is an 'inherently unstable form of society'. He certainly does not apply this logic to his own observations about such a social formation. Lasch indicates that there is good reason to believe that post-industrial society comes into being 'when capital accumulation has reached the point where scarcity is no longer a major social problem – that is, when the industrial system has developed the capacity to satisfy all basic human needs' (Lasch, 1972:36). Obviously, this is not merely a friendly over-generalization but an erroneous claim; at least it is difficult to comprehend why poverty once eradicated by appropriate economic and social means, in fact 're-surfaces'.

The varied and persistent dissent from the theories of post-industrial society may be conveniently divided into objections which, first, address the most general question, namely the very status of post-industrial society in the modern world. How valid a judgment is the assertion that post-industrial society is set to become the world's dominant social formation? Such general assessments can rarely be separated clearly from a critical consideration of specific assertions about the ascent of post-industrial society. However, I will try to discuss, secondly, a number of particular objections, for example, critiques which deal with the role of 'theoretical knowledge' in post-industrial society, the 'new' technology, the composition of the labor force, power-holders, or the possibility of more extensive and effective planning and control of social activities. At times, the comments are constructive elaborations of suggestions found in the theory of post-industrial society and therefore also show the location of implicit agreement between Daniel Bell and his critics. Thirdly, critical responses frequently deal extensively with practical, or political, implications of the theory of post-industrial society and I will refer to a number of these observations. Finally, my review of the critique of the theory of post-industrial society is followed by an assessment of the assembled critical comments and of the theory itself, benefiting from a more distanced perspective, if only in terms of additional time which has elapsed and events which have occurred. Naturally such distance is of some benefit for a re-examination of the theory of post-industrial society and its explicit and implicit projections as well as critical counter-projections.

Is there a post-industrial society at all?

Many critics of the theory of post-industrial society dismiss the idea more
or less outright. They deny that it is justified to speak of modern society in
these terms. However, I will treat such objections with equal brevity and
simply enumerate the range and points of reference of such dissension:
Critics have dismissed the model as 'epigonic' (*nihil novi sub sole*), an
expression of 'intellectual disorientation' (Lenk, 1987:311),[29] as 'unrealistic'
because historically a new type of society never emerges this rapidly
(Kumar, 1989:41), as a right-wing response to industrial class conflict
(Frankel, 1987:3–6), as a 'useful ideology for certain social forces and
interests' (Ferkiss, 1979:91)[30] or, briefer as a 'new ideology' (Frankel,
1987:383), even as a doctrinaire and impoverished Marxist theory (Floud,
1971), as capturing the realities of two or maybe three years in the mid-
1960s (Miller, 1975:28), or as an occasion to affirm the genius of Marx (cf.
Schroyer, 1974). From one historian's point of view (Stearns, 1974), Bell
fails to adduce sufficient historical evidence to 'prove' the existence of a
post-industrial society. That is, the societal framework has not changed in
the way that it changed from agricultural to industrial society[31] and many
of the trends he likens to post-industrial developments had already begun,
according to Stearns, in early industrial society, for instance: the co-
operation between science and industry, as in the case of chemistry, the
emergence of white-collar workers, the increasing tempo in transportation,
etc. But, most importantly, Bell fails to indicate, but as Bell might say
quite deliberately, what the consciousness of the post-industrial society is
and how the mental framework therefore differs from that prevailing in
industrial society (Stearns, 1974:14).

The general thrust of the more serious, comprehensive but still critical
assessments of the theory of post-industrial society, that is, by critics who
do simply want to banish the model outright from social science discourse,
can perhaps best be summarized with the observation that in industrial
societies, profound *economic, social and/or cultural* changes indeed are
underway and are readily observable. In other words, the evidence

---

[29] Lenk (e.g. 1987:329) proclaims, with substantial pride, priority for a number of
'important' observations about advanced modern society that he discovered before Bell's
analysis of these tendencies and theoretical interpretations of comparable events. But Lenk
conveniently overlooks the fact that most of the essential outlines of Bell's theory of post-
industrial society were first published in the form of essays during the course of the 1960s and
not in 1973.

[30] According to Ferkiss (1979:91–94), the ideological function of Bell's theory of post-
industrial society within intellectual politics represents, more specifically, (a) the attempt to
refute classical Marxism; (b) the effort to defend the 'new class' in American society; and (c)
as an apologetic function for rationalism.

[31] In the light of such objections, it is, however, legitimate to ask whether the societal
transformation between agrarian and industrial society for all times and in a definitive manner
set the standard against which all other subsequent changes have to be judged if they want to
qualify as basic societal transformations, that is, as the origin of a novel societal system.

assembled to make the case is convincing but hardly compelling. Evidently important transformations are under way; they are at best necessary but not sufficient conditions to allow for the judgment that we are witnessing or that we have already witnessed a break in modern societal formations. On balance these different trends therefore lack sufficient specificity or coherence and really do not represent satisfactory confirmation to consider industrial society and its dominant social formations at a sudden end (e.g. Badham, 1986). Thus, a kernel of truth, or sometimes even multiple bits of adequate observations, are acknowledged to be part of Bell's theory of post-industrial society but the conclusion which he tries to advance, namely that the sum total of these socio-structural trends represents an emergent and distinctive form of society is not accepted.

These critics therefore would prefer to stress, for example, that 'industrial and post-industrial society are linked, not simply by the persistence of particular trends in social and economic life, but by the most general and abstract principles governing their development' (Kumar, 1978:235).[32] This group of critics often see the trends Bell enumerates as mere elaborations, as a working out, or as an evolution of well-entrenched social formations, many of which are already in place in early industrial society. It is much too early to completely dismiss or disregard the industrial framework as a matter of the past.

Thus, post-industrial society can also be seen as another stage of capitalism and not as a step beyond capitalism (e.g. Heilbroner, 1973:170), or even industrial society. Following much the same logic, other critics deny the efficacy of naming what is still a capitalist society by any other name than capitalism, or at best 'neo-capitalism', because the mode of social organization has not really changed (e.g. Miller, 1975:1–2). In short, it is highly improbable, as Kumar (1978:238) for example stresses, that 'changes of the same revolutionary order could be transforming the industrial societies so soon after the fundamental and long-drawn-out rupture with the feudal, agrarian and peasant societies from which they emerged'.

A second group of critics, also attempting to arrive at comprehensive evaluation of the merits of the basic thesis of the theory of post-industrial society, ultimately advances a somewhat more ambivalent reaction to the scenario Bell outlines. And their criticism is voiced in rather different terms, and ranges from concern with the lack of precision of the basic

---

[32] Kumar (1978:231) explicates and illustrates his conclusions about the persistence of forms of domination of industrial life in the following manner: 'Beneath the postindustrial gloss, old scarred problems rear their heads: alienation and control in the workplace of the service economy; scrutiny and supervision of the operations of private and public bureaucracies, especially as they come to be meshed in with technical and scientific expertise. Framing all these is the problem of the dominant constraining and shaping force of contemporary industrial societies: competitive struggles for profit and power between private corporations and nation states, in an environment in which such rivalries have a tendency to become expansionist and global.'

terms of the model, to the suggestion that the observable changes are, in the final instance, merely an extension of the features of the industrial age, or that the theory has a respectable intellectual ancestry dating back at least to the nineteenth century and therefore is simply an amalgam of the theories of modern society of Saint-Simon, Comte, de Tocqueville and Weber and that Bell's theory can hardly lay claim to having anticipated or captured a new era in human civilization.

Anthony Giddens ([1973] 1980:259), for example, expresses skeptical admiration mixed with severe reservations about the theory of post-industrial society. That is, theories of post-industrial society, which he summarily labels 'technocratic theories' are

> attractive precisely because they appear to encapsulate some of the most striking and distinctive features of the contemporary world . . . And yet the very fact that technocratic theories are not new, that they date back to the early origins of industrialism in nineteenth-century Europe, should warn us to be suspicious of their claim to separate out what is novel in the emergent 'post-industrial' universe from the merely 'industrialized' era of recent past history.

Moreover, the assumption that post-industrial society is a unitary type, that the economy primarily drives the development of society, or that the most 'advanced' type of society shows to other societies what their often unavoidable future will be like, does not constitute a novel theoretical observation because these assertions already firmly govern theorizing about industrial society. Moreover, these assumptions generally resonate with and compound the inadequacies of the orthodox assumptions of nineteenth-century social theory; for example, the fallacious presumption about the level of economic or technological development as determining, in the last instance, societal development as a whole.

In other words, Giddens ([1973] 1980:253–274) objects not so much to observations which emphasize discontinuities between industrial and post-industrial societies but to the remaining and strong methodological and substantive affinities between the theory of post-industrial society and its predecessor, the theory of industrial society.[33] Giddens identifies three premises shared by both approaches:

1 The theory of post-industrial society claims for itself to describe, as does the theory of industrial society, a type of society which is, or ultimately will be, quite common around the world.
2 The development of society and its theoretical identity are primarily determined by the economic system, or formulated in a much more reductionist sense, by the level of its technology and therefore not by other factors and processes, for example, its political and cultural organization.

---

[33] Ralf Dahrendorf (1988:137) reports a similar, though more generalized sentiment upon re-reading Bell's *The Coming of Post-industrial Society*, 'one is struck by its tone, which is very much that of an industrial society, albeit one which has progressed beyond manufacturing to information-led economic growth.'

3   Both social formations are seen by their proponents as special, fully developed types of society anticipating the path of development for all those societies which have not as yet undergone the same transformations. In a continuation of assumptions governing classic sociological discourse on types of society, the observed socio-economic patterns of change are seen as necessary, or 'natural' and obligatory evolutionary structures of development.

As far as I can see, Giddens primarily objects to granting theoretical pre-eminence to economic-technical over normative, cultural, political-ideological or military factors because such a strategy tends to minimize the actual importance of these sectors and their actors to society. Perhaps such an objection is not entirely fair or justified because Bell tries to distance himself, from time to time, explicitly from the idea that technological developments independently induce social changes, or for that matter, that technical innovations are self-generated.[34] A similar note of caution may be seen in Bell's repeated insistence that his interest, at least in *The Coming of Post-industrial Society*, centers on socio-structural transformations in society.

Giddens is not convinced that certain technological and economic developments constitute opportunities or constraints that are iron-clad and will be repeated in society after society. Of course, this also means that Giddens is not impressed that developments observed for the United States are invariably exemplary for other countries. The ability of the United States to successfully generate and sustain the developments Bell describes depends, to a considerable extent, on historically unique conditions and therefore cannot be freely exported. Any influence the United States exercises abroad depends more on its political-military might and the considerable influence of American multinational corporations.[35]

In some ways, these criticisms have also been anticipated by Bell. At least, he insists, in a self-critical and self-restricting fashion, in the introduction to his *The Coming of Post-industrial Society* (Bell, 1973a) that he is not, unlike Marx, a proponent of a deterministic conception of history. That is to say, the fate of the United States does not necessarily preview that of other societies (see also Bell, 1973b:748). None the less, Bell does not always strictly adhere to his own precepts (cf. Smart, 1992:35).

Giddens ([1973] 1980:262) finally doubts that it is possible to translate knowledge into power and that knowledge as a productive force represents a unique attribute of post-industrial society; on the contrary, 'modern technology is not "post-industrial" at all, but is the fruition of the principle

[34] As I have indicated, Bell (1973a:110) repeatedly tries to stress that 'the initiative in organizing a society these days comes largely from the political system.'

[35] Other critics of the theory of post-industrial society express doubts that certain transformations of the labor force in the United States, for example, the growing proportion of scientific-technical personnel, may be considered to be exemplary for other countries since the increase in the number of persons in these occupations is in response to exceptionally high military expenditures (compare, for example, Tilton, 1973:730).

of accelerating technical growth built into industrialism as such.' It is possible, on the basis of these considerations, to describe industrialization and economic growth as the outcome of intellectual efforts in as much as the process of industrialization is linked to the realization of (technical) knowledge, namely knowledge about the ways objects function (cf. Landes, 1980:111).

The critique that the identity of modern society, and therefore the evolution of stages of modern society, is not merely driven by its economic realities, already incorporates an objection to the reality of post-industrial society which makes reference to the normative center and foundation of society as its most distinguishing attribute. Calhoun (1992:225) notes an unfortunate lack of attention by Bell to the question of social integration in post-industrial society. But Bell's account not only displays a lack of concern with the forces of social solidarity in modern society; the assertion about a fundamental discontinuity in modern society is misleading because there has been no 'basic shift in the form of social integration' that warrants the assertion that a new sort of society might 'reasonably be declared to exist'. The normative transformations and changes in cultural dispositions which have occurred and are observable are, as other critics have already emphasized, very much in line with familiar changes that have taken place throughout the modern era. In short, for most critics of the theory of post-industrial society, modernity, capitalism and the modern age generally persist.

Specific objections

The critical objections to Bell's theory not only originate with general theoretical agendas concerned with ways of conceptualizing modern society and its dynamic, or perspectives legitimizing the continued existence of industrial society and its established conflicts. On the contrary, many of the trenchant comments pertain to particular observations about specific aspects of post-industrial society or implications Bell's position appear to have for entrenched theoretical and methodological approaches to social and economic affairs. Some of the assessments also address, broadly speaking, from a sociology of knowledge point of view, how some of the salient attributes of the theory of post-industrial may have originated, or to which 'local' intellectual and/or political concerns, in the sense of national community for example, they may attempt to respond. Particular objections range from comments about Bell's discussion of the impact of post-industrial social developments on social inequality or of working conditions, to the role of values in the transformation of societies and the extent to which developments observed in the United States anticipate trends for other societies.

Bell's reflections on social inequality, for example, are frequently assailed by Marxists as a violation and rejection of their perspective on class relations, or as Stearns (1974:16–22) argues, the class structure of contemporary society has to be understood as an extension of earlier industrial class structure and not as a departure from it. At best, he is prepared to accept that an evolution of class structure has occurred but not a fundamental break in the class structure. The occupational structure in developed societies accordingly is for the most part an extension of the range of structures and positions already in evidence with the emergence of the industrial social structure, some of which took a considerable time to fully develop.

At the same time, Anthony Giddens ([1973] 1980:264) observes that the theory of post-industrial society has an apologetic streak because the language of technocratic theories actually masks the general failure

> to get to grips with problems which need a precise and concrete analysis; the idea that one all-embracing type of social order, that is, 'industrial society', is being replaced by another such overall system glosses over the need to examine the interconnections and sources of conflict between sub-groups and classes of which societies are composed.

The theory of post-industrial society therefore repeats, Giddens concludes, the error of the functionalist theory of industrial society because it too systematically underestimates, even hides, sources and processes of conflict among divergent groups in society. Tilton (1973:730), in his review of Bell's *The Coming of Post-industrial Society*, using an approach critical of the underlying 'ideology' of the theory of post-industrial society, indicates how much, in his view, the theory is affected by its own national context. That is, it has an 'incorrigibly American character' when judged by the fact that most of the empirical examples and most of the statistics draw on US sources. The explicit and implicit message therefore pertains to the exemplary nature of American society for post-industrial society. In fact, some of the developments may be unique to the US, for example, the large percentage of scientific personnel since they may be the result of efforts by the US government to retain its role as the world's dominant military power. By the same token, Goldthorpe (1971:282; also Stearns, 1974:14) asserts that the theory of post-industrial society systematically underestimates the independent influence of values and a change in values as a motor of social transformation in modern society. Specifically, Bell takes the ideology of economic growth for granted and cannot imagine that such value orientations associated with it may be transcended at some future point. However, I will not pursue these criticisms in any further detail here; instead, I plan to concentrate on aspects of the theory of post-industrial society of more immediate interest in the context of developing a theory of knowledge societies.

The axial principle

The axial principle of post-industrial society, or more precisely, its social structure, is the codification of theoretical knowledge. The axial principles of the remaining sectors of (modern) society are self-fulfillment in the cultural system and equality and the right to representation in the political system. As Bell (1974:23) adds, though all societies rely on knowledge, dependence on the codification of theoretical knowledge as a source and mode of innovation is new. This observation is especially fitting for the 'new science based industries . . . computers, telecommunications, optics, polymers, and electronics'. However, any systematic *sociological* reflection on the nature of 'theoretical knowledge' (and its interrelation with technology) is virtually absent from Bell's *The Coming of Post-industrial Society* as well as the many essays and studies which preceded its publication.

I will discuss this omission below and it is not sensible, in my view, to merely substitute knowledge production for the production of goods. Nor is there much reflection in Bell's theory on what would appear to be at least strongly implicit in his thesis, namely the idea that a notion of the axial principle of theoretical knowledge simultaneously constitutes a plea for a historic reversal of the base–superstructure relation. Even if one assumes, as Bell certainly does, that the most immediate impact of the new axial principle is on the economy – resulting in such changes as a shift in the division of labor, the development of specialized occupations, the emergence of new enterprises, the shift among economic sectors and sustained growth – the source of the changes manifest in the economic structure is, in the final analysis, the product of cognitive efforts which lead to the incessant growth in knowledge claims.[36] Therefore, socio-structural processes are not, at least immediately, the motor of social change in modern society. In addition, the symmetry of base and superstructure is reversed.

None the less rather different interpretations of the macro-sociological consequences of post-industrial developments and the axial principle remain, indicating considerable theoretical ambivalence. Is it the case, as Heilbroner (1973:175), for example, emphatically states, that all speculation about 'post industrialism assumes that the causal line of inference runs from the economic changes to the political and social changes' and that the 'primum mobile of "prediction" ' remains the economic process of social transformation?

Knowledge and skills

The same ambivalence does not extend to discussions about the notion of 'knowledge' or 'skills' for there appears to be agreement among commentators and originators that these concepts are not among the essentially contested notions of the theory of post-industrial society. Both in Bell's formulation and in the comments of critics, the nature and role of knowledge and skills are taken for granted. This is not to say that the

---

[36] Cf. my discussion of science as an immediately productive force in Chapter 5.

concept of knowledge, its dimensions and structures, the pace of its growth, how its economic contribution can be measured and what effects it has on the nature of work in modern society are not discussed. On the contrary, these questions are extensively addressed (e.g. Bell, 1968). But in another and more important sense, a discussion of his notion of theoretical knowledge, its relation to technology, the new, instrumental use of knowledge and the 'startling shift' in the character of knowledge itself does not occur at all. It does not occur because there is a tacit consensus about the nature of *scientific* knowledge. The social structure in which such knowledge operates productively is, as is knowledge, 'linear, cumulative, and quantitative for there are specific rules for the process of growth and differentiation' (Bell, [1975] 1980:31). Thus, the absence of controversy on this central dimension of the theory of post-industrial society is not an accidental omission or commission.

The few and largely unexplicated hints which Bell as well as Richta, whose conception of science and technology Bell explicitly endorses, offer about the concept of 'theoretical' knowledge, the reasons for an accelerated societal demand for such knowledge, the conditions for the quickened pace of growth of knowledge, the reasons for its reliability and the manner of its forceful impact on society and so on, indicate, despite their brevity, that the notion of knowledge can be treated in such a shorthand fashion because of an implicit reference to what is assumed to be a widely shared understanding of the nature of science and scientific knowledge. What everyone knows and accepts obviously does not need extensive reflection.

The justification for the abbreviated treatment of the axial principle is that knowledge is introduced and conceived from the point of view of what can only be called a strong version of 'scientism'. Scientism is a comprehensive conception of the nature of scientific knowledge, of the role of the scientific process, of science's impact on society, including its barely recognizable or relevant limits, of the relation between science and (rational) political as well as economic action, and last but not least, of the legitimacy of science. Scientism as used here to describe some of the unexplicated premises in Bell's and Richta's analysis of the distinct role of science, originated in the nineteenth century but is still the most influential and powerful conception of the nature of science and its effects on society. Scientism has become, in its most general outlines, such a widely accepted and persuasive view that it is, for most intents and purposes, superfluous to systematically discuss the reason for the growth and power of scientific knowledge even within sociological discourse, at least until very recently.

Even those critics who would not accept or subscribe to scientism because they are highly critical of the nature of the observed impact of science and technology on nature and society, or because they fear that scientific rationalism born in a fight against superstition has itself become a modern force akin to superstition, none the less accept, with considerable reluctance of course, the premise of almost non-existent limits to the influence of science and technology on society. Paradoxically, critics are almost forced to accept the premise of the lack of any serious and systematic limits to the power of science because their critique feeds on and lives by the same premise. These interdependencies show, at the same time, that the success of scientism as an ideology or image of the social relations of science represents, until this very day, an overwhelming intellectual success.

But how do Bell and Richta conceptualize knowledge and the reasons for its strategic function more specifically? First, for Daniel Bell (1973a:20), as I have indicated already, knowledge is an anthropological constant and has of course been necessary in the functioning of any society. What is therefore distinctive about post-industrial society is the change in the character of knowledge itself. What has become decisive for the organization of decisions and the direction of change is the centrality of theoretical knowledge: the primacy of theory over empiricism and the codification of knowledge into abstract systems of symbols that, as in any axiomatic system, can be used to illuminate many different and varied areas of experience. Every modern society now lives by innovation and the social control of change, and tries to anticipate the future in order to plan ahead. The commitment to social control introduces the need for social planning and forecasting into society. It is the altered awareness of the nature of innovation that makes theoretical knowledge so crucial. By the same token:

> the advances in a field become increasingly dependent on the primacy of theoretical work, which codifies what is known and points the way to empirical confirmation. In effect, theoretical knowledge increasingly becomes the strategic resource, the axial principle, of a society. And the university, research organiz-ations, and intellectual institutions, where theoretical knowledge is codified and enriched, become the axial structures of the emergent society (Bell, 1973a:26).

Elsewhere in *The Coming of Post-industrial Society*, Daniel Bell offers and discusses both more general and more restrictive conceptions of knowledge, depending on the purpose at hand. If the referent is social policy, for example, Bell (1973a:176) proposes to define knowledge in a pragmatic, even utilitarian sense as that 'which is objectively known, an intellectual property, attached to a name or a group of names and certified by copyright or some other form of social recognition (e.g. publication)' and therefore as something whose qualities are evidently not unique to post-industrial society. Given that such knowledge functions like a symbolic commodity in exchange relations, knowledge is paid for and is subjected to the economic judgment of the market. Knowledge is part of the social overhead of society (Bell, 1968:163). But such a notion of knowledge as socially useful symbolic capital, and Bell's more general (academic) conception of knowledge defined below, deliberately refrains, as Bell himself acknowledges, from reflecting on an important range of sociological dimensions of knowledge production, forms of knowledge, the transfer of knowledge and the social consequences of knowledge.

Bell also proposes an encyclopedic conception of knowledge; he defines it as 'a set of organized statements of facts or ideas, presenting a reasoned judgment or an experimental result, which is transmitted to others through some communication medium in some systematic form' (1973a:175). Bell adds that this definition of knowledge allows for the separation of knowledge from mere news or entertainment, in as much as knowledge involves new judgments (i.e. research and scholarship) or new combinations of older judgments (i.e. textbook and teaching). He stresses, moreover, that this encyclopedic conception of knowledge is, in as much as it includes explicit reference to collective and/or 'objective' criteria concerning the validity of knowledge claims, a considerably less general and generous conception of knowledge than Fritz Machlup's characterization of knowledge as that which any individual cares to consider to be knowledge (cf. Machlup, 1962:21).

It is evident that Bell (1973a:345) also wants to emphasize that the defining characteristic of post-industrial society is not merely forms of symbolic or encyclopedic knowledge but particular knowledge claims, namely theoretical knowledge. The power and legitimacy which demarcate theoretical knowledge are not affected by time and place. Independent of contingent conditions, theoretical knowledge can be 'translated into many different and varied circumstances'. Bell therefore highlights what can only be described as ideal outcomes of scientific knowledge production and justification.

The constituent attributes of Bell's discourse on theoretical knowledge originate with and gain currency from rationalist, epistemological discourse about scientific knowledge. More specifically, its constitutive attributes, for example, generality, objectivity and abstractness (cf. Bell, 1979a:209 n. 16) which, in this context, operate as demarcation criteria, are characteristic of an epistemology of scientific knowledge which celebrates the extent to which proper methodological procedures generate knowledge ultimately void of any traces of its origins or originators. Bell's conception of theoretical knowledge bears some family resemblance to Friedrich Hayek's ([1945] 1948:80) early notion of scientific knowledge, although Hayek wants to stress the opposite principle in his discussion of the use of knowledge in economic affairs, namely, the limits of scientific knowledge and therefore the pertinence, even the superiority at times and in some contexts of what he calls the knowledge of the 'particular circumstances of time and place'. That is to say, scientific knowledge distinguishes itself by its ability to transcend time and place and is therefore of general relevance. However, in Hayek's view, the 'opportunity costs' of general knowledge are its inability to address local circumstances which require the command of 'unorganized' knowledge. But such knowledge can and does perform eminently useful functions in specific or unique circumstances.

The conception of knowledge employed by Bell cannot but have some affinity to the entrenched debate about general and individual 'knowledge' as one encounters it, for instance, in the neo-Kantian philosophy of science at the turn of this century, or for that matter, in the context of many other

similar efforts designed to come to grips with the apparent gap between
what is apprehended as unique and what is claimed to be common to many
situations.

In the early 1920s, Karl Mannheim ([1980] 1982:155) had already
characterized the social origins and function of the epistemological
assumptions, which inform Bell's conception of knowledge, in a very
perceptive fashion as the development of methodological views which
celebrate, above all, the extent to which knowledge is 'depersonalized and
decommunalized', the extent therefore to which 'the known is to be
detached from any particular and communically-rooted subject in order to
locate it on a conceptual level accessible only to any conceivable subject.'
As Mannheim ([1980] 1982:163) emphasizes as well, the origins of
rationalist epistemology can only be explained on the basis of a change in
the existential relationship among people and in the relationship between
people and things. In other words, Bell's conception of theoretical
knowledge and the reasons for its authority and power in social relations
are rather distant from a sociological conception of either the construction
of scientific knowledge and technological systems or their varied social
consequences.

The outcome of the pre-eminence of theoretical knowledge, for Bell
(1973a:344), is that 'every society now lives by innovation and growth, and
it is theoretical knowledge that has become the matrix of innovation.' Both
in the context of knowledge utilization but also in the context of the
production of theoretical knowledge for application, knowledge claims
are strongly linked to such fundamental epistemological attributes as
rationality, planning, control and foresight. The development of advanced
industrial society, and more so post-industrial society, is profoundly
affected by the 'extension of a particular dimension of rationality' (Bell,
1971:2).

The theme of an acceleration in the rationality of social action, and of
the conviction that the spread of rationality fosters social and economic
progress, is first elaborated in the eighteenth century. It becomes a
pervasive topic of classic sociological analysis. As well, it became embodied in warfare and industry. The same vision also resonates with a
technocratic ethos which Bell (1973a:349) anticipates will further spread in
post-industrial society. In its emphasis

> on the logical, practical, problem-solving, instrumental, orderly, and precision
> and measurement and a concept of a system, it is a world-view quite opposed to
> the traditional and customary religious, esthetic, and intuitive modes. It draws
> deeply from the Newtonian world-view, and the eighteenth-century writers who
> inherited Newton's thought did indeed believe, as Hume has Cleanthes say in his
> *Dialogues Concerning Natural Religion*, that the author of Nature must be
> something of an engineer, since Nature is a machine; and they believed, further,
> that within a short time the rational method would make all thought amenable to
> its laws.

Bell's description of the intellectual origins of the technocratic world-view is a useful reminder that the instrumental consciousness is not a novel, that is, merely modern historical phenomenon. In addition, the technocratic consciousness of classical positivism has had its counterpart, in some instances to this very day, in Marxism as it too tries to pin its hopes for an emerging society on both the inevitable destruction of the past and the scientific re-construction of the future (cf. Gouldner, 1976). Indeed, such a technocratic consciousness and confidence as well as resemblance to Bell's treatment of theoretical knowledge can be found in Radovan Richta's theory of the scientific-technological revolution. For example, in an essay first presented in 1974, Richta (1977:30) points out:

> Once a closed, exclusive area on the margin of society, science becomes an immense organism operating in all spheres of social life. A new type of science is gradually emerging, differing considerably as to social function and theoretical and methodological principles from both ancient knowledge . . . and the New-Age science originating during the Renaissance and the Industrial Revolution . . . The logic underlying this development is a tendency towards the integration of the process of cognition (and transformation) of the world with the process of self-cognition (and transformation) of the society – the conception of science evolved by Marx, Engels and Lenin.

In a previous publication, with somewhat less deference to the heroes of Marxist thought and more precision, Richta et al. (1969:217) describe the nature of the new type of enabling science as follows:

> Science owes its new status primarily to its exceptional power of *generalization*. In contrast to other products, a scientific finding is not consumed by use, on the contrary it is improved on and then 'it costs nothing'. Moreover, science possesses a peculiar *growth* potential. Every finding is both a result and then starting point for further research; the more we know, the more we can find out. This intrinsically exponential quality distinguishes science sharply from all traditional activities of the industrial type.

Similarly,

> fundamental changes are in progress in the field of technology . . . a new technological basis relying on automation and cybernetics is gradually coming into being. This sets into motion the entire machinery system – thus shifting the focus of man's nature-oriented activities from the mere transformation of nature to the control over the entire process of transformation of nature by society (Richta, 1977:30–31).

In their initial analysis of the scientific-technological revolution, published as *Civilization at the Crossroads*, Richta and his collaborators (1969:212–213) stress that science at present is no longer primarily 'a factor of social consciousness' but a 'productive force', which is 'being converted in one way or another into applications of science'. And ultimately, under the circumstances of the scientific and technological revolution, 'growth of the productive forces follows a law of higher priority, that is, the precedence of science over technology and of technology over industry' (Richta et al., 1969:41). However, Richta and his colleagues (1969:34) also emphasize that a fundamental transformation of human activity occurs through which individuals assume a new position in the world of productive forces. They stress that it would be misleading to see the scientific and technological revolution merely as the result of more scientific knowledge and of more technical application. The truly relevant criterion for the revolutionary character of the impact of science and technology is, therefore, the transformation it brings about in the relation of humans to the forces of production, more specifically, the greater distance of most people from direct production, or the increase in the 'subjective factor' of production. None the less, Richta leaves the strong impression that these profound changes are in the end the outcome of a wider application of science but not necessarily any 'new' form of knowledge production.

Aside from treating knowledge, the axial principle of post-industrial society, as a kind of black box, Bell also does not convincingly address, or propose to treat, the *sociological distinctiveness* and specificity of the production and nature of the claims and use of knowledge in *this type of social order* compared to the general role it is supposed to have had in industrial society. This is not unimportant because some theorists have already assigned to knowledge in industrial society the function it only acquires according to Bell in post-industrial society. Gellner (1964:179), concurrent with the publication of Bell's first exposition of the theory of post-industrial society, suggests that in industrial society knowledge plays 'a part wholly different from that which it played in earlier social forms'. Moreover, the type of knowledge typically found in pre-industrial society is quite a different form of knowledge. Thus, at least for Gellner, modern science is intimately linked to industrial society and industry is closely dependent on science.

The lack of interest in analyzing the sociological dimensions of theoretical knowledge and its startling new qualities is perhaps best explained as a passive acceptance by Bell of the entrenched division of labor in scientific discourse. It is the legitimacy of the same division of labor which has for decades pre-empted the sociology of knowledge from extending its perspective and analytical tools to an examination of scientific knowledge.

New technology

For many social theorists, from Karl Marx to Joseph Schumpeter, without adopting a position of technological determinism, it has long been the case that technological change, through its impact on productivity and the ease with which information flows, is one of the important sources of economic growth and change in the structure of the economy.

The same assumption holds for Bell's theory of the origins and transformation of the post-industrial economy. That is, it is quite evident that Bell's theory of post-industrial society and its equivalents are animated by the conviction that technology, especially *new forms of technology*, transform society, in particular industrial production, but the emphasis remains superficial unless it also provides insight into the comprehensive and original effects new technology has on social relations, including evolving normative conceptions, risks and limits on social conduct. Despite the substantial importance one may assign to the impact of technology and technological rationality, a mere reiteration of its economic significance, and the bland assertion that it is somehow novel, lacks the convincing theoretical force and fails to separate the assertion from its many predecessors in social and economic theory. On the basis of the observations offered about the nature of the new technology, one can only conclude that technological progress in post-industrial society is the expansion of the advance of *Zweckrationalität* already identified by Max Weber as the motor of change and the distinctiveness of Western society.

The frequency with which assertions about the impact of technology on the structure of the economy and productivity have been made in the past is related to the fact that technology generally has to be seen as a means of extending, or as a substitute for, the human body and therefore in many ways is, as is knowledge, a kind of anthropological constant. The challenge posed by modern technology in post-industrial society then is to discern its novel qualities and effects.[37] The question is whether technological change in post-industrial society is merely a further increase in the 'efficiency' of human conduct, or a transformation in social relations, social structure and technology itself.

Much of the discussion of technology, including that of Bell, continues to be shaped by the power of technology as a rational instrument of action. Without doubt, technology represents, from a logical point of view, a capacity for action. From a sociological point of view, however, technology, even conventional technical artifacts, is more than merely a means of action for, in its realization and in its impact, it is assimilated to social structures, joins and becomes conflated with, as it is employed, meaning, purpose and aims (cf. van den Daele and Krohn, 1982). A consideration of technological artifacts as mere means in the performance of social action therefore tends to systematically underestimate the social significance of technology in modern society. Any successful technical innovation and employment of technology requires that certain material *and* social conditions be fulfilled (cf. Schumpeter, [1942] 1950; Dosi, 1984; Radder, 1986; Dosi et al., 1988).

Technology is the material appropriation of nature under conditions which isolate, purify and separate 'natural objects' from the spontaneity of nature and rearrange and assimilate them to socially predetermined functions (cf. Böhme, 1992). At the same time, the implementation of technical innovations implies not only changes in the social structure but in the culture of society. Social conduct is technically patterned. It takes place within the context of a configuration of technologies. Hence, it is not

---

[37] Cf. Charles Sabel's (1991:34–35) attempt to categorize present views on the new role of technology in contemporary corporate settings.

the individual technical object that is socially relevant but its connections with larger configurations or complex networks of objects and social structures.[38] However, these *techno-structures* are diverse, interconnected and most difficult to demarcate *a priori*.

Equivalent considerations apply to the question of technological development, which is assimilated to and guided by contingent considerations and expectations.[39] Based on these considerations, technology, including the trajectory of its development, is not a 'free good' but involves context-specific knowledge accumulated over time and is dependent on localized circumstances including explicitly articulated interests as well as its own inherent limits or potential as a specific cognitive paradigm.

The theory of post-industrial society fails to advance, it seems to me, a convincing and more comprehensive argument which might account for the thesis that technology is (co-)responsible for a break in the framework of society and how and why the new technologies rewrite and reorganize the manner in which life is apprehended, how work is experienced, how illnesses are produced and how forms of life are altered (cf. also Block and Hirschhorn, 1979:391). A theoretical argument has to be developed which shows that technology, especially new technology, has a qualitative impact and not merely a quantitative effect on social relations, for example, in the sense of more consumer objects. Theoretical reflection has to focus on the embeddedness of individual technologies into a network of technologies and social structures, that is, into techno-structures, and that social conduct, social integration and solidarity is increasingly technically patterned and mediated. The production of technology is part of social reproduction; technology involves the production of social structures (cf. Böhme, 1992).[40] Moreover, discussion of the impact of modern technology on society has to engage the dominant accompanying ideology of tech-

---

[38] As Gernot Böhme (1992:43) maintains, 'today the life of the social body is largely determined by these techno-structures and the life of the individual is determined by his potential to connect up and be a customer.'

[39] Several economists (cf. Nelson and Winter, 1982; Dosi, 1982, 1984; Dosi et al., 1988), sociologists (e.g. van den Belt and Rip, 1987; Wynne, 1988) and historians (cf. Constant, 1987) have taken up the challenge to develop theoretical models and adduce empirical cases concerned with the impact of the economic, social, political and cultural context on technological development. In addition, analytical perspectives have been developed, based on the assumption of a fair range of similarities between science and technology, designed to examine the advance of technologies along a path shaped by the technical properties, the problem-solving heuristic of a specific technology and the general cognitive regime of a certain *technological paradigm*. That is, a specific technical development fits within 'a technological trajectory as the pattern of "normal" problem solving activity (i.e. "progress") on the grounds of a technological paradigm' (Dosi, 1984:15).

[40] The suggestion by Jeffrey Alexander (1992b:305) to treat technology as discourse, 'as a sign system that is subject to semiotic constraints and responsive to social and psychological demands', is therefore but a very partial theoretical advance from conventional social scientific discourse about technology as a means–ends rational action pattern since neither considers the social process of the appropriation of nature (or society) nor the development of techno-structures.

nology, that is, the technocratic ethos and its pitfalls. In addition, and importantly, any sociological examination of the role of modern technology should not be restricted to an investigation of its consequences as if any analysis and critique of its formation is *a priori* prohibited or limited to the assertion that technology eternally displays but one set of choices, namely the propensity to dominate and control.[41]

Alvin Gouldner (1976:255) refers quite critically to Bell's (as well as John K. Galbraith's)[42] conception of 'technical rationality'. He objects, in particular, to what he considers to be a short-sighted, even ideological use of the term. Gouldner is convinced that Bell overestimates the extent to which bureaucratic organizations might be committed to efficiency, or that their goals in fact are very much influenced by considerations pertaining to technical rationality. That is to say, Bell and Galbraith underestimate or refuse to recognize the fact that technical considerations are limited to instrumental usages and that they are therefore subordinate to political goals and decision processes: 'the actual structural subordination of technical rationality to managerial power and economic interest is occluded by the ideology of the new technology' (Gouldner, 1976:257). The conclusion for Gouldner is that Bell's theory of post-industrial society is part of the large species of technocratic theories and that there is, in addition, a direct intellectual link between the analysis of post-industrial society and Bell's thesis, formulated in the 1950s, about the end of ideology:

> A technocratic model . . . which sees technicians dominating officials and management, and which sees the modern technologically developed bureaucracy as governed by an exclusive reliance on a standard of efficiency is a fantasy, a utopia, an ideal type. That fantasy, however, was the grounding of the 'end of ideology' thesis, as well as Galbraith's and Bell's vision of the new knowledge-dominated society (Gouldner, 1976:257).

At best, however, Gouldner's critique exemplifies the point I have tried to make about the convergence of the use of the concept of technology and scientific knowledge among both critics and proponents of technocratic world-views because Gouldner evidently subscribes to a strictly instrumentalist view of technology, as I think Bell does. He does not assign to either technology or science the status of an autonomous force in, or

---

[41] The past few years have witnessed initial attempts and discussions extending the theoretical perspectives, approaches and methods developed for the social study of science to the development of technology (e.g. Bijker et al., 1987). However, the sociological turn in technology studies remains in its initial developmental stage. At issue often is how much autonomy can be ascribed to technology. For a first critique of some of these approaches see Hamlin, 1992.

[42] Gouldner refers, as far as I can see, to Galbraith's (1967) examination of the 'new industrial state' (cf. also Galbraith, 1973) in which reference is made, especially with respect to economic enterprises, to the power of newly emerging 'techno-structures'. 'The techno-structures within enterprises are represented by personnel with specialized knowledge; the function of those workers who do not enjoy any rights of participation in the decision making processes is to blindly follow the decisions' (cf. Galbraith, 1973:71).

better, outside society. Indeed, Bell (e.g. 1971:22) repeatedly stresses that
the 'technocratic mind-view necessarily fails before politics'. Thus, not
much is gained from Gouldner's objection except that it constitutes
evidence of how different readings of the theory of post-industrial society
become possible in the first instance.

The service economy

Bell's attempt to formulate a theory of social inequality, which transcends
the theory of social stratification appropriate to industrial society, has
frequently met with substantial opposition, even considerable disbelief.
Critical responses to Bell's observations, for the most part, affirm a
persistence in the socio-economic and cultural conditions responsible for
the differential allocation of power and privileges in society,[43] in particular, the relevance of property and wealth and its social, political and
economic consequences manifest, for example, in the link between access
to political decision-making and patterns of privilege. Daniel Bell (e.g.
1964:54) refers to a *new base of power* in modern society, namely 'skills'
and knowledge and the mode of access to this social power which is
education. But Bell does not suggest that differential skills and knowledge
become the sole arbiter of status and privilege. They constitute a new base
of social inequality *alongside* those linked to property and political
mobilization.

But these remarks already indicate that Bell's theory of social inequality
in post-industrial society is inextricably linked to his views about the
emergence of the service sector as the dominant economic structure and
therefore the kind of work now typically performed by service occupations.
The class cleavages in post-industrial society reflect the changing balance of
economic sectors (see Tables 4.2–4.4). Thus, the critical comments
directed at general patterns of social inequality in post-industrial society
are best discussed in the context of an examination of the nature of the
service sector of the economy.

The first comment which can be made about the status of the service
sector as a central dimension of discourse on the nature of modern society
is that it constitutes, even for most critics, one of the most persuasive, and
in many ways, hardly controversial ideas of the model of a post-industrial
society. The notion of the dual importance of the service sector, representing both the reason for the emergence of post-industrial society, assuming
such a break is accepted as persuasive, and one of the chief characteristics
of the new era has rarely been questioned. Rapidly, society is organized

---

[43] For Jean-François Lyotard ([1979] 1984:14), the somewhat formal assertion that post-
industrial society also sustains a 'ruling class' and that the members of the ruling class continue
to be those who are the decision-makers, although it is no longer the traditional ruling
political class, represents sufficient evidence for the assumption of considerable continuity in
societal formations.

Table 4.2 *Civilian employment in agriculture for selected industrialized countries, 1960–1991 (percentage of the workforce)*

	1960	1965	1970	1975	1980	1985	1989	1991
Canada	13.2	10.0	7.6	6.1	5.4	5.1	4.3	4.5
United States	8.5	6.3	4.5	4.1	3.6	3.1	2.9	2.9
Japan	30.2	23.5	17.4	12.2	10.4	8.8	7.6	6.7
Australia	11.0	9.6	8.0	6.9	6.5	6.1	5.5	5.5
Austria	22.6	17.9	14.6	12.5	10.5	9.0	8.0	7.4
France	23.2	18.3	13.5	10.3	8.7	7.6	6.4	5.8
Germany (FRG)	14.0	10.9	8.6	7.0	5.3	4.6	3.7	3.4
Greece	57.1	49.3	40.8	35.2	30.3	28.9	25.3	–
United Kingdom	4.7	3.8	3.2	2.8	2.6	2.5	2.1	2.2
OECD	21.6	17.4	13.8	11.6	9.6	8.6	7.6	–

Sources for Tables 4.2–4.4: OECD, *Labour Force Statistics*, 1963–1983 (1985), 1969–1989 (1991b); OECD, *Quarterly Labour Force Statistics* (1992d)

Table 4.3 *Civilian employment in industry for selected industrialized countries, 1960–1991 (percentage of the workforce)*

	1960	1965	1970	1975	1980	1985	1989	1991
Canada	32.7	33.2	30.9	29.3	28.5	25.4	25.7	23.2
United States	35.3	35.5	34.4	30.6	30.5	28.0	26.7	25.3
Japan	28.5	32.4	35.7	35.9	35.3	34.9	34.3	34.4
Australia	38.9	38.0	37.0	33.7	31.0	27.6	26.5	24.2
Austria	41.7	42.6	41.4	40.9	40.3	38.1	37.0	36.9
France	38.4	39.9	39.2	38.6	35.9	32.0	30.1	29.5
Germany (FRG)	47.0	48.4	48.5	45.4	43.7	40.9	39.8	39.3
Greece	17.4	21.1	25.0	27.9	37.7	27.4	27.5	–
United Kingdom	47.7	46.6	44.7	40.4	37.7	31.6	29.4	27.3
OECD	35.3	36.8	36.9	34.9	33.8	31.0	29.9	–

Table 4.4 *Civilian employment in the service sector for selected industrialized countries, 1960–1991 (percentage of the workforce)*

	1960	1965	1970	1975	1980	1985	1989	1991
Canada	54.1	56.8	61.4	64.6	66.0	69.5	70.1	72.3
United States	56.2	58.2	61.1	65.3	65.9	68.8	70.5	71.6
Japan	41.3	44.1	46.9	51.5	54.2	56.4	58.2	58.9
Australia	50.1	52.4	55.0	59.4	62.4	66.2	68.0	70.4
Austria	35.7	39.5	44.0	46.6	49.3	52.9	55.1	55.7
France	38.5	38.0	47.2	51.1	55.4	60.4	63.5	64.7
Germany (FRG)	39.1	40.7	42.9	47.6	51.0	54.5	56.5	57.4
Greece	25.5	29.5	34.2	36.8	39.5	43.7	47.1	–
United Kingdom	47.6	49.6	52.0	56.8	59.7	65.8	68.4	70.0
OECD	43.0	45.8	49.3	53.5	56.6	60.3	62.5	–

around the provision of services; hence, post-industrial society is, as Bell (1973a:127) emphasizes, primarily a game between persons. What counts above all is 'not raw muscle power, or energy, but information. The central person is the professional, for he is equipped, by his education and training, to provide the kinds of skill which are increasingly demanded in post-industrial society.'

The pre-eminent proposition therefore becomes that the economy in post-industrial society has moved from the provision of goods, produced mainly by industrial-type jobs, to that of services. This important trend, it is almost universally agreed, also brings with it the sectoral relocation of the labor force.[44] The movement is away from the farm and the factory to the office. Though manufacturing (industry) always required a certain (public and/or private) service supply, as Max Weber points out in his discussion of the origins of modern capitalism,[45] post-industrial society results in the creation of, as a matter of fact constitutes, a 'service economy'. The interdependence of sectors is driven home by the fact that a very significant portion of the output of the service sector, that is up to half of the value added of some service industries, is not immediately 'consumed' but absorbed by the production sector in all industrialized countries (cf. Britton, 1990:531). Such an economy, driven by differential productivity of sectors, increased wealth as well as changing needs and demands of consumers for services, results in a relatively faster growth of such areas of employment as health, education, government, recreation, research, transport, trade and finance. By implication, this can only mean that manufacturing and agriculture become rather less important economic sectors and that the changes in the nature of work in these two sectors of the economy (after all they do not disappear altogether) are also somewhat less significant; that is, work in industry and agriculture does not exemplify the work of post-industrial society. The important changes result, in turn, in a dramatic transformation of the composition of the labor force because in post-industrial society at the heart of the labor force are 'professional and technical' occupations.

As the data in Table 4.4 indicate, one of the widely accepted procedures in accounting for the structure of economic sectors is the inclusion of the government and non-profit activities as service-sector activities. This procedure tends to muddle the issues. Most importantly perhaps, it tends to gloss over the relationships, the boundaries and the dynamics of the market and the state. Obviously market and state activity are interconnected in many ways. None the less, one of the most significant shifts

---

[44] Not all observers agree that the pattern of these sectoral transformations are inevitable and universal. Singelmann (1978), for example, points out that the Canadian and US experience cannot be generalized to Western Europe or Asia where the growth in the service sector occurred *before* labor moved into the manufacturing sector.

[45] For a more recent analysis which also takes the view that a segmentation into services and manufacturing does not necessarily imply that they compete with each other but rather complement and reinforce each other, see Daniels (1989).

Table 4.5 *Government employment*[1] *in selected industrialized countries, 1960–1990 (percentage of total employment)*

	1960	1965	1970	1975	1980	1985	1990
Canada	–	–	19.5	20.3	18.8	20.0	19.7
United States	14.7	15.7	18.1	17.8	16.5	15.8	–
Japan	–	–	5.8	6.5	6.7	6.4	6.0
Australia	23.0	23.0	22.9	26.2	26.0	26.4	22.8
France	–	13.1	13.4	14.3	15.6	17.8	22.6
Germany (FRG)	8.0	8.0	11.2	13.9	14.9	16.0	15.1
Belgium	12.2	12.2	13.9	15.7	18.6	19.9	19.5
Sweden	12.8	12.8	20.6	25.5	30.7	33.1	31.7
United Kingdom	14.8	14.8	18.0	20.8	21.1	21.8	19.2
OECD (unweighted average)	11.2	11.9	13.6	15.7	17.2	18.6	14.8

[1] Government employment includes employees of all departments, offices, organizations and other bodies which are agencies of the central, state or local public authorities. Excluded are other government enterprises and public corporations (cf. OECD, 1992c: 556).

Sources: OECD, *Historical Statistics, 1960–1985* (1987:38); OECD, *Economic Outlook: Historical Statistics, 1960–1990* (1992a: 42)

which has taken place in recent decades in most developed countries is not only the (until recently) persistent growth of government activities, both in terms of state expenditures and in the proportion of the labor force employed by government (Table 4.5), but the rate with which government has increased. As a matter of fact, many of the available national statistical accounts of the proportion of state employees tend to utilize a narrow definition of 'public employment' and therefore underestimate the proportion of individuals in advanced societies dependent for their employment on state-controlled and/or subsidized activities.[46] In any event, government often grew faster than the growth of the national product. The result, of course, is that state activities now command a most significant share of all economic activities. In many countries close to half of the GNP outlays are state expenditures.

The term 'services' and the concept of the 'professional' have long and distinguished careers in social science. The pre-eminence of these terms in social science discourse indicates that they make reference to empirical

[46] Not surprisingly, the definition of 'government employment' is a contentious issue and often has to be answered *ad hoc* in relation to the statistical data made available by governments and/or international organizations. Whether employees of publicly owned enterprises (e.g. banks, telecommunication companies, radio and television stations, power-generating corporations to mention only a few enterprises in the hands of state or local authorities in many industrialized countries) should be counted as employees of the state is one of the main contentious issues. The OECD (1987:541) information used here is a narrow one and includes 'producers of government services', that is, those employed by various state levels in administration, defense, education, social services but *excludes those working for most public enterprises*. Equally difficult to classify are individuals who work for organizations or carry out activities that may not be directly controlled by government but rely heavily on government subsidies, e.g. farmers, miners or physicians in some countries (cf. Alestalo et al., 1991:37–39).

phenomena which have at least a similarly active career in society. The assimilation of the notion of the service sector and of the professional as the typical, representative occupation of this employment 'area' would indicate that the theoretical model is indebted to Clark's (1940) and Fourastié's ([1951] 1960) three-sector hypothesis and the functionalist theory of the professions. The three-sector hypothesis and the analysis of the professions refer, however, to shifts in the structure of employment patterns and skills, which begin early in industrial society (cf. Hartwell, 1973). From an aggregate perspective, the proportion of employees which found work in the manufacturing sector, in the nineteenth century, in most industrialized nations, has not changed as dramatically, if at all, as has the shift in the relative importance of employment in the primary and tertiary sectors of the economy. The greater transformation is in the decline in employment in agriculture and the rise in service-sector employment. Yet, the diminished importance of agriculture is, at the same time, constitutive of the rise of industrial society, while the rise in the importance of the service sector occurs also in response to the changing structure of the manufacturing sector, as will be discussed later in greater detail. The upshot is, at least for Kumar (1978:204), that the conditions for the changes Bell considers as the first and simplest criterion of post-industrial society, namely the shift of the labor force away from agriculture and manufacturing, are 'related both temporally and structurally to the original process of formation of "industrial society" '.

In the meantime, the terms of the discussion have also acquired, not least because they now refer to rather varied and differentiated processes and because of the extraordinary heterogeneity of service occupations, considerable ambivalence as terms of inquiry into labor force changes. In addition, in terms of now accepted measurement,[47] the standard differentiation of occupational position by economic sector (United Nations International Standard Industrial Classification of All Economic Activities) is based on the productive results of the *place of employment* of the employee rather than on the *tasks* the person performs (cf. Braverman, 1974:360). It is perhaps needless to indicate that this procedure creates considerable ambiguities if not outright deception – the nurse employed by an automobile company is counted as working in the industrial sector, while the nurse who works for an elementary school is counted as a service-sector employee. In general, therefore, conventional classifications not only 'understate the extent to which good production is, directly or indirectly, responsible for the generation of services employment and changes to the structure of the economy' (Britton, 1990:532), but fail to reflect the degree to which production itself increasingly is carried out and facilitated by

---

[47] The statistical practices of the United States Census have changed; early in the century, employees who are now counted as service-sector workers, e.g. workers in automobile repair shops or repair work of any description, were included in the manufacturing sector (Stigler, 1947).

'service' occupations, or indicate how important the provision of goods within the service sector is for the service sector (see also Chapter 6 on 'the changing manufacturing sector'). In short, while the productive output of economic activity indeed ranges from pure commodities to pure services, most and perhaps an increasing proportion of goods embody some kind of service, while most services require commodities (cf. Dunning, 1989:4–5).

Furthermore, in terms of pay and skills, for example, what is labeled as the service economy contains a mixture of skilled, well-paid and unskilled, poorly paid labor. The actual composition varies within the service economy from service industry to industry and from country to country (cf. Myles, 1990:285–288). As a matter of fact, the very diversity of occupations, or better, occupational tasks within and among occupations, assimilated to the notion of the service sector, appears to almost force the observer to treat them as unitary. As I will have occasion later to discuss in greater detail, the economist Fritz Machlup spent considerable intellectual energy ascertaining the contribution of 'knowledge' as a force of production in modern society (for example, treating all 'clerical' occupations as knowledge-workers). At best, the definition of the service sector often relies, following premises of labor market segmentation theory, on a few rather broad categories (such as low skill/low wage and high skill/high wage),[48] which have been in place for some time, or even worse, in some discussions becoming a residual category. There is therefore the express danger that service workers are introduced into the analysis of the labor market in modern society in a black box fashion and that their importance is, at times, even exaggerated. The latter certainly would appear to apply to the strategic role and relative importance of professionals. Since the theoretical interest tends to focus on the growth of the service sector *per se*, interest converges on what are possible common features of the service sector and not on its internal differentiation and stratification. Whatever the common factors may be, most existing definitions imply rather abstract and vague similarities between, for example, a heart surgeon, a professional football player and a concierge. Yet, inadequate statistics and diverse categories (for example, what exactly is a service, is the place of employment a sufficient indicator or does it happen to be the task performed which is decisive?) also result in rather sloppy estimates or misleading guesses of the size and composition of the service sector.

In short, instead of merely repeating what is now widely treated as conventional wisdom, that is, as Bell (1973a:133) puts it, 'if industrial society is defined as goods-producing society – if manufacture is central in shaping the character of its labor force – then the United States is no longer an industrial society', this premise of many discussions that accumulation simply has shifted to services should not be taken for granted. But rather

---

[48] Most of the jobs in the service sector created in the US in the past two decades have been 'low-skill' jobs, more precisely, they have been 'low-skill, hands-on, part-time, low-wages, dead-end jobs' (Cohen and Zysman, 1987:10).

than engaging the debates surrounding typologies and classifications of services as such (Fuchs, 1968; Daniels, 1985), it might be more fruitful to ask more fundamental questions about the role of services in modern society. Questions which then remain largely unexamined or unanswered are, for example: what exactly produces a growing demand for services of what kind? Or what type of work characterizes a knowledge society and for whom? Does manufacturing retain its importance? How typical are professionals in the knowledge society? Is it sufficient to argue that people will increasingly perform white-collar work? Generally, it would appear to be more important now to focus on the *interdependence relations of economic activities*, of goods *and* services within and among economic enterprises, on the kinds of organization[49] in which individuals are employed, the kind of work they perform and how the exchange relationships between those who produce and whose who consume evolve. For example, the transactions between consumer and producers are different from those of experts and clients (whereby clients, of course, may be industrial firms or located in the service economy), as is the importance of time and distance in production and consumption patterns. The issues which follow naturally from this emphasis are not concerned with the question of the sector in which individuals happen to be employed but with the tasks they are required to perform and the networks of relationships in which they find themselves immersed. In other words, the change to which attention has to be drawn is perhaps the 'massive sophistication of the labor force' (Wiles, 1971:39–40), and how it affects *all* sectors of the economy, *all* occupations within the economy and *all* exchange relationships in the market.

Leading trends within the economy of the knowledge society are sustained by more than one sector of the economy. They are based on strong links between sectors. As a result, the practical and theoretical value of a simple sector model of the transformation of the economy of modern society is severely diminished.

The centrality of universities and research institutes

For Daniel Bell (e.g. 1973a:116) the primary institutions in post-industrial society are 'intellectual', more specifically, university and research institutes and not, as Max Weber had still anticipated, the office. They will become the dominant institutions of post-industrial society. Their societal influence will not be based on any direct power and influence they may

[49] One important difference in the kind of organization individuals work in already involves the size of the workplace. In the US, and in most other countries, industrial firms tend to be much larger than service companies. Over 60 percent of all service-sector employees in the US work in organizations which have fewer than 100 employees. In contrast, only 30 percent of employees in manufacturing work in such organizations (cf. Bruyn, 1991:161).

command. University and research institutes will 'provide the most creative challenges and enlist the richest talents' (Bell, 1971:4).

The meaning Bell attributes to the concept of domination exercised by research institutes puts its influence close to one of Weber's notions of 'authority' rather than social power. But despite such modifications of the domination exercised by intellectual institutions, Bell clearly wants to assert that the balance of *power* shifts in favor of science and technology, if only because the decision-making will have an increasingly technical character. In relative isolation, this thesis, which we will encounter again in an even more explicit format in Herbert Marcuse's discussion of and warnings about the domination of technical rationality in advanced industrial society and in Helmut Schelsky's grim prognosis about the advent of the 'technical state', situates the description of the role of science and technology in post-industrial society once more close to Alvin Gouldner's (1976:255) reading of Bell's theory of post-industrial society as a form of modern technocratic consciousness; that is, as the 'technologists' wish-fulfilling fantasy of being free from the control of purely political, economic, military, or banking interests is a technological ideology, a project mistakenly defined as an already achieved condition'. In other words, Gouldner is convinced that Bell is incapable of adequately reflecting in his theory of post-industrial society on the profound limitation of technical rationality, the importance of reflexivity and therefore on the subordination of technical rationality to managerial control and economic interests.

The increasing status and influence of the scientific estate, however, is not only the result of the growing penetration of technical rationality into many social contexts but is also due to its exemplary form of life, especially its communal ethic based on a free exchange of information and the non-coercive authority of knowledge. Bell suggests that 'the scientific estate – its ethos and its organization – is the monad that contains within itself the imago of the future society' (Bell, 1973a:378). In much the same way in which the Puritan ethic became the ethos of capitalism, the ethic of science is the emerging ethos of the post-industrial society (Bell, 1973a:386). However, the growing social influence and impact of science implies at the same time a transformation of the scientific community itself toward 'big science' and a greater dependence of science on the state. The *laissez-faire* relation between science and the state, if it ever existed, has vanished. Science becomes 'intertwined with the government in dealing with the social and political issues of the day' (Bell, 1972:379n). The links between science and government become an intensively negotiated sphere of action. The possible outcome of such a transformation of science may well be, according to Bell, that the 'utopian components of the post-industrial society' contained within the ethos of science are in jeopardy. In the end, the shift in power toward science remains ambivalent. Bell repudiates any technocratic pretense (e.g. Bell, 1973a:265, 337). Though scientific knowledge becomes the central resource of society and some political decisions may even become inescapable, increased political conflict and tension likely cannot be avoided in post-industrial society. The problems of post-industrial society therefore remain political problems and cannot be reduced to technical ones.

While it would be inaccurate to assert that Bell merely points to a *quantitative* increase in research and development activities in post-industrial society as the decisive indicator for the new productive role of science and technology, he does not, in his analysis of the shift of societal power toward science and technology in post-industrial society, extensively explicate the *social* dimension of patterns of research and development and its embeddedness into specific national or regional socio-economic and socio-political contexts.

The organization and politics of science

While the relative strength of nations as industrial societies depended on their industrial capacity, chief among them steel production, its successors in post-industrial society will depend on the nature and the kinds of state support for science, the politicization of science, and the social problems of the organization of work by science teams. All of these issues are elevated to 'central policy issues in a post-industrial society' (Bell, 1973a:117–118). In other words, the common source of political problems in advanced society is the relation of science to public policy. In the course of the transformation of science since the Second World War into an inextricable adjunct of military and economic power, the choices of scientists and the scientific community are no longer idiosyncratic personal choices. As a matter of fact, science becomes a polity with identifiable interests, organizations, leading spokespersons and considerable intellectual influence. Given the growth of scientific organizations, its personnel, the amount of research funds required and the centrality of innovation for society, 'the bureaucratization of science is inevitable' (Bell, 1973a:405). A centralized bureaucracy within science poses certain risks for science. The competition for recognition, as the motivating force for scientific activity, may be impeded as recognition no longer goes to individual scientists but laboratories, organizations or bureaux. Free inquiry itself may be stifled and may become more of a response to stipulated social, national and global priorities and political goals. At the same time, the political and economic systems have an agenda *for* science and the sciences undermining central attributes of the ethos of science.

With respect to the link between science and government in the United States, Bell (1973a:403–404) sees the old, elite-based structures of science dissolving as institutes, organizations and specialties proliferate. The dependence of the military on university science is diminishing since the military-industrial complex provides the military with a broad research capacity. And with the growth of scientific personnel and research funds for science, the number of groups and individuals competing for funds has grown considerably, somewhat diluting the concentration of research capacities.

But all these developments lead to the classic dilemmas pertaining to the independence of scientific activity and the social function of science in modern society. For Bell, the tensions between countervailing tendencies and traditions in science will both shape the political realities of science and provide the impetus for a defense of the autonomy of science.

Power-holders

Bell's analysis of the rise of theoretical knowledge has merit in that he does not simply echo the fears or joys of those who have proclaimed that the scientist and the engineer are, in post-industrial society, the power-brokers who replace the entrepreneur, the industrialist, the manager and the politician as the power-holders of industrial society. It is, of course, no accident that the theme of scientists as the priests of a new age and a new religion linked to science and power should be raised from time to time in our society. Harry G. Johnson, for example, uses just such imagery to describe the role of science in modern society:

> To an important extent, indeed, scientific research has become the secular religion of materialistic society; and it is somewhat paradoxical that a country (the United States) whose constitution enforces the strict separation of church and state should have contributed so much public money to the establishment and propagation of scientific messianism (1965:141; cf. Lapp, 1965; Price, 1965:12; Klaw, 1968).

But, as can be seen from the dates of these warnings about the faith-like and church-like features of science in modern society, they issue for the most part from the early and mid-1960s, at least in the United States. Yet Bell's own theory, which dates from the same period, is void of such metaphors. He substitutes more realistic language and analyses and simply suggests, in line with his axial principle, that the 'dominant figures' of post-industrial society are the 'scientists, the mathematicians, the economists, and the engineers of the new computer technology' (Bell, 1971:4). At the same time, he claims that most major societal decisions will at least be mediated by intellectual institutions and the 'theory class', in that sense, becomes, of course, the power-broker for society.

Property

The emergence of the service economy in particular and knowledge-based work in general raises the broader theoretical question about the persistence of patterns of social inequality and institutional mechanisms which transmit and secure the intergenerational transmission of power and privilege. In industrial society, the prevailing institutional mechanism has been property, 'guaranteed and safeguarded by the legal order, and transmitted through a system of marriage and family' (Bell, 1971:19). Daniel Bell maintains that the property system in American society has lost some of its social significance and now constitutes only one of three co-existing modes of power, mobility and influence. In addition to the historic mode, property as an avenue to status and power, there are also knowledge and skills as a route to power and influence, mostly based on educational achievements, and finally, political office as a basis for privilege and power, mostly linked to membership of political organizations or machines. And, it should be added, with the emergence of knowledge, skills and political office as foundations for power, the conventional idea that property is virtually identical with the possession of *objects* begins to be diluted, or what is the same, the relative importance of property in the traditional sense begins to decline significantly.[50] But even if the appropriation of property is not limited to 'things', the relation between owner and the appropriated object changes if the object happens to be knowledge, skills or political office (see Chapter 5 for further discussion of the question of knowledge as property.

The emergence of new elites and new underprivileged groups as the result of differential access to and command of knowledge and skills derives from the 'simple fact that knowledge and planning – military planning, economic planning, social planning – have become the basic requisite for all organized action in modern society' (Bell, 1971:20). The ethos of those who manage to rise under these mechanisms is not merely economic self-interest but includes professional beliefs or the norms of the scientific community.

In addition, the institution of property itself is undergoing an essential correction in modern society. Traditionally, property rights have been the economic basis and symbolic correlate of the rise of individualism. Moreover, these rights constituted relationships between individuals. Today, entitlements, at times precariously based on relations between corporate actors, especially governments and individuals, and titles to symbolic property of entities, for example, bonds, shares, subsidies, grants, contracts, certificates, royalties, 'cultural capital'[51] are not really

---

[50] But as Emile Durkheim ([1950] 1992:138) observed in his lectures on the sociology of ethics, 'there is no reason why incorporeal things may not admit to the power of appropriation. *A priori*, no limits can be set to the power the collectivity has to endow anything that exists with the qualities requisite for juridical appropriation, or to take away those qualities.'

[51] Compare Bourdieu's (e.g. 1979, 1983, 1986) conception of 'cultural capital' which synthesizes ideas that can be traced to Marx, Durkheim and Weber. It posits cultural capital as a universal practice and medium of recognition and identity formation, establishing boundaries of inclusion and exclusion: 'As the objective distance from necessity grows, lifestyle increasingly becomes the product of what Weber calls a "stylization of life", a systematic commitment which orients and organizes the most diverse practices – the choice of a vintage or a cheese or the decoration of a holiday home in the country' (Bourdieu, [1979] 1984:55–56). In contrast to Bourdieu's perspective, if this distinction of the chain of reasoning is

fully controlled by the individual owner but often by corporate actors, for example, insurance companies, or state agencies. These are much more typical property rights. They are not closely linked to individuals any more and have therefore become more and more 'invisible'. They do not confer status and command social deference in any immediate sense as did traditional wealth. Many invisible property rights cannot be sold, given away or inherited.[52] There is further change in the nature of property and the rights the individual may derive from property. This change is connected to the shift in the norms which apply to ownership. While ownership once conferred almost unlimited rights to employ and dispose of property in any way the owner saw fit, today such rights are increasingly restricted on the basis of a variety of norms considered to be superior collective goals.

Planning and control

Optimism and skepticism, even considerable fear, about post-industrial developments often appear side by side. Perhaps this is the case because assurances and predictions about favorable or repressive social and political developments are distilled from the same set of underlying social trends. For example, Robert Heilbroner (1973:176) confesses, although he emphasizes simultaneously that such predictions about social futures are highly precarious, that he is apprehensive that the economic trends pointing toward post-industrialism will be accompanied by 'more authoritarian political structure, by more anomic groups in the undereducated, by increasing restlessness and boredom among the educated "middle class" still subject to the stimuli of a competitive, acquisitive culture'.

Many of the explicit fears or ambivalent hopes for post-industrial society are directly associated with one of the strong themes of Bell's theory of post-industrial society, namely, the prediction that the rise of a professional and technical class signals, especially as far as the character of political and economic decision-making is concerned, the spread of technocratic forms of consciousness and decision-making. But Severyn T. Bruyn (1991:149) expects, in direct contrast to Heilbroner's evident fears, that the growth of the service sector and its typical occupations offers the 'potential for closer interpersonal interaction, less hierarchy and dominance between opposing roles' in the market place. In addition, different modes of orientation based less on economic considerations may come to prevail in the market place of post-industrial society.

meaningful at all, I am trying to argue that knowledge in the sense of cultural practices does not take the place of more traditional attributes of inequality but is employed to acquire, enlarge and reproduce traditional boundaries of figurations of social inequality, given, indeed, a profound transformation in the realm of necessity.

[52] Even good will is not sufficient to pass on symbolic property rights: 'Thus it was appropriate for Jesus to say to the rich youth: "Give away your goods to the poor", but not for him to say "Give your education to the underprivileged"' (Simmel, [1907] 1978:440).

In any event, critics and Bell are in agreement that post-industrial society will usher in a social formation in which at least concerted efforts toward more extensive planning of social, economic and political activity will be quite typical.[53] If planning, assuming that it is sensible to be optimistic toward its promise in the first instance, stands in a definite relation to control, for example, initially in the sense of lower flexibility and less autonomy of social action, then the judgments about Bell's theory depend on one's image of the relation between control and planning and the value one may place on certainty or uncertainty. It is possible to assume that planning and control stand in a kind of zero-sum relation whereby more planning always implies more control and vice versa. However, it is also conceivable that the relationship is exactly the reverse, namely that more planning actually generates more flexibility, more unanticipated consequences and more chances to respond to new circumstances with extensive reflection. However, if planning is merely a synonym for control in the sense of successfully anticipating or pre-determining courses of action, then the relation between control and planning becomes quite straightforward.

As indicated, Daniel Bell (1968:156–157) believes that 'every modern society now lives by innovation and growth, and by seeking to anticipate the future and plan ahead.' Innovations are driven by theoretical discoveries, while the commitment to growth is linked to the need to plan and forecast. Bell is quite optimistic that science is capable of responding in an affirmative fashion, even in the social sciences: 'The rise of macro-economics, and the new codifications of economic theory, now allow governments to intervene in economic matters in order to shape economic growth, redirect the allocation of resources and . . . engineer a controlled recession in order to re-deploy resources.'

For the first time in history, as Bell (1971:5) underlines more than once, we therefore have the possibility, through the use of computers and simulation models, for instance, of conducting large-scale, controlled experiments in the social sciences on economic processes, foreign policy, military interventions, and social action generally, including the simulation

---

[53] It is in the context of such expectations that one also encounters repeated references to rapidly developing information technologies and their force in the transformation toward more effective planning and practical social experiments. For Bell (1973a:344), the development of the computer allows for the possibility 'of large scale "controlled experiments" in the social sciences. These, in turn, will allow us to plot alternative futures in different course, thus greatly increasing the extent to which we can choose and control matters that affect our lives.' In my opinion, the 'causal' chain is exactly the opposite. If we are capable of controlling matters that affect our lives, then we are in a position to change (perhaps with the help of social science) these circumstances (see Stehr, 1992). In line with such reasoning, Bell (1979a:173) adds, in a later analysis, a note of caution about our ability to model society for such efforts may be weakened because 'society is increasingly open and indeterminate, and as men become more conscious of goals there is greater debate about decisions.' That is to say, the circumstances that need to be subjected to control may become more volatile and resistant to attempts to change them in certain ways.

of various decision-making processes. The promise of such intellectual labor is quite simply that we are capable of plotting 'alternative futures', and thus we are 'greatly increasing the extent *to which we can choose and control matters that affect our life*' (my emphasis). The issue of the nature of intellectual experiments and of their translation into practice in particular, that is, the realization of the experimental effects in contexts other than the one in which the same effects are initially produced, namely under controlled circumstances, is not considered by Bell, as far as I can see, in any detail. The lack of consideration would indicate that a transfer of effects is considered merely a technical problem. Yet there can be little doubt that Bell rates the ability of collectivities (and individuals?) to plan and deliberately direct future outcomes as the most important change of our time; that is to say, 'men now seek to anticipate change, measure the course of its direction and its impact, control it, and even shape it for predetermined ends' (Bell, 1971:9). In short, his discussion is animated by a very strong sense of the enabling features of intellectual labor in all of the sciences. The ability to improve dramatically the transparency of events, in particular future events and therefore the confidence that the future can be brought under control, not unlike the way diseases have been conquered in the past, is one of the central messages of the theory of post-industrial society. Rationality, planning and foresight become the languages of the age.

Toward the end of the 1960s, Keynesian economics and interventionist economic policies appeared to have solved, even for the foreseeable future, the problem of managing and controlling national macroeconomic developments. But only a few years later, the economic profession and governments alike had grave doubts that any effective economic policy could be devised to cope with simultaneous unemployment and inflation, or stagflation. The Keynesian consensus gave rise to the persisting intellectual crisis in economics and economic policy. In the case of one of the pre-eminent success stories of the social sciences, the optimism of Bell that the social sciences finally had advanced to the point where they would be able to deliver with certainty useful practical knowledge, and had at their command the necessary codified knowledge, was undermined almost as soon as the prediction about successful planning and forecasting was made. In the end, it seems, the irrationality of politics will not be made more peaceable by planning and the promises of control, for 'politics . . . is always prior to the rational, and often upsetting of the rational' as Bell (1971:23) recognizes.

Social crises, revolutions and historical breaks

Too many of the discussions of the theory of post-industrial society and its subsequent development are excessively fascinated by notions of 'social crisis', 'revolution', 'historical rupture' and by the question of where and how the break occurred with industrial society. Most of these and kindred concerns, it seems, are inappropriate to theoretical discourse about contemporary social, economic and political conditions because it is doubtful that contemporary social transformations necessarily will repeat patterns detected to have occurred in the past.

On the other hand, a related issue merits attention, namely, the alleged, perhaps only implicit, continuity in those premises of the theory of post-industrial society which pertain to 'long waves' of historical change. That is to say, the image of the post-industrial society 'carries much of the baggage of nineteenth century evolutionary thought' (Block, 1990:6) and its once much heralded, and now of course widely discredited typologies of societies developed, for example, by Auguste Comte, Karl Marx and Herbert Spencer. These evolutionary theories were connected, as is well known, to a strong notion of distinct stages of social and individual development and the more or less abrupt jump of iron necessity from one human stage to the next. These notions found their way into everyday thought and may still be found there, but in social science discourse a fast body of scholarship has discredited these evolutionary visions. Bell has tried to emancipate his theoretical approach from these features of classic discourse.[54] But an author has limited control over how his design is interpreted and therefore the extent to which it is moved by critics toward the intentions of these theoretical ancestors. Such readings are a matter of contingent contexts and agendas subject to varied theoretical and practical intentions.

Assets of the theory of post-industrial society

As already mentioned, many of the criticisms and alternative projections critics have offered have, in the meantime, failed equally. At the same time, the critics' own theoretical agenda makes them often oblivious to the fact that the original formulation of the theory of post-industrial society, not least because of its theoretical elasticity, is not adverse to points raised in some of the critical assessments. This appears to be particularly true as far as the persistent claim is concerned that the theory of post-industrial society intends to transcend the notion of capitalism. As far as I can see, the theory of post-industrial society, formulated with considerable open-ness, is quite compatible, especially since Bell operates in direct lineage to Raymond Aron, with the idea that the economy of post-industrial society may be organized according to market principles, or on the basis of state planning: 'Just as an industrial society has been organized politically and culturally in diverse ways . . . so too the post-industrial society may have

---

[54] At times, Bell's mode of presentation does invite reflections about patterns of similarity between his typology of societies (pre-industrial, industrial and post-industrial) and typologies favored by nineteenth-century evolutionary social theorists (e.g. Bell, 1973a:x).

diverse political and cultural forms' (Bell, 1968:158).[55] As a matter of fact, both the critics and advocates of the theory of post-industrial society underestimate the extent to which only a specific organizing principle of economic affairs, as history has demonstrated now, assures both economic success and the survival of forms of political organization.

The theory of post-industrial society does not intend to be a comprehensive theory of modern society. Rather, Bell prefers an analysis of modern society in terms of structure (and politics) rather than values or modes of orientation. Such a disposition is a preference for an examination of tangible matters. In modern society, the study of values and orientations makes reference to much more rapidly changing social features. Even if one is able to substantiate the claim that values matter and that orientations may change, the more important challenge remains to say why values may differ, if in fact they differ, and if the contrast in values makes a difference. But Bell's insistence on focusing primarily on socio-structural changes in modern society and those induced by the social structure in other sectors of society also reflects his analytical decision (cf. Bell, [1979, 1980] 1982) that contemporary society lacks the kind of over-arching, dominant constitutive principle in terms of which the full range of social, cultural, political and economic activities in society are organized. Modern society lacks, assuming societies ever operate on interrelated and totalizing principles, such unity or coherence and therefore the kind of centrality and integration such a canon or code may be seen to effect. I believe that Bell stresses, though not first and foremost, the potential fragility of social relations and the likely disjuncture and conflict among more or less autonomous sectors (subsystems) of society, or as Weber expressed it, the various orders and value spheres of the world.

The use of the term 'post-industrial society' is perhaps deliberately chosen to affirm the lack of a deterministic center by calling attention to the idea that this social formation stands in transition between more distinctive types of society, namely industrial society and a future social formation, not yet endowed with the same degree of specificity.

A further important asset of Bell's theory of post-industrial society is his repeated attempt to assure us that his approach lacks the kind of determinism that classic sociological discourse saw as a virtue of theorizing.

---

[55] In a study devoted to the development of Daniel Bell's ideas particularly in the 1940s, Howard Brick (1986:201) also briefly comments on some of the features of his theory of post-industrial society and observes that the 'elasticity' of its construction owes its origins to diverse intentions embedded in Bell's thought, namely 'his attempt to define an ongoing process of social development in terms of an outcome that is both within reach and yet impossible to grasp. This problem, like that of Bell's descriptive collage, can be understood in terms of his discussion of capitalism and its fate. The sharp tension in the text between the suggestion that tendencies of social organization drive beyond capitalism and Bell's denial of his proximity to "post-capitalist" theories point to the abiding tension that characterizes the interdeterminate transitional society Bell seeks to describe, the tension between evolutionary survivals and prospects which is the real theme of all his work.'

Whether Bell in fact always succeeds in living up to his own commitments is perhaps questionable and whether the degree of flexibility and built-in ambivalence of Bell's conceptual scheme, reflecting modern societal fragility, is sufficient might be open to dispute.

However, the theory of post-industrial society believes itself to have understood the future. It therefore retains, though it may well be in a most ambivalent sense, a measure of the modern spirit, for example, in the sense that it reaffirms and reiterates the conviction that social, political and economic problems can be effectively solved (cf. Bauman, 1991:29). The theory of the knowledge society does not claim to have charted the future in the same spirit.

5

Knowledge about Knowledge

Humans in general are more interested to accomplish something rather than to know how it is done and achieving the former usually preceded insights into the latter.

(Georg Simmel, *Über sociale Differenzierung*)

How should a nation that could not invent the wheel predict the invention of just that wheel?

(Otto Neurath, *Foundations of the Social Sciences*)

The most serious theoretical deficiency of existing theories of modern society which assign a central role to knowledge is, as I have tried to demonstrate, their rather undifferentiated treatment of the key ingredient, namely knowledge itself. The crucial importance of knowledge within these theories has not been matched by extended and enlightened discussions of the concept of knowledge. Even more generally, our knowledge about knowledge is, despite, and for a time because of, the sociology of knowledge (see Stehr and Meja, 1984a), not very sophisticated and comprehensive. I have attempted to argue that the range of knowledge or forms of knowledge that science makes available, the fact that science becomes increasingly the only source of additional knowledge and that the change in the available knowledge dramatically enlarges the available options of social action, suggests that the investment in, the distribution and the reproduction of scientific knowledge also changes and is bound to acquire greater social significance, as does, of course, the production of knowledge. These questions therefore will form the core of the considerations advanced in this chapter.

Scientific discourse developed a kind of natural attitude toward its own knowledge. And for this reason, but not merely for this reason, the number of well-explicated categories of knowledge in sociology has been fairly limited. We really have not moved much beyond the proposals about different forms of knowledge found in Max Scheler's early contributions to the sociology of knowledge. Later explications tend to be quite similar to Scheler's ([1925]1960:13–49) categories of knowledge, namely (a) knowledge of salvation (*Erlösungswissen*); (b) cultural knowledge, or knowledge of pure essences (*Bildungswissen*); and (c) knowledge that produces effects (*Herrschaftswissen*), although that ancestry is not often spelled out or recognized.[1] The most widely employed conceptions of different forms of knowledge are dichotomies. Dominant is the distinction between scientific and non-scientific knowledge. This distinction was taken for granted for such a long time that it has not really been elaborated for decades, except in the sense that non-scientific knowledge became a residual form of knowledge. In addition, the dichotomy between specialized and everyday knowledge has been widely used in sociological discourse, whereby specialized knowledge was often identical with scientific and technical knowledge. On the whole, our knowledge about knowledge was, until more recently, derivative of and deferential to dominant philosophies of science.

Knowledge in knowledge societies

A look at the conceptions of knowledge employed by those who have elevated knowledge to the new axial principle of modern society indicates that these theorists pause but briefly to consider the social nature of knowledge, particularly of scientific knowledge. Although many and elaborate definitions of knowledge are offered, an equivalent effort toward a theoretical analysis of the decisive phenomenon 'knowledge as such' is not thought necessary.[2] The new qualities of scientific knowledge and its social consequences are merely postulated. In short, knowledge is essentially treated as a black box.[3]

The discussion of knowledge in these theories of society is self-exemplifying. The logic of the theory becomes the logic of social relations. Both tend to represent a conception which is governed by considerations of quantity and functionality (e.g. Boulding, 1965; Drucker, 1965). Depending on how mechanistically or lawlike knowledge and knowledge about knowledge is construed in this case, there is of course the danger that the post-industrial society is conceived in terms which subordinate social action

---

[1] The well-known distinction Jürgen Habermas ([1968] 1971:301–317) has offered between discrete knowledge-constitutive human interests, for example, namely the technical, hermeneutic and emancipatory interests of the different sciences, resonates with Scheler's typology of forms of knowledge.

[2] This restriction also applies, in my opinion, to the analysis of the knowledge system developed, from an organizational perspective, by Burkart Holzner and John H. Marx, for post-industrial societies. According to Holzner and Marx (1979:17) what is characteristic for post-industrial societies is the emergence of occupational positions and organizations which attempt to join, intending to affect the efficacy of planning, the development, dissemination and application of technical and specialized knowledge.

[3] Bell (1973a:176–177) is aware of the possibility of examining knowledge more comprehensively since he refers to the sociology of knowledge and the questions it typically raises. However, he hastily relegates these questions to specialists or as outside the purview of his approach.

to laws of absolute power beyond the control of society (c'
1977:114).

The central question posed by those theorists of post-ind'
who have claimed that knowledge has become the agent of socia.
becomes a functionalist one. What are the consequences of objectiv.
knowledge for both society and the individual, and how can these results of
knowledge be apprehended? A second common factor in their approach to
knowledge concerns the observation that the tempo of social change
accelerates and reaches an unprecedented pace and that the rapidity of
societal change somehow parallels the growth in the scale of available
objective knowledge (cf. Price, 1961, 1963; Bon and Burnier, 1966; Tondl,
[1968] 1972; Bell, 1973a:168–174). However, we are not offered, in
deference to the model explicated in the philosophy of science, any
sociological account of the condition for the rapid growth of scientific
knowledge within the contemporary scientific enterprise in contrast to the
scientific community in the past. Nor do we encounter theoretical curiosity
about the reasons for the growing demand for scientific knowledge, in
various societal institutions, especially the economic system. Nor, for that
matter, is there a discussion of the politics of knowledge in modern society.
An adequate understanding of the role of knowledge in knowledge
societies requires one to open up the black box in each instance.

Toward a sociological concept of knowledge

For the purpose of some further explication of the concept of knowledge,
one must distinguish between what is known, the content of knowledge,
and knowing. Knowing is a relation to things and facts, but also to rules,
laws and programs. Some sort of participation is therefore constitutive for
knowing: knowing things, rules, programs, facts is 'appropriating' them in
some sense, including them into our field of orientation and competence.
The intellectual appropriation of things can be made independent or
objective. That is, symbolic representation of the content of knowledge
eliminates the necessity to get into direct contact with the things themselves. One is able, in other words, to acquire knowledge from books (cf.
also Collins, 1993). The social significance of language, writing, printing,
data storage etc. is that they represent knowledge symbolically or provide
the possibility of objectified knowledge. Thus, most of what we today call
knowledge and learning is not direct knowledge of facts, rules and things
but objectified knowledge. Objectified knowledge is the highly differentiated stock of intellectually appropriated nature and society which may
also be seen to constitute the cultural resource of a society. Knowing is,
then, *grosso modo* participation in the cultural resources of society.
However, such participation is of course subject to stratification; life
chances, life style and social influence of individuals depend on their access
to the stock of knowledge at hand.

Knowledge, ideas, and information – to use quite deliberately very broad and ambivalent categories – are most peculiar entities with properties unlike those of commodities or secrets, for example. If sold, they enter other domains and yet remain within the domain of their producer. Knowledge does not have zero-sum qualities. Knowledge is a public good. When revealed, knowledge does not lose its influence. While it has been understood for some time that the 'creation' of knowledge is fraught with uncertainties, the conviction that its application is without risks and that its acquisition reduces uncertainty has only recently been debunked. While it is very reasonable and in some sense urgent to speak of the limits to growth in many spheres and resources of life, the same does not appear to hold for knowledge. Knowledge has virtually no limits to its growth.

Georg Simmel made the same observation, shortly after the end of the First World War, although for him the lack of any real limits to the growth of knowledge (cultural products) above all signals a serious intellectual danger for individuals and society. It signals the danger of a 'tragedy of culture' in which the growing cultural objectifications exceed the ability of the individual to absorb the plenitude of knowledge in any meaningful manner. Human products take on a life of their own while constraining human conduct. But as he stresses,

> everybody can contribute to the supply of objectified cultural contents without any consideration for other contributors. This supply may have a determined color during individual cultural epochs that is, from within there may be a qualitative but not likewise quantitative boundary. There is no reason why it should not be multiplied in the direction of the infinite, why not book should be added to book, work of art to work of art, or invention to invention. The form of objectivity as such possesses a boundless capacity for fulfillment (Simmel, [1919] 1968:44).

For Simmel, the important and dangerous outcome is a broad discrepancy between the volume of cultural products and the ability of the individual to assign meaning to them, as I will discuss below.

Knowledge is often seen as a collective commodity *par excellence*; for example, the ethos of science demands that it is supposed to be made available to all, at least in principle (compare Merton, [1942] 1973). But is the 'same' knowledge available to all? Is scientific knowledge when transformed into technology still subject to the same normative conventions?[4] What are the costs of the transmission of knowledge? Knowledge is virtually never, despite its reputation, uncontested. In science, its contestability is seen as one of its foremost virtues. In practical circumstances, the contested character of knowledge is often repressed and/or conflicts with

---

[4] The answer one economist, for example, provides, is that technology must be considered, in contrast to the convictions concerning scientific knowledge in the scientific community, a 'private capital good'. In the case of technology, disclosure is not the rule and rents which can be privately appropriated for its use can be earned by its producers (cf. Dasgupta, 1987:10).

the exigencies of social action.[5] The apparently unrestricted potential of its availability, which does not affect its meaning, makes it, in peculiar and unusual ways, resistant to private ownership (Simmel, [1907] 1978:438). Modern communication technologies ensure that access becomes easier, and may even subvert remaining proprietary restrictions, although concentration rather than dissemination is also possible and feared by some.[6] But one could just as easily surmise that the increased social importance of knowledge, and not so much its distinctiveness, may in fact undermine the exclusiveness of knowledge. Yet the opposite appears to be the case and therefore raises anew the question of the persisting basis for the power of knowledge.

In a preliminary way, I would like to define knowledge as a *capacity for social action*.[7] In this sense, knowledge is a universal phenomenon, or an anthropological constant. But in many instances, the discussion of the role of knowledge in social action quite surprisingly is restricted to this rather elementary observation. Without wanting to engage in extensive or even excessive terminological discussions, the notion of 'knowledgeability' of human agents, as proposed by Giddens (1984:21–22), for example, characterizes first and foremost practical consciousness and therefore knowledge as an 'ordinary', often widely shared and tacit, component of social action. As such, knowledge is a condition for the possibility of social action. The point Giddens wants to stress is the extent to which knowledgeability is constitutive of, or common to, social action. Giddens, therefore, does not intend to refer, in his usage, to the problems at issue here: namely, how and why knowledge expands, how it may be subject to stratification, how it is mediated by knowledge-based occupations, and how it represents the basis for authority or is the source for economic expansion. Giddens emphasizes the mutuality of knowledge while the concern here centers on its very absence, even if this absence is only temporary. Giddens wants to advance, although not exclusively of course,

[5] As Georg Simmel ([1907] 1978:437) indicates, the intellect (or knowledge) stands in rather close relation and proximity to individualism, as does money. Reason has an individualizing property because it is the essence of its content that the 'intellect is universally communicable and that, if we presuppose its correctness, every sufficiently trained mind must be open to persuasion by it. There is absolutely no analogy to this in the realms of the will and the emotions.' In addition, the contents of the (objective) mind 'do not possess the jealous exclusiveness that is common in the practical contents of life'.

[6] Compare, for example, the conflicting views of Harold Innis (1951) and Marshall McLuhan on this matter.

[7] The *sociological* conception of knowledge advanced here resonates with Ludwig von Mises' (1922:14) definition of *property*, for von Mises suggests that as a sociological category, 'property represents the capacity to determine the use of economic goods.' Based on the idea that knowledge constitutes a capacity for action, one can of course develop distinctive categories or forms of knowledge depending on the enabling *function* knowledge may be seen to fulfill. I believe Lyotard's ([1979] 1984:6) attempt to differentiate, in analogy to the distinction between expenditures for consumption and investment, 'payment knowledge' from 'investment knowledge' constitutes an example of such a functional differentiation of more or less distinctive forms of knowledge.

an ontological argument. Fundamentally, the issue at hand here is that actors not only know but want to know more than fellow actors and that knowledge is a stratified phenomenon of social action. If restricted to this conception, however, knowledge is hardly capable of sociological analysis. Sociological inquiry requires some idea about the extent to which knowledge operates not merely as a condition for social action but as a stratified phenomenon in social action.

The notion of knowledge as a capacity for social action has the advantage, it seems to me, that it enables one to stress not merely one-sided but multi-faceted consequences of knowledge for action.[8] The term capacity for action signals that knowledge may be left unused[9] or may be employed for irrational ends and leaves room, therefore, for a 'dialectical' theory of the use of knowledge. The definition of knowledge as a capacity for action indicates strongly that the material realization and implementation of knowledge is dependent on, or embedded within, the context of specific social and intellectual conditions. Knowledge, as a capacity for action, does not signal that specific knowledge claims always convey or carry a kind of constant and fixed 'value' enabling actors to translate and employ them for the identical purposes and for closely similar outcomes. In as much as the realization of knowledge is dependent on the active elaboration of knowledge[10] as a capacity for action within specific social conditions, a first link between knowledge and social power becomes evident because the control of the relevant conditions requires social power.[11] The larger the scale of the project, for example, the larger the need for social power in order to ensure control over conditions for the realization of knowledge as capacity for action (see also Radder, 1986).

It is important to realize that knowledge, as an element of power

---

[8] Perhaps I should point to a competing definition of 'knowledge' which sets knowledge identical with action or conceives of knowledge as emerging from action. Peter Drucker (1969:269) observes that knowledge as 'normally conceived by the "intellectual" is something very different from "knowledge" in the context of "knowledge economy" or "knowledge work" . . . Knowledge, like electricity or money, is a form of energy that exists only when doing work. The emergence of the knowledge economy is not, in other words, part of "intellectual history" as it is normally conceived. It is part of the "history of technology", which recounts how man puts tools to work.' In a later study, Drucker (1989:251) very much affirms this conception and defines knowledge as information that 'changes something or somebody – either by becoming grounds for action, or by making an individual (or an institution) capable of different and more effective action. And this, little of the new "knowledge" accomplishes.'

[9] The thesis that knowledge invariably is pushed to its limit, that is, is realized and implemented almost without regard for its consequences, as argued, for instance, by C.P. Snow (cf. Sibley, 1973), constitutes of course a view which is quite common among observers, for example, of the nature of technological development. However, the notion that science and technology inherently and inevitably force their own realization in practice fails to give, for one thing, proper recognition to the context of implementation.

[10] Compare Lazega's (1992) essay on the 'information elaboration' in work groups and the relations between information and decision-making in and dependent on 'local' contexts.

[11] Additional elements of the ambivalent equation relating knowledge to power are discussed in Chapter 7.

relations, generates not merely coercive, distorting and repressive consequences, as many traditional conceptions of power would imply, but has
productive and enabling features as well. And a more developed theoretical notion of power requires the ability to incorporate both attributes of
knowledge as a capacity for action. The use of a more differentiated
concept of power, conscious of the constraining and enabling features of
power, becomes all the more relevant the greater the actual amorphous-
ness of power and the greater the malleability of social structures and
conditions become for the realization of knowledge. Knowledge has many
enabling features which allow individuals and groups to organize resistance, avoidance and general opposition. Such an emphasis becomes
important not only because the degree and effectiveness to which knowledge operates as a capacity for action increases but so does the dissemination and access to knowledge among strata which may have been cut off
in the past. Since knowledge and access to knowledge are not evenly
distributed, such a world is not a world without power and inequality.

Obviously, *scientific and technical knowledge* represent such 'capacities
for action' and maybe even quite a special capacity for action in modern
society. However, this does not mean that scientific knowledge should be
seen as a resource which lacks contestability, is not subject to interpretation and can be reproduced at will.[12] The special importance of scientific
and technical knowledge, in any modern society, derives not so much from
the fact that it is at times treated as if it is essentially uncontested (or
objective) but that it constitutes, more than any other form of modern
knowledge, an *incremental* capacity for social action or an *increase* in the
ability of 'how-to-do-it' which, moreover, may be 'privately appropriated',
if only temporarily. In economic settings, incremental knowledge has
particular importance as a source of added value. The strategic importance
of incremental knowledge as an immediately productive force in economic
contexts specifically may effect the ways in which production and the
delivery of services are organized as well as the types of commodities and
services that are produced. Thus, I agree with Dosi (1984:88–89) who, in
the field of industrial innovation, sums up the conditions for the possibility
of technological innovation in market economies as best described and
served by the dual conditions of technological opportunity *and* the private
appropriation of the benefits of innovative activities. The commitment of
private firms to innovation is closely linked to their ability to temporarily
appropriate the marginal additions to knowledge and therefore the
economic advantages which may accrue from the control over such
knowledge.

Generally, knowledge as a capacity for action enables one to set something

---

[12] If knowledge indeed would 'travel' almost without impediments and could be reproduced largely at will, the idea that the creators of what typically constitutes 'new' knowledge
in modern society, namely scientists and engineers, would have to be located at the apex of
power in such societies certainly would make considerable sense.

into motion; at the same time, knowledge need not be perishable. In principle, a consumer or purchaser of knowledge may use it repeatedly at diminishing or even zero cost. Thus, what counts in the sense of gaining advantages in societal formations, which primarily operates according to the logic of economic change (growth) and social transformation, is access to and command of the *marginal additions to knowledge* and not the generally available stock of knowledge. Science and technology constantly *add* (in a non-pejorative sense) to the existing stock of knowledge and therefore the ability of individual and corporate actors to affect their circumstances of action. In this respect, that is in its ability and legitimacy to generate novel capacities of action, science is virtually without a competitor in modern society. None the less, knowledge as a capacity for action cannot be reduced to scientific knowledge.[13]

Other factors aside from knowledge constitute capacities for action and a basis for power because they are, in relation to the potential demand, scarce. Knowledge is not quite such a resource. John K. Galbraith (1967:67) claims, for example, that power 'goes to the factor which is hardest to obtain or hardest to replace . . . it adheres to the one that has greatest inelasticity of supply at the margin.' Knowledge, as such, is not really a scarce commodity, though two features which can be a part of certain knowledge claims may well transform knowledge from a plentiful into a scarce phenomenon. First, what is scarce and difficult to obtain is not access to any knowledge (perhaps even in the sense of random knowledge) but to *incremental knowledge*, that is, not merely to just another additional or 'marginal unit' of knowledge but to a specific knowledge claim. Knowledge as such really is not scarce at all. But the greater the tempo with which knowledge ages or decays, the greater the potential influence of those who manufacture or augment knowledge, and correspondingly, of those who transmit such increments. Secondly, if sold, knowledge enters, as already indicated, the domain of others, yet remains within the domain of the producer, and can be spun off once again. This signals that the transfer of knowledge does not necessarily include the transfer of the cognitive ability to generate such knowledge, for example, the theoretical apparatus or the technological regime which yields such knowledge claims in the first place and on the basis of which it is calibrated and validated. Cognitive skills of this kind, therefore, are scarce. But they are not the only skills in demand since knowledge constantly has to be made available, interpreted and linked to emerging local circumstances. This is the job performed by experts, counselors and advisers. The group of occupations

---

[13] Such a conclusion already follows from the theorem that knowledge is a kind of anthropological constant. But it also follows from conceiving of knowledge as a capacity for action because knowledge then becomes, as Lyotard ([1979] 1984:18) stresses, 'a question of competence that goes beyond the simple determination and application of truth, extending to the determination and application of criteria of efficiency (technical qualification), of justice and/or happiness (ethical wisdom), of beauty of a sound or color (auditory and visual sensibility), etc.'

designated here as counselors, advisers and experts is needed to mediate between the complex distribution of changing knowledge and those who search for knowledge enabling to act because 'ideas travel' as 'baggage' of people whereas skills are embodied in people (cf. Collins, 1982). A chain of interpretations must come to an 'end' in order to become relevant in practice and effective as a capacity of action. This function of ending reflection for the purpose of action is largely performed by experts in modern society.

Whether scientific knowledge is particularly effective in practice, as most of its proponents would argue, is not at issue. The collective capacity to act, the extent to which our existential circumstances are socially constructed, has increased immeasurably in modern society. But one should not deduce from that, perhaps in an almost linear fashion, that the capacity to act of units of the collectivity, for example the individual, small groups or even large entities such as nation-states has simultaneously been enlarged immeasurably. On the contrary, the potential to transform and construct at the collective or cumulative level goes in fact hand in hand with an increasing inability even of large social entities to affect their fate. That is, the capacity of the whole to make its history should not be misread to mean that this ability necessarily can be parlayed into planned, anticipated or even desired change. The fact that the human species makes its own evolution does not easily, if at all, translate into the ability of parts to do the same. Assuming the opposite constitutes a kind of 'ecological fallacy'.

Science as an immediately productive force

Science and technology began as a marginal enterprise of amateurs in the seventeenth century; but modern science, especially since the Second World War, has received a large proportion of the public budget and constitutes a major source of investment for private capital. Individuals, trained as scientists or engineers, are a growing part of the labor force in modern society. The growth in the system of modern higher education is both the result and the motor of the increased importance of science and technology. Institutions which produce, distribute or reproduce knowledge are now comparable in size to the industrial complex. Furthermore, it is now often emphasized that no area of social life will remain unaffected by the impact of natural science and technology although this does not mean, as will be discussed later, that scientific knowledge and technology will eradicate totally, as many theorists of the nineteenth and early twentieth centuries expected, the 'traditional' forms of knowing and conventional world-views even in advanced society.

The changes in and for science take place in three steps. First, and up to the end of the eighteenth century, the scientific community had the function of enlightenment, that is, it was a producer of *meaning*, social consciousness and a critique of world-view. Secondly, in the following century, during the emergence of the industrial society, science became a *productive* force and shifted position in the structure of basis and superstructure. It was a productive force in as much, as Karl Marx observed, as it was frozen into machines.[14] However, in as much as science, during the nineteenth century, developed as a 'pure' science, it was not a productive force. And, thirdly, in this century science has increasingly become an *immediately productive* or 'performative' force.

In my view, the major change in the production of scientific knowledge, in turn providing one of the foundations of the possibility of a knowledge society, is the expansion of the social function of scientific knowledge and this expansion in functions served takes place without the elimination or a significant reduction of the earlier functions scientific knowledge has had in society. Science also produces knowledge which, at least in the short run, serves no particular social or extra-scientific function. Science is perhaps the only institution in modern society which in the course of its development does not appear to lose some of its original purposes to other sectors of society, for example, as the result of structural differentiation. On the contrary, science increasingly absorbs certain functions in society. In addition, it expands by generating or taking on new purposes. The institution of science therefore appears to be somewhat immune to the incessant forces of social differentiation and specialization.

Obviously, it is quite difficult to propose novel terms for each of these categories of knowledge produced by the scientific community. However, the following concepts might be a first approximation:

1 *Meaningful knowledge*: The knowledge of most of the social science disciplines and the humanities is knowledge which in its primary social function affects mainly the (social) consciousness of members of society (*Deutungswissen* or *Orientierungswissen*).
2 *Productive knowledge*: Most of the traditional disciplines in the natural sciences generate productive knowledge (*Produktivwissen*) in that such knowledge can be converted into ways of directly appropriating natural phenomena.
3 *Action knowledge*: The most recent form of knowledge, as an immediate productive force, may be considered to be action knowledge (*Handlungswissen*) because such knowledge is already a direct form of social action. It is the immediate capacity for action and this includes the capacity to generate more (new) knowledge.

Since science became a productive force in the nineteenth century, it has ceased to belong exclusively to the superstructure of society. The change from functioning as a producer or critic of world-views to functioning as a

[14] As Marx ([1939–1941] 1973:706) observes, 'nature builds no machines, no locomotives, railways, electric telegraphs, self-acting mules etc. These are products of human industry; natural material transformed into organs of the human will over nature, or of human participation in nature. They are organs of the human brain created by the human hand; the power of knowledge, objectified.'

productive force means, as indicated, that important aspects of science are now part of the material basis of society. Earlier science was not mature enough to be applied to problems of production, while the material appropriation of nature in the sense of efficient control over boundary conditions or production of pure materials was not developed far enough to enable a realization of scientific results in dimensions relevant for production. In short, a change in the material and cognitive appropriation of nature in the nineteenth century turns science into a productive force and assists society to evolve into industrial society.

The material appropriation of nature aided by science means more specifically that nature as a whole is gradually transformed into a human product by superimposing a new structure, namely a social structure. The social structure in essence is objectified knowledge, that is, an explication and realization of what we know are the laws of nature extended by engineering design and construction. Nature is scarcely experienced otherwise than as a human product or within human products. Because the appropriation of nature is driven by science, scientific knowledge attains a pre-eminent position in society. Scientific knowledge as productive knowledge becomes the dominant type of knowledge.

In this century, science becomes an immediately productive force. 'Immediacy' means that science now may, contrary to the relation between production and science in the nineteenth century, be relevant for production without being mediated by living, that is, corporeal labor. Hence one might be able to speak about the possible abolition of manual labor, especially of factory labor which requires strength and physical dexterity, and the removal of human labor from production to that of the preparation and organization of production. Labor in the conventional sense of the term will become a kind of residual category and primarily knowledge based. Science produces society directly. Most of the knowledge produced and employed in production is no longer embodied in machines. The effects of this are enormous. It crucially extends to diffusion patterns of technology, the decisions affecting the location of production, the inter-relation between organizational structures and labor, patterns of conflict and co-operation, comparative advantages and the mounting contingency of economic activity.[15]

---

[15] In the early 1960s, during the de-Stalinization period, orthodox Marxist philosophers, for example, in East Germany, discussed the notion of science as an 'immediately productive force', not least as a corrective to the 'undialectical' conception of science advanced by Stalin (cf. Klotz and Rum, 1963:27). But aside from the work the notion of science as an immediately productive force had to accomplish in the ideological struggle underway, the concept mainly referred, as far as I can tell, to the idea that production becomes the material realization of scientific discoveries (e.g. Stoljarow, 1963:835; actually, it is claimed that Walter Ulbricht initially employs the term, cf. Klotz and Rum, 1963:26). Later, somewhat more elaborate conceptions of the notion of science as an immediately productive force are also in evidence. For example, labor is described as a form of scientific work (e.g Lassow, 1967:377); yet, such discussions continue to be embedded in the struggle against 'narrow' Stalinist conceptions of the forces of production.

Although Daniel Bell (1979a:167–168) makes reference to the need to conceive of a 'knowledge theory of value' succeeding the obsolete labor theory of value because 'knowledge and its applications replace labor as the source of "added value" in the national product', his conception of the role of knowledge in the productive process ultimately reduces it to an 'instrumental', dependent source of value or to a function in which knowledge itself is not as yet productive and capable of adding value independently. Bell (1979a:168) rather tersely stresses, 'when knowledge becomes *involved* in some systematic form in the *applied transformation of resources* (through invention and design), then one can say that knowledge, not labor, is the source of value' (emphasis added). The role and the importance of scientific knowledge in production goes beyond the limits assigned to it by Bell.

The notion of the sciences as an immediate productive force is not easily understood, even if the thesis about the impending abandonment of traditional factory labor and labor largely based on (practical) experience is accepted. It may be objected that the work of the engineer must be 'realized', that is, applied by the traditional labor of artisans or factory workers in producing machines for production. One has to ask: what does science actually produce as an immediately productive force?

Theorists of post-industrial society speak about the scientific penetration of labor and social practice. They hint at a process of analyzing, rationalizing and generating data about labor and social practice. Realms of social life become subject to planning and control. Further, they expect a structural change of labor in the sense of a change in the composition of the working class. It can be observed that there is an increase of higher qualification, in particular, of the proportion of scientific-technical intelligence, a quantitative shift from the group of laborers employed within the sector of production to the sector of preparation, planning and regulation, and, of course, to services. Finally, the Richta group (1969) conceives of science as a productive force because the leading branches of industry, that is, chemical and electric industries, are to a large extent science based. The result is that the level of contemporary productive forces is largely determined by scientific-technological developments.

But why is science an immediately productive force and what is the product of science? The answer must be that science increasingly produces action knowledge, that is, data and theories, or better, data and programs. Hence science can be called an immediately productive force only in cases where data and programs as such become components or even constitutive of society, a society in which the production of knowledge is immediate social production. Indeed, this is the case today. A considerable part of the total work within advanced societies already takes place on the meta-level; it is second-level production. Production to a large extent is not metabolism with nature any longer, that is, material appropriation typical of industrial society. Part of production presupposes that nature is already materially appropriated; it consists in rearranging appropriated nature according to certain programs. The 'laws' which govern the appropriation of appropriated nature, or secondary production, are not the laws of nature but the rules of social constructs. At the level of social practice we *potentially* meet an analogous situation. Some fields of the social sciences whose subject is society in the state of being appropriated are, for instance, operations research, cybernetics, theory of planning, decision theory, rational choice theory etc. However, social sciences of this kind presuppose, in order to be successful and able to produce action knowledge as well, that society is bureaucratically conditioned and prepared for data processing. That this precondition in fact is lacking is one of the theses of this analysis, or paradoxically, the appropriation of society by the social sciences produces the opposite effect, namely, fragility rather than opportunities for planning and regulation. In other words, the social sciences are never as efficient as material productive forces as is a science that produces machines or living copper as labor.

As science becomes an immediate productive force in our century, it does not lose any of its previous possibilities but adds a decisive new one. Contrary to the situation in the nineteenth century, the production of knowledge now also becomes immediate social production unmediated by labor. In contemporary society a secondary structure on the basis of already appropriated nature is established. As Jean-Jacques Salomon (1973:50) points out, 'science is no longer applied, in Comte's sense, to the organization of production, but society itself is organized with a view to scientific production.' The rules which govern 'secondary' production are social constructs rather than the laws of nature. The consequence is that new disciplines emerge whose output serves as an immediate productive force, e.g. operations research and programming, computer science etc. The production of data and systems is immediately productive because it tends to reproduce the knowledge structure of society. Production of knowledge is consequently social production. Reproduction of society means, to an increasing degree, reproduction of appropriated nature and of the self-appropriation of society. The outcome of these developments is also that scientific knowledge in the sense of an immediate productive force becomes a societal resource with functions comparable to those of labor in the productive process. But unlike labor under capitalism, the owners of the resource 'knowledge' in a knowledge society acquire power and influence because owners of capital cannot, as was still the case for corporeal labor, reduce its content in production through substitution of capital; at best, knowledge can be substituted through other knowledge. Notwithstanding the mechanization of brain work, there also always remains an irreducible amount of 'personal knowledge', which can be converted into and valued as 'intellectual' or 'cultural' capital.

Knowledge as an individual/collective capacity for action

What distinguishes a knowledge society above all else from its historical predecessors is that it is a society which is to an unprecedented degree the product of its own action, or a society in which our secondary nature far outpaces and outgrows our primary nature.[16] Interventions by nature are, increasingly, the result of prior human interventions into nature. The balance of nature and society (cf. Stehr, 1978) or of facts beyond the control of humans and those subject to their control has shifted strikingly.[17] In the Richta Report (Richta et al., 1969:244) certain analogous observations may be found when the authors of the report for example underline that

> the scientific and technological revolution is essentially a part of the process of constituting the subjective factor, that is to say, the subjectivity of society, and then of man, who through its medium comes to master the processes by which the productive forces of human life are created . . . these subjective factors discover that their own development offers radically new opportunities to intervene in the march of history.

In as much as I attempt to stress the greater ability and range of social action as a constitutive feature of the knowledge society I reject naturally the idea that such a society can be or is necessarily a 'technocratic' enterprise, that is, a society which witnesses almost helplessly the inversion of technical means into social ends as sketched, for instance, by Helmut Schelsky (1961) and many others on the left and the right of the ideological divide in social science (cf. Freyer, 1955, 1960; Marcuse, 1964) as the 'general law of scientific civilization' (see also Krämer, 1982). In Chapter 8 I will critically examine the notion of the technical state, as it emerges from these visions, as anti-thetical to the theory of the knowledge society.

Contemporary society has shifted more and more toward capacities which are socially constructed and allow society to operate on itself. More

---

[16] Keeping in mind, of course, that this enlarged capacity to act is not necessarily evenly distributed throughout society and among institutions. I will discuss the stratified nature of knowledge and the consequences of extended capacities to act in Chapter 9.

[17] The increasing capacity of society to act upon itself should, in the end, reduce the probability that knowledge societies will converge to form some kind of common form of society because the greater capacity to act, made possible by the growth of scientific and technical knowledge, has to 'pass through' the filter of local conditions as it is being implemented. Such a process, under normal circumstances, assures that the variety of societies will not be limited to but a handful of exemplars (on the topic of convergence cf. Mills, 1958; Tinbergen, 1961; Levy, 1966; Meyer, 1970). In the context of describing and justifying his choice of the term 'post-industrial society' rather than some other designation for the emerging form of society, Bell (1973a:37) also notes that the new post-industrial societies will fail to achieve the kind of unity 'of the economic system and character structure which was characteristic of capitalist civilization from the mid-eighteenth to the mid-twentieth century.'

specifically, the material appropriation of nature means that nature *in toto* is gradually transformed into a human product by superimposing on nature new, socially constructed designs. This structure is objectified knowledge, namely, an explication and realization of what we know are the laws of natural processes extended by engineering design and construction. The same applies to social processes and social institutions. The horizon of human action and potential social action expands considerably in a knowledge society as already indicated; however, the process I have in mind is one which applies first and foremost at the *intermediate* level of action, that is, at the level of small groups, social movements, smaller corporations and not necessarily at the so-called institutional level of social action, referring for example to the state agencies, the political system, the economy, the educational system or even society and the nation-state. I am not suggesting, therefore, that such an extension in the range of social action is evenly distributed and extends necessarily, and does so invariably, to all individual actors in a knowledge society. The principle of stratified social action does not become inoperative. In a knowledge society many groups and individuals continue to face severe constraints on their range of social action. Nor does the concept advanced here mean that nature or natural facts have had to retreat totally, although these constraints will now be rooted in their restricted access to knowledge. On the contrary, and perhaps paradoxically, our increasing distance from nature may mean that nature can affirm itself catastrophically in knowledge societies.[18] I conceive of a knowledge society as a society in which science and technology have extensively heightened the capacities of society to act upon itself, its institutions and its relation to the natural environment.

But the increase in possible courses of action, that is, in the ability of social organizations, for example, to adapt rapidly to changes (including the need to adapt to problems which represent unprecedented challenges and changes) and enlarge its range of conduct does not result merely from an increase in knowledge about society. The practical usefulness of natural science did not result only from more knowledge about processes 'out there' in nature, at least not only and not most importantly. Natural scientific knowledge became useful only in technical contexts, that is, in contexts in which nature was already available materially. But the 'veneer' of the socially constructed material culture is, in an important sense, quite thin; advanced technology and complex economic relations demand a sophisticated level of quality control and relatively stable social environments (cf. Ravetz, 1987). In an analogous sense, the growing usefulness of social science knowledge is dependent on a prior rationalization of societal contexts, which many argue is the case already in contemporary society. Societal contexts, individual and group capacities of action are increasingly transformed through the utilization of scientific knowledge. These are the

---

[18] Compare our analysis of the interrelation of climate and society in Bray et al., 1994.

processes which must be analyzed under the general heading of the 'scientification' of social action. The increase in the ability of society to act upon itself is by no means restricted to a transformation in the social means of production but extends also to its relations of production. The unprecedented increase in the ability of society to transform itself increases the contingency of social, political and economic relations and has the dual effect of implying both emancipation and the real danger of new forms of dependencies.

Science and technology are, therefore, not merely emancipatory forces, as has been one of the prevailing romantic images throughout history, but also socially constraining forces. One of the elementary constraints issuing from the 'growth' of scientific knowledge is that it has no visible or conceivable term.

These transformations definitely imply that 'all visions of a future without conflict and struggle are doomed to disappointment' (Richta et al., 1969:257) unless, of course, society uses its ability to change itself as a means to drastically inhibit changes which result in social and political conflicts. But such a program would be highly unrealistic. The source of the increase in the ability of society to act upon itself is, for the most part, the consequence of the expansion of scientific knowledge in the broadest sense of the term. The destinies of modern societies are inextricably bound to science and technology. Therefore, one can only reiterate the observations of Radovan Richta and colleagues (1969:213) that science in advanced society does not operate merely

> as a factor in the production of things and as an instrument for satisfying wants; it serves equally as a source generating new types of human endeavor, as an initiator and producer of new wants. That is to say, it is a productive force that can create new demands, conflicts and outlooks.

The concept of knowledge in a knowledge society advanced here does not imply, therefore, that the expansion of knowledge encroaches somehow on 'ideology' and produces a society less affected by ideological thinking. Science multiplies possibilities: 'For every want satisfied and every advance in knowledge, it breeds a multitude of new questions, a spate of human dissatisfaction' (Richta et al., 1969:214).

Importantly, knowledge is not merely enabling, as many would want to stress, it is also constraining, as its critics are prompt to point out. Often the enabling and constraining features of knowledge are closely intertwined. The duality in the consequences of knowledge may, for example, be seen in its effect on the social organization of work: on the one hand, the 'information revolution' or the increased use of microelectronics may indeed be viewed with alarm, since they enable a most sophisticated, centralized and comprehensive monitoring and inexpensive storage of output data or even more generally work behavior, for example. On the other hand, the same artifacts also allow for a high degree of decentralization, local initiative, flexible location, personal responsibility and even the effective and inexpensive monitoring of the monitors.

The political economy of knowledge

The nature of the changes I have described as changes leading to a knowledge society are, above all, changes in the intellectual appropriation of nature and society. There is now an immense stock of objectified knowledge which mediates our relation to nature and to ourselves. Nature is and can scarcely be experienced other than as a human product or within human products, and social relations are mediated by an increasing stock of arrangements of an administrative, legal, or technical kind.

From the point of view of the production, distribution and reproduction of knowledge, the first characterization we are able to give of our contemporary societal condition is a mere quantitative diagnosis: the superstructure of society and nature is now so immense that the greater part of the overall social activity is not production but reproduction, in particular, of knowledge itself, and that implies of the conditions which make specific effects and processes possible in the first place.

The kinds of constraints which operate in a knowledge society differ from those analyzed in theories dealing with more traditional forms of power relations in general, and political power in particular. In the case of traditional notions of power, its possession and use is deliberate and intentional; responsibilities can be traced to its sources, and the benefits or costs associated with its employment are, in many instances, assigned quite unambiguously. The kinds of emerging power in knowledge societies are not merely the constraints which issue from the exclusive possession and control over specific resources or persons, which compel those subjected to the exercise of power because they lack the same means of power and have, therefore, but limited choices at their disposal in the face of overwhelming odds against them in carrying out certain actions or tasks. In knowledge societies, constraints circulate, as Rouse (1987:246) puts it convincingly:

> throughout our relations with one another and our dealings with things and pervade the smallest and most ordinary of our doings. They shape the practical configuration within which our action makes sense, both to ourselves and to one another. This shaping occurs most directly through their effects upon the kinds of equipment available to us, the skills and procedures required to use that equipment, the related tasks and equipment that use imposes upon us, and the social roles available to us in performing these tasks. Through this process, they change our understanding of ourselves and our lives.

The social and material contexts of social action are altered in fundamental ways. The choice of alternatives, especially sensible alternatives in a given situation, are affected and redesigned. As Rouse (1987:246) puts it in the same context:

> it is not so much that these power relations compel specific actions from us (although they certainly do that) as that they re-configure the style and interconnectedness of what we do. There are still many possible actions and self-interpretations open to us. But these are drawn from a field of possibilities that

increasingly displays characteristic features reminiscent of laboratory micro worlds.

But these changes are also related to changes in the fundamental characteristics of knowledge itself and the way knowledge is shaped by the means of its production and dissemination. The differences at issue concern the rise in the need to interpret knowledge and therefore the extent to which knowledge has lost, or appears to have lost, the characteristic of being secure, certain, definitive and even truthful. The progressive elimination of time and space as relevant elements in the production of knowledge has paradoxically injected the importance of time and place in the interpretation or use of knowledge. Since the validation process of knowledge cannot refer back, except in rare circumstances, to the original author of the claim, the interpretative task once again becomes crucial. Anthony Smith (1986:162–163) ascribes the loss of authority of knowledge and the concomitant rise in the importance of processes of interpretation partly to the means of dissemination and production of augmented knowledge; that is, in

> an electronic era . . . there is no longer any certainty in knowledge. In the new global Alexandria of computerized information there is no ultimate perceptual security, no ultimate validation of a text back to an original writer or to an original authority. It is a culture based upon a ceaselessly interpretative notion of knowledge . . . There occurs a kind of paradigm shift when we move from the analog to the digital. It is a shift from the objective to the relative, from certainty through the representation of knowledge as objective to a different kind of certainty derived through a satisfying interpretation of varying reasons of information. It is a shift from precision to probabilism, and it echoes many other recent shifts in the sphere of science and culture.

In the view of some observers, part of the political economy of knowledge in modern societies concerns the possibility that knowledge becomes the basis for class formation in general or the emergence of a 'knowledge class' in particular. Since I have already extensively examined the relations between knowledge and inequality, I will, at this point, restrict further observations about social inequality and knowledge to a few comments mainly intended to express skepticism toward the notion that we are witnessing the emergence of a 'knowledge *class*' in modern society. Peter Berger (1987:66), for example, has recently argued that the modern middle class is increasingly divided into the old middle class consisting of the 'business community and its professionals as well as clerical affiliates' and the newer part, namely the 'knowledge class'. In other words, the former segment of the middle class consists of individuals who derive their 'livelihood from the production and distribution of material goods or services' while the knowledge class includes people whose occupations 'deal with the production and distribution of symbolic knowledge'.[19]

----

[19] The term 'class' for Berger (1987:51) includes all those attributes which for Marxists make classes-for-itself *and* classes-in-itself.

For the purposes of specifying this modern social stratum in greater detail, Berger refers affirmatively to Helmut Schelsky's description of the emerging group of knowledge-producers and knowledge-disseminators in modern society. Schelsky (1975:14) labels this group as the class of the 'distributors and mediators of meaning and purposes' (*Sinn- und Heils-vermittler*). Given Berger's inclusive definition of social class, he maintains that the knowledge class has common material and political interests and a common consciousness. For Berger, the knowledge class tends to be, at least in the United States, on the left of the political spectrum while their economic interests include firm support for an extension of the welfare state – which happens to be the employer of the majority of the knowledge class.

These claims for a knowledge class appear exaggerated but also too restrictive as I will attempt to show in describing some of the fundamental transformations of the modern labor force in Chapter 6. Individuals who are in the business of distributing and disseminating knowledge are by no means confined to membership of the 'middle class'. The probability that this stratum develops a 'class consciousness', or in fact has an incipient class consciousness, is remote. As a matter of fact, Schelsky maintained that the group of knowledge-producers and knowledge-disseminators has every interest in hiding its rule. Since the new class Schelsky discerns tends to dominate education, the media and the public relations field – in short, all those spheres in modern society which somehow have to do with the formation of the public's consciousness and identity – it is relatively easy for this class to deceive the public about its inordinate influence and its interests. One of the most effective strategies employed in this deceptive process is the maintenance of the old myth of the continued existence of the old class conflict between proletariat and capitalist. Such a stance precludes the formation of class-based political organization and the explicit struggle for power. Finally, there is no certainty that this segment of the labor force will really grow any more.

Knowledge as a commodity

It would appear to be almost self-evident that, in a society in which knowledge becomes the dominant productive force, that knowledge, or certain types of knowledge at least, turns into a commodity and can be appropriated, recognized and treated as property. Of course, knowledge has always had its price and has never been available in an unlimited supply, that is, knowledge has been, not unlike other commodities, scarce, and in order to utilize it, one had to sometimes buy it. However, what precisely determines the value of knowledge is by no means self-evident. The value of knowledge depends, for example, not merely on the utility it may represent to some individual or firm but is linked to the ability or inability of others actors, for example competitors, to utilize and exploit it to their advantage as well. In the context of traditional economic discourse, knowledge is treated in a peculiar and often less than plausible fashion, ranging from assuming 'perfect' knowledge of market participants to treating knowledge merely as an exogenous dimension or efforts to argue that knowledge can be treated in a reductionist manner, that is, as a conventional economic category to which orthodox concepts such as utility, fixed and variable costs apply with benefit and without restriction.[20]

It would seem that economists tend to prefer a conception of the value of knowledge which closely resembles their conception of value in the case of any other commodity, namely, value derives from the utility of the 'product' knowledge (use-value), although there remains a considerable range of indeterminacy when it comes to the expected value of knowledge (e.g. Bates, 1988).

For a significant part, the service sector of society lives off selling knowledge. The educational system employs millions who make a living by disseminating socially necessary knowledge. The control of the free circulation of knowledge cannot only be hampered by limited access to the preconditions for its acquisition but also, in a legal way, by assigning property rights to it. One only has to refer to patent and copyright laws. In many countries, patent and copyright laws are no longer confined to technical artifacts and processes but include intellectual ownership in art, music, literature and, increasingly, scientific inventions.

In short, the fact that knowledge is treated as a commodity and is traded is not a new phenomenon. However, some observers would assert that we are witnessing, as the result of technological transformations, especially in conjunction with the proliferation of information-processing machines, a radical 'exteriorization' of knowledge with respect to the 'knower'. With it, the relationship of the

> suppliers and users of knowledge to the knowledge they supply and use . . . will increasingly tend to assume the form already taken by the relationship of commodity producers and consumers to the commodities they produce and consume – that is, the form of value. Knowledge is and will be produced in order to be sold, it is and will be consumed in order to be valorized in a new production: in both cases the goal is exchange (Lyotard, [1979] 1984:4).

What counts according to Lyotard, therefore, is the exchange and not so much the use-value of knowledge. None the less, there is still not an

---

[20] In an effort to arrive at ways of determining the value of information as an economic good, Bates (1988:80), for example, argues that there is an inherent imbalance in the fixed-cost and variable-cost component of producing (and reproducing) information. The production of information has an exceptionally high component of fixed and a very low, even non-existent variable-cost component (the costs associated with the replication of the information) because information is infinitely reproducible and consumes all other resources. Such a treatment of 'information', of course, is only plausible as long as one is convinced that reproduction is virtually unproblematic (e.g. transcends the initial conditions of production including the costs associated with it) and can be repeated at will because production is definitive and does not require any intermediaries or subsequent interpretation.

economic theory of knowledge in analogy to a theory of location for land as a factor of production, capital or labor. Economists have taken knowledge for granted, as have most of their fellow social scientists, and often introduced it as an exogenous or external factor or, put simply, as a black box.

The development of an economic theory of knowledge is by no means an easy task; for one thing, knowledge is, as I have argued, inherently a collective, rather than primarily a private good or property. Knowledge is embedded in social relations.[21] 'Knowledge of various kinds, while it is differentially allocated and a scarce resource, is not, like so many other goods, diminished, decreased in value, or consumed in the process of exchange' (Holzner and Marx, 1979:239); also Georg Simmel ([1907] 1978:438). The absence of any ready ways of dividing (in theory and practice) knowledge into 'units' has perhaps also limited the enthusiasm of economists to treat knowledge as a commodity among other commodities (cf. Boulding, 1966). For the most part, the actual possession and legal definition of *property* is exclusive: 'A thing over which I exercise the right of property is a thing which serves myself alone' (Durkheim, [1950] 1992:141). The exclusive legal command and personal possession of knowledge or a kind of isolation of knowledge as an object is much more difficult to realize if possible at all. However, the legal system has provisions and presumably may evolve in the future, giving certain forms of knowledge an apparently exclusive status. More importantly, the (meta)-capacity to generate new increments of knowledge – which are most likely to confer comparative advantages – is not a collective property. In other words, knowledge is neither strictly comparable to property nor is without attributes which move it, under certain conditions, nearer to property and commodities.

Charles Derber and his colleagues (1990) arrive at a somewhat different conclusion in their analysis of the societal authority and influence of professional occupations in the United States. On the basis of the assumption of the enormous historical variability of what passes for and is accepted as knowledge, and therefore the suspicion that almost anything may be sold as 'knowledge' as long as this group is successful in persuading clients that they in fact have use and a need for the knowledge controlled

---

[21] Daniel Bell ([1979] 1991:237–238) also observes that knowledge in the form of a '*codified theory is a collective good*. No single person, no single set of work groups, no corporation can monopolize or patent theoretical knowledge, or draw unique product advantage from it. It is a common property of the intellectual world.' Bell's characterization of the main reasons why (codified) knowledge constitutes a collective rather than a private good allows the inference that such qualities derive, on the one hand, from their peculiar epistemological attributes and, on the other hand, from the effective operation of the ethos of the scientific community, especially its negative sanctions against secrecy. In contrast to Bell's views, I attempt to stress that it is the social nature of knowledge itself, its production and reproduction, which eliminates the possibility that it becomes the exclusive property of individual or of corporate actors.

by a certain occupation and that this knowledge is superior to everyday knowledge, 'professional' knowledge takes on the typical attributes of the construct of 'property'. Knowledge becomes a commodity because the peculiar nature of the demand (as well as the needs it serves) and the strategies to meet the demand are fully controlled by those who offer the knowledge in question.

Among the crucial strategies is the privatization of knowledge. The prohibition barring lay practice is one of the most powerful strategies to 'privatize' knowledge. In a kind of self-created enclosure and self-policed circle knowledge becomes a commodity (cf. Derber et al., 1990:16–18). Even if one assumes that it is relatively easy in practice to legitimize and monopolize knowledge, Derber and his colleagues overestimate the passivity of the consumer and the solidarity of the professional fraternities. A more significant drawback of their position, it seems to me, is the fact that they once again discard any concrete analysis of the knowledge base of the professionals and rest their case on fairly formal attributes of the knowledge of professionals. The status of the attributes Derber and colleagues invoke appear to be applicable to any knowledge claim and the case boils down to a question of power enabling professionals to set and control cognitive agendas. It is not clear, for example, why scientific knowledge claims have displaced magic since both are functional equivalents as a source of control for the powerful. However, knowledge is not always identical.

The growing supply of and demand for knowledge

An issue which almost immediately follows on the heels of the question of knowledge as a commodity is how one accounts for the growth and therefore for a continuous supply of knowledge and, by the same token, how one explains any unrelenting demand for knowledge. The competing answers to the first question would see the answer as either resting with an inherent logic of scientific and technical progress or with a specific demand for knowledge driven by socio-economic and socio-political requirements and needs. One of the fundamental questions which the emergence of knowledge societies in addition raises concerns, of course, the very reason for the shift to knowledge as a crucial dimension in production. The theory of post-industrial society takes it for granted that the demand for theoretical knowledge increases to the point where it becomes the dominant dimension for production and fashions the kinds of skills required of labor in a knowledge economy. Perhaps it is useful to review briefly some of the suggestions which go beyond trivial conclusions and indicate that the demand for knowledge simply reflects a shift or leap in the economic return of scientific research, although the practical economic results from science may occur in a most roundabout fashion. Undoubtedly, this utilitarian argument is used most frequently and it is the most persuasive one to justify the growing commitment of resources spent on scientific research by the state and business.

Conventional wisdom has it that the industrial revolution 'was set in motion by a set of interests engendered by the self-expansion of capital' (Richta et al., 1969:70–71) and, more precisely, by the surplus value or profit generated by capital. While this is at least the motive force which holds for the owners of the means of production, others have theorized that the Protestant ethic may well have propelled the industrial revolution. While this debate continues, the process or factors responsible for the dynamics of knowledge production remain largely unanalyzed. Daniel Bell (1973a:26) suggests that 'a modern society, in order to avoid stagnation or "maturity" . . . has had to open up new technological frontiers in order to maintain productivity and higher standards of living . . . Without new technology, how can growth be maintained?' Radovan Richta's (1977:48) argument is quite similar, although he restricts his claims to socialist society and asserts a kind of pre-established harmony between scientific knowledge and 'necessary' societal development. This assertion culminates in the plea and conviction that in socialist societies 'there is an ever-growing need for further expansion and acceleration of scientific and technological progress' (Richta et al., 1969:75–81). Thus, the question remains why it is that 'where once science followed in the wake of industry and technology, the tendency today is for it to control industry and lead technology' (Richta et al., 1969:216). Both Bell's and Richta's assertions about the rise of knowledge do not really claim that there is any novel motive force peculiar to post-industrial society which stimulates the expansion of science and its extensive use. The rise of knowledge is at best related negatively to factors which threaten the maintenance of certain motives, desires and particularly economic (material) wants already prominent in industrial society. In this sense, post-industrial society represents but an extension of industrial society.

Similarly, the discussion of knowledge within the context of economic discourse does not appear to advance the matter much. In order to critically examine the role of knowledge within the context of conventional economic discourse, I will confine myself at this point to an analysis of the ways in which economic investments are defined and measured. For the purposes of accounting for investments, economists employ a definition of what constitutes an investment which limits such expenditures to tangible capital, that is, to either machinery or physical plants. Knowledge cannot be an investment unless it is embedded in tangible capital. Knowledge as frozen into machinery is an investment. Within conventional national accounting schemes, expenditures for research and development, for training and the purchase of certain types of services do not constitute an investment component. It follows that the purchase of a personal computer or acquisition of the hardware by a business represents, for the purposes of these national accounts, a capital investment, while the purchase of the requisite software, perhaps a program tailored to the needs of the company and possibly much more expensive than the machine(s) itself, is considered a cost of doing business and not an investment. Such a differentiation is a striking anomaly since 'it is well known that software will play an ever-increasing role in the computer industry as hardware costs continue to decline' (Block, 1987:156–157). Not only is the number of people who are software developers growing at an exponential rate but so is the turnover of firms producing and selling software. The expenditure of individuals and corporations on advice, counseling and expertise is also growing at a rapid rate; however, such services are not treated as an investment.

Since economic discourse has treated knowledge mostly as an external variable, and since the history of science has rarely inquired into the extent to which scientific progress is driven by or responds to economic forces, the possible impact of economic processes on the supply of scientific knowledge has hardly been investigated. Despite the scarcity of analysis, one has little difficulty discerning two disparate positions. First, it is asserted that scientific progress occurs in splendid isolation from economic demand and interests. The utilization of scientific knowledge for productive purposes is driven by the supply of knowledge which happens to be at hand. Utilization follows opportunistic principles. Secondly, the growth in the supply of scientific knowledge is induced by the forces and the specifics of the demand for such knowledge. More precisely perhaps, one can assume that human needs, especially economic needs, determine the path of scientific development.

In his study *Invention and Economic Growth*, which is concerned with an economic account of inventions and their dissemination, Jacob Schmookler (1966:184), for example, argues that economic demand 'induces the inventions that satisfy it'. Schmookler's assertion about the origins of inventions resonates quite closely with the well-known saying that 'necessity is the mother of invention'. The supply of inventions, it would appear, is almost totally elastic and independent of time and place. Each need generates almost concurrently the invention it requires.

One of the basic difficulties with this thesis, of course, is that you cannot really explain the perplexing persistence of many individual and collective needs. Why has it been impossible to satisfy these needs with appropriate scientific discoveries? Schmookler tries to escape this difficulty by concentrating on existing or successful inventions, more concretely, patents which have been issued. But this approach does not assure a clear separation and independence of the demand factors which are supposed to generate appropriate inventions. Therefore, Rosenberg (1974:98) points out that it is only possible to explain the needs which might have been met by certain discoveries if one concentrates on the supply side and examines the available knowledge at any given time. Available knowledge is structured in a certain manner and not evenly distributed in relation to different external needs and requirements.

With respect to the assumption that scientific progress is not propelled by a specific self-regulating logic and that economic interest may well impinge upon scientific development, Rosenberg (1974:100) supports the idea that economic motives and processes 'have played inevitably a major role in shaping the direction of scientific progress . . . but within the changing limits and constraints of a body of scientific knowledge growing at uneven rates among its component sub-disciplines.'

Rosenberg's conclusion makes evident how important it is to base the analysis on a solid understanding of the nature and function of knowledge. Schmookler's observations are too closely tied to the idea that knowledge puts things into motion rather than that knowledge is the capacity for action and not yet identical with its realization. Knowledge also can be seen as the capacity for avoidance. However, Schmookler sets out from 'successful' inventions, in the form of patents granted, and therefore is unable to identify and define the role of demand forces 'independently of the evidence that the demand was satisfied' (Rosenberg, 1974:97).

A novel hypothesis about the reasons for the growing need for knowledge in modern society is argued by Peter Drucker who suggests that the impetus for the increasing demand has to do less with more difficult and complex job skills and more with the considerable extension of the working life span of individuals. Thus, it is not so much the demand for labor and particular skills, but the *supply* of highly skilled labor that underlies the transformation of society into a knowledge society. Drucker's (1969:278) thesis therefore is that the nature of work changed with the arrival of highly educated workers. Because knowledge work is demanded, knowledge jobs have to be created. Thus, Drucker proposes a 'supply side explanation' of the transformation of industrial society into a knowledge society. The extension of education is itself a reflection of a drastic lengthening in the work life expectancy.

A more conventional but also more realistic account is offered by Jean-Jacques Salomon (1973:49), who offers the suggestion that the change to post-industrial society is the result of a convergence, or much more directly, the result of a symbiosis between science and the public authorities (and the economy). Knowledge becomes the objective of power because power is nourished by knowledge. That is to say, the convergence of 'their interests has set off a massive production of new knowledge and technologies of which the advanced societies make deliberate use.' The convergence between state and science is derivative of the nature of modern science (it is quite expensive and basic research does not yield immediate economic returns) and the nature of modern society, especially the exercise of authority which comes to rely increasingly on knowledge. For these reasons, Salomon (1973:67) is able to argue that the 'pursuit of science fits the ends of power itself, however remote it may be from any purpose outside itself and however remote its own purposes may be from those of the state.' Salomon (1973:51) refers both to military research and research for civilian purposes, although he claims that 'science policy is historically the child of war and not of peace.' Basic science carried out to serve national interests and prestige, on the often interdependent fronts of

Knowledge societies

Table 5.1   *Public expenditure on education, 1975–1988 (US dollars)*

	% of GNP				Per inhabitant			
	1975	1980	1985	1988	1975	1980	1985	1988
Africa	4.6	5.2	5.8	6.6	19	41	37	39
Asia	4.3	4.5	4.3	4.4	20	41	43	71
Europe[1]	5.7	5.5	5.5	5.4	197	336	285	435
Oceania	6.5	6.0	5.8	5.6	334	464	436	635
North America[2]	7.4	6.7	6.7	6.8	550	802	1108	1349
Latin America	3.6	3.9	4.0	4.4	42	91	71	90

[1] Includes the former USSR.
[2] Data for the United States refer to total public and private expenditure on education.
Source: UNESCO, *Statistical Yearbook* (1990)

both the military and the economy, is viewed increasingly as a good investment by the state. The arms race in peace times leaves the pattern of science policy essentially unchanged.

Although the debate about the relative importance of different factors on the growth and demand for knowledge is inconclusive, since one lacks a widely recognized standard of measurement, Salomon (1973:57) concludes that the economy 'would not be so marked by technological innovation as it is today without the spur of military programs'. Yet Salomon also recognizes that the spin-off from military and space research may well be less important in the future, or more generally, that research motivated by military designs may not be the only handmaiden of the demand for knowledge.

Expenditure on knowledge production

Despite the almost heroic efforts of Fritz Machlup and his students to quantify expenditure in the United States on knowledge production (and distribution), attempts to legitimize the theoretical and empirical analysis of the economic value and role of knowledge, at least among professional economists have met with little if any resonance (cf. Machlup, 1979). The difficulties connected to such an enterprise are undoubtedly immense and one should perhaps be prepared to concede from the beginning that such an undertaking is futile. The process of quantification, and therefore the extension of conventional economic bookkeeping to knowledge, is fraught with methodological problems because one has to rely on information or guesses that otherwise proceed from the assumption that knowledge is not a common factor of production. But aside from the immense difficulties of generating empirical information about different categories of knowledge, in the final analysis, one will be forced to treat knowledge as a kind of *black box* in the process of measuring the economic value of knowledge.

The expenditure of a country on education (see Table 5.1), or the public

Table 5.2 *Expenditure on knowledge production in the United States,*
1958–1980 (percentage of adjusted GNP)

	1958	1963	1967	1972	1977	1980
Education	11.8	13.3	14.7	14.8	13.7	12.5
R&D	2.2	2.6	2.6	2.2	2.1	2.2
Media	7.7	7.5	7.7	7.9	8.1	8.0
Information machines	2.0	2.4	2.6	2.3	2.7	3.2
Information service	4.9	5.2	5.7	6.7	7.6	8.4
Total	28.6	31.0	33.3	33.9	34.2	34.3
Adjusted GNP (in billion $)	485	648	872	1275	2052	2823

Source: Rubin and Huber (1986:19)

and private appropriations and investment in research and development, are only capable of providing an indirect measure of the societal costs of knowledge production. None the less, internationally comparative data are informative because they can offer a rough picture of the concentrations of educational and research effort of different nations and regions of the world.

From a theoretical point of view, attempts to quantify knowledge are difficult to justify because knowledge is less as well as more than a conventional commodity and its value. In a strictly economic account, the value of a commodity can only be determined on the basis of the price it generates in market context. But knowledge rarely acquires such an exchange value.

Data generated as part of a research programme to quantify the overall expenditure on knowledge production in the United States may be found in Rubin and Huber's (1986) study. Their attempt to measure knowledge income and expenditure connected with commodities and services constitutes the deliberate effort to extend Fritz Machlup's 1962 investigation into the proportion of the Domestic Economic Product that goes to knowledge production (Table 5.2).

Rubin and Huber (1986:3) sum up their findings by indicating that the proportion of knowledge production as a percentage of the (adjusted) gross national product (GNP) in the US increased from 29 percent in 1958 to 34 percent in 1980. Such a rate of growth is, of course, when judged against some extravagant expectations and when compared to the average increase in the rate of growth of other elements of the GNP, 'an extremely modest rate of growth'.

How controversial these figures can be and how closely related their interpretation is to the prevailing theoretical perspective of the researcher becomes evident by comparing the estimates of Machlup with Braverman (1974). In attempting to estimate the proportion of expenditure on knowledge in modern economies and the role of knowledge in the production process, Machlup (as well as Bell and Drucker) arrives at numbers which differ considerably from Braverman's results. Braverman bases his estimate of the proportion of 'knowledge work' (in distinction to the cost of knowledge production referred to earlier), as does Machlup (1962), on the occupational classifications of the US Census. Braverman (1974:241–242) arrives at the conclusion that there is a remarkable concentration of technical expertise in the United States in a relatively small group of occupations. On balance, therefore, 'it is probably proper to say that the technical knowledge required to operate the various industries of the United States is concentrated in a grouping in the neighborhood of only 3 percent of the entire working population – although this percentage is higher in some industries and lower in others.' Machlup's (1962) estimates for the same period and the same economy differ, however. He puts the proportion of 'knowledge workers' at about 40 percent of the working population, while Drucker (1969) estimates the proportion of 'knowledge work' to reach up to 50 percent of the gross national product in the US.

It is evident that Braverman employs an extremely narrow definition of what constitutes the mobilization of technical knowledge and expertise in industry and in the service sector, that is, he confines his estimate to those occupations labeled 'technical engineers' and 'technicians' (that is, occupations responsible for the design of the production process) by the US Census Bureau because he wants to stress the persistence or emergence of new forms of degrading work and exploitation, for example, the separation of the conceptualization from the execution of work, under monopoly capitalism. The engineering profession as a result is viewed by Braverman (1974:243) as subject to the well-known constraints of other forms of mass employment, namely 'rationalization and division of labor, simplification of duties, application of mechanization, a downward drift in relative pay, some unemployment, and some unionization'.

Where Braverman emphasizes the growing homogenization of the workforce, Bell and others observe an expanding scope for occupational differentiation in the modern economy. Where Braverman notes an increase in the intensity of the subordination of labor to capital, Drucker and others conclude that the sphere of autonomy and self-determination of employees is enlarged. In both instances, however, rather little attention is paid to the actual processes of work, the organization of work and of whatever control may possibly be exercised.[22] Knowledge and expertise are treated as black boxes.

---

[22] Newman and Newman (1985:499) stress that with respect to the impact of information technology 'little attention has been paid either to ascertaining how central internal control problems actually are in determining the use of Information Technology by firms, or to the question whether particular instances of fragmentation or de-skilling do in fact result from management strategy, or from other causes such as the limited capabilities of current technology, or the selling strategy of equipment suppliers which may in fact be designed to present these defects of their products as if they were virtues.'

Knowledge and information

Finally, in this chapter, I should take up the question of the relation between knowledge and information. The first question perhaps has to be whether it is still possible and sensible to distinguish between information and knowledge (information and *Erkenntnis*), for this would appear to be a conceptual distinction quite difficult if not impossible to sustain in light of the fact that these notions are often used as virtual equivalents. The extent to which usage has made them indistinguishable raises, last but not least, the problem of the futility of any alternative effort which detects merit not in conflating but in distinguishing their meaning and referents. It is likely, however, that prevailing practices will prove to be more persuasive.

An equally formidable barrier against any new or renewed attempt to separate knowledge and information sociologically and point to their common features is the almost impenetrable mountain of competing conceptions of knowledge and/or information indebted, moreover, to multiple epistemological and ontological perspectives. I will refer to some relevant conceptions of knowledge and information. Perhaps the conception advanced by Daniel Bell (1979a:168) is worth referring to at some length: 'By information I mean data processing in the broadest sense; the storage, retrieval, and processing of data becomes the essential resource for all economic and social exchanges (in post-industrial society).' Bell's conception of information is indistinguishable from the technical conception of communication in which the meaning, exchange and transfer of a piece of information is independent of the carriers (source and receiver) of information. By knowledge, in contrast, he means 'an organized set of statements of fact or ideas, presenting a reasoned judgment or an experimental result, which is transmitted to others through some communication medium in some systematic form' (Bell, 1979a:168).

It would appear that the technical conception of communication applies to knowledge as well, although Bell makes implicit reference to the distinct epistemological status (or value) of knowledge and information which results in a hierarchical and asymmetrical gradient between knowledge and information. None the less, the dichotomy has strong disembodied strains, that is, there is no reference to the contingent character of information and knowledge and the need to interactively render knowledge and information intelligible and negotiate whether it is valuable or appropriate. Given Bell's technical conception of communication of knowledge and information, the assumption is of course that both knowledge and information travel virtually unimpeded. Finally, what links if any may exist between information and knowledge remain ambivalent. At best, it would seem that Bell's conception of knowledge and information contain the claim that information is the handmaiden of knowledge. Moreover, it is overly confident about the (uncontested?) authority, trustworthiness and power of information and knowledge. It seems to me that Bell's interpretation raises more questions than it answers.

None the less, a discussion of the interrelation of knowledge and information provides an opportunity to summarily rehearse some of the comments I have made about the role of knowledge in social affairs. Knowledge, as I have defined it, constitutes a capacity for action. Knowledge enables an actor, in conjunction with control over the contingent circumstances of action, to set something in motion. Knowledge allows an actor to generate a product or some other outcome. But knowledge is only a necessary and not a sufficient capacity for action. As indicated, in order to set something into motion or generate a product, the circumstances within which such action is contemplated to take place have to be subject to the control of the actor. Knowledge which pertains to moving a heavy object from one place to another is insufficient to accomplish the movement. In order to accomplish the transfer, one needs control over some medium of transportation useful for moving heavy objects, for example. But the value which resides in knowledge is linked to its capacity to set something into motion. Yet, knowledge always requires some kind of attendant interpretive skills and a command of the situational circumstances.

The function of information is, as I would see it, both more restricted and more general. It is more general because information is by no means as scarce as is knowledge. In addition, access to and the benefits from information are not only or as directly restricted to the actor or actors who come into the possession of information. Knowledge use is more restricted and more limited in its use-value because knowledge alone does not allow an actor to set something into motion though information may be a step in the acquisition of knowledge. A good example of information is price advertising and other market information such as availability of a product. Such information certainly can be useful; in the context of the modern economy it is very general and easily as well as widely available, but the consequences of having such information as such are minimal. From the point of view of a consumer, price information combined with knowledge about the workings of the market place may constitute a capacity to effect some savings. Information has attributes assuring that it constitutes, certainly to a greater extent than is the case for knowledge, a public good. Information is self-sufficient. It is not enabling in the sense of allowing an actor to generate a product. Information merely reflects the products from which it is abstracted.

6

The Economic Structure of Knowledge Societies

There are, in the context of this study, several important reasons for addressing the nature of the changing economic structure of modern society. First, development of knowledge societies is connected to basic transformations in the structure of economic activity. The engine of much of the dynamics of economic activity and the source of much of the growth of added economic value can be attributed to knowledge. Paradoxically perhaps, the self-transformation of the economy diminishes the importance of the economy to individuals and society. Of course, it does not eliminate it. But from the point of view of the individual, for example, the economy of knowledge societies has the enabling quality of allowing central-life interests to progressively drift away from purely economic ones or, from a macro-perspective of social conflicts, for instance, a shift toward more generalized struggles not primarily driven by material clashes can be discerned. The conditions which allow for such displacements also render traditional economic discourse (and policy derived from such premises) less powerful. At the same time, natural, social and cultural conditions, namely scientific-technical, environmental and institutional change, often treated as exogenous factors by neo-classical economics, become increasingly important to economic activity.

Secondly, the emergence of a primarily knowledge-based labor force cannot be understood apart from a profound transformation in the economic system; and, thirdly, public debate and political discourse on modern society is still captivated and impoverished, perhaps dominated but certainly often limited, by reference to economic considerations. Prevalent popular orientation and a frequent basis for political judgments are references to economic imperatives and therefore how policies and conduct generally fit with 'free' market forms; that is, political realities are frequently defined in a most restrictive fashion.

A fourth reason is the quality of the link between the economic system and other societal sectors, for example the private world, which is changing and justifies a re-examination of the assumption of a self-propelled development of economic change, on the one hand, and the firm separation between the economy and other sectors of society, on the other. In addition, the extent to which situational and contingent rather than transcontextual and universal effects play a role in economic relations justifies a theoretical approach to economic relations informed by socio-logical considerations.

Fifthly, sociological discourse, in the past few decades, has been increasingly separated from economic discourse. It is possible to conceive of this distancing as a matter of the increasing differentiation of social science discourse. Economics lost interest in the analysis of social institutions, while sociology conceded the study of socio-economic phenomena to economics (cf. Swedberg, 1987; Granovetter, 1990).[1] Finally, both economic analysis and sociology lost interest in the study of the societal and socio-economic impact of science and technology. However, it is now, in the light of existing economic conditions, less certain that such a state of affairs represents a proper cognitive priority and intellectual division of labor. The sociological contribution to the analysis of economic relations should not merely be peripheral nor should the treatment of scientific and technical change be considered exogenous to economic analysis (cf. Dosi et al., 1988).

Central to my analysis is the thesis that the origin, social structure and development of knowledge societies is linked first and foremost to a radical transformation in the *structure of the economy*, including a set of novel and largely unintended consequences, for example in the area of terms of trade, inflation, productivity, competitiveness and employment. Moreover, the ways in which society is affected and co-ordinates its economic activities and agents are changing. Although the central thesis will be that we are witnessing the emergence of a new structure and organization of economic activity on the basis of a new combination of the forces of production, Emile Durkheim's specification of the general status of economic factors within a primarily sociological analysis, first introduced at the end of the nineteenth century for his own central theoretical category of the division of labor in society, remains valid. That is, Durkheim ([1893] 1964:275) draws a distinction in the use of the category of division of labor by sociologists and economists; for the latter, 'it essentially consists in greater production. For us, this greater productivity is only a necessary consequence, a repercussion of the phenomenon. If we specialize, it is not to produce more, but it is to enable us to live in new conditions of existence that have been made for us.' Attention in this instance indeed centers only secondarily on outcomes. The primary focus is on how outcomes become possible, are sustained, organized and perhaps even continue to grow.

Productive processes in *industrial society* are governed by a number of factors all of which appear to be on the decline in their relative significance as conditions for the possibility of a changing, particularly *growing*

---

[1] As Christopher Freeman and his colleagues (1982:ix), for example, resolutely stress: 'The development of industrialized economies cannot be reduced to statistics of the growth of GNP, of industrial production, of capital stock, investment, employment etc., valuable though these statistics undoubtedly are. Underlying these statistical aggregates are the growth of entirely new industries and technologies and are the decline of old ones and many social and institutional changes in the structure of industry and government.'

economy: the dynamics of the supply and demand for primary products or raw materials; the dependence of employment on production; the importance of the manufacturing sector which processes primary products; the role of labor (in the sense of manual labor); the close relation between physical distance and cost and the social organization of work; the role of international trade in goods and services; and the nature of the limits to economic growth. The most common denominator of the changes in the structure of the economy seems to be a shift from an economy driven and governed, in large measure, by 'material' inputs into the productive process and its organization to an economy in which transformations in productive and distributive processes are determined much more by 'symbolic' or knowledge-based inputs and outputs. However, social science discourse and official data collection still tend to think of economic activity primarily in terms of the production of commodities.

The economy of industrial society is initially and primarily a material economy and then changes gradually to a monetary economy. Keynes' economic theory, particularly as outlined in his *General Theory* (1936), reflects this transformation; it becomes, as evident recently, a symbolic economy. The changes in the structure of the economy and its dynamics are increasingly a reflection of the fact that knowledge becomes the leading dimension in the productive process, the primary condition for its expansion and for a change in the limits to economic growth in the developed world. In short, the point is that for the production of goods and services, with the exception of the most standardized commodities and services, factors other than 'the amount of labor time or the amount of physical capital become increasingly central' (Block, 1985:95) to the economy of advanced societies.

A close examination of the literature in economics indicates, however, that the function of knowledge and information in economic activity is, for the most part, ignored by economists. Either that, or they introduce knowledge as an exogenous variable, as an expense and generally treat it as a black box.[2] There are significant exceptions of course, and I will refer to them.[3] But the general and disparaging observation by Stigler (1961:213) is still close to the mark: 'One should hardly have to tell academicians that

[2] The economic concept of *capital* is narrowly defined and refers to fixed, physical capital equipment in plant and organizations. Such capital is recognized as *investment*, that is, as objects which must be purchased. However, the acquisition of knowledge, for example, in the sense of research and development, creating of organizational structures, educational programs or the development of skills are treated as *expenses* and not as contributing to the capital formation of organizations.

[3] One of the significant exceptions among economic theorists is Friedrich von Hayek (e.g. [1945] 1948) for whom the central problem of economic theory is the problem of knowledge and who, despite his methodological individualism, views social institutions such as economic markets as knowledge-bearing phenomena. Markets are not allocative mechanisms but rather epistemological devices 'in which knowledge that could not be collected by a single mind is yet rendered accessible and usable for human purposes' (Gray, 1988:55). Markets embody tacit knowledge.

information is a valuable resource: knowledge *is* power. And yet it occupies a slum dwelling in the town of economics.' Knowledge is a residual, even invisible component of production and assets. Knowledge has many 'qualitative' components and quality has not yet prospered within economic discourse. Despite its apparent ascent as a source of added economic value, for example, knowledge remains elusive.

The specific changes in the economic *structure* may be described briefly as follows. The important changes in the relations of production, the nature of work and the composition of the labor force will be dealt with in greater detail below.

The diminishing role of primary materials

The striking change here is the 'uncoupling' of the raw material economy from the industrial economy.[4] The uncoupling has been accompanied in recent decades, perhaps slowed, by a secular decline in the price of commodities when compared to the price of manufactured goods. The decline of commodity prices has been uneven. It has been particularly strong in the case of metals (Figure 1; cf. Grilli and Yang, 1988; for trends see IMF, 1992:86–87). In general these developments imply that the recent 'collapse in the raw materials economy seems to have had almost no impact on the world of industrial economy' (Drucker, 1986:770). The traditional assumption of economists has of course been that changes in the price structure, most surely dramatic changes, ought to have a profound impact on the cycle of economies.

However, the significant decline in the price of most raw materials has not brought about an economic slump, except perhaps in those countries which rely to a large degree on trade with raw materials. On the contrary, production has grown (Figure 2). As the regression lines in Figure 3 for example show, in the case of the (apparent) consumption of aluminum in OECD countries from 1962 to 1990, the increase in consumption departs, or slows more and more from the growth of the manufacturing sector in these countries. What accounts for the uncoupling is the decline in demand for primary commodities[5] and the simultaneous increase in the supply of, for example, food.

---

[4] In the context of this section, attention will focus on the fact of the uncoupling process itself and on the possible reasons for such a development; however, I will not draw attention to and discuss national, regional or even global environmental consequences of the uncoupling process in some countries (cf. Simonis, 1989), or the overall impact of a shift in material intensive production from some regions of the world to other groups of countries.

[5] Although these particular estimates should be taken with a grain of salt, Peter Drucker (1986:773) relates that 'the amount of industrial raw materials needed for one unit of industrial production is now no more than two-fifths of what it was in 1900. And the decline is accelerating.' These estimates need to be viewed with some skepticism simply because they are unusual ways of viewing production costs when compared to more conventional methods of accounting among economists. But this also ensures that such comparisons are challenging perspectives.

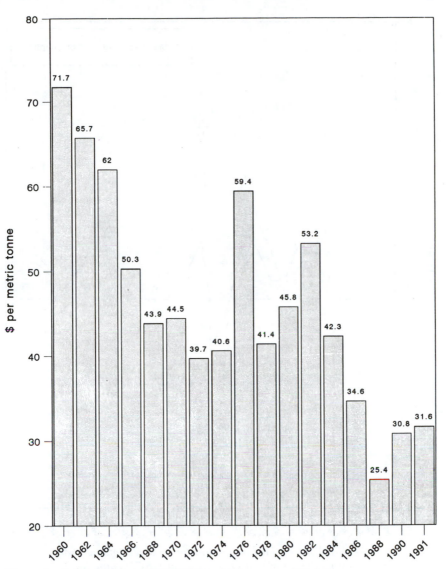

Figure 1 *Iron ore prices, 1960–1991 in 1990 constant US dollars (deflated by G-7 consumer price index)*

Source: World Bank, *Market Outlook for Major Primary Commodities*, volume 2. Washington, DC: World Bank, 1992: 139. Reproduced with permission

The demand for raw materials in manufacturing diminishes 'not only because of miniaturization (e.g. chips) and the reduction of energy requirements, but also because of the revolution in material science. One asks less for specific materials . . . and more for the properties needed (e.g. tensility, conductivity) and the material combinations that can provide those properties' (Bell, 1987:9). In terms of the sheer quantity of the

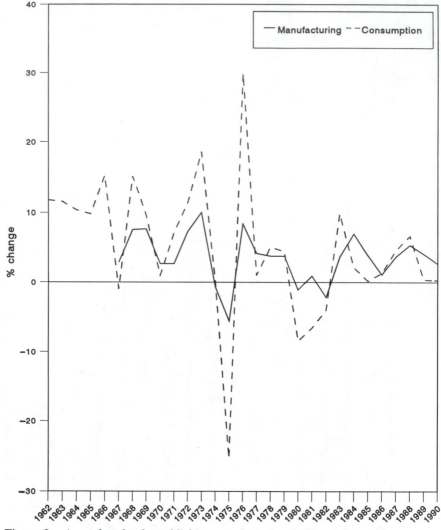

Figure 2   *Annual real value added in manufacturing and annual growth
in (apparent) consumption of primary aluminum in OECD countries,
1962–1990*

Sources: Real value added in manufacturing: OECD, *Historical Statistics*, 1992a:
48, 50; 1983: 44, 46; consumption of primary materials compiled by World
Bank. Reproduced with permission

consumption of primary materials, the amount of primary aluminum
utilized in the OECD countries has not risen much since 1979. In the case
of steel it has declined in the same period[6] as exemplified in the United

[6] According to World Bank data, in 1979, the total consumption of primary aluminum in
OECD countries was 11,422,000 tonnes and in 1990 it had reached 11,994,000 tons; even in

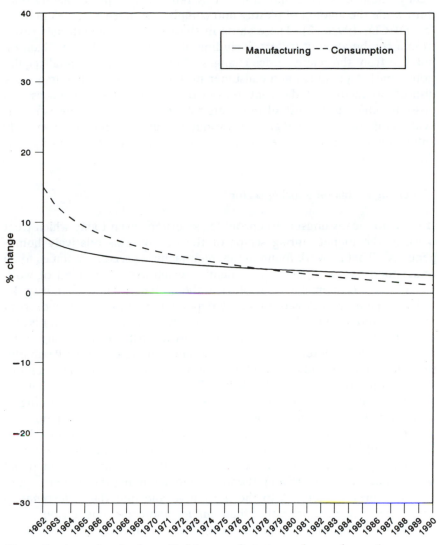

Figure 3   *Annual real value added in manufacturing and annual growth in (apparent) consumption of primary aluminum in OECD countries, 1962–1990 (log regression)*

Sources: Real value added in manufacturing: OECD, *Historial Statistics*, 1992a: 48, 50; 1983: 44, 46; consumption of primary materials compiled by World Bank. Reproduced with permission

---

low and mid-income countries it increased by a small percentage. The steel consumption in OECD countries declined from 428 million tons in 1973, to 395 million tons in 1979 and to 358 million tons in 1990.

States motor industry; from the mid-1970s to the mid-1980s, the iron and steel content of cars manufactured was reduced by approximately one-third while the amount of plastics and composites increased by 33 percent (cf. OECD, 1992e:22). These shifts in the input of raw materials result from a combination of factors, including of course technological changes, but also from the relative price changes of factors, environmental regulations, market pressures and consumer preferences. It is, of course, very difficult to factor out the contribution of each of these influences and possibly others to the use of raw materials in production. However, it is evident that the thesis that growing production and consumption invariably entails increasing natural resource use has to be re-examined in light of these developments.

The changing manufacturing sector

It is by no means unusual to encounter assertions even today which treat work in the manufacturing sector of the economy as relatively homogeneous.[7] That is, work found in the manufacturing sector continues to be understood as one of the few remaining examples of the kind of work which classic economic and sociological theory had in mind when it spoke of labor, namely work carried out by dependent and exploited laborers in industrialized settings. This type of work in the manufacturing sector is also often perceived as one of the last bastions against the increasing trend toward greater differentiation, new rationality, more extensive flexibility, self-determination and increased reflexivity of work in the service sector of the economy (cf. Offe, 1984: 24–25). The upshot is, of course, that the worlds of work and economic sectors are seen as operating according to different rationalities, one technical, or perhaps better, 'functional' rationality and the other a kind of 'substantial' rationality (cf. Mannheim, [1935] 1940:51–56).[8] Consistent with some of the traditional general assumptions of contemporary theories of society, especially the notion of functional differentiation, the governing theme in understanding the modern economy becomes a reference to the normative and material *differentiation* among economic sectors rather than *linkage* and complementarity.

Assuming that the differentiation of the modern economy into three

---

[7] Affirming this perspective, Claus Offe (1984:23), for example, contends that 'by far the largest proportion of the work carried out in the "secondary", that is, the industrial, commodity producing sector can be reduced to the common abstract denominator that such work is subject to the common technical-organizational productivity regime as well as the criteria of singular profitability while these standards of the work and evaluation process lose their (relative) definite character where labor becomes reflexive, namely within the largest segment of the "tertiary" sector of service industry.'

[8] The upshot according to Offe (1984:27) is that we are faced with a significant 'doubling of the term labor, with a proximity and an opposition of dual and contradictory standards of rationality corresponding to the images of the "efficient producer" or the "effective safeguarding of accomplishments" and therefore with an evident loss of the once unequivocal conception of work.'

sectors remains plausible, what is less contentious is that the character of labor in modern society is changing. The central questions for analysis become whether the changes in work are mainly confined to a specific sector of the economy or whether the transformation occurs in all sectors, perhaps driven by similar forces and constraints and whether the pattern of labor found in one sector increasingly extends into other sectors of the economy?[9]

By the same token, it is widely postulated that the overall economic importance of, or the capacity to add value to, the manufacturing sector is declining and that the primary significance of economic activity has shifted to the service sector. These conjunctures at times have been discussed under the heading of 'de-industrialization' (for example, Bluestone and Harrison, 1982). It is worth noting that Daniel Bell does not, as far as I can tell, ever expressly advance, in the context of his extensive comments on the nature of the post-industrial economic structure of society, the thesis that the manufacturing sector actually *shrinks* in economic importance. Bell (1979a:163) explicitly contends that post-industrial society involves a 'change from a goods producing to a service society'. As a result perhaps, the frequent reading of his theory that the aggregate importance of the manufacturing sector diminishes under post-industrial conditions acquires a certain credibility. As a matter of fact, the designation 'post-industrial' itself supports such an image. And the almost 'logical' inference of that kind of interpretation is that the industrial sector of the economy becomes largely dispensable in an affluent economy.

But exactly the opposite is the case. Contrary to many assumptions, the manufacturing sector and industrial production are not declining in importance in contemporary society.[10] Since several observers have seen fit to assert with some urgency that *manufacturing matters* (Cohen and Zysman, 1987), and have done so quite convincingly, it is evident that the post-industrial economy thesis has been widely interpreted to mean that

[9] I take it that the latter is the position argued by Cohen and Zysman (1987:xiii) in their book *Manufacturing Matters*. Summing up their position, Cohen and Zysman observe that the new technical division of labor has 'extended the production processes outside the confines of the traditional manufacturing firm. We are experiencing a transition not from one kind of industrial economy to a service economy, but from one kind of industrial economy to another.'

[10] This conclusion can be expressed quantitatively in a number of ways. One interesting set of figures (Forstner and Ballance, 1990: 38–39) which confirms the consistent importance of manufacturing is its almost constant share between 1970 and 1986 among countries with 'developed market economies (this is a group of twenty-five countries from Australia to the United States) of the value of total exports of these countries. In 1970, approximately three quarters of the value of total exports comes from manufacturing; in 1986, the figure has risen slightly. During the same period of time, in the case of developing countries, the share of manufacturing increases from 25.9 to 63.7 percent (exports excluding oil).' According to Forstner and Ballance (1990:38), the rising share of 'manufactures in the exports of developing countries cannot be attributed primarily to price effects, but was the result of more fundamental changes in the structure of production.' The figures dispel the notion that these countries are dependent on the export of agricultural commodities.

Table 6.1　*Percentage of gross domestic product (at 1985 prices)[1]
generated by manufacturing activity,[2] 1978–1990*

	Canada	US	Japan	Australia	Austria	France	Germany (FRG)	UK
1978	19.0	22.7	25.6	19.6	26.4	24.9	33.2	26.1
1979	19.0	22.7	26.3	19.8	26.8	24.8	33.5	25.0
1980	17.8	21.8	25.9	19.7	26.7	24.2	32.5	23.2
1981	17.8	21.7	27.3	19.4	26.4	23.7	32.1	21.4
1982	16.0	20.9	27.4	18.4	26.3	23.3	31.3	21.1
1983	16.6	21.3	27.9	17.9	26.1	23.3	31.2	20.4
1984	17.6	22.3	30.0	17.6	26.5	22.6	31.8	20.5
1985	17.7	22.4	29.5	17.3	26.9	22.1	31.4	20.7
1986	17.3	22.3	28.0	17.8	26.7	21.5	31.4	20.7
1987	17.4	22.4	28.9	17.5	26.0	20.8	30.4	19.8
1988	17.5	–	29.7	17.6	27.0	21.0	30.3	–
1989	17.5	–	30.6	17.4	27.4	21.1	30.4	–
1990	16.1	–	31.3	16.7	27.9	20.9	30.4	–

[1] Canada at 1986 prices; United States at 1980 prices; Australia at 1984–85 prices; France at 1980 prices and United Kingdom at current prices.
[2] The manufacturing activities include: (1) food, beverages and tobacco; (2) textile, wearing apparel and leather industries; (3) wood, and wood products, including furniture; (4) paper and paper products, printing and publishing; (5) chemicals and chemical petroleum, coal, rubber and plastic products; (6) non-metallic mineral products; (7) basic metal industries; (8) fabricated metal products, machinery and equipment; and (9) other manufacturing industries.

Source: OECD, *National Accounts: Detailed Tables, 1978–1990*, volume 2 (1992c)

the secondary economic sector not only loses out as a source of employment but is also a loss leader in terms of its contribution to the overall material well-being of the modern economy. In other words, is the composition of the relative contribution to the gross national product across economic sectors really changing? When did the change commence and how significant is it? In addition, what exactly is the linkage between sectors of the economy? Do we have to assume that *economic* connections too are driven by the process of differentiation, or is it the case that the service economy, for example, perhaps represents more of a complement rather than a substitute or successor to manufacturing?

As the distribution of the contribution of the manufacturing sector (at *constant prices*)[11] to the GDP of selected economies in Table 6.1 indicates,

[11] Using constant rather than current prices and therefore focusing on quantity rather than both volume changes and price changes generates a somewhat more accurate picture of the relative position of the manufacturing sector. When measured in current prices, the share of manufacturing in the US has constantly *fallen* since 1978; at constant prices, however, its contribution remains stable as Table 6.1 demonstrates. The difference in the two trends reflects the higher productivity in the manufacturing sector relative to other sectors and therefore a relative decline in its prices, for example, compared to prices in services. By the same token, the decline in the contribution of the manufacturing sector to the GDP in the United Kingdom, measured in *current prices*, could be a consequence of the same factors. But in the case of the United Kingdom, constant prices were not available.

the share of the manufacturing sector between 1978 and 1990 has declined somewhat in some of the countries, remained stable in others and increased in the case of the Japanese economy. In other words, the repeated observation that the 'shift to services' represents a change toward an increased consumption of services *at the expense* of manufactured (or agricultural) products is mistaken. The data indicate that there has not been a significant shift in the relative contribution of the different sectors of the economy to the total output (see also Baumol et al., 1985).

However, within the manufacturing sector rather significant trans-formations are taking place. First and foremost, production is switching away from commodities which are material intensive. Although Peter Drucker (1986:773) does not offer a precise source for his estimate, he relates that the raw materials in a semi-conductor microchip account for 1–3 percent of total production cost; in an automobile their share is 40 percent, and in pots and pans it is 60 percent. But also in older industries the same scaling down of raw material needs goes on, and with respect to old products as well.[12] The result is, for the time being, that two forms of manufacturing are emerging:

> one is material based, represented by the industries that provided economic growth in the first three quarters of this century. The other is information- and knowledge-based: pharmaceuticals, telecommunications, analytical instruments and information processing such as computers (Drucker, 1986:779).

And, most of the economic growth in the manufacturing sector, in terms of value added, occurs in the knowledge-based industries.

Secondly, connected with these changes is a persistent modification in the kind of employment activity typical of the manufacturing sector. Most available official statistics on employment reflect only insufficiently con-tinuing changes in predominant occupational skills and employment patterns in manufacturing. However, information on the percentage of 'administrative, technical and clerical workers' in the manufacturing industries, for example in Great Britain between 1959 and 1982, indicate an appreciable shift in the balance of occupations within the manufacturing sector (cf. Cutler et al., 1986:77). In the case of other countries for which the same type of information is available, consistent shifts toward a larger proportion of 'administrative, technical and clerical' employees as a proportion of all employees in manufacturing can be observed (Table 6.2) (cf. also Roach, 1991).[13] None the less, these figures should only be

---

[12] Peter Drucker and Daniel Bell refer almost in unison, though without citing a source for their information, to the following relations for illustrative purposes: (a) Drucker (1986:773) contends that 'fifty to 100 pounds of fiberglass cable transmits as many telephone messages as does one ton of copper wire'; and (b) Bell (1987:8) recounts that 'one hundred pounds of optical fibers in a cable can transmit as many messages as one ton of copper wire'. I assume that both authors found their information in a newspaper or magazine.

[13] The OECD statistics on the proportion of 'administrative, technical and clerical' employees are limited to a few of the member countries. Statistics for Germany and France as well as a number of other countries are not available or limited to just a few years of reporting.

Table 6.2   *Percentage of administrative, technical and clerical workers in manufacturing industries in selected industrialized countries, 1962–1989*

	Canada	US	Japan	Denmark	UK
1962	–	25.9	25.1	21.7[1]	22.6
1965	25.6	25.6	26.8	22.9	23.4
1970	27.5	27.5	28.4	24.6	26.5
1975	29.4	28.8	33.1	27.2	27.8
1980	30.1	29.9	34.1	28.1	30.0
1985	–	32.0	34.3	29.4	–
1989	–	31.8	35.3	35.8	–

[1] 1963.

Source: OECD, *Labour Force Statistics, 1963–1983* (1985); OECD, *Labour Force Statistics, 1969–1989* (1991b)

considered as representing a crude quantitative approximation and likely significant underestimation of a trend toward knowledge-based manufacturing and therefore a demand for skills very much unlike those traditionally expected and practiced in industry.[14] Most importantly, these figures do not show the transformation of job skills and tasks faced by employees in manufacturing who are not, based on conventional typologies, classified as 'white-collar workers' or as 'administrative, technical and clerical workers'. A disaggregation of the information for the manufacturing sector as a whole would, in addition, show that the scale of the shift toward a greater proportion of 'administrative, technical and clerical' personnel and the extent of the substitution of knowledge-based occupations depends on the type of industry.[15] But what is needed even more urgently, independent of conventional occupational labels, is a detailed examination of the actual work tasks carried out by employees in industry.

Moreover, the proportion of the production cost in the industrial sector

[14] By the same token, Wolff and Baumol (1989:table 3) estimate that the total percentage of '*information workers*' in the 'non-durable manufacturing' (and 'durable manufacturing') sector of the US economy increased from 28.0 (32.0) per cent in 1960 to 35.8 (38.2) percent in 1980. Wolff and Baumol (1989:33) indicate also that a substantial portion of the total increase in the number of information workers, namely 53 percent, is the result of the *substitution* of information workers for non-information employees in production.

[15] The classification of employees in industry into 'administrative, technical and clerical' and 'operatives' has been used for a considerable time in the British *Census of Production*. Census returns indicate that the ratio of administrative, technical and clerical employees to operatives in British industries already begins to rise in the 1920s and 1930s. In 1924 the ratio is 9.5 and in 1935 it has risen to 12.9 (Florence, 1948:142). Disaggregating these figures already indicates that the shift is least pronounced in coal mining, metal mining, jute, slate quarrying, tin-plate, non-metal mining, cotton spinning, linen, wool, brick making, coke, shoes, china, shipbuilding and building, while the highest ratios may be found, in the 1920s and 1930s, in oil and tallow, ink, gum and sealing-wax, starch and polish, brush, wholesale bottling, chemicals, electrical engineering, aerated waters, fur, butter, preserved foods, scientific instruments, musical instruments, aircraft, plate and jewelry and mechanical engineering (see Florence, 1948:142).

Table 6.3 *Aggregate hours of work by sector in Germany (FRG),
1960–1991 (millions of hours)*

	Agriculture		Manufacturing		Service		State	
	Total	%	Total	%	Total	%	Total	%
1960	8478	(100)	26 101	(100)	17 032	(100)	4259	(100)
1965	7027	(84)	25 868	(99)	16 894	(99)	5172	(121)
1970	5141	(61)	24 632	(95)	16 343	(96)	4468	(105)
1975	3909	(46)	20 438	(79)	15 869	(93)	6105	(143)
1980	3084	(37)	19 922	(77)	16 355	(96)	6553	(154)
1985	2943	(34)	17 379	(67)	16 226	(95)	6735	(159)
1990	1973	(23)	18 186	(70)	17 148	(101)	6754	(159)
1991	1898	(22)	18 359	(70)	17 728	(104)	6711	(158)

Source: Kalmbach, 1988:174 and private communication

which accrues to knowledge grows and assumes remarkable proportions. In other words, the major source of revenue increasingly comes from software rather than the production of hardware. As a case in point, and as Peter Drucker (1986:778) points out:

> the manufacturing costs of the semiconductor microchip are about 70 percent knowledge – that is, research, development and testing – and no more than 12 percent labor. Similarly with prescription drugs, labor represents no more than 15 percent, with knowledge representing almost 50 percent. By contrast, in the most fully robotized automobile plant labor would still account for 20 or 25 percent of the costs.

A distinction which becomes quite central in this respect, therefore, is between technical means of production characteristic of industrial society which were, for the most part, experience-based or craft-based technologies and the means of production of the knowledge society which are based, also for the most part, on a 'scientification' of skills. New industries within the manufacturing sector will be derivative of knowledge rather than experience. The skills most valued in manufacturing will not be (practical) experience but systematic knowledge.

The analysis of employment trends exclusively based on the number of *jobs* or the aggregate of employment and unemployment has the disadvantage of failing to capture important transformations in the form, content and volume of work. Information about the number of jobs does not reflect changes in the type of work; for example, a growth in part-time work. If one is interested in the volume of work an economy requires or provides and how the volume of work in different sectors of the economy may have changed over time, a better measure to consider is total number of hours actually worked (cf. Block, 1987:130–134).

The total aggregate number of hours worked, based on the actual number of hours worked in different sectors, has steadily declined in Germany since 1960 (Table 6.3).[16] The volume of work has been reduced

[16] For an analysis of working-time development after the war in Germany that uses the individual worker as its unit of analysis compare Hinrichs (1991).

during the past thirty years by 20 percent. The only sector that has experienced an increase in the number of hours worked is the state sector. However, the initial rapid increase in the 1960s has slowed since 1980 and stagnates at the present. Aside from the agricultural sector of the economy in Germany, the number of hours worked in the manufacturing sector during the past three decades has declined by a third while it has remained at the same level in the (private) service sector. The data presented demonstrate how important it is to separate, within the service sector, what rarely is disaggregated, namely state employment and employment trends in private service industries.

The 'scientification' of the manufacturing (and the service) sector of the economy is reflected in a dramatic shift in the type of investment and therefore the kind of capital formation typical of industry. Such trends can be documented despite the fact that, as I have already indicated, the conventional accounting of capital formation is quite restrictive. Investments only count as capital formation if the investment involves tangible capital, that is, investments in either machinery or physical plant. Such a procedure underestimates, to a considerable extent, the degree and volume of likely structural shifts in investments in a knowledge society. Given the conventional approach, in the United States, between 1983 and 1988, the manufacturing sector capital formation was quite low; however, 'this sector's spending on information technology has risen at about an 8 per cent average since 1982' (Roach, 1991:120). These gains were sufficient to account for the entire additional capital formation in the industrial sector in the United States. By the same token, within industry, the technology intensity declines significantly with commodity-based manufacturing.

These changes, characteristic of the change from industrial society to knowledge society, and the different systems of production in each, are differences in the wake of growing mutual dependence and integration during the twentieth century of scientific knowledge and technical practices and objects (Böhme et al., 1978). Production becomes increasingly an extension and specification of laboratory knowledge and leads to the construction of 'idealized' technical objects, which makes it possible to transcend, to some extent at least, more technical and craft-based knowledge in production (cf. Layton, 1976; Channell, 1982). The greater the comprehensiveness of scientific models and idealized technical objects, the 'more scope they offer for rationalizing technical expertise and practices since they provide a measure of efficiency for machines, and hence designs, which are not derived from current practices' (Whitley, 1988:394). Estimates about the impact of these developments on the production process, changes within sectors of the economy or employment patterns which utilize rather conventional statistical data, for example, the relative presence of 'white-collar' occupations within the manufacturing or service sector of the economy, likely tend to seriously underestimate the transformations because these categories themselves, inherited from industrial society, become obsolete.

Moreover, and also contrary to many conventional assumptions, the normative and material differentiation of economic sectors in modern society is by no means the most significant or important observation one is forced to advance on the basis of the evidence about the pattern of interrelations among economic sectors. For in this instance too, linkage, complementarity or interdependence among sectors is the more incisive observation. For example, service-type inputs are needed at every stage of the production process in the manufacturing sector, or the delivery of most service-type jobs directly or indirectly requires products which originate in the industrial sector of the economy.

In many respects, therefore, the well-established conceptual distinction between the economic sectors, especially between the service and the manufacturing sectors is misleading, at least under contemporary conditions. More specifically, most *goods* purchased are intended to provide a service or a function and there are few 'pure' *services* unconnected to certain commodities. The distinction between goods and services becomes even more ambivalent when one takes into consideration the option of the consumer to purchase, lease or rent (and thereby enjoy the service of) a commodity. In short, 'the output of economic activity may range from that of pure goods to pure services. However, most – and indeed an increasing proportion of – goods embody some non-factor intermediate services, and most services embody some intermediate goods' (Dunning, 1989:4).

Production against employment

The future of work has been a central concern of social theorists for centuries ever since employment in the sense of a commitment to paid work, in eighteenth-century Europe, became not only an existential imperative but an emblem of civilization. In the eighteenth and nineteenth centuries, the notion of the future of work for most social theorists meant an emancipation *from* the worst physical drudgery and toils associated with work at the time, namely a reduction in work time, greater autonomy and generally more challenging work tasks, whereby liberation from work was thought to be more likely than emancipation *within* the work context. Indeed, the emancipatory potential of industrialization has been fulfilled in the sense that the average work week has been reduced dramatically from more than 80 to less than 40 hours.[17] But in this century too, skeptics remained convinced that workers would find self-fulfillment outside work (e.g. Friedmann, [1956] 1992). That is to say, the standard account of the (inherent) constraints of production and the implicit coercive if not exploitative consequences of a concentration of ownership continued to

---

[17] A consideration which may play a role in the future, though it clearly did not in the past, is that further reductions in working hours may be negotiated or legislated as a means of securing places of work for the unemployed (cf. also Hinrichs et al., 1988).

provide the apparently persuasive background for the thesis that labor in the end is really only another *means of production*.

In the context of the theory of post-industrial society (Bell, 1976: 148–149), however, new hopes seem to be raised about the chances of an emancipation of workers within the context of work because post-industrial society is a *communal* society in which the social unit is the community organization rather than the individual, a world in which the modalities are 'cooperation and reciprocity rather than coordination and hierarchy'. In the salient experience of work, 'men live more and more outside nature, and less and less with machinery and things; they live with, and encounter only, one another.' The question and the reality of any changes in the *quality* of the work context and the demands placed on workers, for example in terms of skill requirements, will be briefly discussed in the next section and at greater length once I analyze the fastest growing segment of the labor force in modern society, namely the group of knowledge-based occupations or 'experts, counselors and advisers' (see Chapter 7).

The issue which should be taken up first concerns the question of the future of work in a different sense, though not new to discussions about labor in this century, namely the relative *scarcity of work*, the threat of persistent secular unemployment and therefore the much strained relation between economic growth and full employment. The grim question becomes whether, in a knowledge-intensive economy, technology and knowledge not merely eliminate jobs but also work since not so long ago the much more positive conclusion reached after intensive study was that technology destroys jobs but not work (cf. United States National Commission on Technology, Automation and Economic Progress, 1966).

The specific change I have in mind concerns the extent to which employment, especially but not only in the manufacturing sector of the economy, ceases to be a (positive) function of output in this sector; that is, 'increased manufacturing production in developing countries has actually come to mean *decreasing* blue-collar employment. As a consequence, labor costs are becoming less and less important as a "comparative cost" and as a factor in competition' (Drucker, 1986:775). In traditional terms, this development is of course a reflection of increased productivity in the manufacturing sector and therefore of a decrease in the labor/output ratio.[18] The output of the manufacturing sector in advanced economies increases and retains its relative economic importance while its contribu-

[18] A study prepared for the United States Department of Labor (1984) documents these developments for the four industries of hosiery, folding paperboard boxes, metal cans and cleaning for the period 1962–1982. In each of the four industries, advances in technology are responsible for a significant increase in productivity, a decline in employment and a rise in the overall output as well as the output per person employed in these industries. During this period, employment in hosiery manufacturing in the US declined by 41 percent, in metal cans 16 percent, and in laundry and cleaning the decline amounted to 34 percent in twenty-two years.

tion to employment declines. Drucker (1986:776) predicts, therefore, that developed countries will in twenty-five years 'employ no larger a proportion of the labor force in manufacturing than developed countries now employ in farming – at most, ten percent'.

But the uncoupling of production from labor is more general since the overall increase in the number of unemployed persons has been soaring in the past two decades. The traditional close link between output and employment ceases to accompany shifts in the economy and creates the 'paradox' of growth and unemployment (cf. Therborn, 1986). While the evidence in this regard for the manufacturing sector is clear and can draw on a heritage of information dating back a number of decades, there is no comparable experience for the service sector and its growing efforts to search for efficiencies. For the time being, productivity gains in the area of service-type occupations appear to be confined to the manufacturing sector.[19] However, it is very likely that the search for efficiencies will be concentrated in the service sector in the future.

Between 1970 and 1989, the number of unemployed increased from 10 million to more than 25 million in the Organization for Economic Co-operation and Development (OECD) countries (Table 6.4).[20] Unemployment rates and patterns over time differ across countries (cf. Therborn, 1986) because similar economic policies and constraints or straightforward patterns of persistent growth during this period cannot be found in all countries. According to OECD figures, in the United States, for example, the unemployment rate during the same period actually declined, while in Japan it continued to remain virtually unchanged (see Table 6.4). However, in absolute terms, the number of the unemployed in Japan doubled; it increased from 680,000 in 1973 to 1,420,000 in 1989 and 1,390,000 in 1991.

One might of course, in the light of these figures, be prompted to offer the entirely correct observation that, despite the increase in unemployment

[19] According to results reported by Roach (1991:119), who defines service-type occupations as while-collar jobs, in the United States the 'service industries could have doubled their white-collar productivity growth over the past five years if they had matched the employment efficiencies realized in manufacturing' during the same period.

[20] There is a persisting controversy among economists whether the rise in unemployment in the past three decades is also the result of a structural transformation of the economy and especially the outcome of 'technological' changes. Some recent econometric studies (e.g. Jackman and Roper, 1987) report that structural changes do not account for the rise in unemployment in the 1970s and 1980s or that such changes represent but a small portion of the total variance (Layard and Nickell, 1985). In the end, however, these studies do really manage to demystify the reasons for the dramatic rise in unemployment. According to the theory of long-term, Kondratiev economic cycles, technical innovations have long been associated with long-run economic waves. Each cycle lasts about fifty to sixty years. At the present time, we are in a 'downswing' of the wave during which 'information technology' matures and cost-saving investments increasingly, as has been the case before in previous cycles, tend to displace labor (cf. Freeman, 1979). However, these conceptions are much too crude to allow for sensible inferences about the impact of technology on economic activities, let alone the task of forecasting its effect on employment.

Table 6.4   *Annual unemployment rates for selected industrial countries,*
1960–1993[1]

	1960	1965	1970	1975	1980	1985	1991	1993
Canada	7.0	3.9	5.6	6,9	7.4	10.4	10.2	10.0
United States	5.5	4.5	4.8	8.3	7.0	7.1	6.6	6.5
Japan	1.7	1.2	1.2	1.9	2.0	2.6	2.2	2.3
Australia	–	–	1.6	4.9	6.1	8.2	9.6	9.9
Germany (FRG)	1.0	0.4	0.8	3.6	2.9	7.2	4.5	4.8
France	0.7	1.5	2.5	4.0	6.3	10.2	9.4	9.8
Spain	2.4	1.5	–	3.0[2]	11.1	21.1	15.2	–
Belgium	3.1	1.6	2.1	5.0	8.8	11.3	9.3	9.6
United Kingdom	1.6	1.2	3.0	4.3	6.4	11.2	9.4	9.4

[1] The rates are not strictly comparable among countries (cf. for example, Freeman et al.,
1982:4–5).
[2] 1974.

Sources: United Nations, *Economic Survey of Europe in 1991–1992* (1992); OECD, *Main
Economic Indicators: Historical Statistics, 1969–1988* (1990); OECD, *Employment Outlook*
(1992b)

in the past three decades in OECD countries, both the *total labor force*
(that is, the number of people registered as working or available for work)
and the number of individuals employed or *total employment* has increased
substantially. The dramatic increase in unemployment rates, it could be
noted further, might therefore at least also be the result of a rapid growth
in the supply of labor. However, a growing supply of labor must not
invariably, as least as far as relevant historical precedents in the United
States, Japan and Germany are concerned, go hand in hand with rising
unemployment. A rapid growth in the labor force has been associated with
sustained rates of low unemployment. Yet, given the now widely institutionalized expectation in advanced industrial societies that the state and
the economy must find ways to guarantee their citizens acceptable and
perhaps steadily improving standards of living (cf. Dahrendorf, 1987:110–
111), growing and significant rates of unemployment constitute a serious
political challenge to governments. Moreover, sustained and consequential
unemployment represents a critical challenge to the maintenance of social
citizenship rights. In short, it is possible that we are confronted with a new
and sustained volume as well as a new structure of unemployment and
novel political consequences.

The nature of unemployment has definitely changed in the past two
decades. The number of persons who have been long-term unemployed
(given the standard definition, those unemployed for more than one year)
has tripled to 9.4 million. The increase in both the absolute number of
long-term unemployed as well as the rapid increase in their share of total
unemployment was one of the main transformations of the labor market in
the 1980s. At the beginning of that decade, the proportion of long-term
unemployed in OECD countries was on average around a quarter of the
total unemployed. By the end of the decade, it had risen to about a third.

Table 6.5   *Long-term unemployment in industrialized countries,*
1973–1991 (percentage of unemployed workers out of work for more
than 12 months)

	1973	1979	1983	1986	1989	1991
Belgium	51.0	58.0	62.8	68.9	76.3	–
France	21.6	30.3	42.6	47.8	43.9	3.73
Germany (FRG)	8.5	19.9	28.5	32.0	49.0	–
Italy	–	35.8	41.9	56.4	70.4	–
Netherlands	12.8	27.1	43.7	56.3	49.9	–
United Kingdom	26.9	24.5	36.2	41.1	40.8	–
Sweden	–	–	10.3	–	6.5	–
Canada	–	3.5	9.5	10.9	6.8	7.2
United States	3.3	4.2	13.3	8.7	5.7	6.3
Japan	–	16.5	15.5	17.2	18.7	17.9
Australia	–	18.1	27.5	27.5	23.0	24.9

Source: OECD, *Economic Outlook* (1992a) and *Employment Outlook* (1992b)

The rise and the persistence of long-term unemployment is both related to, but also independent of, the overall unemployment rate. During the 1980s, long-term unemployment grew despite economic recovery and expansion during the later part of the decade. Obviously, the personal and social costs of long-term unemployment are enormous. In the case of many countries of the European Union, high levels of unemployment are now often associated with declining chances of finding a job at all (cf. Bean, 1990). Thus, if the experience of the 1980s is any indication of future patterns of unemployment, the incidence of long-term unemployment will continue at a high level, or even increase in times of more significant economic downturn *and* growth. The rise and the persistence of long-term unemployment is likely due to a number of factors,[21] such as the increase in non-standard work (part-time and short-term employment), and produces different patterns of exposure to long-term unemployment depending, for example, on the age, education, gender or regional residence of workers.[22] In the long run, however, the most significant factor may well be reduced requirement for labor as a result of fundamental transformations in the economy preventing entry into the workforce in the first place, changing skill requirements displacing workers for extensive periods of time and a mismatch between competencies in demand and those available among unemployed persons.

None the less, as the figures in Table 6.5 indicate, there are some

---

[21] For some economists (e.g. Rahman and Gera, 1990:2), however, the matter is much more straightforward: 'One major reason for the increase in the duration of unemployment is the increase in the proportion of individuals experiencing prolonged unemployment.'

[22] According to OECD (1992b:271) figures, during the 1980s, the proportion of relatively young men (25–44 years of age) among the long-term unemployed in most industrialized countries rose (the proportion of 'youths' under 25 years of age and older workers tended to decline) while the ratio of men to women among the long-term unemployed remained, for the most part, fairly stable.

countries in which long-term unemployment is relatively low.[23] This is the case for some Scandinavian countries, Canada and the United States. In Japan, the long-term unemployment rate is about three times higher than it is in Canada. Whether these differences in long-term unemployment rates are primarily the result of distinct accounting (or state-labor market)[24] regimes, or whether they reflect, in North America for example, as the OECD (1991a:41) maintains, differential rates of flows into and out of unemployment, is open to debate. Across OECD countries, as Kolberg and Kolstad (1992:185) observe, the incidence of 'long-term unemployment follows the general level of unemployment closely, and seems to be independent of the sex- and age-specific distributions of unemployment.' This allows, it seems to me, the interpretation that long-term unemployment reflects a specific secular trend in the economy of these countries and will not disappear with the regular economic fluctuations (cf. Walsh, 1987). The increase in unemployment and long-term unemployment, at this point referring to the management of the process of entering and exiting the labor market only, will likely hasten the decline in the autonomy of market forces and increase the *fusion* of welfare-state regimes and the labor market. This has consequences both for our understanding of the welfare state and the principles which govern economic conduct (cf. Kolberg and Esping-Andersen, 1992). Part of the same structural change in employment patterns is the rapid increase in the proportion of part-time workers and temporary employees as a proportion of the total labor force, suggesting an increase in the 'precariousness' and 'flexibility' of employment patterns (cf. OECD, 1991a:53).

The data on which most of these observations are based are aggregate unemployment rates. The structural composition of unemployed individuals according to different criteria and on reasons for unemployment are not easy to obtain; nor is the comparative analysis of unemployment rates without serious problems since unemployment is conceptualized and politically managed in very different ways across OECD countries. Aside from national unemployment regimes, for example, the *links* between the welfare state and the labor market, the result is that both the level and the development of unemployment rates will be structured differently. How-

---

[23] The standard measure for long-term unemployment is twelve months. The available information about longer durations of unemployment confirms the trend about a rising proportion of people who are out of work for extensive periods of time.

[24] For example, while Belgium reports one of the highest incidences of long-term unemployment, not only is it without a waiting period after which insurance benefits commence, but it also provides an unlimited unemployment benefit duration; in the United States, in contrast, the maximum duration for unemployment benefits is 26 weeks and in Sweden it is 60 weeks (cf. OECD, 1991a:200–201). Thus, it is not surprising that there is an overall close correlation between the duration of benefits and the duration of unemployment (United Nations, 1991:201) and that economists begin to refer to the existence of a 'culture of unemployment'.

ever, this does not mean that observers are completely immobilized in discerning certain fundamental employment changes.[25]

But it is not the welfare state which contrives, especially in the strong sense of producing, such a 'secular' or structural trend in unemployment rates, for example, as some social critics maintain, by offering disincentives to work; nor is the welfare state any more in a position today to achieve full employment with the aid of national aggregate fiscal and monetary policies, as envisioned say by Keynesian economic policies (cf. Stehr, 1992). The decline in employment in both the agricultural and industrial sectors of the economy in developed economies is taken for granted by economists. Further, it is assumed that this pattern will continue. The question therefore becomes, given the premise of the three-sector differentiation, whether the service sector is able to compensate for the losses with employment growth and how significant its ability will be to create jobs. William Baumol's (1967) answer is a negative one.[26] But the weakness of his argument may well rest with introducing the notion of the service sector as a black box (cf. Scharpf, 1988; Esping-Andersen, 1992).

In any event, the degree to which economists and other social scientists as well as policy-makers are seriously alarmed about rising and persistent unemployment in advanced industrial societies in recent decades depends on the degree of faith they display in the compensatory significance and the efficacy of market mechanisms (or, for that matter, intervening policies) to secure conditions approaching full employment and therefore an equilibrium in the demand and supply of labor. But even from a purely economic point of view, it is of course widely recognized that markets in general and labor markets in particular are far from perfect (and economic policies are distant from aiding the self-adjusting mechanism of the market). Thus, the 'lags' and disequilibrium in labor markets already observed for an extensive period may not only constitute a prolonged stalemate because the conditions responsible are not merely frictional, cyclical and short term, but the labor market dislocations could last for an unprecedented time and even grow considerably.[27]

[25] Among the most remarkable differences in unemployment rates is that between *skill levels*. In Great Britain (1985) and the USA (1987), for example, the unemployment rates of semi- and unskilled workers was approximately four times that of professional and managerial workers (see Layard et al., 1991:286–287).

[26] Baumol (1967) distinguishes between economic activities in which productivity is relatively constant and technologically progressive activities in which a cumulative rise in productivity can be observed. The former class of activities includes, for the most part, service-type jobs in which labor is an end in itself. Such a differentiation between sector productivity is also part of Jean Fourastié's (1950) classification of economic sectors. In addition, Baumol assumes that labor costs of both types of activities increase in concert. It follows that unbalanced productivity growth threatens to drive many services, as ultimately too costly, from the market (including a growth in self-service activities), or the state has to finance (subsidize) these services.

[27] In one study, designed to estimate the economic effects of computer-based automation technology on the American economy, Leontief (1985:39) forecasts, assuming considerable investment into the new technologies, that the labor force required in the year 2000 would be

It may be objected that the experience with profound labor market dislocations and shrinking employment due to technological changes is not really novel. The plight of the coal, steel and textile industries in many countries in recent decades provides relevant examples; similarly, technological inventions in the nineteenth century produced the first such severe shocks and labor market dislocations. But each time, discussions about the specter of technological unemployment abated.[28] Concern usually diminished as each of the dislocations was absorbed and *compensated* for by re-organizations, migration, a growing demand for labor in other industries and sectors, re-training and other measures.[29] The present problem, therefore, boils down to the question, as Adolph Lowe (1986:3) for example asks, 'whether the employment effect of the new technology basically differs from those earlier impacts'.

There is serious reason, I believe, to assume that restoring full employment – and I do not mean to refer to the more demanding traditional definition of such a state – is no longer feasible in knowledge societies. Economic processes which in the past may have compensated for severe dislocations of the labor market cannot be counted on anymore. Because the technological changes under way will ultimately impact with special force in the private and public service sector, this sector is no longer capable or can no longer be expected to absorb displaced employees from the other economic sectors, but will itself contribute to a decline in the quantity of available work.[30] Governments and companies in almost every field of economic activity are forced and determined to do more with fewer employees. The repercussions of such a development are considerable. They are significant because full-time paid labor in industrial society was not merely a matter of existential necessity but basic to citizenship rights of individuals and because the volume of the compensatory fiscal activities of the welfare state is dependent on the employment performance of the economy.[31]

---

significantly smaller than today. The new technology would require approximately 20 million fewer workers to produce the same bill of goods. Similarly, the composition of the labor force would be different; the proportion of professionals would rise while the percentage of managers and clerical workers would decline.

[28] Early discussion of the impact of technological change on employment may be found in Hobson (1910), Emil Lederer ([1931] 1938) and Salz (1932).

[29] Compensation theories suggest, as Marx for example already maintained in the first volume of *Das Kapital*, that technological progress, in the final analysis, adds to the aggregate quantity of work (cf. zur Nedden, 1930). But chronic, persistent unemployment invariably undermines the intellectual and political status of compensation theories (e.g. Salz, 1932:1608).

[30] The image of the dilemma of the laboring society increasingly losing work but also of being emancipated from the burden of work may be found in Hannah Arendt ([1960] 1981).

[31] Karl Hinrichs and his colleagues (1988) offer a number of resolutions and options to this dilemma which do not simply either reduce the legal claims individuals are allowed to make on the income-maintenance programs of the state or increase the contributions of employers and those still employed to the welfare state. The option which assumes particular significance

The social anatomy of work

A discussion of the relevant changes of labor and of the workplace in the economy of knowledge societies may be separated into two more or less distinct considerations. First, there is the question of the *quantity* of labor which likely obtains in knowledge societies, and associated with specific structural trends in available work, changes in the meaning of the social construct of 'work'. I have already discussed this issue briefly. Secondly, there is the question of the *quality* of work activities, particularly the required qualifications, typical work activities and the social organization of production. But in each instance, the most significant common issue is whether labor in knowledge societies primarily consists of an extension of trends established in industrial societies, though some of the conditions which justify speaking of a continuation of entrenched patterns may not be the same any more. In the case of the quality of work activities, for example, one might conclude, although low-skilled manual labor may not be the typical work activity in knowledge societies anymore, that so-called 'intellectual labor' is subject to the same processes of rationalization, coercion and control that affected manual labor in industrial society. In this section, I will concentrate on the second set of issues although a few observations of the social construct of labor are in order.

The meaning associated with the term 'work' today is a product of industrial society. What constitutes work in industrial society is much more narrowly defined than was the case in pre-industrial society. In a number of ways, work activities in industrial society became more clearly separated from non-work activities. The emergent boundaries between the economic and social spheres correspond to the distinction between work and non-work activities: the *spatial* division between the place of work and the location for other types of conduct is among the most important distinction in industrial society. Equally self-evident is the differentiation of work *time* and leisure. Finally, the use of the term 'work' is often restricted to work associated with *employment*, or self-employment.

One of the potentially contentious but also crucial questions of contemporary society is whether the primary meanings associated with the term 'work', especially its narrowness, will or can persist in a world in which work, in the traditional sense of the term, will likely become much more scarce.[32] In knowledge societies, individuals who never join the 'regular'

---

in the context of their considerations is the working time and the possibility of devising ways to reduce it across the board in order to generate additional employment.

[32] One social theorist who has reflected on the appropriateness of the narrow, employment-centered term of work and offered suggestions for a broader understanding of work is Enzo Mingione. For example, he proposes that work should include 'all types of formal employment, but also a variety of irregular, temporary or occasional activities undertaken to raise cash and various activities that produce use values, goods and services for direct consumption either by the individual and his/her household or other individuals or households, which are more or less necessary for the survival' of the individuals and households

workforce, who are forced out of work, or decide to be unemployed, do not simply drop out of society. They are integrated into society by knowledge as the new principle of sociality. However, they are likely to be mainly *objects* of knowledge and not subjects of knowledge.

It is by no means a novel observation that the social organization of work is changing and that the nature of the change has to do with what originally constituted, at least according to Marx and Engels, the condition for the possibility of the division of labor in society, namely, the separation of labor into manual and intellectual labor (cf. Marx and Engels, [1932] 1960:28). The shift is away from manual to intellectual labor, and therefore to a corresponding increase in the role knowledge and learning play in shaping work and the ability to work.

Within this set of issues, at least two distinct questions may be identified. First, the extent to which, in the course of these changes, the nature of work *activities*, of work organization and experience with work undergoes changes; secondly, the changing conditions of production raise questions about the relation between work and other social arrangements, for example, social inequality, education, culture, leisure, the family, and their respective boundaries. These issues will be dealt with separately.

As Karl Marx ([1939–1941] 1973:705) outlines in his *Grundrisse*, with the advance and application of technology and science,[33] the worker is no longer the principal agent of production and what appears to be the mainstay of production and wealth is neither the immediate labor performed by the worker, nor the time that he works, but the appropriation by man of his own general productive force, his understanding of nature and the mastery of it; in a word, the development of the social individual. In contrast, the productive forces of industrial society are based, for the most part, 'on the direct labor of workers, measured and exploited in terms of labor time' while the productive forces of advanced society are 'based on the capacity of people to learn' (Block and Hirschhorn, 1979:367). The quality or, as Marx formulates it, the 'power of the agencies', rather than the quantity of labor and the social organization of work, becomes crucial. For Marx, this transformation already signals the end of bourgeois society

---

(Mingione, 1991:73). One of the purposes of the new broader definition of work is to join conceptually more closely what already has been joined in practice, namely the social and economic spheres of activity. Another consequence of the broader conception, then, is to offer an analysis of the importance of the 'informal' economy. The notion of work, as Sabel (1991:24) therefore agrees, refers to 'such disparate and rapidly changing experiences that it is at least as reasonable to treat the word as a popular shorthand for survival as to regard it as a category of activity that gives similar contours to our different understandings of life.'

[33] It should be noted that Karl Marx, in tracing the evolution of the capitalist mode of production, was always careful to trace, in contrast to many of his followers, both the 'negative' and the 'emancipating' effects of the forces of production. However, as long as the advance of science and technology occurs within the frame of capitalist relations of production, their development fosters, at the expense of the workers, the profits of the owners of the means of production. After all, for Marx, socialist modes of production do not involve scrapping modern technological means of production (cf. Sohn-Rethel, 1978).

and the demise of an economy based on exploitation and of exchange value as the measure of the use value of commodities.

However, as most of the categories used by economists and others still indicate, the unit of production which is still invoked is primarily the *individual* employee and the time spent on the job by the individual; that is, the leading assumption that remains dominant to this day is that the crucial components in the determination of the 'quality of labor', for example, are the individual characteristics that workers or employees generally bring to their place of work 'rather than of the organizational environment in which the labor is employed' (Block, 1985:441 n. 62). The 'discovery' of the importance of the *social* organization of work dates at least to the 1930s and the Hawthorne studies of Roethlisberger and Dickson; but today the importance of institutional features for productivity and profitability have increased to the point that Fred Block (1985:95), for example, elevates it to the 'determining role' of the factor of labor quality.[34]

One cross-national survey of attitudes to technological change in the workplace, carried out in the second half of 1982 in six industrialized countries, namely, the United States, Britain, West Germany, Sweden, Japan and Israel, indicates that respondents who have experienced technological changes on the job generally appear to rate the effect quite favorably. They report not only that their jobs have become more interesting, responsible, cleaner, but also involve less physical strain. None the less, a large number of respondents sense that monotony or loneliness, dependence and difficulty have increased. In Japan, unfavorable reactions predominated (cf. Yuchtman-Yaar, 1987).

The increased 'scientification' of work has already been emphasized. However, Whitley (1988) has cautioned against excessive estimates of the extent to which new scientific knowledge is transforming working procedures and practices in all sectors of the economy and at all levels of labor. The extent to which labor is affected by new scientific knowledge depends, as Whitley (1988:415) for example observes, on a range of factors which either facilitate or present obstacles to the adoption of new knowledge. The diffusion of knowledge is, of course, not independent of the 'organization and control of occupational practices and expertise, the type of the new knowledge and its relations to current practices and the degree to which the objects and systems being treated are separable from their environment and/or the latter are controllable' (Whitley, 1988:415). At the same time, Whitley's note of caution and his enumeration of factors which influence the 'scientification' of work does not extend to forces which may quite severely constrain an organization or corporation finding

---

[34] As Block (1985:95–96) therefore asserts, 'two factories might be quite similar in the "quality" of their labor forces and the nature of their capital stock, but their output might differ greatly because of institutional differences that lead in one factory to greater downtime and poorer quality control.'

itself, not in splendid isolation, but in a competitive environment, as the result of market forces.

In a more general sense, in recent years the focus of the sociology of work, the sociology of organizations and industrial sociology has been on the extent to which the work environment and the social organization of work activities have been transformed enough to justify the conclusion that work in advanced industrial society justifies either the label of a perpetuation of trends already in place in industrial society (perhaps even a worsening of some attributes of work activities), or whether, as a result of the changing working conditions, work and its environment changes dramatically and constitutes a break with the kind of work typical of industrial society.

In the case of the dominant perspective of industrial society in which a certain kind of technological progress or regime is closely linked to mass production systems, intensive productivity gains and the capacity to produce an abundance of goods as well as hierarchical forms of work organization and control, the answer is almost self-evident. In the end, the (capitalist) logic at work always contributes, as emphasized at one time, to a massive alienation of workers, or as argued more recently, to an extensive de-skilling of the work force (e.g. Braverman, 1974).[35] The ability of management to preserve and exercise domination is assured by virtue of holding on to or monopolizing *knowledge* about the conceptions on which production is based. That is, the successful separation of execution and conception is the key to the control and persistent degradation of the worker. The new version of the oppression thesis also generalizes about the workplace without any credit to the imagination of the worker and specific conditions of work. The thesis minimizes, consistent with Marx's portrait of the labor process in capitalist society, the ability of the worker to affect his or her working conditions. Technological developments simply reproduce the domination of capital over labor, often on a more repressive scale[36] and contribute, as Merton (1947:80) already

[35] Although the de-skilling thesis is often associated with the work of Harry Braverman, there are numerous predecessors, reviewing developments in production processes of industrial society, that conclude, as Helmut Schelsky (1954:20), for example does: 'The closer we approach automation, though without ever fully reaching it, the greater the degree to which work becomes spiritless and stressful and the lesser the extent to which it requires interest in technical matters and skills or, even initiative of any sort.' However, Schelsky anticipates a further state in the evolution of work in which, after automation has been achieved, the worker will be required to perform highly skilled tasks, for example, in the course of supervising and controlling highly complex production equipment.

[36] The authority for and classic example of Marx's view of the role of technology in the labor process in capitalist society, as outlined in volume 1 of *Capital*, is the alleged displacement of textile workers in England as the result of the introduction of the self-acting mule in cotton spinning. As Marx ([1867] 1967:435–436) puts it, 'machinery not only acts as a competitor who gets the better of the workman, and is constantly on the point of making him superfluous. It is also a power inimical to him, and as such capital proclaims it from the roof tops and as such makes use of it. It is the most powerful weapon for repressing strikes . . . It would be possible to write quite a history of the inventions, made since 1830, for the sole

expresses it, to an 'enforced obsolescence of skills'.[37] These observations
tend to make inferences about processes from outcome. In general,
therefore, the much discussed Braverman thesis, developed decades later,
about the irreversible de-skilling process of labor treats the change in the
nature of technological paradigms, the specificity of the workforce, the
dynamics of work and local conditions as a black box. But one might also
ask whether it is something inherent in the process of material production
which requires the detachment of planning and execution, or whether the
disconnection stems rather from the desire of management to control and
exploit labor?[38]

Today, fascination with the constraining features of the conditions which
give rise to more hierarchy and control have been replaced by equally
strong convictions about a *new* technology and a logic of organizing
production which is essentially permissive (cf. Hirst and Zeitlin, 1991;
Sabel, 1991:24). These views are linked in turn to the distinction between
the declining regime of mass manufacturing ('Fordism') and the growing
system of 'flexible specialization' in production (cf. Piore and Sabel,
1984).[39] As a result, technology is no longer seen as a dehumanizing force
but as one which enables or at least holds the promise of participation in

---

purpose of supplying capital with weapons against revolts of the working-class. At the head of
these in importance, stands the self-acting mule, because it opened up a new epoch in the
automatic system.' Lazonick (1979:257) has examined the historical evidence in the case of
Lancashire in England and concludes that the case of the self-acting mule 'does not
demonstrate the unfettered triumph of capital over labor through the use of the division of
labor and machinery'. Marx's misleading portrayal of the effects of this particular invention, it
would appear, relied too much on the views of the ideological proponents of the technical
change in question.

[37] Merton assumes, as do the proponents of the later de-skilling thesis, that the obsolescence of
skills is irreversible. In the light of the kind of production technology used, a compensation
process is presumably not considered likely. The increasing employment of labor-saving
technology produces the enforced obsolescence of skills among the workers. The social and
psychological consequences of discarding acquired skills are mainly connected to the
demotion of status (including the possible loss of the public identity of the job) and the
destruction of the positive self-image of the worker, stemming from the once confident use of
those skills. In short, as Merton (1947:80) anticipates as well, 'alienation of workers from
their job and the importance of wages as the chief symbol of social status are both furthered
by the absence of a social meaning attributable to the task. Increased specialization of
production leads inescapably to a greater need for predictability of work behavior and,
therefore, for *increased discipline in the workplace*.'

[38] For Theodor Adorno (1969) and André Gorz ([1971] 1976:170), for example, the answer
can only be, at least as long as one examines the issue from the (interested) point of view of
the owner of the means of production, that it is *not* technical progress 'in the true sense' which
requires hierarchy and a fragmented division of labor in industry but the effort and
determination of the class of owners for maximum exploitation. In addition, such aims are not
necessarily compatible with the most efficient use of production techniques and work
organization. The relations of production still dominate the forces of production.

[39] In much the same sense, Kern and Schumann (1983:357) sum up some of the relevant
findings of their research into rationalization and the conduct of industrial workers by noting
that workers increasingly are seen, at least among the more flexible and enlightened segments
of management, 'as persons with complex abilities and varied developmental potential that

the affairs of work. In the sphere of work, the profound anxiety about the destructive ways of technology are now replaced by animated discussions about the freedoms from control. The vocabulary of intentionality and agency, thought to be obsolete, reappears in discussions of work, production and the social organization of work (e.g. Cavestro, 1989). Paradoxically, the technology once feared to have become self-regulating now regulates itself in the sense of negating regulation. None the less, perspectives which emphasize the enabling features of new technology should not commit the same fallacy associated with assertions about the inherently repressive nature of production technologies, namely, to declare, as Karl Marx for example did, that technology invariably reproduces domination. Even if new technologies allow for greater flexibility and require it for greater efficiency, they do not thereby automatically also foreclose the possibility, depending on local circumstances and the nature of (economic and political) 'partnerships' that technology happens to find itself lodged in, that versatility and innovative capacity is restricted in the interest of sustaining hierarchical control of owners and managers.[40] There is not a natural role for technology as such in all of this.

But there is a counter-conception which accepts the fact that the conditions of work have changed but is not convinced that modern technology primarily is enabling and permissive. This perspective asks whether intellectual labor will not be subordinate to the same processes of rationalization and control that affected manual labor in industrial society and create a kind of 'intellectual assembly line', that is, a division of labor in which the 'rationality of the bureaucratic organization acquires the mechanized efficiency of the factory, and in which mental labor is subjected to both the rationalization of its knowledge and the gradual automation of its productive activity' (Perrole, 1986:111).

The deep divisions in the theoretical assessment of the nature of the impact of new technologies, in this case on work and the organization of work, attest that it is impossible to factor out effects which would indicate that these technologies by themselves are determining factors.[41] The essentially contested concept about the impact of technology also displays, in other words, the variety of *empirical* situations and interpretations about the effects of new technologies to which reference is made.

---

one is able to employ with particular effectiveness if one endeavors to utilize their capacities on the job extensively rather than merely minimal segments by discarding the remainder of their ability; in other words, achievement expectations are not lowered but the utilization of the intellectual and motivational capacities is increased.'

[40] Summing up a number of case studies in this area of research, Jones (1990:306) arrives at such a cautionary note when he observes that 'in general the prospect of using these systems [flexible specialization] to tighten hierarchical control over final operations may prove more appealing to many managers than the surrender of detailed powers to the shop floor *that is necessary* for versatile and innovative productive capability.'

[41] That is, Alain Touraine ([1984] 1988:108) is probably correct to infer from the essentially contested view about the status of new technologies that it is 'impossible to isolate a primary cause of technological origin as the determining factor of all programmed society'.

From the employment society to the consumption society

Compared to virtually all other prior historical societies, the modern capitalist societies that emerged in North America and Europe during the eighteenth and nineteenth centuries have been most concerned with the conditions of employment. The extraordinary and consistent preoccupation with paid work and the emergence of paid labor as a social activity separate from the household justify the label of 'employment societies' (Keane, 1988). Not surprisingly, economic discourse, too, is preoccupied with concerns directly linked to the worlds of production (of goods and services), work and incomes (in the form of rents, interest and wages). In other words, economic discourse today continues to be linked to the eighteenth-century definition of the *major* factors of production, namely, capital and labor, its mix and consequences measured in monetary units. The world of work finds its mirror image in the sphere of consumption. Society produces in order to consume and it consumes in order to produce. For many purposes, such a focus indeed may still be quite appropriate. For example, if one is concerned with the productivity of capital or labor, such an arithmetic is sufficient. Even though in modern societies 'less than one sixth of the total time of the average fit adult' (Gershuny, 1988:6) is devoted to paid work, paid labor as a separately institutionalized activity continues to constitute the major social activity of large segments of the population and much of the energies of modern society are still geared toward efforts to constantly expand the production of goods and services.

However, if the focus and the implied equivalence as well as equilibrium between production and consumption shift, both in the case of those who are still part of the realm of labor and those who are not, namely, from work in the narrow sense of the term, to *forms of life* of employees and households in modern society, then an analysis, as Niklas Luhmann (1988:164–166) for example has emphasized, of the *consumption* side – especially in relation to the total wealth (*Besitzstand*) – is more pertinent than is the mere income of individuals or households.[42] Consumption acquires greater independence from production. Undoubtedly, work provides meaning to consumption. As the aggregate of work shrinks and as the relative amount of time individuals devote in their lifetime to work for which they are compensated is reduced and as consumption is less immediately tied to labor, the meaning of consumption changes as well.

The growth in the total wealth and entitlements of individuals and households has accelerated enormously. Many individuals and households become, through pension funds for example, indirect owners of the means of production as well, though such ownership of course has lost much of its traditional attributes. What is meant here, therefore, is not related to the

---

[42] Among sociologists who emphasized rather early the growing importance of the consumer position of individuals in modern society, at the expense of the importance of the occupational position, for their consciousness and status, are Helmut Schelsky (1956:65) and Ralf Dahrendorf ([1957] 1959:273).

shift, although quite real, in the quantity of time spent outside the work environment and therefore a shift in central-life interests (Dubin, 1956) to leisure activities. The focus still remains with the material or economic well-being of individuals and households; however, forms of life, in as much as they are dependent on material well-being, are not driven any more by considerations directly linked to the value of income but consumption patterns and their determinants, namely the *Besitzstand* of the actor(s). The determinants of the consumption patterns are related to the specific circumstances of the individual and the household unit. Structures of social inequality resonate with such circumstances as well.[43]

Among the outcomes of such a change in the circumstances which affect forms of life and material well-being is a closer link between the economic and social spheres, or a shift in the economic dependency relations of individuals and households. But even more importantly, the specificity of social conflicts in knowledge societies changes dramatically. The displacement of concerns and struggles which primarily revolve around the satisfaction of economic needs, the allocation of monetary income, interests and rents, shifts the locus of major societal conflicts to more generalized and global needs. The primary role in terms of which social struggles take place no longer involves *workers as workers* and the owners of the means of production as capitalists. The locus of the conflicts shifts to the individual as a configuration of roles, or as Alain Touraine ([1984] 1988:11) puts it, to the *social actor* in any one of his or her roles: 'One could almost say that it is the human being as living being.' One of the principal axes of conflicts pits the consumer against production regimes of all sorts.[44] The generalization of issues contested in societal conflicts deprives knowledge societies of a central locus and arena in which these struggles take place.

The emergence of the symbolic economy

A further major change in the structure of the economy of post-industrial societies is the emergence of an (internationalized)[45] symbolic economy[46]

---

[43] Niklas Luhmann (1988:165) illustrates this proposition as follows, 'whether one is married or not and whether one has children or not, whether the spouse works or not and whether, as the case may be, one may have to support divorced spouses, whether one lives in an inherited home or has to rent – all these factors contribute more significantly to the economic life chances than collectively agreed upon wage rates or, as the case may be, insurance or pension payments.'

[44] More concretely, the new social conflicts have involved consumers in quite a spectacular and many-faceted way. They have spoken out against 'schools or against the university in the name of education, against the scientific-political complex in the name of public good, against hospitals in the name of health, against urban planning in the name of interpersonal relations, against the nuclear industry in the name of ecology' (Touraine, [1984] 1988:110).

[45] 'This means that few countries, if any, are able to control their own currency. There is a loss of one of the main levers of power and influence' (Bell, 1987:9).

[46] In an analogous sense, Alain Touraine ([1984] 1988:104) records that the passage to post-industrial society takes place 'when investment results in the production of symbolic goods

which 'deals' in monetary and non-monetary symbolic commodities. Peter Drucker (1989:127) assumes that the symbolic economy, in the form of money flows, already shapes and rivals the transnational material economy.[47]

Initially, the term 'symbolic commodities' should be put into quotation marks, lest one simply assumes that the full range of symbolic commodities has *economic*, *legal* and *practical* qualities not unlike any other commodity, for example durable goods which have a certain utility independent of the specific context in which the product is produced, exchanged or consumed, and a legal status, especially property rights attached to it. None of these attributes applies, at least in the strict sense, to a number of the symbolic commodities. Most importantly perhaps, the identity and utility of the symbolic items are often highly context sensitive and cannot be 'understood' or estimated separate from the context in which they originated and were 'consumed'. The proximity of the context of production and utilization of symbolic commodities is often quite close; the life expectancy of symbolic commodities is fairly limited. Property rights to symbolic commodities are virtually absent. The regulative principles which govern market exchanges and intervention into the market do not apply in full force to exchange processes involving symbolic commodities.

Symbolic 'commodities' of a monetary nature, in particular capital movements, cross-rates, exchange rates, interest-rate differentials and credit flows, are to a considerable extent 'unconnected to trade – and indeed largely independent of it' and 'greatly exceed trade finance' (Drucker, 1986:782); they are more important now for the world economy than the traditional flow of goods and services.[48] The gold exchange standard which operated for much of the life span of industrial society has been replaced by the electronic information system of today.

Symbolic commodities of a non-monetary nature are, for example, data ('sets of numbers'), technological trajectories, statistics, fashion regimes,

---

that modify values, needs, representations, far more than in the production of material goods or even of "services". Industrial society had transformed the means of production; postindustrial society changes the ends of production, that is, culture.'

[47] Following the 'currency crisis' in the third week of September 1992, the *New York Times* (September 23, 1992, Section C1) was prompted to observe that 'on a dull day, hundreds of billions of dollars' worth of marks, yen, dollars and other currencies change hands, as speculators bet on the direction of currency markets and money managers seek opportunities overseas. On a busy day, volume can top a trillion dollars. That is a lot of money. And as last week proved, the combined power of all these traders can overwhelm the power of governments, even when all of Europe is trying to act in concert. The events provided a bitter reminder to central bankers and finance ministers around the world that the power of governments to control economies and currencies has eroded.'

[48] Drucker (1986:782) provides the following figures to illustrate the claim: 'World trade in goods is larger, much larger, than it has ever been before. And so is the "invisible trade", the trade in services. Together, the two amount to around $2.5 trillion to $3.0 trillion a year. But the London Eurodollar market, in which the world's financial institutions borrow and lend to each other, turns over $300 billion each working day, or $75 trillion a year, a volume at least 25 times that of world trade.'

programs, product marketing and organizational 'knowledge' as well as the growing flow of information within and across national boundaries. The acceleration of the flow of information increases uncertainty; more precisely, it reduces the length of those moments in which certainty appears to prevail. The rapid dissemination of symbolic goods accelerates their obsolescence. In the manufacturing industry, for example, the growing importance of symbolic commodities for the provision of products and their production raises costs and demands larger markets to absorb these expenditures. Commodities and services, to a growing extent, embody knowledge.

Developments of the monetary symbolic economy, changes in its trends and abrupt shifts occur often in response to anticipated political events or are driven by unanticipated crises in different parts of the world. Indeed, not only trade in goods and services is very much affected by the symbolic economy, the dynamics of the symbolic economy often have political repercussions. In addition, in the traditional realm of international trade and services, the movement of *symbolic commodities*, that is, knowledge, has become a more salient factor in the world economy (cf. Dickson, 1984:163–216).

The eclipse of time, distance and place

One further significant effect of the production of goods and services more dependent on knowledge is the growing irrelevance of time and place (and therefore distance) as a constraint for production;[49] that is, competitive advantages increasingly are expressed in symbolic terms and such capital is much more mobile within and across national boundaries. The potential for spatial reorganization and the redisposition of time in production, distribution and consumption activities arises from the ability of information technology to 'overcome' time and distance constraints. However, the uneven mosaic of existing spatial divisions of firms and enterprises, that is, the existing high geographical concentration of industries within and among nations, will not suddenly give way to a less structured and unequal location of economic activities. Nor does the increasing emancipation of the productive process from time and place mean that production is no longer taking place within country or region-specific social and political contexts and constraints or that only decentralization effects will be observable. While constraints on place do not disappear altogether, changing spatial and time constraints allow for *many more locational configurations* than was the case under previous regimes with much more restrictive constraints (e.g. Hepworth, 1986). As a matter of fact, new constraints including the compression of time are added as production

_____

[49] Geographers, economists, planners and other social scientists have enumerated many of the specific conditions which give rise to the greater 'locational capability' of firms and enterprises (cf. Storper and Walker, 1983).

becomes knowledge-based manufacturing,[50] and others, such as the existing services and the infrastructure generally in a particular location, remain significant in decisions to abandon or position enterprises.

None the less, contemporary 'locational capacities' of firms and enterprises, although not equally distributed across the range of manufacturing and service industries, have multiplied considerably. Companies have more choice as to where they decide to combine mobile and relatively immobile, i.e. country or region-specific, endowments. Specific decisions of course will depend on a host of factors, for example, the reasons for investing in the first place, the product characteristics, the behavior of competitors, the regulations and policies of host countries and social and cultural factors (cf. Dunning, 1989:33–36). Most importantly, however, the relative eclipse in the importance of scarce locational features, distance and time for productive processes, and in many instances, services, represents a radical inversion of the governing calculus compared to the importance of locational configurations which count for economic production processes in industrial societies. In industrial societies production is in principle still tied closely to location (region) and/or time by virtue of the weight and cost of moving crucial productive ingredients, factors which allow for manufacture of commodities in the first place. In contrast, knowledge, in principle, is highly mobile and travels well. Under the proper conditions, especially in the presence of economic incentives, knowledge not only travels well but fast. This also means that an efficient communication infrastructure will be quite important for the economy in the knowledge society (cf. Nicol, 1985:192; Henderson and Castells, 1987). The choices of potential contexts for production have multiplied immeasurably and have become, as some economists begin to name it, 'global'. It also means that the kinds of considerations which enter into the determination of the location of production extend beyond those crucial in the past, namely a calculus primarily, though rarely only, driven by considerations of economic efficiency.

---

[50] In terms of the relative contribution to any increase in the locational capacities of firms, the flexibility of production processes, the mobility of capital or other factors *not* directly related to 'labor' costs, such as the decline in transportation and communication costs, may be of particular significance. At the same time, these changes imply increases in the skill requirements of jobs and therefore a relative increase in the importance of labor to location. The locational choices of high-tech firms, for example, are constrained by the need for highly trained labor and different types of labor depending on the kind of production phase (cf. Glasmeier, 1990). In a world in which labor is scarce, the increase in the importance of labor to locational decisions would mean a more powerful voice and higher rewards for labor. However, such would not appear to be the case. A leveling in unequal patterns of location would require that labor, too, becomes highly flexible and mobile. Unless one excludes labor almost entirely from production, such a development is unrealistic (cf. Storper and Walker, 1983:34). Existing empirical information, based on conventional classifications of industries, trade patterns and employment structures, are somewhat of a handicap in producing compelling and comparative empirical evidence about changes in locational constraints (cf. Krugman, 1991).

Historically, location theories which tried to explain the distribution of employment in manufacturing, for example, have emphasized the constraints related to the costs of transportation, access to the means of production, especially labor and the relative rigidity of production methods. At the same time, the relevant boundaries within contemporary economic discourse still presume that the decisive boundaries are those of the (sovereign) nation-state. The growing irrelevance of location and time for production, distribution and consumption also means that the link between what were once thought to be norms or 'rationalities' of *different* social systems, for example leisure and economics, converge or are confronted in decisions about production facilities. Location is more than merely an allocation problem (cf. Storper and Walker, 1983:34).

In knowledge societies, production and enterprises are, or will be, largely emancipated from the geographical features of a location. The redefinition and rearrangement in the location of enterprises or production are related, on the one hand, to the 'enabling developments in the service components of goods production, and information handling and communication technologies' (Britton, 1990:536) and, on the other hand, dramatic changes in the production regimes themselves. Important consequences follow from this. In many instances, the specific location for production, while independent of a certain *natural* geographical location, as was often the case in the past, in fact has to exist or be created in the first place. In that respect at least, the choice of location remains rather closely tied to the idea of a specific context and particular locations, constraints which then account for the spatial division of labor. In the United States, 'high-tech industries are likely to be found in states with traditions of innovative manufacturing, and within major metropolitan areas where business services and other urban amenities are ample' (Glasmeier, 1990:73). It is a (socially) constructed context in which these firms decide to locate, a context which can be provided for production, in principle, almost anywhere, especially if one assumes that the calculations which lead to a particular location of economic activities are not based exclusively on economic dimensions.

The efficiency of economic activities that are functionally interdependent will, in the future, not decrease despite increasing physical distance between parts of production activities (cf. Nicol, 1985:198).[51] Similarly, a decentralization of organizational activities should not seriously interfere with the ability to communicate and co-ordinate tasks. The ability to more freely divide activities spatially actually turns into an asset for economic activities. As long as the determination of location can emancipate itself from the now dominant close relationship between costs and distance,

---

[51] As Glasmeier (1990:73) indicates, in 'high-technology industries, the division of labor facilitates such decentralization. High-tech products can be segmented; firms locate technical activities in core regions, but move production to other regions where appropriate pools of labor can be found.'

other factors such as the availability of skills and composition of the labor force will influence locational decisions. As a result, it is probably safe to assume that urban concentration, for example, will not decline; on the contrary, it may continue to increase despite the diminishing importance of the cost of transportation for goods and services.[52]

The growing irrelevance of time to production does not mean that time becomes unimportant altogether either, but rather takes on a very different kind of importance. For example, the possibility of a closer co-ordination of production schedules, even over a great distance, means that questions of the storage of parts and the like declines, and production is closer to actual needs. It is therefore more important now to have a specific item available at a precise instant, yet to live up to that requirement becomes easier as production schedules 'communicate' with each other.

New production technologies often imply that a major economic factor is not so much the time spent producing, but the time during which equipment is idle, including 'downtime' because of malfunctions. Thus, the irrelevance of the time of year or day in production renews the issue of total time of production and of working hours. Knowledge-based pro-duction is more flexible and allows for, some would argue requires, a much greater flexibility in working hours.

The reasons for the irrelevance of time and place for production and the provision of services have to do, on the one hand, with technologies, or better technological regimes, which 'diminish' space and 'shrink' time and, on the other hand, with the qualities of the object that need to be moved in order to produce and in order to consume. Limits to the speed and ease with which the prerequisites of production and the 'products' can be moved are increasingly disappearing. The *enabling* technologies (Dicken, 1992:103) which overcome the limits to movement in industrial society (and generate different frictions of space and time in knowledge societies) are the new media of communication and transportation. For much of human history and a considerable portion of the life span of industrialized society, the speed with which materials, products and individuals were transported was identical to the speed and obstacles faced by entities which had to be communicated across distances. In addition, the costs of both moving tangible and intangible goods was quite sensitive to the distance which had to be traveled and the volume which had to be moved. Today, the mobility of 'information' and the speed with which tangible goods are moved are increasingly at odds. Much of the cost of communication is virtually independent of distance (cf. de Sola Pool, 1990:34–39) and volume, while the cost of the transport of goods is still contingent on distance and volume. Moreover, the cost of communication has fallen sharply. The gap in the

---

[52] Florence (1948:128, 136–140), in his study of *Investment, Location, and Size of Plant*, already anticipates that a decline in transport and communication costs will probably exercise a considerable influence on the mobility of location but these and other technical changes continue to favor a further growth of large cities.

time, ease and cost it takes to move information and tangible products represents one of the constraints on production or incentives to reduce the amount of tangible entities used in production. In addition, some of the same enabling technologies have altered the rigidities of production regimes and corporate organization, making both potentially more divisible and adding further to the process of emancipating production from constraints of time and place.

New limits to growth

Ralf Dahrendorf (1988:123) makes the point that the 1970s were a time of 'enormous exaggeration. The exaggeration of gloom and doom.' Not since José Ortega y Gasset's *The Revolt of the Masses* and Oswald Spengler's *Decline of the West* in the late 1920s and early 1930s have so many books been written about the pending descent and dissolution of a way of life. But no title better reflected and symbolized the spirit of the discussion and concerns than the study of the Club of Rome on the *Limits to Growth* (Meadows et al., 1972). The despairing prognosis of the 1972 Report was that present growth trends in world population, industrialization, food production, environmental decay (in particular, pollution) and the exhaustion of natural resources have to come to a halt within the next century.

The thesis that the world will reach the limits of resource availability on a global scale is self-evident or a tautology. For practical purposes, what is relevant is the time scale. And in this respect at least, discussion about the limits of growth, both then and probably now, continues to suffer from simply extrapolating established trends into the future. The limits-to-growth discussion of the early 1970s was, of course, based on certain premises about the nature of the modern productive and distributive process, with trends extended into the (near) future given specific assumptions, especially about not only scarce but finite resources and a growing world population (cf. Meadows et al., 1972). The outcome of such reflections was the conviction that continued economic growth in industrial societies, and efforts of Third World pre-industrial economies to catch up, is not sustainable and will, in fact, soon lead to catastrophe. But these predictions were soon contradicted by competing analyses (e.g. Leontief, 1977) and events. But at issue here is not whether economic growth is desirable[53] or whether the ratio of resources to population trends and the impact of economic growth on the environment will lead to a sudden reversal in secular advances in economic well-being in the near future, but, rather, the changes in the nature of the productive process itself (not only driven by

---

[53] One of the consequences of the 1972 Report was to stimulate a discussion about the socio-economic principle and desirability of economic growth, in the first instance, as well as debate about the ways in which growth ought to be conceptualized. Vigorous voices reject current economic theory and policy if its orientation boils down to mere efforts to ensure increases in the gross domestic product (GDP). The denial of a growth-orientation is usually based on three considerations: (a) conventional assumptions about economic growth confuse

economic considerations) and the political agenda on any discussion about the limits to economic growth.

One of the crucial deficiencies of the Meadows Report is not so much the notion of constraints on economic activity and patterns of growth, or even 'limits', but concerns the determination of such limits, namely the simple extrapolation of existing trends into the future. Mere extrapolation ignores a whole range of dynamic economic, social and political processes which determine future outcomes, including self-fulfilling and defeating conduct.

The growing centrality of knowledge to the productive process alters the import of certain resources and accelerates the significance of others with different limits. The outcome is that new or different but not necessarily no limits to growth become relevant. One of the commendable outcomes of the *Limits to Growth* has been to affect the agenda of political discourse and policy. The issue of environmental consequences of human activity is now part of the political agenda in many countries.

The changing limits to the growth of national economies or to the global economy also raise the question of the contribution of 'knowledge' to production and increases in output. Available aggregate estimates from economists tend to be fairly imprecise as well as ambivalent; perhaps such figures will never be very precise. One estimate available for the United States credits 'knowledge', which in this instance includes advances in technological, managerial and organizational knowledge, as a source for 54 percent of the total gain in economic growth during the period of 1948–1973 (Denison, 1979:2), while knowledge accounted for only 26 percent of the growth in the years between 1929 and 1948 (Denison, 1979). But as the author of these figures points out himself, these percentages are obtained as residual figures 'because there is no way to estimate it directly' (Denison, 1979:131). In fact, the economic growth due to knowledge is therefore, following the advice of Solow (1957), merely that 'percentage of the measured growth rate in output that cannot be explained by the growth rate of total factor inputs and by other adjustments made for other types of productivity increases' (Feller, 1987:240). Since the different 'variables' typically taken into consideration in these estimates tend to be interrelated, but no theory about their interdependence is available in economic discourse, decompositions of the relative contributions to economic growth only constitute mere illustrations of the growth process (cf. Nelson, 1981). For the most part, estimates of the contribution of knowledge (or technology) to economic growth in the long term are just beginning to be researched more comprehensively (e.g. Fagerberg, 1988, 1991). For the time being, many dimensions of the use and change produced by knowledge in the economy are not taken into consideration in these estimates. It

---

means and ends; (b) they fail to take the reality of the finite state of the planet into account; and (c) the pursuit of such a perspective, paradoxically, assures that some of the very problems, such as unemployment and inflation, that it hopes to cure will actually become worse (e.g. Elkins, 1986).

is, therefore, quite possible that the contribution of knowledge is systematically under-represented to date. And since the estimates are aggregate
figures, it is far from clear which sectors and what commodities are
knowledge-intensive and which are not; at least these numbers do not
allow for any inferences about such questions. In addition, the increased
importance of the knowledge factor does not imply that the 'welfare' of
society benefits, assuming one has a definite notion of what constitutes a
contribution to the welfare of society. But it is entirely possible that much
of the growth attributed to knowledge occurs as a result of the production
of weapons, other destructive means, commodities which have detrimental
environmental impact, nuclear energy or reflect work done in the area of
space exploration, all with dubious social utility. In short, the figures need
to be much more carefully dissected, although the question of the social
utility of economic growth raises difficult, contentious questions (cf.
Heilbroner, 1973).

The fragility of the future

Although much effort has been invested in the reduction of the contingencies
of economic affairs and in the improvement of the possibilities of planning
and forecasting, the economy of the knowledge society is, as much as the
rest of global society, increasingly subjected to a rise in indeterminacy.
While success may at times justify the high hopes of many that techniques
and technologies will be developed to reduce if not eliminate much of the
uncertainty from economic conduct, sudden and unexpected events almost
invariably disconfirm, almost cruelly, such optimistic forecasts about the
possibility of anticipating and therefore controlling future events. As a
matter of fact, and paradoxically, one of the sources of the growing
indeterminacy can be linked directly to the nature of the technological
developments designed to achieve greater certainty. The new technology
contributes to and accelerates the malleability of specific contexts because
of its lower dedication (limitation) to particular functions. Technological
developments add to the fragility of economic markets and the need of
organizations operating in such a context to become more flexible in order
to respond to greater mutability in demand and supply. In the sphere of
production, as a result, a new utopian vision arises, a vision which Charles
Sabel (1991:24)[54] sketches in the following and deliberately enabling
terms:

> Universal materializing machines replace product-specific capital goods; small
> and effortlessly re-combinable units of production replace the hierarchies of the

---

[54] Sabel acknowledges that he has been seen as the major author and therefore responsible
for this utopian vision; however, he prefers to subscribe to a more 'prudent version of these
caricatures'. This is a perspective which accounts for the 'diversity and similarity of efforts to
adjust to the new competitive environment' (Sabel, 1991:24–25).

mass-production corporation; and the exercise of autonomy required by both the machines and the new organizations produces a new model producer which view of life confounds the distinction between the entrepreneurial manager and the socialist worker-owner.

Much of the standard discussion of these matters, at least until recently, has been animated by opposite expectations. Bell (1973a:26), for example, confidently asserts that the 'development of new forecasting and "mapping" techniques makes possible a novel phase in economic history – the conscious, planned advance of technological change, and therefore the *reduction of indeterminacy* about the economic future' (emphasis added).

But the factor of greater fragility, malleability and volatility is not confined to the economy, the labor market and the social organization of work and management, nor does it merely have 'positive' effects on social relations and individual psyches. Greater vulnerability corresponds to greater fragility and greater flexibility is linked to new regimes of exclusion.

7

Experts, Counselors and Advisers

> Work, in the main, is no longer the manipulation of things, but of meanings.
>
> (Ernest Gellner, *Nations and Nationalism*)

The aim of this chapter is to outline the theoretical significance and practical importance of the growing stratum of experts, counselors and advisers, or of *knowledge-based occupations*, in contemporary society. The basic claim is that this stratum of occupations is the fastest growing segment of the labor force. This growth and the increase in the dependence on 'experts' has to be seen as part of a more profound transformation of modern society into a knowledge society. Central to the character of knowledge societies is a knowledge theory of value rather than a labor theory of value (cf. Bell, [1979] 1991:237).

A halt or end to the accumulation and concentration[1] as well as growing demand for novel and more and more specialized knowledge, and therefore the growth of occupations which are disseminating such knowledge, can only be imagined for a society which, due to its volume, density and size of the economic structure is much closer to societal formations in which 'expert knowledge' is distributed much more equally.[2] Such a reversal in the development of society is hardly possible and the demand, therefore, for an end or halt to the growth of experts is quite unrealistic.

Any assertion about the explosive growth in knowledge-bearing occupations can easily be misunderstood also to mean, indeed it is still viewed in this fashion in a number of important theoretical perspectives to which I plan to refer subsequently, that the engine of these transformations in modern society continues to be a drive propelled by the competitive market forces toward greater *efficiency* and *rationalization* of social life and/or greater social (functional) differentiation of societal institutions in which the incline of each of its rationalities and everyday life becomes

---

[1] These terms may be found in Georg Simmel's ([1907] 1978:440) analysis of the role and distribution of knowledge in modern society. Simmel contends that the apparently relentless expansion of knowledge is accompanied, despite an appearance of equality, by a parallel and growing stratification of individuals who are knowledgeable and those who are not, which leads to the pessimistic conclusion that the general 'rise in the level of knowledge as a whole does not by any means bring about a general leveling, but rather its opposite'.

[2] Compare, for example, Ivan Illich's (1977, 1980) demand to do away with occupations which foster 'invalidity' in individuals.

steeper by the day.[3] However, such need not be the case. Any greater reliance on experts, advisers and counselors does invariably spell greater impoverishment of the life-world, a fully autonomous development of the 'inner logic' of a specialized cultural sphere such as science, efficiency or a significant expansion in the ability to control and manipulate individuals and groups.

In any event, there are contradictory, normative ways of interpreting these developments. On the one hand, the rise of experts is seen in a strictly negative fashion. It is interpreted as a response to the disabling and debilitating effects of modern society, or as the dark side of functional differentiation. These effects have been captured with the help of many terms, for example alienation, anomie and displacement. But counseling, therapy and advice do not heal the negative impact of modern institutions, they only placate them and produce new dependencies. This view is perhaps the more prominent expression. On the other hand, the growth of knowledge-based occupations and greater access to counseling, advice and expertise is seen as a positive feature of modern society. For example, access to advice and counseling has enabling effects; it allows individuals and groups to mobilize and organize their life chances and life styles in productive ways. A realistic assessment of the function of experts in modern society would not, I believe, want to confine itself to a single normative judgment about their role and their impact on individuals and groups.[4]

---

[3] The idea that substantive reason expressed in religion and metaphysics in modern society evolves into autonomous institutional spheres of science, morality and art each endowed with its own rationality, namely truth, normative rightness and authenticity and beauty and the development of these cultures firmly under the control of its own experts, results, if one is prepared to fix the boundaries between institutions and the distance between them and everyday life as particularly firm and steep boundaries, in the threat that with 'cultural rationalization of this sort, the danger increases that the life-world (civil society), whose traditional substance has already been devaluated, will become more and more impoverished' and in which therefore the 'hermeneutics of every day communication' are progressively split off from the powerful culture of the specialists (Habermas, [1980] 1981a:9). Needless perhaps to indicate, such a development gives rise to efforts to combat the 'culture of expertise'. The same diagnosis implies that the life-world or civil society 'has to become able to develop institutions out of itself which sets limits to the internal dynamics and to the imperatives of an almost autonomous economic system and its administrative complements' (Habermas, [1980] 1981a:13). It goes without saying that the case Habermas advances rests to an important degree on drawing narrow and exclusive boundaries among social institutions. The result is, for example, that the life-world appears to be, for the time being, a rather passive and submissive institution in modern society deprived of cognitive resources, for example, to combat the influence of other societal institutions, while the economic and scientific systems have rather narrow inner logics – which in many ways actually resemble more affirmative descriptions of modern science and the economy.

[4] Anthony Giddens (1991:33–34) also pleads for a balanced assessment of the role of counselors and advisers in modern society because 'therapy is not simply a means of coping with novel anxieties, but an expression of the reflexivity of the self – a phenomenon which, on the level of the individual, like the broader institutions of modernity, balances opportunity and potential catastrophe in equal measure.'

The central focus of this chapter is, however, on the peculiar place of experts in knowledge societies, the reasons for the demands for expert knowledge, the nature of expertise, the peculiar attributes of knowledge-bearing occupations (avoiding the inappropriate term 'class' already at this point, cf. Lopata, 1976) and, generally, the culture and power of knowledge in contemporary society as it is mediated and represented by knowledge-based occupations.

Given conventional typologies and classifications of occupations, or conceptions about the realities of work in different economic sectors, it is very difficult to produce compelling evidence from existing empirical information, using secondary analysis, that this is how the world of labor is transformed and increasingly works. The viability of the general assertion at the present time can be illustrated. Based on a variety of research designs, one finds particular approximations of the underlying trend toward jobs which are more knowledge-intensive. For example, Myles (1990) and Hunter (1988) report that the shift to employment in services has led to a general upgrading of skill requirements for the economy as a whole. Moreover, using a 'subjective' assessment of required job skills by workers who occupy these positions and comparing these responses with 'objective' skill measures of occupations developed in the late 1960s, Myles and Fawcett (1990) indicate that workers in the manufacturing sector report in the early 1980s that their skill levels are higher than those attributed to the same jobs two decades earlier. Indeed, these findings are suggestive, but far from definitive, and certainly allow for alternative explanations which need not imply any overall increase in skill requirements.

This requires a critical analysis of the existing literature which is sensitive to the issue and has registered, in various ways, the phenomenon of knowledge-bearing occupations. It is necessary to point out the inadequacies of existing categories but it is also possible to peel off useful ideas. It is neither the aim of this chapter to re-animate nor even to resuscitate the increasingly obsolete notion of a 'new' class (cf. Bell, 1979b), for it is rather doubtful that emerging societies will have the kinds of masters past societies had. Experts are far too fragmented intellectually[5] to perform such a historical role. They also have the most diverse

---

[5] An empirical study of the ideological predispositions and of the correlates of the political beliefs of members of professional occupations in the United States, in comparison to that of the group of 'managers', arrives at the conclusion that 'predictions of a homogenous professional-managerial "class" unified around core ideological tenets appear premature' (Wuthnow and Shrum, 1983:485). That is to say, even if one employs a fairly restrictive definition of the group of professional occupations, as is the case for the occupational categories adopted by the US Census, it becomes evident that variance of attitudes *within* each of the two groups of occupations, namely professionals and managers, is considerable. As a result, and based on these findings, it would appear to be dubious to conclude that a cohesive and coherent 'class consciousness' is emerging among professionals in the United States.

allegiances.[6] Nor is it the goal of this discussion to resume the 'de-skilling' or the 'de-professionalization' debate.[7] Clearly, efforts to revive the notion of class are related to the controversy about the distribution of skills and the role of the professions in modern society. But my analysis is not about skills, it is about knowledge. The notion of 'experts' is a difficult one and requires considerable reflection. However, the variety of claims to expertise suggests that while experts at times try, for obvious reasons, to embrace the cognitive authority of science, their 'knowledge' most often is not submitted to the authority of science and is therefore conterminous with what is accepted by the scientific establishment (cf. Barnes, 1985:90-112).

Knowledge and expertise

As I have emphasized, the use of and dependence on knowledge in all spheres of human activity has reached an unprecedented level and has produced far-reaching and virtually irreversible social consequences. In manufacturing, for example, knowledge is increasingly replacing the classic factors of production. At the same time, our conceptual clarity and insight into the nature of knowledge is deficient. Though the importance of knowledge is stressed almost everywhere, it is also, at the same time, often simply treated as a black box and introduced into many discussions in a narrow fashion without much theoretical reflection (e.g. Eulau, 1973).

If one defines the kind of knowledge which is particularly influential in modern society, for example as represented by the knowledge of the research front in science (and technology), then such knowledge, of course, is not only easily set apart from everyday knowledge but becomes identical with 'elite knowledge' (Freidson, 1986:4). Taken to its extreme, this thesis leads, so it seems, to the notion of the *technical state* in which the logic of technology becomes the logic of political action (e.g. Schelsky, 1961). Correspondingly, the emerging groups of experts, especially scientists and engineers, are often narrowly located at the apex of the social hierarchy in contemporary society and are seen, therefore, as something akin to an almost exclusive elite of specialists mostly in the employ of the already powerful and influential who can afford to purchase their services. In a more positive sense, the notion of a 'class' of experts which will become increasingly powerful and influential in society has already been used for some time as a building block in the design of modern utopias. For example, this thesis is advanced by Warren Bennis and Philip Slater in their *The Temporary Society* (1969), and in Heinz Eulau's (1973) idea of a

[6] As Rueschemeyer (1986:139–140), for example, underlines and cautions, 'taken together, the power sharing of the different knowledge-bearing occupations has probably diluted the concentrations of power based on property, coercion and popular appeal; but that is a far cry from saying that the power of partial interests and the conflicts between them have become irrelevant or even muted.'

[7] My reluctance to consider these topics relevant in this context does not mean that the issues have ceased to be the basis for lively disputes (e.g. Esquith, 1987).

'consultative commonwealth', which is the probable outcome of the interrelation between the 'skill' revolution in contemporary society and some of the social consequences of modern technology. But even in more tempered, less technocratic and utopian theoretical blueprints of contemporary social scientists, the fascination appears to be with a 'class of high status "brain workers"' (Ladd, 1970:262; Benveniste, 1972), rather than, as will be the case in this instance, on a much broader and richer spectrum of knowledge-based occupations found in *all* sectors of the economy, not merely the tertiary sector, and on all socio-economic levels. Even today, a preoccupation with high-level experts, with those who advise the 'prince', is in most analyses the primary conception of the expert in modern society. Such an image may well be to the liking of many experts and resonate with their own self-conception; however, it is quite unrealistic.

Our knowledge about knowledge is often taken for granted. Among the paradoxes of a knowledge-based society is, therefore, not only 'how much of the communication of knowledge falls to specialized agencies and channels outside any social control or visibility' (Birnbaum, 1971b:431), but also how limited or one-sided theoretical attention to these matters has been.

New knowledge appears to be almost always better than old knowledge. One might of course presume that the new knowledge drives out old knowledge because it is more adequate. But this need not be the case. At least, it might be difficult to find criteria which allow for a reasonable comparison. In contemporary society, knowledge is, in any event, changing rapidly. Constantly, worlds are lost and worlds are produced. Rapid changes produce fear but also opportunities to translate knowledge, that is, to construct different worlds. But how and by *whom* knowledge is translated into social action, thereby acquiring authority and influence, remains largely hidden.

The unprecedented growth (and decay) in the volume of knowledge, fueled by expanding sites for the production of new knowledge, especially universities and research organizations, corresponds to the rise of a new, increasingly influential and rapidly growing group of occupations of various types of 'experts' or of knowledge-based work. The work experts perform is not simply a passive, almost mechanical task. Experts do not merely pass on pieces of knowledge which remain largely unaffected by the mediation process.[8] The constitution of experts always requires the parallel constitution of a certain clientele or public. Clients and experts have certain minimum common features, be it only the conviction that specialized knowledge is functional under certain circumstances.

[8] In his seminal *The Philosophy of Money*, Georg Simmel ([1907] 1978:603) makes use of a somewhat different metaphor implying that knowledge travels quite effortlessly and virtually unimpeded: 'It has been rightly suggested that theoretical notions . . . are like a torch whose light does not become dimmer by igniting innumerable others from it. In as much as their potential boundless dissemination has no influence whatsoever upon their importance, they elude private ownership more than any other contents of life.'

Despite evidence of considerable disenchantment about the merits of expertise, even fear about a 'tyranny of the experts' and the loss of citizenship in modern societies (cf. Lieberman, 1970), everyone must (still) defer, and is, under circumstances, forced to defer to the authority of experts today, not only in matters of grave and far-reaching consequences, but also in many of the most mundane routines of everyday life. For example, we all express our doubts about the validity of daily weather forecasts, yet the planning of daily activities and routines are to a considerable extent affected by such forecasts. Even at such a mundane level, it becomes evident therefore that the social constitution of (and the response to) experts and expertise always presupposes the parallel body of and socio-intellectual division between variously constituted 'lay' publics (clients) or audiences and experts.

Although there is, on the surface at least, nothing novel about the influence of experts, the role of knowledge and the occupations which mediate access to knowledge take on rather different qualities in advanced societies than heretofore, even in what are known as industrial societies. As a matter of fact, the noun 'expert' did not come into usage until the middle of the nineteenth century.[9] In a society where experts and expert knowledge are indispensable, it seems that the extent to which one has to invoke and blindly rely on virtues of another age, namely to *believe* in the solidity of such knowledge and *trust* expert advice, has by no means diminished; as a matter of fact, the ability to believe and trust has become an even more urgent private and public necessity (cf. Lübbe, 1987). Ordinary and extraordinary life in a modern society are held together by the 'cement' of expert knowledge and trust in the solidity of expert knowledge (cf. Giddens, 1990c:88–92). But that is not to say that the increase in the dependence on expert knowledge has somehow slowed the growth of problems or eliminated many of them, rather, the opposite appears to be the case (cf. Perl, 1971; King and Melanson, 1972). Moreover, there is likely to be a relation between both trends. Experts may be instrumental not only in sustaining demand for expertise but in producing needs which call for their intervention. But is it accurate to suggest that knowledge once produced need not be reproduced or that the marginal cost of the reproduction of knowledge, as some economists have argued (e.g. Bates, 1988), tends to approach zero?[10] Indeed, knowledge

[9] Haskell (1984:xii) relates that the term 'expert', which signifies a distinctive social role, did not come into use until the middle decades of the nineteenth century, for it was only then that 'ascending levels of population density and per capita income made it possible for substantial numbers of people to make a living by selling advice and specialized services, rather than by producing food or other tangible goods.'

[10] From a purely economic point of view it may indeed be appropriate to claim that 'a piece [!] of knowledge does not need to be produced more than once' and that the same 'piece' of information can be used repeatedly by as many individuals as desirable or possible (Dasgupta and Stoneman, 1987:3). However, such a conception of knowledge presupposes a most restrictive conception of knowledge production, its distribution and use, namely one entirely free of controversy and contention.

may only be produced once and then *re*-produced innumerable times. However, reproduction often becomes a form of production of knowledge and it in fact constitutes the salient tasks experts perform.

Under rare circumstances only is knowledge a medium which travels easily and unimpeded, that is, uncontested and not subject to interpretation; the growing stratum of 'experts' therefore commands considerable social influence and even honor in contemporary society, although the extent of this influence tends to be underestimated or masked. The very nature of the tasks performed by this new stratum already signals its potential power over the lives of many individuals in contemporary society, especially by way of a determination of the priorities of their action and definitions of the situation, in the first instance. As Rueschemeyer (1986:104) therefore underlines, experts have considerable impact on the lives of many:

> they define the situation for the untutored, they suggest priorities, they shape people's outlook on their life and world, and they establish standards of judgment in the different areas of expertise – in matters of health and illness, order and justice, the design and deployment of technology, the organization of production.

It is dubious whether assertions about the growing importance of knowledge-based occupations in advanced societies can immediately be translated and examined, with any benefit, into categories designed for the analysis of a very different kind of society, namely *industrial society*. Talk about a new class, different forms of class antagonism and new styles of political and economic conflict (cf. Galbraith, 1967; Larson, 1984:29) is not of significant help. New phenomena require a displacement of theoretical perspectives, and new perspectives generate novel insights. The central issue in advanced society, or what is called the *knowledge society* here, is *not* that power is changing hands, but that the nature or the content and substance of exercising power, and therefore the means and the scope of social control, is changing, as well as the ways in which society reproduces itself and stays integrated.

The knowledge of experts and the power of knowledge

Among the difficult, even notorious, issues in this context is the thesis that knowledge represents power. One needs a much clearer sense of the meaning of the components of this all-encompassing and consequential equation before a sensible discussion about the interrelation of power and knowledge can be developed fruitfully. How is power held, and who holds power where? Why and what knowledge might engender advantages? And, finally, the question of knowledge and power always is, as C.W. Mills ([1955] 1967:606) reminds us, the problem of the relations of women and men of knowledge with men and women of power, or of their possible identity.

It is not surprising to find observers who make quite contradictory global assertions about the effect of knowledge in advanced societies on power or of power on knowledge. Anthony Giddens ([1973] 1980:262), for example, cautions against over-generalizations in this area: 'The "functional indispensability" of the expert in the political and economic administration of the contemporary advanced societies no more necessarily gives him power than was the case in the pre-industrial world.' Other observers, of course, suggest that the identity and nature of modern society is determined by experts whose command of specialized knowledge or technical expertise provides for their control of societal institutions and regulation of individual identities.[11]

Somewhat more narrowly, the emergence of intellectuals as a new social class has been identified as the characteristic feature of advanced societies in which science and technology assume a powerful role (cf. Gouldner, 1979; Konrád and Szelényi, 1979). Whether this social stratum constitutes a power elite or even a new social class depends on more detailed theoretical reflections and empirical examination of the relevance and status of these traditional notions. However, it is most likely that the term social class is inappropriate to the system of social inequality in knowledge societies. Daniel Bell (1979a:204), for example, indicates, 'such an elite has *power* within intellectual institutions . . . but only *influence* in the larger world in which policy is made' (my emphasis). But these and other critical observations about the limits to the power of this new stratum, or the very idea of a 'new class' as an essentially 'muddled concept' (Bell, 1979b),[12] has not discouraged others from boldly sketching, perhaps not without self-exemplifying intentions, the dawn of a new age as the result of the construction of 'political knowledge' (e.g. Brzezinski, 1968), or an era in which professionals not only wield immeasurable political muscle but even greater power in the market and the workplace and in public discourse generally (Derber et al., 1990:5).

---

[11] Derber et al. (1990:4–5) are among recent observers who contend that knowledge-bearing occupations, in their case the professionals, constitute a most powerful class: 'Professionals have infused both capitalism and socialism with a modern mandarin logic. By creating a belief in their own knowledge as objective expertise, and helping to organize schooling and the division of labor to suit their own ends, professionals have essentially turned modern knowledge into private property.' Historical events would appear to have shown that at least the mandarin class of professionals in the socialist world lost their touch in no time, unless of course one cares to argue that the transformation of these societies was a revolution by the ruling class.

[12] Bell (1979b:169) suggests that the notion of the emergence of a new class in modern society mixes two trends, which may not be related at all: the emergence of a new social *stratum* and the stridency of a cultural *sentiment*. And, if there is reason to speak about the idea of a new class, it refers at best to an emergent consciousness or cultural attitude but not to the development of a coherent socio-structural basis (Bell, 1979b:186).

It does not take merely hindsight to know that these images were driven more by wishful thinking than rigorous analysis. For the central point about experts of the emerging knowledge society is that they will not be masters of this society. At best, experts constitute or will be part of rather loose associations of individuals and groups. This is not so much the result of their humility or unwillingness to assume power but the outcome of the substance of the forces they master. The very employment of these forces, namely knowledge and expertise, unwittingly perhaps, diminishes the ability of any group to assume a 'master position' in society. In as much as knowledge is enabling, and if it only de-mythologizes itself, clients of experts also always lose a measure of their dependence. Even if the emergent 'knowledge stratum' had sufficient coherence and community of interest, which is doubtful, it would be unlikely to be able to form a social class, in the sense in which the term has been understood in the nineteenth century in social science discourse, because the 'scientification' of social relations generates an essential fragility of social structures which dissipates and operates against formations attempting to monopolize decisions and usurp social futures.

Traditional accounts of power stress that it is employed by individuals or collectivities on occasion only. That is, power is not seen as a persistent, always present, feature of social action, as say certain beliefs of individuals, but as a resource utilized under special circumstances which warrant use and determine the specific form it takes. Under such circumstances the threat of its use, which alone is always present, is not sufficient any more. Conformity, punishment, revenge, conquest, even slaughter, are seen as the typical manifestations of the exercise of (brutal) power. Finally, repressive, coercive and distorting features, as the main outcome of the exercise of power, and specific collectivities or individuals, which are its victims, are examined primarily in the study of power.

It would be misleading to suggest that expert knowledge is, for some reason, void of these features of power and that, therefore, traditional accounts of power are impotent in the face of the influence, control and authority exercised by experts, counselors and advisers. And it would be equally misleading to maintain that the power of knowledge fully displaces power based on other resources in modern society. Nevertheless, in knowledge societies, the balance in the uses of different forms of power changes; knowledge, rather than the more traditional forms of coercive power, becomes the dominant and preferred means of constraint and control of possible social action.

Thus, one surely needs to emphasize that the kind of power which may in fact flow from specialized knowledge – the extent to which access to such knowledge can be restricted and is in turn somehow in demand – should not be confused with a more traditional and more consequential form of power, namely political power, in the sense in which one typically encounters this term in political theory. Political power, at least in the context of most liberal political theories, involves the ability to restrict or otherwise circumscribe individual freedoms, the raw capacity to impose one's will even against the will of others, to enforce obedience and to threaten and administer coercion, which includes the use of physical force. Political power is also personal power.

Obviously, this is not, or at least not primarily and directly, the kind of power which experts, advisers and counselors wield. Because they do not control the means of political power, one is even more justified in questioning the ability of this group to monopolize and control society in any direct way. The form of power which may flow from specialized knowledge or the appropriation of discourse (Foucault, 1970) is predominantly, and thus by no means exclusively, of a different nature. It is primarily cognitive or theoretical, and at times can also be material, for example, as the result of the introduction of technical artifacts into the situation, but it likely primarily affects the self-conception of individuals. It does not have an overtly coercive influence, at least in most instances, and one can expect, as a result, that this form of power is not perceived as repressive, and is therefore quite distant from the exercise of more traditional forms of (political) power. Expert knowledge provides its clientele with a different grasp and hold upon the world and, in the final analysis, transforms both the world and the individual.

In an analogous definition, Rouse (1987:211) stresses that he proposes to examine power, in this case the power of science, which has to do 'with the ways interpretations within the field [of practices] reshape the field itself and thus reshape and constrain agents and their possible actions'. However, Rouse (1987:244) argues as well that it is no longer possible to sustain, in the light of the increasing application of scientific knowledge and technical artifacts, a 'political distinction between the exercise of power over human bodies and the development and use of capacities to control and manipulate things'.

The presence of expert knowledge is rarely circumscribed, and therefore, only called for occasionally, and its effectiveness somehow is not limited to specific, for example, political or economic conduct. Knowledge-bearing and knowledge-disseminating occupations exercise cognitive authority and influence by restricting courses of possible action of individuals and groups, by setting and defending certain normative standards which enable individuals to construct sensibilities of and for social action,[13] by defining what counts as knowledge, by restricting the circulation of relevant knowledge and by imposing means for assessing the efficacy of expert knowledge. But individually, experts, counselors and advisers may at times, indeed appear to be, rather powerless. However, the general nature of the change in the mode of exercising power is evident, for

---

[13] Compare Shearing and Ericson's (1991) well-reasoned conception of culture as a figurative resource made available through stories that enable constructions of sensibilities of social action.

in advanced societies influence, authority and power are increasingly mediated by knowledge.

From a different vantage point, the same development is, of course, expressed as a shift in the mode of exercising power in modern society from, under normal conditions, coercion to manipulation (e.g. Birnbaum, 1971a:402). Whether such terminology is preferable should be left open for the time being. However, as the balance in the mode of exercising power shifts, the use of coercive power becomes the exceptional case and should not completely color the discussion of power relations in advanced society.

The kind of knowledge which may convey power has to be specified too, for it is unlikely that all forms of knowledge function as resources which yield power, or function equally well in generating power in all contexts. Knowledge that in general most likely confers power is control over incremental knowledge. The power knowledge may or may not convey depends, therefore, on available alternative or competing forms of knowledge, as well as on optional capacities for action. The power of specific knowledge depends on the weakness of its contenders and not so much on any inherent authority it can or must invariably command.

A suggestion by Alfred North Whitehead (1926:282) in his *Science and the Modern World* is perhaps a first useful departure in this search for forms of knowledge that may more likely be associated with power, for in the context of a discussion of the emergence of specialization in science, he comments that 'effective knowledge is professionalized knowledge' but warns at the same time of the dangers inherent in a loss of 'directive wisdom' which is the outcome of more comprehensive and therefore less specialized reflection. However, Whitehead's observations are probably a more useful reminder that it is most difficult, theoretically and empirically, if not impossible, to disentangle either knowledge from the social organization in which it originates since its form and content are affected by the context of its production, or to try to disassociate knowledge from the context of its 'transmission' to a particular clientele. Who holds power should be analyzed in conjunction with the question of how power is held where. The issue whether 'men of knowledge exercise power by virtue of their intellectual capacities and educational attainments, or are these ancillary to other aspects of their roles when they do occupy posts of power', or what is but the same, 'whether power accrues to institutions primarily concerned with producing knowledge, or whether other institutions use knowledge acquired from other sources' (Birnbaum, 1971b:420) may, of course, be posed in this fashion. It is doubtful, however, that one thereby formulates a sensible empirical and theoretical set of issues that can be resolved in an uncontested manner. Knowledge and its context tend to be fused. One can and must, however, discuss the various interrelations between knowledge and institutions. But it would appear to be futile or unnecessary to attempt to resolve, with some finality, whether it is knowledge itself which is the institutional basis for invariably dispensing power in modern society.

Experts, counselors and advisers

The terms 'counselor', 'adviser' and 'expert' all lack precise and well-established meanings. It would not be sensible, therefore, to argue or attempt to maintain meaningful and consistent definitional distinctions *among* these terms. I shall use the terms 'counselor', 'adviser' and 'expert' interchangeably. In each case, however, the labels signify an increasingly important way of life – and of course social divisions – in knowledge societies. With the considerable growth in their number, kind and demand in contemporary society, the meaning of these terms has also undergone a notable and multiple inflation.

Advising and counseling in some sense are by no means novel activities. Many have made a living as experts or advisers, especially to the powerful in the past. But the adviser is no longer merely someone whose advice is proffered to a political leader with whom the expert is in close personal contact (cf. Goldhamer, 1978). This conception is exemplified for example by Ibn Khaldun, Machiavelli, Francis Bacon, Metternich, Bismarck, Lord Cherwell and Henry Kissinger. This form of advice still flourishes, however, in all political jurisdictions. But much more characteristic of our age is the 'democratization' of counseling. It accounts for the growth of the number of advisers and counselors, and for the transformation of the tasks associated with these long-established occupations. Expertise is, in principle, available to everyone (cf. Larson, 1990).

The democratization of advising produces a parallel growth in lay audiences. In all modern societies, not only are the state and large business corporations major consumers and employers of knowledge-bearing and knowledge-disseminating occupations, but so are groups and individuals in virtually all situations of the life-world. This includes guidance in the conduct of mundane and also rather personal affairs of individuals and their families. Moreover, the terms expert, counselor, consultant or adviser, which are descriptive of certain forms of occupational activity, are not necessarily widely employed as the identifying labels of occupations or professions. Rather, the traditional identifying labels remain – priest, banker, nurse, travel agent, teacher, social worker, economist, lawyer, engineer, police officer, mediator, real estate agent, insurance broker – even though the institutional settings in which these expert services may be rendered have been transformed, the recruitment process substantially changed, the advisory process altered, and the function of these knowledge-based services changed considerably.

Social theorists have, of course, for a considerable time been fascinated by the relation of power and knowledge. The works of, for example, Henri Saint-Simon, Auguste Comte, Karl Marx, Thorstein Veblen, Max Weber, Emile Durkheim, James Burnham and Raymond Aron have described or prescribed the political influence of experts, social engineers, scientists, engineers or systems analysts, particularly in industrial society. Various recent theories of contemporary society have identified, as already indicated, a new stratum or social class that challenges existing traditional sources and representatives of power and influence in industrial society. In particular, those who fashion, interpret and directly employ knowledge are seen as the emerging new rulers in society. Scientists, engineers, social scientists or 'intellectuals' are generally identified as the new powerful stratum (cf. Lapp, 1965; Klaw, 1968; Lieberman, 1970; Gouldner, 1979; Konrád and Szelényi, 1979).

More recently, in the context of theories of society, which postulate the end of industrial society, the importance of experts or scientists has been similarly underscored. However, opinion is divided as to whether the 'new class' is merely legitimating or symbolically ratifying decisions of the political power elite, or whether we are witnessing the formation of a genuine shift in societal power relations to a new group of agents of social change. Yet these discussions center, for the most part, on views and issues that are not immediately relevant to our concerns. Most importantly, classic and contemporary discourse on experts (and many equivalent categories) *underestimate* the quantity of occupations which come under their jurisdiction and *overestimate* the efficacy of their influence. In addition, to date most of the theoretical discussions concerned with agents of knowledge are linked in one way or the other to more common notions of intellectuals and their role in society (cf. Mannheim, [1929] 1936; Dahrendorf, 1969; Coser, 1970; Feuer, 1976). Not only has the stratum of intellectuals and its influence in society been identified as based on knowledge, but so has modern bureaucracy, for it represents, according to most standard conceptions, a form of authority based on the command of abstract knowledge.

Before describing the group of experts, advisers and counselors in greater detail, a number of other possibly competing occupational categories must be considered, since they could be seen to encompass the former group of occupations. Of particular pertinence is, of course, the category of *professionals*. The functionalist account of the professions, long dominant in sociology, has close intellectual affinity to Max Weber's discussion of non-economic domination in modern society (cf. Gipsen, 1988) and, therefore, to his ideal type of legal authority, its bureaucratic organization and its class of civil servants.

Herrschaft kraft Wissen

One of the most famous and consequential analyses of the authority of knowledge and experts is, of course, Max Weber's theory of bureaucracy or, more generally, his theory of the intrinsically rationalizing instruments of modern political power, for 'bureaucratic administration means fundamentally the exercise of control on the basis of knowledge' ('*Herrschaft kraft Wissen*') (Weber [1922] 1964:339). Without question, Weber stresses, in this context, the efficiency and power of specialized knowledge derived from a thoroughly old-Prussian conception of the efficacy of the military and civil service apparatus (cf. Spittler, 1980; Niethammer, [1989] 1992). The primary source of the 'superiority of bureaucratic administration lies in the role of technical knowledge which, through the development of modern technology and business methods in the production of goods, has become completely indispensable.' Therefore, as Weber ([1922] 1964:337–338) argues, 'it makes no difference whether the economic system is organized on a capitalistic or a socialistic basis.' Bureaucracy is capable of attaining levels of efficiency, reliability, precision or modes of rational control which no other form of authority is able to attain.

The authority of the administrative apparatus derives from legal norms[14] and continuous work carried out by officials in offices generates and is based on technical knowledge. Thus, there is a convergence of legal norms and knowledge; the effective application of general, legal norms requires the use of general, abstract knowledge. *Rational bureaucratic knowledge* thrives in a social environment which has been 'dehumanized'. Bureaucracy provides the sentiments demanded by the external apparatus of modern culture most effectively and develops its characteristic features especially well:

> the more it is 'dehumanized', the more completely it succeeds in eliminating from official business love, hatred, and all purely personal, irrational, and emotional elements which escape calculation. This is appraised as its special virtue by capitalism. The more complicated and specialized modern culture becomes, the more its external supporting apparatus demands the personally detached and strictly objective *expert*, in lieu of the lord of older social structures who was moved by personal sympathy and favor, by grave and gratitude (Weber, [1922] 1968:975).

Modern bureaucracy succeeds in rationalizing the irrational. It is decisive for Weber ([1922] 1968:979), therefore, that despite the realm of relative unregulated conduct, even in highly rational settings (for example, in the legal system), that 'in principle a system of rationally debatable "reasons" stands behind every act of bureaucratic administration, namely, either subsumption under norms, or a weighing of ends and means.'

Legal authority becomes subject to routinization and antinomies, and conflicts can arise. Bureaucracies not only accumulate knowledge, but attempt to protect it from access by 'outsiders' (cf. Weber, [1922] 1968:990–993), and while political leaders are increasingly 'dilettantes' the experts can only be controlled and kept at bay by other experts (Weber, [1922] 1968:994). Who controls the administrative apparatus? According to Weber ([1922] 1964:338), such control is only to a degree possible by the non-specialist; in general, the 'trained permanent official is more likely to get his way in the long run than his nominal superior, the Cabinet minister, who is not a specialist.'

---

[14] The 'belief in the "legality" of patterns of normative rules and the right of those elevated to authority under such rules to issue commands' constitutes the foundation of legal authority (Weber, [1922] 1964:328).

But the ability of the state to effectively implement its action, and the relative superiority of rational bureaucratic knowledge is, however, limited, as Weber already knew. The only group which can escape the control of rational bureaucratic knowledge most surely is the capitalist entrepreneur. At least he is the only one able to maintain relative immunity from legal authority. However, it is interesting to note why Weber ([1922] 1968:994) believes that the capitalist is, more or less, beyond the reach of state bureaucracy. The ability of the state to intervene in economic affairs is, according to Weber, on the whole not very effective because of the superior knowledge of the facts by the capitalist enterprise and the ability of the corporation to shield pertinent information from outsiders even more effectively than civil servants.

A question which also needs to be posed is whether, once bureaucratization and 'rationalization' in large-scale organizations have reached a state of 'maturity' in the later part of this century, assuming that such organizations ever achieve a notable measure of rationality, further structural changes in organizations or authority relations are still primarily driven by market forces and considerations of efficiency. A large amount of empirical work on modern organizations indicates that these corporate actors are far from blueprints of efficiency and rationality. Moreover, organizational change is not always driven by efficiency considerations nor does it necessarily result in gains of effectiveness and rationality (cf. DiMaggio and Powell, 1983).

The large and varied group of workers laboring to disseminate knowledge in modern society, however, is not only employed by the state. As a matter of fact, many workers are self-employed. The classes of civil servants and *professionals* display considerable kinship, not only from a theoretical point of view, but also from a comparative historical perspective. Therefore, they can be discussed in conjunction. For example, despite important differences in their historical careers, the German bourgeoisie and the Anglo-American middle classes had many features in common because both 'rose to prominence largely on the strength of those qualities that are shared by the models of profession and bureaucracy' (Gipsen, 1988:563).

Professions, professionals and experts

The range of occupational tasks I would like to combine into the group of knowledge-bearing and knowledge-disseminating occupations is not identical with the widely used concept of the professions, or better, referring to the dynamic process in question, the 'relentless drive in every field of human employment' (Gross, 1971:277) toward some form of professionalism. The concept of professions should also not be limited to the notion of professions and professionals associated particularly with the self-understanding of professional associations in North America and England. That notion, and its theoretical counterpart, chooses to ignore many other and historically specific forms of 'professionalization' (cf. Rueschemeyer, 1986). But even if one tries to work with the dominant theoretical model, one has to acknowledge, as Wilensky (1964:141) urges, that while there may well 'be a general tendency for occupations to seek professional status, remarkably few of the thousands of occupations in modern society attain it' (also Goode, 1969:267).

But, more significantly, most of the scholarship concerned with professionals, especially the work associated with the functionalist conception of the nature and the position of the professions in modern society (cf. Parsons, 1939, 1968; Goode, 1957),[15] has chosen to ignore the knowledge base of the professions. The recent impressive critiques of the functionalist perspective on professions have, for the most part, also avoided examining the convergence between the alleged ethos of the professions and their faith in science as a powerful utilitarian force, as a motor of social evolution and as a source of historical progress.[16] The ideological critique of the ethos and the position of the professions in modern society[17] has rarely extended to a critical analysis of the very resource which is said to legitimize such a special role in society. The unanalyzed knowledge base is assumed to be mainly 'scientific', in the narrow sense of the term, and, therefore, immune to sociological analysis, in particular, a sociology of knowledge of professional knowledge (cf. Stehr and Meja, 1990). In the most recent literature on the role of professions, emphasis and interest evidently begins to shift toward calls for an analysis of the knowledge base of professions, the conditions under which it is produced and applied (e.g. Larson, 1990:32) and an analysis of the legitimation of professional knowledge (Derber et al., 1990: 59–75).[18]

Although some of the traditional professions may well be much more differentiated today and transformed as a result of their numerical growth and the new demands placed on them, and the changes in the knowledge

[15] For an early critique of the functionalist approach to the professions compare Bucher and Strauss (1961) who emphasize, using what they call a process or emergent approach, the diversity and conflict of interests within the professions rather than the homogeneous character of the normative and cultural world of the professions.

[16] Parsons (1968:545), for example, argues that the most advanced segment in the course of social evolution of Western society is found in the 'professional complex . . . the most important single component in the structure of modern society' and the members of this stratum are bound to emerge as the leaders in advanced society.

[17] The virtues of the modern scientist as depicted in the deeply rooted image of science in the late nineteenth century, at least in North America and Britain, correspond quite closely to the virtues of professionals. In Victorian times, the modern scientist was widely portrayed as a 'humble and honest man with steady habits, laboring patiently, diligently, selflessly, and without prejudice in the interests of truth' (Hollinger, 1984:142).

[18] Since Derber and his colleagues (1990:59) are convinced that the professionals, at least in the US, form a class, they employ the metaphor that professionals are engaged in a 'class struggle for the mind' to describe the efforts of professionals to legitimize their knowledge base.

base as well as in their institutional setting, their impact on society continues to be a result of their collective organization and their ability to mobilize politically. The category of occupations at the center of attention here, experts, advisers and counselors generally, provides, in this respect at least, a much more diffuse picture. The result is probably that its influence occurs much more via the work of individual practitioners than collective organization and the constraints an organization may impose and enforce. From the point of view of the impact of the professions on society at large, it is of interest to note that some groups among the professions appear to have withdrawn from public discourse – at least in some cultures. Academic professionalization in North America, for example, is associated with privatization or de-politicization, a concentration of intellectual energies and resources on the narrow audience of fellow specialists (cf. Jacoby, 1987). But the differentiation which goes hand in hand with professionalization at the same time increases the importance of the knowledge-bearing occupations identified here since the withdrawal from public discourse of certain producers of knowledge does not reduce the demand and the need for some of their products. As a matter of fact, it may well heighten the importance and power of those who mediate between specialists and the public.

Despite the differences in emphasis, the extensive theoretical discussions and empirical research concerned with the professions is of value for my purposes because it provides initial insights into the societal function and conditions for the growing demand for skills which are based primarily on the control of certain forms of knowledge. From a *comparative historical perspective*, both the groups of professions and bureaucrats are not so much a phenomenon *sui generis* as they are part of a development which encompasses both social formations. They are part, although the efficacy of instrumental rationality is exaggerated, of the

> rise of expertise and certification as specifically middle-class techniques for advancement and for legitimizing privilege, rank, and power (vis-à-vis aristocratic resistance and democratic pretensions alike), intertwined with ideologies of 'culture', science, and public service that function in a context of all-pervading instrumental rationality, specialization, and secularization' (Gipsen, 1988:564–565).

The stress on the enabling features of bureaucracy and professionalization has to be balanced, however, with a view of the constraining features of these social formations, as well as with the ambivalence of professional, bureaucratic and formal knowledge.

Intellectuals and experts

For this reason, and the fact that the role of the intellectual is, perhaps, best described as emerging in a particular form of society and as representative of that historically specific form of society, a clear delineation between the intellectual and the expert should be drawn. Experts are not intellectuals, although intellectuals may at times be experts. In many ways, experts do not displace intellectuals. Yet, both intellectuals and experts live off a disjuncture between common-sense knowledge and expert or general knowledge. The disjuncture is, of course, largely the creation of, or is maintained by, intellectuals and experts. Experts emerge as a separate stratum and ultimately exceed, by a large margin, the number of intellectuals in modern society.

But more important is the observation that experts (and counselors, advisers etc.) comprise typical occupations in a society which has become a knowledge society. For the sake of simplification, intellectuals are creatures of industrial society, while experts are the fastest growing segment of the labor force in knowledge societies. Intellectuals stress general knowledge, experts specialized knowledge. Intellectuals therefore tend to employ communicative skills and rely in their reasoning on 'symbols of general scope and abstract reference' (Shils, 1968:399–400). In the same sense, as Shils also stresses, although in a somewhat ambivalent manner, intellectual interests arise from the 'need to be in cognitive, moral and appreciative contact with the most general or "essential" features of man, society, nature and the cosmos'.

Not surprisingly, but in contrast to most other, more conventional, groups of occupations, discussions concerned with intellectuals typically emphasize specific cognitive attributes, as indicated, for instance, by the extent to which intellectuals engage in and rely on general and abstract notions in their work. Similarly, the rather common idea that intellectuals contribute, above all, to the construction and elaboration of the tradition of 'high culture' in a society signifies that the function of intellectuals is of a specific cognitive quality.

The distinction which should be drawn between the strata of intellectuals and experts becomes even clearer when one considers Merton's ([1945] 1957:209) brief but succinct delineation of the social role of intellectuals in his discussion of the place of intellectuals in public bureaucracy. Merton limits the term 'intellectual' to persons who 'devote themselves to cultivating and formulating knowledge'. Intellectuals, therefore, may be said to have an explicit, and publicly sanctioned, active role in the creation and development of knowledge. The extent to which their active contribution to the formation and development of the public fund of knowledge is their defining characteristic becomes especially clear if one contemplates the role of a teacher or an announcer; if one *merely* communicates the contents of a textbook or reads the script prepared by someone else, one does not function as an intellectual. In fact, one is then merely 'a cog in the transmission belt of communicating ideas forged by others' (Merton ([1945] 1957:210).

But contrary to Merton's strict separation between forging and communicating ideas, which relies, of course, on the idea that 'objective' knowledge travels easily, it is by no means self-evident that the announcer or the teacher refrains completely from transforming the knowledge to be delivered. One has to allow for the possibility that, in most instances, the transmission of ideas does not occur without being affected by the kind of transmission and the context in which it takes place. However, what remains significant is that the teacher or the announcer is not expected to be a producer of knowledge. For intellectuals the latter is a most legitimate activity. The at times disparaging observation that experts typically have 'tunnel vision' becomes relevant. The notion of tunnel vision simply alerts one to the fact that experts, in contrast to intellectuals, are, for the most part, trained to 'examine specialized aspects of problems that blinds them to other issues' (Pacey, 1983:36).

The service sector and the service class

The group of advisers, consultants and experts is by no means based exclusively in the *service sector* of society (which is, at best, a very elusive term), nor does it necessarily perform *services*. These persons may also be found employed, if one uses the well-known three-sector division of the modern economic structure (or development) and the associated occupations in each of these sectors of the economy, in the primary or manufacturing sector of the economy of a society.[19] If the performance of services, especially in contrast to the manufacture of goods, is not seen as restricted by its institutional location, namely to the tertiary sector of the economy, then the work and the function of the category of knowledge disseminators may well be much broader. In any event, much of the discussion of the diverse structure of the service industries and of service occupations in modern society, their size and prospect, really does not shed much light on the issue identified here as more significant both to the growth of the economy and the structure of its labor force.

From a neo-Marxist perspective, the emergence of a group of occupations said to form the *service class*, or third force within the structure of social inequality, constitutes a particular theoretical challenge because these groups may be located between capital and labor. Hence, considerable effort is expended to assimilate such an intermediate stratum of occupations to either side of the ledger. However, aside from their elusive

---

[19] Some of the early discussions about the division of the industrialized economy into three sectors may be found in Fisher (1939) or Clark (1940); more recent and somewhat critical, though ultimately affirmative, discussion of the notion of the importance of the service sector and of the reasons for its growth may be found in Gershuny and Miles (1983) as well as Offe (1984:227–320). However, it is telling that the subtitle of the Gershuny and Miles study reads 'The transformation of employment in industrial societies', that is, their discussion of the changes in the labor force of service industries is, for all intents and purposes, animated by and dependent on the theory of industrial society and the dynamics of its economic structure and sectors rather than a conception of an economy which has transcended, or is about to transcend, that of an industrial society. But then, Daniel Bell's image of post-industrial society is one dominated by the 'service economy' (cf. Bell, 1973a:127–128).

class position in advanced societies, the notion of a service class is, on the whole, rather vague. This group represents, according to Goldthorpe (1982:162), the 'class of professional, administrative and managerial employees' both in the public and private sector of the economy. Among the common characteristics of occupations comprising this class are, for example, their location within a set of interlocking institutions serving capital, discretion and autonomy, superior work conditions and entry regulated by credentials. For Lash and Urry (1987:162–163), the origin of this class can be traced to a loss suffered by capitalists, first at the turn of the century in the United States and later in other industrial societies. The loss occurred in a 'class struggle' between capital and 'modern management' in which the latter, a version of Taylorism, won. Thus, the service class today represents, following these conceptions, for the most part, 'modern, scientific, rational "management"' and therefore a much smaller segment of the labor force than the group of experts, advisers and counselors.

Knowledge workers

One of the still somewhat unknown and relatively unexplored suggestions for a new way of categorizing modern occupations and for analyzing the structure of the labor force may be found in Fritz Machlup's (1962) work on *The Production and Distribution of Knowledge in the United States*. Its main aim was to quantify the contribution of 'knowledge', in the broadest sense of the term, to the post-war economy. For Machlup (1962:7) 'knowledge' encompasses anything 'that is known by somebody and "production of knowledge" any activity by which someone learns of something he has not known before even if others have'. Machlup (1962:363, 382–387) concludes that the 'knowledge industry' accounted for some 29 percent of the gross national product in the United States in 1958 and that 'knowledge workers' made up slightly less than 32 percent of the labor force in 1959. In 1970, the percentage of all knowledge-producing occupations in the economically active population had grown to 39.7 (Table 7.1) (cf. Machlup and Kronwinkler, 1975:755).

Knowledge workers are defined by Machlup broadly as workers in occupations which produce and transmit knowledge. Machlup recognizes the value of disaggregating occupations involved in knowledge work because knowledge work may entail the transportation, transformation, processing, interpretation or analysis of knowledge as well as the 'creation' of knowledge (cf. Machlup, 1981:17). However, Machlup does attempt to statistically differentiate between 'levels' of knowledge work and since the occupational statistics of the US Bureau of the Census do not produce the necessary information directly, the occupational categories the census uses are re-classified by him into 'knowledge-producing' and 'non-knowledge-producing' groups. In some cases, somewhat arbitrary decisions had to be

Table 7.1 *Percentage of the US labor force participating in knowledge-producing activities, 1900–1980*

	Knowledge workers	Non-knowledge workers
1900	10.7	89.3
1910	14.6	85.4
1920	18.3	81.7
1930	21.6	78.4
1940	23.4	76.6
1950	28.3	71.7
1960	33.3	67.7
1970	39.7	60.3
1980	41.2	58.8

Source: Machlup and Kronwinkler (1975); Rubin and Huber (1986)

made. For example, 50 percent of all physicians and surgeons were excluded from the group of knowledge-producing occupations on the assumption that 'only half of their work is diagnostic and therapeutic advice and prescription'. The result is that Machlup classifies, of the census category 'professional, technical and kindred workers', some 20 percent as non-knowledge-producing in 1950 and approximately 19 percent in 1970. Among 'managers, officials and proprietors (except farm)' the percentage of non-knowledge-producing occupations was, in 1950, 41.7 percent and in 1970, 21.6 percent. All 'clerical and kindred workers' are classified as knowledge workers, approximately half of the 'sales workers' and, finally, a small percentage (in 1970, for example, 3.6 percent of the total) of the class of 'craftsman, foreman and kindred workers' as knowledge-producing. However, Machlup classified as knowledge workers occupations located both in the manufacturing and the service sector although none of the occupations found in agriculture qualified. Since 1970, in a further attempt to update the same line of inquiry, Rubin and Huber (1986:3,197) conclude that the proportion of the GNP devoted to knowledge production increased to 34 percent in 1980 and 41.2 percent of the United States labor force were knowledge-producing employees. These figures suggest, therefore, that the size of the 'knowledge-producing labor force' has doubled in twenty years.

The definitions Machlup and his collaborators have employed are, on the one hand, rather broad. For instance, it is doubtful whether it is meaningful to count, without differentiation, all clerical and kindred workers as knowledge workers. In 1970, the group of occupations the Census Bureau groups as 'clerical and kindred workers' alone accounts for 45 percent of the knowledge workers Machlup identifies in total. At the same time, Machlup's effort to re-categorize the census data is probably too restrictive. Especially noteworthy in this regard is his attempt to assign occupations, in an either/or fashion, mostly on the basis of the occupational title, to the class of knowledge- or non-knowledge-producing workers. The outcome could well be that the proportion of 'craftsmen, foremen and kindred workers' or 'operatives and kindred workers' (none classified as knowledge workers) who perform 'knowledge work', at least as part of their required tasks, is much too small. One has to recognize, of course, that Machlup tried to make the best out of an unsatisfactory data base. The occupations enumerated by the US Bureau of the Census are simply not a very reliable statistical basis for efforts to discern trends which ignore occupational titles.

Bell (1973a:212) argues that the figures on the proportion of the GNP spent on knowledge production and transmission would have to be much smaller than Machlup's estimates, although he employs Machlup's term and indicates, for instance, that the 'manual and unskilled worker class is shrinking in society, while at the other end of the continuum the class of knowledge workers is becoming predominant in the new society' (Bell, 1971:4). However, Bell (1973a:213) insists elsewhere that the proportion of the GNP allotted to education, given a more narrow definition of educational expenditures, should be about half of what Machlup allows, namely 7.5 percent in 1969 rather than 14.7 percent. Yet even Bell's more conservative figures imply a doubling of the GNP proportion of education expenditures in twenty years.

In a more recent attempt to estimate the size, composition and growth of the labor force in the United States engaged in activities that are information related and those that are not, Wolff and Baumol (1989) arrive, at least as far as the growth rate is concerned, at conclusions quite similar to those calculated by Machlup, namely that in 1980 the percentage of 'information workers' in the labor force had increased to 52.5 from 42.2 per cent in 1960. The estimate of the total employment in information-related work in all three periods is, however, much higher than the estimate Machlup presents.

Wolff and Baumol's estimates are also based on a classification of occupational titles utilized by the US census. The authors refer to the robustness of the estimates, stating that they vary little despite substantial changes in the pattern of classifying occupations. The increase in information-related employment has been so substantial during the period surveyed that it will show up in the data regardless of the taxonomy employed (Wolff and Baumol, 1989:18). The novel aspect of the observations reported by Wolff and Baumol (1989:35–36) is their attempt to attribute the increase in the share of information-related occupations in the labor force to specific processes. The first and more important factor is the

> *substitution* of information workers, particularly knowledge producers, for non-information workers within production. This factor accounted for over half of the increase in the share of information employees in total employment. The second is relative *productivity movements* among industries, which accounted for over a third of the relative growth of information workers and over 40 percent of the relative growth of data workers (Wolff and Baumol, 1989, 35–36; emphasis added).

Labor force statistics are a difficult, even contentious, matter; they are, of course, socially constructed categories and most of the categories commonly in use do not make reference, at least not on the surface, to such matters as the time spent on, let alone relative importance of, 'knowledge production' or 'knowledge transmission' and changes over time, as part of the task typically associated with conventionally classified or labeled occupations. In the light of these shortcomings, it is, of course, not surprising that the question of the form of knowledge associated with specific occupations is not addressed at all.

Knowledge-based occupations

The definition and discussion of the role and importance of experts is typically narrow in a number of relevant senses: first, it tends to be mostly concerned with those who advise people at the apex of power, that is, in executive positions of influential societal institutions. Exemplary of this would be individuals who command political power. One of the issues to which too much attention has been paid, as a result, is whether experts, in fact, replace the powerful, and therefore constitute the real source of power in a society increasingly dependent on expertise of various kinds. Of course, experts advise the powerful; however, one misses the peculiar growth of advisers, experts and counselors if the focus is restricted in this manner. Secondly, there is the widespread assumption that experts, as clients of science and technology, are limited to and empowered by offering versions of instrumental or technical rationality. And this means that the potent influence of experts is said to derive from the very nature of such knowledge, in particular its definite character, its workability, the ease with which it 'flows' across boundaries and the decisive and penetrating insights it conveys to those who deal in such knowledge and to those who are able to avail themselves of expertise. The flow of knowledge from above to below and the kind of knowledge which is exchanged or imparted is, at best, taken for granted. The axiom simply is that scientific knowledge passes, virtually unimpeded, first from the producers to the experts, then from the experts to clients.[20] As long as one assumes that the kind of knowledge in which experts deal is unequivocal, it becomes difficult, in some respects at least, to understand why there is a growing demand for advice and counsel.

Thirdly, concerns are rarely with the advisory process itself, that is, they are seldom linked to the immediate and broader social configuration of clientele and experts. The question is: are experts merely the media of knowledge or do they play an intellectually much more active role in the 'transfer' of knowledge? Moreover, what social processes account for the apparently rapidly growing need for expert knowledge? Fourthly, the consequences of the transaction between clientele and experts are rarely

---

[20] For a critique of what amounts to a widely held and defended 'instrumental' model of dissemination and application of knowledge produced in science cf. Stehr, 1992.

examined in the context of most existing discussions. They are not made a
focal point of discussion because the advice, on the whole, is presumed to
be efficacious. In short, the discussion of the power or lack of power of
experts is typically informed by premises which could well be erroneous.
One needs to examine critically each and every one of these views and
therefore whether experts decide or legitimate. Past discussion of the role
of experts proceeds on the basis of well-worn dichotomies such as the
distinction between means and ends of social action or scientific-technical
and political knowledge. Finally, one cannot ignore the changing societal
context in which these developments are taking shape; in particular,
whether advanced society, for example, in the form of the knowledge
society or post-industrial society, is really a novel type of society that
constitutes a break with industrial society and poses unique costs and
benefits to occupations which deal in knowledge.

Conflating the thesis that experts advise, for the most part, the powerful,
with the conviction that the means and ends of social action can be
separated decisively as well as the affirmation that it is primarily coercive
power which makes for the defining characteristics of power relations
because it, in the final instance, produces the decisive difference, leads to
rather sterile discussion. It leads to reflections on whether experts are
really the new power elite or whether the shift to expert power alone
constitutes a sufficient change in the nature of society, for example for a
change from industrial to post-industrial society. An excellent example in
this respect is Birnbaum's (1971a:403) observations that

> those who command concentrations of power and property are able to employ
> technical experts – for good or for ill. That expertise is bought, either in the form
> of bureaucratic organizations producing knowledge, or in the services of
> individual technical experts. When technicians do rise to actual command
> positions, they cease to function solely as technicians but function as men in
> command, men with power.

Using a label Giddens ([1973] 1980:263) proposes for consideration,
such an analysis may be best served if one labels the kind of high-level
experts, technocrats and kindred advisers as a nascent 'ruling class' in
advanced societies. But even Giddens does not consider the evidence in
the case of advanced capitalist or state socialist societies sufficient to
warrant such a conclusion.

In an attempt to delineate more clearly the unique characteristics of the
growing segment of the labor force in modern society which I have in a
general way designated as knowledge-based occupations, it is perhaps
helpful to clarify, first, their status with respect to knowledge itself, and,
secondly, their relation to clients and the institutions and sectors of the
economy in which they may be typically found. Finally, I would like to
offer a few preliminary observations about the nature of the advisory
process in which these occupations find themselves engaged daily in their
work.

I would like to define those who consult, provide guidance to others, counsel or give expert advice, as the group of occupations engaged in *transmitting* and *applying knowledge*. It is of course the case that the verbs 'transmit' and 'apply' usually convey a meaning which is not quite the meaning they ought to have in this discussion. In this instance, the terms 'transmit' and 'apply' do not mean that knowledge flows, is passed on or communicated in a manner which leaves it virtually untouched and unaffected by the work of knowledge-based occupations. On the contrary, the transmission and application of knowledge is an active process. The reproduction of knowledge involves almost invariably the production of knowledge. It is difficult not only not to learn in the process of applying knowledge (Dasgupta and Stoneman, 1987:3) but it is also virtually impossible to leave knowledge, as it is transmitted and applied, unaffected and untouched by this very process.

These first outlines of how knowledge-based occupations relate to the currency in which they deal, namely knowledge itself, is probably not very satisfactory. It is not very satisfactory because the outlines of what differentiates experts, counselors and advisers from other and larger segments of the labor force are still rather vague and inconclusive. For one thing, one can, of course, argue, perhaps must argue, that all occupations are somehow knowledge based. Knowledge is an anthropological constant. Knowledge has and always will play a role in all occupational activities, as it does in most other human activities. It is therefore important to further differentiate with respect to knowledge and the typical product or output.

There are several categories available which aim for distinctions of relevance here; for example, the distinction between theoretical and practical knowledge would appear to be such a distinction. That is to say, knowledge-based occupations would then refer to that growing part of the labor force which deals in theoretical knowledge. However, neither this nor similar distinctions are quite satisfactory because even occupations which may be said to deal in theoretical knowledge cannot do without practical knowledge. Thus, any distinction with respect to knowledge has to recognize from the beginning that certain practical craft-like skills and procedures are essential to all occupations. But the segment of the labor force of interest to us, above all, acquires, manipulates, organizes and communicates knowledge, more accurately knowledge about knowledge. That is to say also, that the typical product or output of knowledge-based occupations obviously is knowledge and not a technical artifact. The execution of the job is identical with the consumption of its outcome, namely knowledge.[21] Therefore there is, in contrast, the more traditional segment of the labor force which *leaves its knowledge in place*. In many instances, such knowledge cannot even be communicated, but can only be acquired by observation, imitation, participation or trial and error. Such

---

[21] The degree of control exercised over the work process depends, one might suggest with Larson (1977:26–27), on the lack of separation between work process and output (cf. also Whitley, 1988:401–404).

knowledge, *skills* would probably be a better term, manifests itself in, or better, is invested in artifacts, processes and products. Skills are robust, specific and concrete while knowledge, especially contemporary knowledge, is much more fragile, general and abstract.[22]

But the skills of workers and craftsmen (cf. Montgomery, 1979) and the knowledge of experts are functional equivalents with respect to the power (or functional autonomy) they confer on those who possess knowledge and skills. In short, the peculiar relation to knowledge of knowledge-based occupations has to do with the fact that knowledge itself becomes the focal point of its activity. But that activity is, of course, dependent in turn on skills not communicated but 'objectified' in the outcomes of the work experts, advisers and counselors do. For experts, advisers and counselors, knowledge is an *immediately productive force*. These distinctions make evident as well why the discussion of knowledge-based occupations is not germane to the debate about the transformation of the working class in capitalist society as the result of a de-skilling process of the labor force (Braverman, 1974) and similar efforts or critiques of attempts to revitalize the notion of class (e.g. Stark, 1980; Hunter, 1988).

In addition, it is important to emphasize that the group of occupations of interest in this context stands in a *peculiar relation* to the clients of the services offered by a 'knowledgeable' stratum (cf. Lerner, 1976). The labor and the knowledge claims of experts need to be legitimized. Experts derive their legitimacy from the relationships into which they enter and particularly from the recognition that comes from their clientele with its demand for the expertise of knowledge-based occupations. Bauman's important suggestion of treating the notion of 'intellectuals' as a structural element within a social configuration rather than as a category which has certain and possibly lasting intrinsic qualities, is therefore of theoretical interest, at least in an analogous sense, and deserves to be considered in some detail. His treatment of the role of the intellectual and of intellectual strategies in many ways is quite close to our terminology of advisers, experts and counselors. Bauman does not require, for example, that intellectuals be the producers of the knowledge they command. He suggests that social configurations which do have the intellectual category as their structural element are certain to possess at least four major characteristics.

> First, a major dependency among those which weave together into a major figuration in question is grounded in the socially produced incapacity of individuals (singly or in the groups they form) to conduct their life business on their own. Some stages of their life activity, material or spiritual, in their practical or ideational aspects, must be beyond their control, and hence they need advice, assistance or active interference of someone else.
>
> Secondly, this influence makes for a genuine dependency, as it casts the

----

[22] Collins (1993:105) notes that skills have to be learned by example, that is, they 'have to be transferred through interpersonal contact or "socialization" rather than through book learning'.

'helpers' close to the sources of uncertainty, and thus into a position of domination . . .

Thirdly, what the dominated are lacking . . . is knowledge or the resources to apply knowledge to their acts. By the same token, the dominating possess the missing knowledge, or mediate and control its distribution, or have at their disposal the resources needed to apply the knowledge they possess and to share the products of such application. The dominating are therefore sages, teachers, or experts.

Fourthly, the intensity and the scope of their domination depends on how acute is the sense of uncertainty or deprivation caused by the absence of knowledge in an area serviced by a given group of sages, teachers or experts. More importantly, it depends on the latter's ability to create or intensify such a sense of uncertainty or deprivation; to produce, in other words, the social indispensability of the kind of knowledge they control (Bauman, 1987:19–20).

In addition to Bauman's proposal to treat and examine intellectuals as part of a larger social configuration, it is important to emphasize further *relational structures* within which experts find themselves: (a) the relation of knowledge-based occupations to (socially constructed) forms and stocks of knowledge itself; and (b) their location in specific discourse communities of experts, advisers and counselors. That is, experts are not isolated individuals but derive and defend their claims to expertise by virtue of their membership and standing in communities of experts. Although the stratum of experts consists of various and increasingly larger communities of knowledge-based occupations, as a whole they do not form and cannot be analyzed as a *social class*. Even if one concedes that 'classes are never united' (Gouldner, 1979:31), knowledge-based occupations do not form a class. The social and political organization and consciousness of experts as experts simply does not exist in contemporary society. The variety of occupations which are knowledge based is very large and diverse indeed. Experts are found in all sectors of the economy and represent all levels of inequality. One cannot even treat experts as part of some social movement. It is simply an open question, and will remain open, whether the kind of tasks and for whom one performs these skills is still a crucial, let alone sufficient, source of political solidarity in modern society.

I assume that the knowledge these occupations employ is not, under most circumstances, directly of their creation. That is, these occupations serve as mediator between the knowledge producers and the knowledge users, between those who create a capacity for action and those whose job it is to take action. There are, of course, instances in which the function of knowledge producer and knowledge transmitter is, by and large, carried out by the same individual. But the peculiar relationship that experts create or are expected to maintain does not imply, as emphasized already, that their function is somehow limited to that of mediation in the narrow and perhaps even neutral sense of a simple flow of information from a source to a receiver. Their function is, in other words, by no means passive; they are not merely convenient and efficient vehicles transmitting knowledge. On the contrary, it can be assumed that their influence, as well as their esteem, derives from the transformative activity they perform.

What is meant by the metaphor of an active transfer of knowledge by knowledge-based occupations becomes more precise if one considers the various meanings of the Latin verb *consultare*. Heinz Eulau (1973:169) has examined this verb in some detail and describes its associated meanings, depending on the context in which the term is used.

> The term *consultare* means to consider, deliberate, cogitate, reflect, think over, advise with, take advice from, and so on. The variety of these meanings is less helpful, however, than the meanings of the more primitive Latin verb *consulere*, which directly calls attention to the reciprocal character of the consulting relationship. On the one hand, *consulere* means to ask questions, or examine; on the other hand, it means to give counsel. The reciprocity appears even stronger in the German translation of *consulere* where it simultaneously means to ask someone (*jemanden befragen*) and to advise someone (*jemanden beraten*) . . . Interestingly, *consultare* refers to a second family of meanings that define the consulting relationship. In some contexts, *consultare* is used as a synonym for *curare* – to care for or worry about – and for *prospicere* – to provide for. In this usage, then, both an empathetic and a providential aspect of consultation are emphasized. Thirdly, the related adjective *consultus* – one who is consulted – may be used as a synonym for *intellegens*, *peritus* or *eruditus* – intelligent, expert and learned; and the process to which *consultus* applies is supposed to be *dilegens* or *accuratus* – careful or accurate.

The varied meanings of the verb *consultare* already signify how manifold and complex the process of consultation is and how entangled the cognitive and social relations of the participants and practitioners in practice are.

Most importantly, however, knowledge-based occupations should not be seen as passive media obtaining, collating, systematizing or in some other way neutrally 'operating' on knowledge and then transmitting that knowledge to various publics. Of course, they engage in all those activities. But the outcome is that their work on knowledge changes it. Knowledge is never an unproblematic 'currency' which can be easily exchanged. The exchange controls and restrictions are often formidable and enforced. Experts selectively invoke their interpretation of knowledge. Therefore, the definition of the priorities of action and the definition of the situation by clients is often mandated by experts consulted for advice. The knowledge which is passed on, in some way, undergoes changes as it is transmitted. Experts transmit and apply knowledge but they do so in an active fashion. It is this activity which needs to be examined quite closely for the transformative activity is one of the keys to any comprehensive and systematic understanding of the function and conditions for the demand for experts and their knowledge in advanced societies.

Institutions and expertise

Not only are the processes by which, and the knowledge in which, experts deal often taken for granted, but equally unexplored are the institutional contexts within which knowledge is employed, and how these contexts may, in turn, affect the very mediation between knowledge, social action and the kind of authority knowledge may have. And from a socio-historical and comparative point of view, we have but limited insights into the changing roles and cognitive strategies employed by experts, counselors and advisers in response to changing social and intellectual conditions.

Germane observations may be found in Bauman's (1987) study of changing intellectual practices. He distinguishes between modern and post-modern experiences which correspond to distinct views of the (social) world, one in which order is thought to be possible and the other, the post-modern view of the world, in which an almost unlimited number of models of order is seen as a lasting attribute of the world. The corresponding intellectual practices are, according to Bauman, best described with the help of the metaphor of the 'legislator', in the case of the modern world, and that of the role of the 'interpreter' in the post-modern world. More precisely, the most characteristic strategy of the *modern* intellectual practice 'consists of making authoritative statements which arbitrate in controversies of opinions and which select those opinions which, having been selected, become correct and binding', while the

> typically post modern strategy of intellectual work . . . consists of translating statements, made within one community based tradition, so that they can be understood within the system of knowledge based on another tradition. Instead of being oriented towards selecting the best social order, this strategy is aimed at facilitating communication between autonomous (sovereign) participants (Bauman, 1987:5).

Whether the primary intellectual strategy in a world characterized by multiple and incompatible but legitimate world-views is, in fact, mediation and translation generally or only that of having a small 'elite' of inter-preters remains an empirical question, as is the possibility that one of the characteristic features of post-modernity is a decline in the authority of experts or a legitimation crisis which may go hand in hand with the appearance of uncertainty. None the less, the distinction between modern and post-modern experiences which Bauman advances is useful because it alerts us to the possibility that the role of experts has changed, perhaps even considerably, depending, for example, on the nature of the knowledge-based resources they are able to call on and the nature of the social context they are expected to serve. At the same time, different strategies may co-exist within the same period of time and result in distinct modes of conflict among experts, as well as between clients and experts. Bauman's observations suggest also that it might be important to attempt to reconstruct, from available records, how the advisory process may have functioned in the past.

Historically, the function and authority of knowledge, as well as the type of knowledge, varies from institution to institution. Max Weber ([1922] 1968:29), as indicated already, has described modern political power and the type of social organization which supports and sustains political power as a type of 'authority based on knowledge'. At the same time, Weber ([1922] 1968:994) recognizes certain limits to political authority which is based on knowledge, in particular, 'the expert knowledge of private economic interest groups in the field of "business" is superior to expert knowledge of the bureaucracy. This is so because the exact knowledge of facts in their field is of direct significance for economic survival.' Private enterprise, Weber argues, is relatively immune to the intervention of bureaucratic authority. Effective intervention by the state in the capitalist epoch into the spheres of business and commerce is restricted and often takes on unanticipated consequences. Private enterprise is able to guard 'secrets', as a means of power, much more closely while the consequences of 'errors' in judgment are immediate and severe, paid for by losses or, in the extreme, the very existence of the business.

The resource of knowledge generates conflicts between experts and their clients. Whether the conflict between counselors, advisers and experts, on the one hand, and practical politicians, on the other hand, being for example,

> over and over again represented by the latter as a conflict between those who think they 'know better' and hence would have no scruples in forcing their ideals down the throats of those whom they rule, and the politicians, pragmatists by nature, who beware of moving forward too fast for the 'people' to follow them, and who put the 'art of the possible' above any stiff doctrine (Bauman, 1987:105).

is, indeed, the best description of the nature of the conflict between these groups remains to be examined empirically. Bauman's description of the conflict between experts and politicians, however, does point to the need to carefully analyze the contingent (situational) features faced by each of the two groups as a source of potential conflict between them.

Conditions for the growth of experts

Discussion among social scientists of the need for and the place of expertise in modern society generally is an established theme of theoretical analysis. It is linked, moreover, to the analysis of the rise of science and industrialization and the consequences both are seen to have for the social structure, culture and politics of society, specifically, and the very fabric of social relations, generally. The analysis over the years is affected by salient historical events and trends discerned by social scientists, for example, the rise and defeat of fascism, and the emergence of state socialism and its economic failure. The views of social scientists oscillate between hope for and fear of experts, professionals, intellectuals and knowledge workers in these changing historical situations, and are crucial forces for society. In addition, the discussion easily falls victim to the assumption that the reasons for and the result of the growth of knowledge-bearing occupations is a drive for efficiency and a growth in rationalization.

First, I will try to collect a variety of often imaginative perspectives that share the goal of accounting for the growing presence of knowledge-based occupations in modern society. It will become clear, however, that discussions about the conditions that may give rise to the growth of knowledge-based occupations can hardly be separated from observations about the functions experts, counselors and advisers are, according to a variety of perspectives, assumed to fulfill in modern society.

In the inter-war years, the British sociologists Carr-Saunders and Wilson (1933:485–486), in a discussion of the role of the professions, animated by an almost undiluted faith in the disinterestedness of the professional, emphasized the special, societal significance of expert knowledge for the very survival of modern democracy:

> The association between scientific inquiry and the art of government has become a prime necessity. Knowledge is power. Authority without knowledge is powerless. Power dissociated from knowledge is a revolutionary force. Unless the modern world works out a satisfactory relationship between expert knowledge and popular control the days of democracy are numbered.

The state has to establish proper relations with the professions as their main source of knowledge and 'a right relationship between knowledge and power is the central problem of modern democracy.'

But despite the vigorous call for the knowledgeable professions to serve the state and for the state to establish good relations with the professions, it remains ambiguous why the state (increasingly) needs the knowledge controlled by professionals, what knowledge the state might find useful in the first place, and why the professions are capable of controlling the knowledge the state requires to survive. However, the corrective the professions were seen to offer at the time, not only to Carr-Saunders and Wilson, but also to reformers such as Emile Durkheim ([1950] 1957), R.H. Tawney (1920), and C.S. Peirce, is one which resonates with the unrelenting change brought about by capitalism. That is, concerned, even stunned, by the tempo of social change generated by the economy in the first part of this century, advocates of the professions

> depicted the backdrop of commerce and industry as a scene of such unrelieved selfishness that once the professional was thrust into the foreground he could hardly fail to look selfless in comparison . . . Since the market released individuals from what were perceived as healthy and proper social obligations, the reformers identified capitalism with individualism, and morality with the restoration of communal bonds. On all counts, the professions seemed to offer solutions to the problem of self-interest, and for that reason professionalization could seem a cultural reform of vital importance (Haskell, 1984:186).

Similarly, the work of Karl Mannheim ([1929] 1936, [1935] 1940), in its different phases (cf. Kettler et al., 1984), echoes, despite its ambivalence, the hope that intellectuals or planners may come to the rescue of the political sphere which is under siege and attack from different and destructive forces.

In the 1960s, social scientists once again turned to the analysis of 'experts' or, more to the point, the representatives of 'technical rationality' and their pervasive and apparently irreversible dominance of all spheres of society, including a 'scientification' of politics and, therefore, the end of politics because technical necessities transplant political decisions (cf. Habermas, [1968] 1971). Both Helmut Schelsky (1961) and Herbert Marcuse (1964), on the right and the left of the political spectrum respectively, painted the picture of the dawn of a 'technical state' as the outcome of the dominance and authority of science and technology and, therefore, the power of experts silencing all other voices and purposes, other than those given by technical rationality itself.

But what all these divergent 'expert' conceptions about the hopeful or dangerous role of 'experts' share, despite their many differences, is a largely uncritical and unexamined conception of the nature and source of the expertise. Moreover, all these theoretical visions also agree, as is evident in the ensuing 'technocracy debate' (cf. Koch and Senghaas, 1970) in Germany in the early 1960s for example, that the power of expertise is, in the end, in modern society an overwhelming force to be reckoned with. Depending on how the holders of expertise are conceptualized, the likelihood that they will, even against the will of other groups, assume the center position in the core institutions in which decisions ought to be or will be made in modern society, is widely taken for granted. In addition to sharing a largely scientistic conception of knowledge, these varied, sometimes hopeful, at others times skeptical, examinations of the virtue and function of expertise have in common also an 'elitist' conception of experts; that is to say, there are usually assumed to be but a few experts, at least those who really count are rather small in number, and those few typically migrate to the top of the relations of power and authority in society. For the most part, even the more recent relevant literature which makes its topic the unprecedented growth of knowledge, takes the demand for such knowledge for granted, or simply postulates, but leaves unanalyzed, the growth in the use of knowledge and, therefore, the increase in knowledge-based services. Much of the literature reiterates confidently a linear relation between the extent to which the 'amount' of knowledge increases, often seen as a cumulative process, with the corresponding growth of ignorance, at least among most segments of the population of modern society (e.g. Merton, 1975).

Another example of broad and confident assertions which fail to raise, let alone analyze, the issue of the reasons and conditions for the growth of expert knowledge is the bold and ultimately uninformative assertion by Stich and Nisbett (1984:236) that it is the hallmark 'of an educated and reflective person that he recognizes, consults, and defers to authority on a wide range of topics'. It is, therefore, in an even more general sense, simply an essential and quite straightforward feature of the evolution of civilization, as represented by an incessant increase in the complexity and volume of knowledge, that individuals are increasingly forced or constrained to defer, on more and more issues, to the judgment of experts.

Kenneth Boulding (1967:691–692), in contrast and in an analogy to the economic assertion that 'specialization without trade is useless', holds that the same principle applies to knowledge. Specialization in the production of knowledge permits greater productivity but if such growth is not accompanied by intellectual exchange relations, 'the bits of specialized knowledge do not add up to a total knowledge structure for mankind.' The conclusion becomes that the conditions for the necessity and growth of experts is related to the need to circulate or disseminate knowledge.

Georg Simmel ([1919] 1968:44) considered the immense growth in the quantity and impact of knowledge on the life of individuals to be a most salient feature of modernity.

> But, more important, the infinitely growing supply of objectified spirit places demands before the subject, creates desires in him, hits him with feelings of individual inadequacy and helplessness, throws him into total relationships from whose impact he cannot withdraw, although he cannot master their particular contents. Thus, the typically problematic situation of modern man comes into being: his sense of being surrounded by an innumerable number of cultural elements which are neither meaningless to him nor, in the final analysis, meaningful. In their mass they depress him, since he is not capable of assimilating them all, nor can he simply reject them, since after all, they belong *potentially* within the sphere of his cultural development.

Thus, under contemporary conditions, so much information is available that 'mere accessibility is not better than invisibility' (Dennett, 1986:145). But even a vague awareness of the potential availability of more and more knowledge affects individuals. The separation between the knower and the known is seen to accelerate. At the same time, the gap between the two also takes on different qualities and has novel social consequences.

Moreover, public policy is, Simmel ([1909] 1984:92–93) notes pessimistically, for the most part quite impotent or incapable of increasing the ability of the individual to absorb the rapidly growing complexity of modern culture. The discrepancy between 'subjective' and 'objective' culture could perhaps be lessened by measures of the state which may be designed to enable individuals 'to turn the experienced objective culture faster and more reliably than heretofore into materials of the subjective culture that alone carries the definitive value of the former'. One may infer, therefore, that experts, counselors and advisers perform urgently needed tasks in modern society and that the persistent growth in their ranks and functional importance corresponds to or signals a continuation of the trend in the gap between cultures Simmel noted at the turn of this century.

However, as suggestive as Simmel's assertions may in fact be, his observations about the place of expert advice in society and its apparently growing importance to most individuals does not satisfactorily address the question of the reasons and conditions for the apparently increasing social utility of experts and of the various social consequences this may in fact have.

On the most general plane, possible answers to a search for the *conditions for the possibility* of a rapid demand for expert advice in many social institutions and situations, including many contexts in everyday life, might be linked to the nature and tempo of the development of technical-scientific knowledge, especially as it is rapidly translated into practice and therefore becomes quickly relevant to social practices and increasingly even transforms and dominates such practices. Taken to the extreme, perhaps the demand for expertise is a function of the production of expertise, and presumably, the success in generating or transforming social conditions in the image of such 'expertise'. The demand for experts in a society which is becoming increasingly a society molded by science could be seen, in this sense at least, to be self-generating; that is, more and more decisions call for the rhetoric of rationality and efficiency which science and technology promise (cf. Nowotny, 1979:119).

An analogous and relevant thesis is advanced by Peter Drucker who argues that the crucial reason for the observed increase in the demand for knowledgeable employees, and perhaps, therefore, for the shift to a knowledge society, has nothing to do with more exacting and complex job skills and subsequent adjustments in the demand for such qualifications by employers. Rather, Drucker considers such a hypothesis merely a widely held myth. The effective reason for the considerable growth in job skills and knowledge is linked, according to Drucker, to the immense increase in the working life span of individuals. Thus, it is not so much the *demand* for labor and particular skills, but the *supply* of highly skilled labor that underlies the transformation of society into a knowledge society. In other words, the thesis Drucker (1969:84) expounds, a variation of the theorem of Jean-Baptiste Say that every supply creates its own demand, is that 'the arrival of the knowledge worker changed the nature of jobs. Because modern society has to employ people who expect and demand knowledge work, knowledge jobs have to be created. As a result, the character of work is being transformed.' Drucker proposes therefore a kind of 'supply side explanation' of the transformation of industrial society into knowledge society. Higher-educated entrants into the labor force expect upgraded jobs,[23] but the extension of education is itself a reflection of a drastic lengthening of work life expectancy. The dramatic growth in the average number of years spent in schools, apprenticeships and various other learning institutions, such as colleges and universities, since the Second World War has altered irreversibly the 'supply of labor'.[24]

By the same token, the growth of the social utility of experts may be a response to profound changes in the social organization of society, in particular, its escalating rationalization, social differentiation, segmentation and compartmentalization. Increasing rationalization implies an escalation

---

[23] 'Long years of schooling make a person unfit for anything but knowledge work' (Drucker, 1969:284).

[24] Drucker must first have developed the supply-side account of the growth of knowledge-based labor in 1969 since only a year or two earlier he advocated the more conventional account of the relation between education and the labor market in an essay which deals with the nature of technology and society in the twentieth century. For in this context Drucker (1967:27) argues that the 'stress on education is creating a changed society; access to education is best given to everyone, if only *because society needs* all the educated people it can get' (my emphasis).

in societal complexity and, at least according to many observers, that decisions about normative solutions to everyday problems or the technical availability of relevant objects have to take a 'detour' via science and technology since they cannot be extracted directly from the repertoire of solutions and resources of everyday life (e.g. Habermas, [1968] 1971). Greater differentiation goes hand in hand with a much more complex distribution of social knowledge. It reduces the accessibility of many parts of social knowledge because these parts become, at best, only relevant under special conditions. In situations which do not recur frequently, access to knowledge or the need to know is mediated by relevant advisers and counselors who deal in those context-related stocks of knowledge suddenly of urgent relevance to an actor or group of actors; or, as others have suggested (e.g. Weingart, 1979), the expansion of the functions of the state increasingly takes over experts, even produces needs for experts and advisers to serve the state, for example, within new areas of regulation, or within traditional fields of governmental practice.

But even before the recent attention, among political scientists, of possibilities of ungovernability, of an overload of governmental capacities or of a de-legitimation of the state (cf. Birch, 1984)[25] as a result of the increasing demand for and growing responsibilities of the state, social theorists assigned a special role in society to the professions or similar groups. The professions were seen, under certain conditions, as an effective answer to the crises of liberal democratic societies and as a much needed barrier against moral disorganization in the form of excessive individualism in modern society. T.H. Marshall (1939), in the inter-war years, saw the professions as 'exemplars and bulwarks of social stability', while Parsons (e.g. 1968) assigned to them, in the post-war years, the functions previously fulfilled by religion and its social organization. The inability or ineffectiveness of the modern state, in the face of growing demands to intervene, leads Halliday (1987:28), on the other hand, to expect that the state may volunteer, or be forced to delegate, responsibilities to the professions. But these and kindred observations tend to be restricted by their very focus, the role of professionals.

Finally, theoretical ideas pertaining to questions about the conditions for the growth of knowledge-bearing occupations in modern society not infrequently designate knowledge itself as the motor of an accelerating demand for special intellectual skills. But such a link is both a dubious and attractive proposition. It is dubious because it may well amount to a circular proposition. As well, the same thesis resonates closely with the now discredited 'internalist' account of the dynamics of science. Yet it is, despite its simplicity, attractive because it raises the possibility that the growth of knowledge is self-sustained, at least at the juncture where the knowledge-producing institutions have reached a certain critical mass in society.

---

[25] I will analyze the thesis of the growing ungovernability of modern societies in Chapter 9.

None the less, linking the growth of knowledge-disseminating labor merely to the growth in the quantity as well as a more and more differentiated stock of knowledge fails to inquire, as I have stressed, into the nature of the knowledge in demand. In addition, the sources of the demand itself have to be examined as well as the possibility that such demand is not merely the result of a growth of knowledge itself. In the latter case, useful suggestions in fact already exist. They are perspectives that produce a shift in the focus of sociological inquiry concerned with the transformation of the economy in modern society. Emphasis increasingly is on economic processes driven by symbolic rather than material input and knowledge as an immediately productive force that displaces the traditional means of production which dominated industrial society.

The functions of expertise

At least two general approaches are imaginable in response to the question of the social function of advice in society. One approach might examine the function of advice for the individual recipients of counsel while the second would attempt to gain insights into the function of advice by employing a more macro-sociological analysis. These points of departure in fact may not lead to incompatible accounts because the two levels of analysis refer to interrelated phenomena. However, the conception individuals subjectively may have about their reasons for seeking advice may well differ considerably from those which one could theoretically assign to the expertise and counsel on a macro-sociological plane. Similarly, the self-conception of the knowledge-bearing occupations may differ from those one may be able to assign to this segment of the labor force on the basis of a particular theory of society.

In the latter tradition, some observers have spoken of modern society as a society which has rapidly been transformed from a 'performance' to a 'learning' society. In a performance society individuals will practice in adulthood skills which were acquired in youth. In a learning society, abilities and skills are practiced in adulthood which were not acquired in youth. Instead, one might expect to have several distinct careers within the course of one lifetime (Anderson and Moore, 1969). Given the assumption of the rapid obsolescence of (occupational) skills in modern society, one function of the various occupations offering counsel and advice could be to provide direction in precisely these circumstances, including the training of further experts. In many circumstances, it is, given this perspective, the accelerating tempo with which knowledge, perhaps more importantly, *knowledge in need of interpretation*, develops which forms the motor for the rising demand for advice and guidance by individuals whose ability to adapt to what are novel circumstances is challenged repeatedly.

Everett C. Hughes (1958:141) describes the person who seeks out advice in the following straightforward manner: 'The client comes to the pro-

fessional because he has met a problem which he cannot himself handle.'
The apparently simple equation to which Hughes' observation alerts us is
the distinct possibility, easily discounted in the context of a discussion
which continually stresses the growth in the volume of knowledge and its
relevance to most affairs of everyday life, that learning in advanced
societies often does not result in the acquisition of even elementary
cognitive skills, let alone additional mental abilities, enabling us to
independently cope with the intellectual requirements of many situations.

A discussion of the number of individuals in advanced societies who are
functionally illiterate serves as a useful reminder that the growth in the
stratum of experts, advisers and counselors may, paradoxically, be partly
the outcome of the practical inefficiency of those charged with imparting
these skills. The failure at the level of learning potentially represents a gain
of a larger clientele at the other end. If the conditions for the growth of
experts are indeed the outcome of the ineffectiveness of 'experts', or the
failure of teachers and others to transmit the necessary knowledge and
cognitive skills necessary for acquiring a measure of intellectual independence, any empirical analysis ought to be able to shed some light on this
possibility by examining the composition of the experts' clientele,
especially by examining the proportion of repeat clients among all clients.
If experts do not create, in the sense just discussed, their own clientele, one
has to consider the possibility that experts themselves manage to produce a
demand for the knowledge or the services they offer. In either case, the
omnipresent notion of a diffusion of knowledge to the population at large,
which is such a large part of democratic utopias, would require a
fundamental correction.

The attempt by Claus Offe (1984) to provide a *functional* definition of
the service sector of the economy may prove to be helpful for a definition
of the general function of knowledge-based occupations in society. Offe
distinguishes between two basic functions which have to be fulfilled in
society: (a) the need to physically reproduce and assure the survival of
society (this function is accomplished in the producing sector of the
economy); and (b) the need to culturally reproduce the forms and
conditions under which efforts directed at the physical reproduction of
society are accomplished. These activities secure the 'infrastructure' and
the 'cultural resources' of a society which provide the societal frame within
which physical reproduction takes place. This latter function is performed
by service occupations of all kinds, ranging from physicians and security
men/women and sales personnel to artists and teachers. The common
denominator of service occupations, according to Offe (1984:233), is,
therefore, the social construction and maintenance of the specific institutional and cultural preconditions (for example, the nature of exchange
relations).[26] Service occupations not only maintain the stock of knowledge

[26] As is the case for any functional definition, this attempt too has its difficulties with the
dynamic dimension of its object, although Offe (1984:233) suggests that his definition of the

in society but add to it. The plausibility of Offe's definition of the function of service occupations rests to a considerable extent on the distinction between symbolic (reflexive) and material (producing) occupational tasks as is already evident from his categorization of reflexive work as part of the service sector and productive work as part of the industrial sector of the economy. Symbolic and material work may not constitute some kind of hierarchy but exists in reciprocal dependence, as Offe (1984:235) stresses. None the less, the two forms of work are conceived as largely mutually exclusive activities – and as such representative of distinctive functional activities. Service occupations *maintain* while material work *produces*. Such a distinction and definition of the societal function of service work has the drawback that it is linked too closely to the nature of industrial society. The differentiation, for example, does not allow for a mixing of tasks and functions. It therefore fails to be cognizant of the possibility that many occupations require the manipulation of symbols even if they are located in the industrial sector of the economy because material production in the sense of any direct transformation of nature is less and less characteristic of production. In addition, the conflation of knowledge-producing and knowledge-disseminating tasks produces a rather undifferentiated category of 'symbolic' work.

The classic empirical studies which have shown and pointed critically to the fact that experts and expertise may at times merely serve to provide and underscore the legitimacy of goals or decisions previously taken by officials who ask for advice (e.g. Wilensky, 1956, 1971), perhaps can be subsumed under the function of providing 'cultural resources'. But the possibility of such a categorization only indicates how ambivalent as well as suggestive the notion of 'cultural resources' happens to be. The functions advisers, experts and counselors perform in advanced society can best be conceptualized as rather diverse and varied. They may include such tasks as resolving conflicts among contending parties, or providing legitimacy for decisions taken in controversial debates, for example, in the case of serious disputes about the development of nuclear energy in which expert knowledge is employed as a symbolic medium for the resolution of fundamental social conflicts (cf. Nowotny, 1979:25–28) and as a basis for legitimizing decisions ultimately arrived at. If knowledge-based occupations in modern society can be said to perform any specific function rather than a most diverse range of purposes, it has to be the function of providing capacities for action to those who desire or require knowledge.[27]

So, in more concrete terms, knowledge-bearing occupations perform

---

function of service occupations in modern society can somehow accommodate aspects other than the static features of the service sector of the economy.

[27] The perspectives under which knowledge-bearing occupations dispense knowledge may be a clue for the function(s) these occupations assign to themselves. An example of such a model would be the 'therapeutic' model of the 'helping-healing-human service professions', in which 'the highly directive, authoritarian, and manipulative application of knowledge is made legitimate through the healing, curative intent' (Holzner and Marx, 1979:322).

many significant functions, for example, the formation and transformation of individual identities, or more mundane needs, for example, dispensing advice on activities ranging from taxes, travel arrangements, investment opportunities, housing alternatives, clothing choices, preventive health measures and marriage contracts.

Finally, Holzner and Marx (1979) propose an *institutional* approach to the analysis of the centrality of knowledge to modern society. Although the application of knowledge to human problems is by no means a novel phenomenon, according to Holzner and Marx what is unique in contemporary society is 'the emergence of role statuses and processes self-consciously and intentionally designed to link the production-discovery of new knowledge with its application-use in a coherent, integrated, purposive, and pervasive knowledge system' (Holzner and Marx, 1979:17). While this image of how knowledge travels in modern society may well be too suggestive of largely planned, well-controlled and easily traceable routes of influence, it does indicate that the perception of knowledge is affected by the perception of the knowledge-bearing and disseminating, and not only knowledge-producing, occupations. But whether the developments sketched by Holzner and Marx (1979:18) 'go hand in hand with heightened public ambivalence about experts, scientists, professionals, and academics' remains, to a large extent, an empirical issue. As the same authors further indicate, the authority of experts 'in relation to practical affairs, programs, and problems is particularly under challenge. Nearly everyone has had a few frustrating encounters with the representatives of specialized, technical expertise. . . .' And since this indeed is an increasingly common perception, the question of the conditions for and the function of expertise in contemporary society becomes an even more pressing matter.

The culture of advice and expertise

Advisers, experts and counselors obviously perform multiple roles and functions; for example, they may be called to serve as witnesses, advocates, managers of crises and risks, referees, arbiters, judges, or simply as individuals who transmit knowledge in some fashion. Whatever the particular role they may be called upon to perform, of interest in this context is the routine manner and, at times, innovative ways in which counselors, advisers and experts provide their services in specific social settings.

Since the advisory process is a reciprocal one, involving a dual flow of 'messages', attention has to focus on a complex set of modes of conduct. Counselors advise someone on the basis of obtaining advice from someone else. Advisers and experts are part of a social configuration in which they not only relate to other individuals (and groups), but more importantly, to existing stocks of knowledge. Part of the analysis of the advisory process, therefore, is the way in which experts select, legislate, organize and transform knowledge in the course of pursuing their routine occupational or professional tasks.

In a preliminary sense, one can distinguish between formal and informal settings in which advice and expertise is offered and 'consumed' in some way. The extent to which settings are not explicitly mandated to offer advice and in fact, dispense expertise, is considerable in contemporary society. For example, the media are a resource for advice on many issues to readers, listeners and viewers. On the other hand, the advisory process is, of course, often embedded in a particular institutional pattern designed for the dispensation of knowledge-based services. In such a context, specific forms of knowledge are offered as pragmatically useful knowledge. However, earlier optimistic pronouncements to the contrary – in the form of theories which suggested the possibility of a fairly singular and homogeneous organizational and normative pattern for 'professional work' to evolve in modern society (e.g. Tawney, 1920; Parsons, 1939, 1968; Goode, 1957),[28] – these conceptions do not recognize the diversity of institutional settings and the range of persons who are engaged in counseling, consulting and advising.[29] Although the image of the disinterested professional retains some of its public credibility, more recent sociological theories concerned with the professions[30] emphasize the extent to which professionalization is a strategy to enlarge the autonomy, ensure dominance, control access to, and improve the social status of the occupations in question, rather than the extent to which professional activities are governed by a set of widely shared normative standards, which have the effect of subordinating self-interest to higher ends such as the welfare of the client or public interest, universalism, disinterestedness, the truth or technical competence and training (e.g. Johnson, 1972; Parkin, 1979; Willis, 1983; Haskell, 1984).

In his exposition of the ethos of science, Merton ([1942] 1973:275–276) stresses disinterestedness as a basic *institutional* norm of the professions,

[28] Very instructive in this context is Burton J. Bledstein's (1976:87) discussion of the 'professionalization of American lives', which he dates from the 1840s and which he defines as the comprehensive socio-cultural transformation of the identity of the middle class in the United States. The culture of professionalism 'emancipated the active ego of a sovereign person as he performed organized activities within comprehensive spaces. The culture of professionalism incarnated the radical idea of the independent democrat, a liberated person seeking to free the power of nature within every worldly sphere, a self-governing individual exercising his trained judgment in an open society.'

[29] A possibly typical institutional setting, if there is indeed a modal pattern even for the established professions, may not be of great assistance since the patterns of institutional forms within which knowledge-bearing occupations operate vary greatly even within societies, let alone among societies.

[30] In the 1960s a shift in the predominant emphasis and interest in the professions among social scientists took place. The general sense of approval, even the idea of moral superiority, of the role of the professions in society gave way to a view which emphasized failings as well (cf. Freidson, 1984:4–5), and began to exhibit considerable skepticism toward moral assumptions of the professions that once commanded wide assent.

however, 'disinterestedness is not to be equated with altruism nor interested action with egoism. Such equivalences confuse institutional and motivational analysis.' That is to say, a wide range of personal motives are compatible in principle, for instance, with the institutional control of the action of scientists.[31] One result of these changes in emphasis and interest is that the degree of theoretical agreement among social scientists about the nature of the professions has decreased considerably. Freidson (1984:5) goes so far as to conclude that 'scholarship concerned with the professions is in an intellectual shambles' and, therefore, a fresh approach broadening the domain of inquiry with respect to the occupations, the function and nature of the tasks they perform might be helpful.

Another outstanding characteristic of the functionalist theories of knowledge-based occupations, in the narrow sense of professions, has been to take for granted the knowledge the professions rely on and dispense. At best, a few abstract features of the knowledge base are highlighted, such as its 'systematic' character.

Predominant in the functionalist analysis of the professions is an examination of changes in the institutional setting of the advisory process. The prevailing institutional standard or setting against which developments in knowledge-bearing occupations have been analyzed is the theory of *bureaucracy*, on the one hand, and what can only be described as a *market-oriented model of professional work*, on the other. The prevailing assumption becomes that bureaucratic control and professional work, in particular, are incompatible (cf. Kornhauser, 1962; Glaser, 1964; Thompson, 1969; Eulau, 1973). From a variety of theoretical perspectives, the diagnosed decline in the autonomy and discretion of professional work is attributed to bureaucratic and managerial control, the corresponding decline in self-employment, and to an unfavorable demand for certain knowledge-based occupations. These conceptions then result in the notion of a generalized crisis which includes a revolt of certain segments among the clients of professionals (cf. Haug and Sussman, 1969), or perhaps, even the proletarianization or de-professionalization of the professions in contemporary society (cf. Johnson, 1972; Oppenheimer 1973; Haug, 1975; McKinley, 1982). As one analysis from a neo-Marxist perspective defines it, 'by proletarianization we are referring to the process through which the work activities of those occupying professional and specialist positions at lower levels of professional hierarchies within large legal and accounting offices, for example, are increasingly fragmented and routinized' (Clegg et al., 1986:192). Though other observers see the restriction in the ability of professionals to determine their client's agenda to be less severely affected, in this instance, however, only those in the upper positions of the

---

[31] Merton adds that the differentiation between 'institutional compulsives' and 'motives' is, as far as he is concerned, a significant, though largely implicit, conception of Marxist sociology.

professions can possibly be exempt from the general decline in the autonomy of the professions in modern society.[32]

The discovery of de-professionalization in the late 1960s and early 1970s coincided with the political demands of the day for a de-institutionalization and de-professionalization of knowledge. However, whether many professionals will become ordinary workers in contemporary society might rather be a function of the underlying theory of society and less a matter of actual developments in employment conditions of professionals. Ironically, many neo-Marxist views of a decline in the nature of the position of professionals take their cue from the market-oriented model of professional work. In addition, the notion of the alleged iron control of bureaucracy and the loss of discretion is, in all likelihood, at least in such a generalized manner, a myth of the potency of bureaucratized organization, probably perpetuated by bureaucracies themselves. Thus, other studies of professional occupations, though they use a similar theoretical perspective, come to a less dramatic conclusion and suggest that these positions do not generally face a significantly reduced range of discretion and autonomy (e.g. Derber, 1982). Moreover, the most eminent theorist of modern bureaucracy, Max Weber ([1922] 1968:225), did not conceptualize knowledge and bureaucratic organization as contradictory elements; on the contrary, he stressed that 'bureaucratic administration means fundamentally domination through knowledge.' Weber recognizes the structural similarities of workers and bureaucrats, namely that both are deprived of control over the means of production and subject to the control of the class of owners of the means of production. A study from a neo-Marxist perspective makes essentially the same claim:

> It is clear that certain professional occupations have considerable discretionary powers over the political and ideological determination of the bases of class struggle. However, it is important to note that this discretion is structurally subsumed by the economic relations of capital and is also limited to the particular institutional sphere which is accepted to be their professional domain (Clegg et al., 1986:193).

Industrial workers and employees of bureaucracies are not invariably members of the same class and they do not necessarily share the same interests. Nor is the structural location of professionals sufficiently homogeneous; as a matter of fact, it is 'characterized by a range of differentiated market and status positions for which there can be no common ground for class identification on the basis of interests' (Clegg et al., 1986:200). The logic of bureaucracies is, for the most part, based on technical expertise; the degree of technical knowledge that employees of bureaucracies command leads to their employment and advance in the organization. One should not simply assume, finally, that ordinary workers today are the

---

[32] It is no accident that these conclusions closely resonate with the de-skilling thesis diagnosed among industrial workers, as I discussed in Chapter 6.

same as ordinary workers of the dawn or the peak of the industrial age of a few decades ago.

What applies to industrial workers, namely, that in contemporary society they find themselves in a great diversity of workplaces, and are, at times, endowed with considerable discretion, which can be translated into influence and even power, surely not only holds for professionals but more generally also for the large groups of counselors, experts, advisers and consultants:

> Expert practitioners of various kinds generally have greater leverage in the market and at work than industrial workers do; but on a more privileged level they probably match manual workers in the diversity of work arrangements. Different professional groups vary greatly in the degree of autonomy they can maintain for individual practitioners and for the profession as a whole, and there are considerable differences in the power they derive from their respective places in the social division of labor (Rueschemeyer, 1986:127).

The advisory process should be an area of critical reflection and empirical research in need of more attention than has been the case in the past. Many issues remain to be examined. For example, the advisory process is subject to routinization because problems are repeatedly encountered and responses are institutionalized (cf. Berger and Luckmann, 1967). Evolving routines are an important object of study since they constitute the ways in which counselors and advisers deal with uncertainty, as genuinely new problems, for which no ready-made solution is at hand, are confronted (cf. Fox, 1967). Another issue which needs to be examined is, of course, the kinds of knowledge used by different groups of knowledge-based occupations. From the point of view of those who request and receive expert advice, prominent issues are related to the question of how experts are found, the credibility of the advice, what calculus is employed to determine the believability of experts, or on what basis judgment can and must be suspended about the counsel obtained. What is done when conflicting advice is obtained? Under what circumstances can one be discouraged from following expert advice? In other words, difficult questions of deference, disability, dominance, trust, control, disenchantment with expertise, personal autonomy, authority and power abound and in all likelihood will acquire greater practical importance in the future and often serve as a basis for social conflict in knowledge societies.

8

The Technical State

The capabilities (intellectual and material) of contemporary society are immeasurably greater than ever before – which means that the scope of society's domination over the individual is immeasurably greater than ever before.

(Herbert Marcuse, *One-dimensional Man*)

In the 1960s, although these conceptions had their intellectual predecessors, both conservative and neo-Marxist thinkers conjured up an image of the impending spiritless technical state as technical rationality extended its relentless influence to all sectors of modern life. The domination and closure achieved by science and technology were seen to mark the beginning of a singular type of society and the end of individual freedom and subjectivity. Individuals were thought to be in danger of being totally absorbed into a repressive set of productive relations and absolute domination exercised by the state with the help of new forms of control.

Attention will be drawn here to two prominent accounts of the possible rise, the internal make-up and the consequences of the technical state, namely, to Herbert Marcuse's influential statement of the theme found, most fully developed, in his *One-dimensional Man* (1964) and to Helmut Schelsky's thesis that advanced industrial society is a powerful instance of 'scientific civilization' as first expounded by him in a lecture in 1961 entitled 'Man in scientific civilization' (*'Der Mensch in der wissenschaftlichen Zivilisation'*). Though Marcuse and Schelsky stood for radically opposed political philosophies and goals, they arrived, in their description of the social consequences of modern science and technology, at essentially the same position.

Both descriptions are self-exemplifying in that they display some of the very intellectual practices, namely universality, control and prediction, the authors otherwise castigate as representative of a scientistic spirit out of control. Although Marcuse's and Schelsky's theories of advanced society are today essentially forgotten and rarely invoked when attention turns to the key features of modern society, especially its built-in flaws and risks, I will ask whether such amnesia is really justified. In addition, the vigorous debates among social scientists that the theories helped to generate at the time are still of interest as is the question of the reasons for the peculiar convergence in Marcuse's and Schelsky's intellectual positions. Among the most notable cognitive confluences is their conception of the nature of modern technology as an instrument of social and political action.

In Chapter 9 I will sketch some of the core attributes of the knowledge society; paradoxically, these attributes would appear to represent the realization of the implicit historical alternatives Marcuse and Schelsky had in mind when they warned about the social and cultural consequences of science and technology and the extension of the intellectual and material capacities of modern society. However, these features of society and effects on the life of many individuals come about as the result of, rather than despite, the penetration and transformation of contemporary social relations by scientific knowledge and technologies.

The scientific civilization

Schelsky's lecture is of considerable interest for a number of reasons. First, it represents one of the earliest theoretical efforts to chart the rising influence of science and technology on social life generally, and the political sphere in particular; in that respect it pre-dates, but is not referred to in, the later theories of post-industrial society or scientific-technical civilization, as developed outside Germany. Secondly, Schelsky's theory dealing with the 'scientification' of life initiated a vigorous and acrimonious intellectual dispute, which was confined for the most part to Germany, and is now known as the *technocracy debate*. The label chosen for the dispute indicates already that not all themes of Schelsky's theoretical polemic were taken up with equal vigor. Other topics found less resonance at the time but deserve more attention today. The questions and warnings which found immediate resonance were those related to the emergence of the politics and political culture, or better, the lack of such a superstructure in the case of the technical state. Thirdly, the theory of scientific civilization represents the effort of a more conservative social scientist and social philosopher to state his political concerns about the impending loss of individual autonomy and freedom as the result of the spread of technical rationality throughout societal institutions, while Marcuse's views, of course, are those of a more radical social and political thinker who, in a way, shares Schelsky's fears. It is remarkable, therefore, to see the extent to which the two accounts of the impact of science and technology on modern society converge in the end. The two theorists appear at least to have no difficulty in agreeing on the conditions for the possibility of the emergence and the dangers represented by the technical state.

In the 1960s, both Schelsky's and Marcuse's conceptions resonated quite closely with themes which dominated intellectual discourse, namely the power and authority that humans exercise over humans and reflections on how such power could perhaps be eradicated either substantially or completely. Both Marcuse and Schelsky pondered ways in which this might be achieved; although the kind of social transformation in authority relations they anticipated did not find much affirmative response, their views did pertain, none the less, to one of the governing themes of intellectual and political discourse of the day. Perhaps this also accounts for the partial convergence of their conceptions and the vigorous interest extended in debate to both theories.

Schelsky enumerates what he considers to be the most salient and consequential outcomes of the growing impact on society of science and technology. In each case, the list, which is reproduced fully below, is preceded by the question of 'What does it mean that. . .?' But his listing is linked to what he considers to be the elementary proposition of his analysis, which he also describes as basic anthropological fact, namely the increasing 'scientification of our world and life in it' (p. 5).[1] However, these developments are still accompanied by widely held views about the function of science and technology in society, which Schelsky considers to be rather dubious conceptions. That is to say, the perceived view of the role of science in society, which can be traced to the Enlightenment or is mediated by nineteenth-century natural scientific positivism, must be replaced by a comprehensive theory which proceeds from and is based on the assumption that the pervasive scientification of our existence requires a completely new understanding of the role of science in the context of the relation between man and world.

The questions raised by such a point of departure for a theory of society, of course, have to be: what specific changes occur in society as the result of the increased impact of science and technology, for example, in the thinking and acting of individuals and groups, and the world-views they hold? And what does a scientific civilization look like in general terms? As indicated, Schelsky provides us with an extensive enumeration of consequences which read as follows: What does it mean that . . .

- 'Natural' illnesses are increasingly replaced by civilizational diseases?
- Death is no longer experienced as a matter of inevitable fate of human existence but as a technical accident?
- The birth of children is more and more the outcome of voluntary decision-making?
- The material needs of humans are increasingly satisfied on the basis of artificial products?
- The organic or natural is replaced successively by artificial products?
- Humans are more and more threatened by man-made processes?
- Disputes about social issues do not revolve around the question of existential minimum anymore but participation in civilizational needs?
- Man lives increasingly in an artificial environment?
- Natural conditions and nature become administrative objects?
- Humans no longer perceive themselves as subjects limited or restricted by nature (for example, man transcends natural limits of movement and sense experience)?

---

[1] For the sake of simplicity, I will give only the page reference to Schelsky's lecture when I cite him specifically in the subsequent discussion of his views.

- Power based on technology has become the destructive force of mankind?
- There is an unlimited threat to men of man-made scientific-technological weapons?
- Personal experiences are rarely immediate experiences?
- Human abilities are objectified increasingly in machines and technical devices?
- Increasingly, political and economic decisions and processes are subject to rational calculation (that means, decisions are more and more based on deductive reasoning)?
- Social technologies are employed increasingly to manipulate the psyche and social relations?
- Institutions and configurations of the 'objective spirit' are planned today and deliberately designed?
- Space is incorporated into production?

With a few exceptions, and these tend to be relatively unimportant components, the list is formulated as a catalogue of social 'losses' due to scientific-technological change. As a result, there can be no doubt as to the standpoint of the author himself; he is rather skeptical, even pessimistic about the impending era of scientific civilization. The list of consequences can be reduced to a basic or general feature of scientific civilization. However, in order to characterize the essential characteristic of scientific civilization, it would be helpful to know what image of society Schelsky employs as a contrasting model. Yet, the type of society he uses as the contrast emerges as but a faint shadow; what he must have had in mind appears to be a much more traditional form of society because the operating term he uses in efforts to create the contrast always happens to contain the adjective 'natural', as in 'naturally occurring conditions' and 'natural forces'. Finally, Schelsky refers to 'naturally evolved historical institutions' (p. 13). In explicating the dichotomy, he refers to Gotthart Günther, who defines the frequent reference to 'nature' that Schelsky employs as follows: 'Living consciousness understands nature in its essential being as incomprehensible contingency, a super-human realm of unmutable laws and a self-contained being which existed prior to all consciousness and individual being.'

The dominant world-view prior to scientific civilization, therefore, is a dualistic conception of society, individual and nature in which individuals were virtually helpless victims in the face of natural conditions and constraints. Modern technology, then, constitutes a world-historical break in the unbalanced relation of man and nature; as a result, this relation is almost reversed. More precisely, for Schelsky, *modern* technology represents not merely an adaptive capacity to the constraints of nature, but a reconstruction of nature by society, and therefore of society, with the aid of man-made technology. In the context of modern technology, man no longer confronts nature with the assistance of organs aided, improved and developed in their capacity by technology, but on the basis of a 'detour' via the brain, or the application of theoretical knowledge in practical contexts. The outcome is that, using the language Schelsky employs, 'artificial' nature as well as an 'artificial' change of man himself becomes a fact, that is, the result is a 're-construction and re-creation of man . . . in his corporeal, psychological and social existence' (p. 16). In short, we produce, as Schelsky stresses, 'the scientific civilization not only as technology but necessarily also in a much broader sense continually as "society" and as "soul" ' (p. 17). Modern technology changes the relations of man to nature, to himself and to others. The result of this dual transformation is the 'circulation of self-determined production' (p. 16), which is the real foundation of scientific civilization according to Schelsky. The self-regulated and self-propelled nature of this process (*Eigengesetzlichkeit*), the constant production and reproduction, evolves into a self-steering process which does not appear to allow for any escape. In addition, Schelsky describes the self-propelled development of scientific civilization as follows:

> Every technical problem and every technical solution invariably becomes also a social, a psychological issue because the self-propelled nature of this process, created by man, confronts humans as a social and psychological dictate which in turn requires nothing but a technical solution, a solution planned and executed by man since this is the nature of the condition to be tackled (pp. 16–17).

Modern technology represents a particular logic and this logic necessarily becomes the dominant logic of human life. One of the significant consequences of such a conception of technology is that the traditional 'logic' of technology reverses itself. That is, technology as a producer of mere means of human action becomes a producer of ends or meaning, or what is but the same, 'means' of action determine its ends and prefigure the direction of social change. Schelsky describes technology as an intellectual process which dissects varied natural objects into their elementary parts in order to re-assemble them according to the principle of the least effort or maximum efficiency. The result of modern technological construction, therefore, is a novel product or process with *artificial* features and, in analogy, an *artificial* human being.

It is noteworthy that Schelsky's prophecy about the role of technology does not extend to technology's ability to lessen or even resolve the dilemma at the heart of economic affairs, namely, the problem of distributing scarce resources, because a technocratic consciousness may well presume economic solutions first (cf. Ulrich, 1987:157). That is to say, others have focused on this point and have maintained that our age may become an age of endless surpluses, which more or less automatically provide solutions to those aspects of political life concerned with conflicts about the allocation of scarce resources. However, Schelsky is for the most part silent on matters related to production and preoccupied with matters of ideology.

Schelsky makes use, of course, although for the most part implicitly of a long conservative, romantic, intellectual tradition of a particularly critical and skeptical analysis of the impact of technology and science on culture and social relations. These critics of science and technology have long expressed severe reservations about the forces unleashed by technology, the destruction it leaves in its path and the range of ideologies it may serve. A single example may suffice.

Georg Simmel refers in his *The Philosophy of Money* ([1907] 1978) as well as in a number of his essays to the existence of a 'tragedy of culture'. Simmel employs this term to refer to the objectification of human products, especially cultural creations, and its psychological and social consequences. Thus, he diagnoses the probability of deep estrangement in modern society between the creative processes of individuals and their contents or products. Simmel observes that there is an evident parallel to the 'fetishism' Marx assigned to the appearance of economic commodities. But the fetishism of commodities is only a special case of this general fate of contents of culture. With the increase in culture these contents more and more stand under a paradox: they were originally created by subjects and for subjects: but in their intermediate form of objectivity, which they take on in addition to the two extreme instances, they follow an immanent logic of development. In so doing they estrange themselves from their origin as well as their purpose. They are impelled not by physical necessity but by truly cultural ones (which, however, cannot pass over the physical conditions). What drives forth the products of the spirit is the cultural and not the natural scientific logic of the objects. Herein lies the fatefully immanent drive of all technology as soon as it has moved beyond the range of immediate consumption. Thus the industrial production of a variety of products generates a series of closely related by-products for which, properly speaking, there is no need. It is only the compulsion for full utilization of the created equipment that calls for it. The technological process demands that it be completed by links which are not required by the psychic process. Thus vast supplies of products come into existence which call forth an artificial demand that is senseless from the perspective of the subjects' culture (Simmel, [1911] 1968:42–43). In other words, we are confronted with a 'demonical rigor' of a law which ensures that objects, in their development,

> have a logic of their own – not a conceptual one, nor natural one, but purely as cultural works of man; bound by their own laws, they turn from the direction by which they could join the personal development of human souls . . . Man becomes the mere carrier of the force by which this logic dominates their development and leads them on as if in the tangent of the course through which they would return to the cultural development of living human beings (Simmel, [1911] 1968:43).

The tragedy of culture Simmel diagnoses is not so much the result of a reversal of means and ends in human conduct but an outcome of an intrinsic logic of cultural forms and the inability of individuals to absorb and internalize them as meaningful:

> It is the concept of culture that the spirit creates an independent objectivity by which the development of the subject takes its path. In this process the integrating and culturally conditioning element is restricted to an unique evolution which continues to use up the powers of other subjects, and to pull them into its course without thereby raising them into their own apex. The development of subjects cannot take the same path which is taken by that of other objects. By following the latter, it loses itself either in a dead end alley or in an emptiness of its innermost and most individual life (Simmel, [1911] 1968:43–44).

Schelsky's conception of modern technology is much more extensive than is customary in the case of more conventional notions of technology. Usually even the notion of *modern* technology is restricted to the idea that technology merely offers more efficient means or artifacts for social action on the basis of a deliberate transformation of existing materials according to a specific plan for definite purposes (cf. Parsons, 1970:607; Popitz, 1986:107–108). The more conventional notion of the role of technology in industrial society is also reflected in Theodor Adorno's (1969:19) characterization of the instrumental function of technology under capitalism: 'It is not technology itself which represents the calamity, it is rather its entanglement with the surrounding societal relations.' On the other hand, Lipset (1981:22) considers it a hallmark of apolitical Marxism to champion the idea that the means of production reflected in the progress of technology determine class relations in developed countries and that technology, therefore, is more than merely a contributor of resources or means for social action. But a more common conception of technology reduces the idea, as Heidegger (1978) outlines it in his lecture on 'The question of technology', to a couple of essential features: (a) technology represents means for a purpose; and (b) technology is human action. Knowledge is turned into instrumental uses in the pursuit of goals and purposes, however, 'the significance of which is not given in the body of knowledge itself' (Parsons, 1970:607). The crucial point, therefore, is that one need not fear that technology has a life of its own; there is no immanent logic of technology, no 'imperative that must be obeyed' (Bell, [1975] 1980:28).

Heidegger considers the conventional definition of technology as both adequate and short-sighted or 'untrue'; that is, he emphasizes that means of action, e.g. technology, co-determine the relationship of humans to the world, to objects and to nature. Using different means implies a novel relationship to the environment. Means are not neutral media which mediate social action in a neutral fashion. Technology is part of and is implicated in the constitution of the world. Especially for the power hidden in modern technology, it is true that 'it determines the relationship of men to what is' (Heidegger, 1977:19), or to cite another of Heidegger's typical formulations in this context, 'Technology is not merely a means. Technology is a form of discernment. If one is attentive, then a whole new realm opens itself as the essence of technology. It is the realm of discernment, namely that of truth' (1978:16).

The dominant conception of technology does not necessarily postulate that technological artifacts are totally faceless and soulless instruments of human action and that these instruments simply do not display human intentions despite the fact that these are outcomes of human construction. However, if one is able to discern any concession to the fact that technical instruments are the products of human activity, or as one might formulate it today, that technology is socially shaped or socially constructed (e.g. MacKenzie and Wajcman, 1985; Pinch and Bijker, 1987), then the concession tends to be extremely narrow and typically is confined to the thesis that the knowledge guiding interests which may shape the design and execution of technology primarily display an interest in the potential of control and domination, or as Theodor Adorno (1969:19) expresses it, the 'clogging' of technology with the dominant societal reality is responsible for the fact that technological development occurs and is channeled with respect to and in a dependence from existing power and profit-based interests, that is, 'at times it fatally conforms to the needs to exercise control.'

Perhaps taking their cue from Adorno's theoretical premises, or for that matter, Edmund Husserl, who criticized the objectivist notion that in science links between knowledge and interests from the life-world have been overcome, social scientists have generated a number of case studies which document the extent to which interests in controlling and constraining conduct are built into the design and construction of technological instruments and production processes (cf. Winner, 1980; Noble, 1984; Barker and Downing, 1985). Technological design has a political dimension. The technology is designed 'not only to perform a material function but also to express and coercively reinforce beliefs about the differential allocation of power, prestige, and wealth in society' (Pfaffenberger, 1992:283). But such a conclusion amounts almost to a reification conflating particular designs and specific socio-historical contexts as universal. In addition, it is sociologically more productive to bear in mind that control always presupposes or generates resistance. Thus, it would be more accurate to state that what these studies show is not necessarily that technological artifacts invariably foster control, surveillance, domination and repression, but that such purposes may effect technological designs as presumably could, depending on the circumstances, other purposes. In the first sense, however, the conclusion about the closeness between technological design and political realities resonates – and I will expand on this – with the theorems advanced by Schelsky and Marcuse.

In the context of his theory of scientific civilization, Schelsky offers a much broader and more consequential conception of technology. In the case of Schelsky's vision, technology almost fully fuses with and dominates the social 'support system' in which it is embedded.[2] His concept is based, although he only refers to the first tradition explicitly, both on Jacques Ellul's notion of technology and the philosophy of technology of a variety of conservative German writers, especially Hans Freyer (1960) and Arnold Gehlen ([1957] 1980; [1940] 1988), but also Martin Heidegger. According to Gehlen ([1957] 1980:10), for example, in modern society a 'super-structure' is emerging made up of an interpenetration and functional interdependence of industry, technology and science. The consequential development of modern technology has, according to Heidegger, the result that modernity is a reality co-constituted by technology and that, there-fore, alternative possibilities of relating to the environment recede into the background and decisively lose any importance. Heidegger (1978:42) concludes: 'What *exists* at present is formed by the power of modern technology. . .'.

Following Ellul, Schelsky incorporates the 'techniques of organization' and the so-called 'human techniques', as the logical extension of the production of artifacts, into his extensive conception of modern tech-nology. On all fronts, therefore, man subjects himself 'to the constraints, he has produced himself as his world and his identity' (p. 18). While human intentions are seen to be built into the design and execution of tech-nologies, it is remarkable that the exact scope and therefore the range of the kinds of constraints which potentially issue from the employment of technology are conceived in very confined and compressed fashion. In as much as the constraints built into technology are somehow fine-tuned to enable and enforce interests bent on domination, control and order, technology becomes a political vehicle in which the values of the powerful are embedded. And as one observer, therefore, affirmatively sums up this perspective, technological instruments and processes are designed 'not only to perform a material function but also to express and coercively reinforce beliefs about the differential allocation of power, prestige and wealth in society' (Pfaffenberger, 1992:282). Given such a conception of the built-in social origins of technology and the constraints which come with its application, the analysis of the social construction of technology, of course, has not moved beyond the convictions expressed about technology as a means of production mechanistically perpetuating the rule of the powerful.

---

[2] Daniel Bell ([1975] 1980:28) also adopts the idea of a social support system in which technology is embedded in order to counter views of critics of the social consequences of tech-nology in modern society. A social support system or the social organization of the use of technology channels the particular employment of technological systems. The relation between the two may vary considerably because a specific technology is compatible with a variety of ways of organizing social action. In other words, Bell rejects the idea that technologies predetermine and prescribe their uses in a narrow sense and then almost come to dominate the social environment in which they become embedded.

The reversal of the means/ends relationship[3] is particularly noticeable in the arena of the authority or power relations in society. More specifically, Schelsky postulates, as a decisive feature of scientific civilization, that power relations are de-personalized; traditional relations of power between individuals and groups, as well as the legitimating belief systems in modern society, exercise power based on political norms and laws, and are replaced by 'iron necessities' (*Sachgesetzlichkeiten*) of the scientific civilization and these, which is crucial, are 'not arrived at as political decisions and are incomprehensible as based on normative or ethical considerations' (p. 22). These developments imply, of course, that democratic decision-making becomes impossible because the place of the sovereign citizen is taken by technical necessities (*Sachzwänge*) which make political contest and discourse superfluous. Power relations take on qualities which make them appear unassailable. Schelsky predicts a concentration and consolidation of state power which therefore evolves into a 'technical state'. The reason of the state requires that the state increasingly monopolizes all means of power based on technology, the necessary financial resources and the (technical) necessity for co-ordination within its control. These developments imply, in the final analysis, that one can no longer comprehend the state as an entity, as Max Weber was able to do, which monopolizes the use of the means of violence. Rather, as Schelsky indicates, 'it determines the degree of efficiency of all technical means at its disposal' (p. 24). It follows that such a state no longer needs politics and politicians in the conventional sense of the term because decisions are taken or occur in an almost automatic and self-regulated process. They are pre-programmed since they are dependent and only possibly based on inherent, necessary technical, principles.

Social action is no longer in need of any orientation or meaning since such orientation is now *a priori* built into, as a constraint, courses of social action. The view that action is largely self-propelled coincides, to a considerable degree, with the self-conception of certain professional occupations such as lawyers, engineers or physicians. The notion that one acts on the basis of certain interests or even as the result of such profane goals as an interest in power, is rejected by professionals; instead they make reference to inherent necessities, the logic of the question under consideration, technology or conditions of action which cannot be

---

[3] As Hans Freyer (1955:167) puts it: 'Humans no longer approach technical mechanisms asking whether they are useful but are instead approached by the machine asking to be used since the human being is capable of it. Buttons which can be pushed are tempting and fascinating. They almost predetermine the decision; this becomes more likely the greater the effect they are able to produce. The question whether, one day, humans will want to act *for the mere reason* that they are in a position to do so has now at least been posed, and posed in earnest too.' The views in turn resonate and reiterate visions of conservative intellectuals contributing to what might be called the cyclical genre of *Zivilisationskritik* ('civilization critique') who fear and detail numerous even demoniac social, political and economic consequences of an increasingly 'perfected' technology (e.g. Jünger, 1946).

controlled but which one cannot avoid taking into consideration or which, in fact, predetermine decisions (cf. Rueschemeyer, 1986:107). As Schelsky, therefore, stresses, ideas and ideologies lose their previous function because 'the technical demands succeed without reference to ideological matters' (p. 31).[4] The state vanishes and, therefore, the well-known Marxist expectation about the demise or death of the state comes true. In other words, 'the more efficient science and technology, the smaller the scope for political decisions' (p. 28). The gap or void between reason and decision, which critical theory in particular considers character-istic for modern science and technology as well as detrimental for social life (cf. Habermas, [1963] 1974:253–282),[5] has been transcended in favor of technical rationality which becomes the dominant part of the equation of reason and decision-making. The exercise of power over humans is now based on the authority of technical rationality, a form of consciousness seemingly void of ideology. Therefore, as Habermas ([1968] 1978:349) emphasizes, all problems which challenge and confront us today to actively take charge of history have now turned into questions of the appropriate technology; perhaps, as Habermas adds, this technocratic consciousness may well constitute the system-independent ideology of the elites in advanced industrial society that rule by way of bureaucratic authority.

Schelsky's conception of modern society, in particular its authority relations, indicates that the conventional notions of the conditions for and the development of social inequality in advanced society are turned up-side down. Dahrendorf ([1967] 1974:69), for example, describes the relevant historical stages as follows: 'In feudal society, man was what he was born; in industrial society of the nineteenth century, man was what he owned . . . Industrial society depends on completely new ascription criteria: now man is what he is capable of doing.' Schelsky's vision of the ascendancy of the technical state[6] can only mean that a society in which inequality is to a great degree based on achievement is replaced by another basis for inequality. However, Schelsky does not outline its principles, except if one

---

[4] But as C. Wright Mills ([1955] 1967:609), in the mid-1950s and with reference to the US Secretary of Defense of the day who, when asked to justify certain decisions in public, invoked the judgments of experts or God, notes rather pessimistically: 'More and more, as administration has replaced politics, decisions of importance do not carry even the panoply of reasonable discussion in public, but are made by God, by experts, and by men like Mr Wilson.'

[5] In opposition to Schelsky, Habermas ([1963] 1974) regards it as typical for the 'scientific civilization' that (political) decisions are differentiated from reason. The consequence is, therefore, the widespread appearance of *decisionism* in the choice of ruling goals and purposes in society.

[6] As indicated, democracy under conditions of the technical state becomes unnecessary, that is, 'technical and scientific decisions cannot be subjected to democratic decision-making, as a matter of fact they would become ineffective. Once political decisions of government are determined by scientifically controlled inherent necessities (*Sachgesetzlichkeiten*), govern-ment becomes an administrative agent of such necessities and parliament an organ of control for its objective appropriateness' (p. 29).

takes his reference to experts and specialists of the technical state as a hint as to what inequality might be based on primarily. But as far as their political position is concerned, the experts would represent, according to Schelsky, more likely than the politicians, the interests of the average citizen because the politicians are seen or act as lobbyists of special-interest groups.

Schelsky's theory of scientific civilization is meant as a dire warning and he hopes to inaugurate fundamental changes to avoid or reverse the developments he predicts are in store for modern society. But how is any escape possible? Ironically perhaps, Schelsky's own theory of scientific civilization is, despite – or even because of – its emphasis on the possibility of control and prediction, characterized by an essential helplessness.[7] Schelsky appears to be forced to submit to the future he sketches for he pleads, in a very ambivalent sense, for a metaphysical change in the identity or self-conception of man in an age of scientific civilization. He urges us to institute a permanent metaphysical reflection which ensures that individuals can guard themselves spiritually against the constant danger of self-objectification by engaging in anticipatory reflection about this process, and thereby assure or remind themselves of their 'superiority'.

Schelsky's theoretical design of the technical state converges, in significant respects, although convergence does not signal identity, with the analysis and thesis of the increasing societal dominance of technical rationality in advanced society by a number of authors who belong to the group of critical theorists. My brief description and critique of these ideas are limited, for the most part, to the conceptions developed by Herbert Marcuse, though similar views may be found in the writings of other members of the Frankfurt School.

The influential thesis of the omnipotence of technical rationality Marcuse advanced and defended is repeated to this day in the writings of quite a few observers concerned with the nature of contemporary society. Peter Ulrich (1987:152) has summarized these views in a concise and telling fashion for he makes use of virtually all the key phrases invoked by critical theory in the 1960s when writing about the dominance of nomological science. The portrait of modern society he sketches is also suitably deterministic:

> In the name of scientific rationality both technical systems and social relations are indiscriminately examined and changed with respect to their *function* in fulfilling set goals that themselves cannot be rationalized. Scientification tends to constitute therefore, based on technologically rationalized systems, the methodically most disciplined formation of the *colonialisation of the life-world*. Scientific experts dominate opinions in a growing number of life spheres; their expertise and even more so their credibility turns into the 'Achilles heel of the industrial system'. The layman (seemingly) does not have to offer anything that can compete with the specialized knowledge of the experts: The judgment of experts terminates any discussion of a problem as long as their competence is taken for

---

[7] Cf. the vivid and original discussion of modernity (and post-modernity), for example, its emphasis on prediction and control, in Borgmann (1992).

granted. Hand in hand with the growing scientification (and therefore 'objectification') of the life-world increases the dependence of decision-makers on the advice of experts. The decision-makers, be it in industry or in the political system, retain the formal authority of their office but in fact they lose their *functional authority* to the experts.

Herbert Marcuse's (1941:421) very early warning, written under the impression of the destructive capabilities of the Nazi regime, that 'today the apparatus to which the individual is to adjust and adapt himself is so rational that individual protest and liberation appear not only as hopeless but as utterly irrational', seems to be an appropriate comment on, as well as affirmation of, the evident futility and self-contradictory nature of Schelsky's call for permanent metaphysical reflection in response to the dominance of technical rationality in advanced societies.[8] Paradoxically, the same dilemma applies to Marcuse's own theoretical reflections about the nature of advanced society and his insistence that technical rationality and the technical apparatus totally govern industry and the state, as well as the life of everyone in society. Using, of course, a very different primary intellectual heritage as his point of reference and departure, and aiming for a different audience, Marcuse nevertheless arrives at conclusions about the dominating role of technology in modern society which are virtually identical to Schelsky's diagnosis of scientific civilization. Marcuse (1964:169) emphatically asserts for instance that 'the world tends to become the stuff of total administration, which absorbs even the administrators' and that 'transcending modes of thought seem to transcend Reason itself.'

At the decisive stages of Marcuse's critique of technical rationality, he not only postulates an indivisible scientific rationality, but he also conflates non-technical rationality with irrationality and irrationality with rationality and becomes himself, unwittingly perhaps, a victim of the alleged total dominance of technical rationality. The rationality of the dominant 'ideology' of technology does not allow, so it seems, for any rational escape anymore; it has become totally dominant and self-exemplifying: 'The rationalized world contracts to a "false" totality' (Habermas, [1981] 1984:368). The result is that Marcuse, as well as Schelsky, can only escape to a kind of *Kulturpessimismus*. In the case of Schelsky, it is some form of heroic metaphysical effort which emerges as the main answer to what would appear to be futile resistance to the inevitable on-rushing march of scientific-technical civilization, while Marcuse banks on a kind of irrational

---

[8] Marcuse (1941:419) underscores this point further, in a very affirmative description of the pervasive power of science and technology, by observing that an attitude which 'dissolves all actions into a sequence of semi-spontaneous reactions to prescribed mechanical norms – is not only perfectly rational but also reasonable. All protest is senseless, and the individual who would insist on his freedom of action would become a crank. There is no personal escape from the apparatus which has mechanized and standardized the world. It is a rational apparatus, combining utmost expediency with utmost convenience, saving time and energy, removing waste, adapting all means to the end, anticipating consequences, sustaining calculability and security.'

reversal to an otherwise irreversible technocratic development, at the apex of its evolutionary path, although this too, paradoxically, requires a technical solution.

Instrumental rationality and new forms of control

Herbert Marcuse's *One-dimensional Man*, subtitled 'Studies in the Ideology of Advanced Industrial Society', first published in 1964, does not once refer to Helmut Schelsky's theory of scientific civilization. But even if Marcuse had known of Schelsky's insistent warnings about the impending modern technical state, he might have chosen, I suspect, to ignore that analysis, given Schelsky's reputation within the post-war sociological community, especially among émigré scholars (cf. e.g. König, [1984] 1987; 1987).[9] Marcuse's ideas and observations about the role of technology in modern society can be traced back to political and intellectual interests in the early 1940s. For as he observed at the time (Marcuse, 1941:414), 'National Socialism is a striking example of the ways in which a highly rationalized and mechanized economy with the utmost efficiency in production can operate in the interest of a totalitarian oppression and continued scarcity. The Third Reich is indeed a form of "technocracy".' However, in the case of National Socialism, politics is still a decisive force; yet, technical knowledge is already an indispensable instrument of political control.

But later, Marcuse assails the scientific mind and the transformation of its knowledge into scientific-technical rationality to have produced in advanced industrial society an ensemble of things and objectified social relations which have turned the project of emancipation from the domination of nature and control into its opposite. Marcuse (1964:146) does not hesitate to argue that these outcomes are inherent in pure science and that 'scientific-technical rationality and manipulation are welded together into new forms of social control.' Outside the world of objective things and social relations one only encounters a world of values but since they or their metaphysical basis cannot be verified, the subjective domain is not real, but is objective and weak and ultimately counts little in the affairs of life.

The technical presumption of science becomes a political presumption and has consequences for the social organization of humans because the transformation of nature, according to the logic of technology, also involves changes in the social relations of individuals. Whatever claims may be made on behalf of the essential political neutrality and potential of

---

[9] Kellner (1984:241), on the other hand, contends that Marcuse's students during the time in question relate that he rarely if ever made explicit reference to the texts and ideas of other contemporary social scientists such as C. Wright Mills, Daniel Bell or Vance Packard; if Marcuse alluded to these theories of society at all, he used them to illustrate his own theoretical conceptions.

technology, Marcuse (1964:154) stresses emphatically, even against Marx, that a technology which has become the *universal* form of material production, 'circumscribes an entire culture; it projects a historical totality – a "world".' In other words, the relation and respective implication of science and its technical application, and of the nature of the society which is created as a consequence, can only be viewed, in the final analysis, as an intimate connection which operates under the same logic.

Technological reason and its universals, namely, the discipline and control of production resulting in regimentation, the pursuit of narrow goals or specialization and the absolute uniformity of regimented and specialized labor or standardization, are bound to predominate throughout society.[10] The universes of scientific and ordinary discourse are soon propelled by the same inherent force, namely, the rationality of domination. All sectors of society, all social activities and all subjectivities are brought under the control of technical forms of discourse. The domination of nature and society go hand in hand. Science and society become reflections of the logic of technical rationality. Marcuse (1964:158) concludes, therefore, that the

> scientific method which led to the ever-more effective domination of nature thus came to provide the pure concepts as well as the instrumentalities for the ever-more-effective domination of man by man *through* the domination of nature . . . Today domination perpetuates and extends itself not only through technology but *as* technology, and the latter provides the great legitimation of the expanding political power, which absorbs all spheres of culture.[11]

The resulting lack of freedom and autonomy appears neither as irrational nor as the result of political forces but as a 'rational' submission to the technical necessities of existence. In the final instance, therefore, instrumental reason becomes ubiquitous and turns society into a 'totalitarian' existence. The political becomes, as is the case in Schelsky's scientific civilization, the technical – 'the incessant dynamic of technical progress has become permeated with political content' (Marcuse, 1964:159) – and rationality becomes irrationality. The state becomes merely an expression of the technical base and is depoliticized. Social change will be arrested, for the most part, by virtue of the power and the primacy of the society's administrative apparatus, and this containment of social transformations is perhaps the most singular achievement of advanced industrial society.

Marcuse's prophecy of the poisonous nature of scientific rationality is even more abstract than that advanced by Schelsky. Marcuse does not provide and discuss any examples of how technological means are turned

---

[10] The decisive outcome of these developments is that the workers are incapable of acquiring a critical view of the repressive social order. The 'masterly enslavement' is pervasive throughout society, affecting all individuals at all levels of production.

[11] Theodor Adorno's ([1966] 1973:320) image about the extension of the rule of nature to a rule over man by man is very similar since he warns that the 'unity of the control over nature, progressing to over man and finally to that over men's inner nature' is one of the enormous dangers of the present age.

into mere means of social control and domination, for example, how the telephone or television invariably furnish the stuff out of which domination is fashioned. The reluctance of dictators to promote a modern telephone system in the early part of this century would indicate that they feared its subversive possibilities. To this very day, differences in economic and demographic factors do not satisfactorily account for the large disparities in the dissemination of the telephone between state socialist and capitalist societies after the Second World War (cf. Buchner, 1988).

However, before attempting to critically analyze Schelsky's and Marcuse's theories of society, it might be useful to briefly refer to some of the grounds for convergence in the observations of Marcuse and Schelsky, especially their thesis that there is the distinct danger that technology in modern society will increasingly displace spontaneous social and political action. Marcuse and Schelsky were by no means isolated in their assessment of the paths of social, political and economic development of advanced industrialized societies in the 1960s and early 1970s. Nor were they alone in attributing the changes to intrinsic 'laws' of science and technology. On the contrary, Schelsky's and Marcuse's observations and warnings resonate with quite a broad intellectual trend which actually began to take on its peculiar characteristic in the 1950s when social theorists first noted distinctive trends in industry and production which appeared to be both clear and irreversible to them. Social scientists thought that they discerned a tendency in industry toward increasing technological progress manifesting itself in the rapid mechanization or *automation* of production. While greater automation of production, which is, as Marcuse (1964:35) observes, inherent in technological progress itself, would enlarge the output of commodities enormously, it would not, as many observers despairingly noted, succeed in making work more meaningful, demanding or challenging. The result, as outlined for example by David Riesman and his collaborators in the *Lonely Crowd* (1950), was, now that industry was succeeding in producing masses of bored workers through simplified work routines, that the central meaning of life would shift and henceforth be sought in the creative use of increasing leisure time.

Schelsky's and Marcuse's observations resonate, to some degree at least, with Daniel Bell's (1960) thesis about the end of ideology or the prognosis by Robert Lane (1966) that we are about to enter an age in which scientific knowledge will increasingly displace the significance of the political element from politics. However, any effect and influence of ideological factors, or for that matter, political attributes, on science and technical developments remains unanalyzed as part of these observations about the course of modern society. The imbalance in question suggests that the conventional central theoretical categories employed in the analysis of modern society, partly inherited by contemporary social science from the past century, such as class or the economy but also the notions of capitalist or socialist, have lost their crucial role in social theory. They lost their appeal because observers, for example, were increasingly convinced that the distinction between capitalist and state socialist economic order was becoming obsolete. At the same time, however, confidence in the power and special character of scientific knowledge remained unimpeded. Raymond Aron both embraced and highlighted these assumptions in his theory of industrial society. At the same time, questions about the motor of 'social change' or the centrality of the economic system for societal transformations in modern society were raised anew, independently of conventional responses. And it was at this time that theorists began to advance the thesis that technology and science rather than economy form the real motor of societal change in modern social systems (cf. Parsons, 1970:619).

More generally, however, both Schelsky's and Marcuse's accounts of the social and political force of modern science and technology suffer from what might well have been an unintended but none the less misplaced confidence in the practical efficacy of scientific reasoning and quantification.

Toward a critique of the theory of scientific civilization

There are at least two elementary but interrelated considerations which form the core of Schelsky's argument about the threatening rise of the technical state. But it is not necessary to take up both of his predictions in detail. There is, first, the realm of political action, politics and the political system, whose significance according to Schelsky but also Marcuse is ultimately reduced to that of a secondary realm which becomes almost superfluous, for it is only in the case of 'imperfections' which at times could issue from and might accompany action based on technical rationality that genuine political decision-making becomes an exigency in the technical state. The very conception and practice of politics and political action is at stake in Schelsky's discussion of modern society. However, I will defer the question of whether Marcuse's and Schelsky's views with respect to the demise of politics are much too narrow and short-sighted – as could easily be argued (cf. Hennis, [1971] 1977). Nor will I explore the related question of whether the injection of more and more technical and scientific expertise into the political decision-making process ironically enhances the probability that policies which emerge in such a context in fact are based on anything but technical conclusions.[12]

Schelsky's elaborate conception of modern technology, which includes, it will be recalled, the notion of the emergence of a potent social technology, constitutes the second essential attribute of his theoretical conception of the dynamics of modern society. Because of the centrality the notions of technology and instrumental rationality generally occupy

---

[12] With the addition of more and more research findings, the decision-making process becomes less and less straightforward for the 'role of scientific research and analysis is therefore not the heroic one of providing truths by which policy may be guided, but the ironic one of preventing policy being formulated around some rival technical conclusions. Research on one hypothesis ought to cancel out research on others, enabling policy to be made which is insensitive to all scientific conjectures' (Collingridge and Reeve, 1986:151).

in Schelsky's theory of scientific civilization, I will examine Schelsky's understanding of technology, its origins and pretensions in greater detail.

Schelsky's conception of the power of technology is based on at least two dubious assumptions. First, it assumes the almost unlimited and un-problematic malleability of social processes based on the logic of technical construction and, therefore, on the questionable premise that human history can be made at will. Secondly, Schelsky's definition of modern technology, in particular its self-sustaining and autonomous development, may be appealing because it offers such a comprehensive logic for the direction and conditions of social change; however, its very closure is also its greatest weakness. It is in all likelihood, and empirical evidence appears to support such an assertion, questionable to assume that the development of modern technology is nursed by a single and self-referential logic of growth, namely, the 'one best way' or the most efficient solution to a given problem. The premise is that technology is self-sufficient in the sense that it contains its own pattern of rationality or that it is capable of providing meaning to yet another 'technical solution'. The development of modern technology is dependent on other systems for references, which inject meaning of yet further marginal or dramatic technical improvements of a process, or choose the best solution from multiple best solutions (cf. Krohn and Rammert, 1985).[13] That this is, or better, must be, the case can also be shown by virtue of the fact that Schelsky's argument focuses almost exclusively on the consequences of modern technology for politics and the political system. However, his notion of a self-propelled and self-referential technology should, in principle, extend to the use of technology in the economy. But Schelsky does not really address the impact of technology on the economy. The introduction of new technologies in business is hardly driven by its own logic. It follows a variety of references including rather conventional motives but also the particular relations of production. However, Daniel Bell (1973a:344), in his analysis of the interdependencies of business decisions, production and government, indicates that he is convinced that, on the one hand, the economy will be increasingly subordinated to government decisions and these will have, on the other hand, a more and more technical character. In other words, Bell seconds Schelsky's notion of the self-referential dynamic of technology and the spread of its logic to other forces in society including business decisions.

The same argument can and has been attacked as short-sighted and as an effort to portray technocratic rationality as non-ideological. The thesis

---

[13] These objections are much more consequential that the disapproval voiced in an early response to Schelsky by Habermas ([1968–69] 1970:59). Habermas objects to the thesis of the autonomous character of technology by suggesting that the 'pace and *direction* of technical development today depend to a great extent on public investments' (emphasis in the original; an equivalent for the term 'pace' does not appear in the original German formulation of the essay, only the term 'direction' [*Richtung*]). Such disapproval, of course, does not really assail the strong assertion of Schelsky's about the autonomous *cognitive* development of technology.

that a technocratic point of view is self-sufficient, that is, can be solely technocratic and therefore only concerned with instrumental efficiency, tacitly accepts the 'end of ideology thesis'. A rejection of such a possibility implies that technocrats cannot be technocrats alone. As Gouldner (1976:265) argues: 'A conception of technocratic ideology that reduces it to instrumental rationality is an illusion of philosophical idealism' because it 'ignores technocrats' "material" interests, including their *political* interests.'

Thus, one of the Achilles' heels of the theory of scientific-technical civilization and of instrumental rational control, in which 'technology becomes the subject of history', to use a formulation by Günther Anders ([1956] 1980), is the rather conventional notion of the nature of advanced technology and technological expertise, which animates all of its utopian promises and rationalistic designs. Domination by technology and by technical expertise requires a degree of cognitive coherence and community of interest, which in fact cannot be observed among technical experts, or in discourse which rests on the authority of scientific knowledge claims. Experts do not act in a unified manner, nor is expertise undivided, or for that matter, will it ever be if such consensus is to emerge on a voluntary basis. It is important to recognize that most 'technical controversies have the form of a competition between two plausible *interpretations* of a situation . . . and technical expert controversy has many of the features of theoretical controversy in science' (Barnes, 1985:106). Scientists, engineers, experts and counselors are far too fragmented intellectually and display allegiances to too many varied groups in society to seriously represent a stratum on the verge of collectively dominating society. Barnes (1985:11) concludes that modern society, though dominated by science, is not ruled by scientific experts: 'Expert assertions today must be expressed in a scientific/technical idiom; that is essential, just as centuries ago a religious idiom was essential. But it no more guarantees that a scientist will be believed today than it guaranteed that a priest would be believed long ago.'

A related and equally dubious assumption of the utopian designs of the impending technical state concerns the conviction that the growth in knowledge and information occurs in patterns which assure its orderliness and therefore prompts greater transparency and rationality of conduct in situations drenched in intelligence. However, the proliferation of knowledge does not invariably mean the reduction of ignorance and increase in certainty. On the contrary, a gain in mere intelligence may well constitute an explosion in confusion, uncertainty and unpredictability. As a result, in the sphere of organizations, for example, an 'increasing share of organizational resources goes to intelligence function; structural sources of intelligence failures become more prominent; doctrines of intelligence – ideas about how knowledge should be tapped and staff services organized – become more fateful' (Wilensky, 1971:174). I will deal with these counter-intuitive effects of the growth of scientific and technical knowledge in the next chapter.

9

The Texture of Knowledge Societies

> The universality of intellectuality, in that it is valid for each individual intellect, brings about an atomization of society. By means of the intellect and viewed from its standpoint, everyone seems to be an enclosed self-sufficient element alongside every other, without this abstract universality somehow being resolved into concrete universality in which the individual person only forms a unity in combination with others.
>
> (Georg Simmel, *The Philosophy of Money*)

This chapter will describe and critically analyze some of the central features of knowledge societies. In particular, I will ask what are some of the salient consequences for knowledge societies as social *collectivities* now that the individual capacity to act is considerably enlarged? It cannot be taken for granted that the ability of major social institutions in knowledge societies to act is also expanding in a corresponding fashion. As a matter of fact, I will argue that the extent to which capacities to act are enlarged occurs at an uneven pace depending on the volume of the social formation. The outcome is a new contradiction: an increasingly large proportion of the public in modern societies, for example, acquires political skills, while the ability of the state and its agencies to 'impose its will' or to exercise its sovereignty is arrested, even decreased.[1] The evolving clash is not between, as was the case in industrial society, culture and civilization resulting in a cultural lag, or between subjective and objective culture ensuing in a cultural tragedy, but between individual and collective capacities to act. This certainly would appear to lead to a much more fragile and volatile form of legitimate authority and power of the state and possibly other major social institutions in modern society. And in that sense it may be said that the growth and the broader dissemination of knowledge paradoxically produces greater uncertainty and contingency rather than a resolution of disagreements or the basis for a more effective domination by central societal institutions.

I interpret the considerable modern enlargement of the informal economy, crime, corruption and the growth of wealth in modern society as evidence of the diverse capacity of individuals, households and small groups to take advantage of and benefit from contexts in which the degree of social control exercised by larger (legitimate) social institutions has diminished considerably. However, much of social science discourse has

---

[1] Ronald Inglehart (1990:335–370) examines the enlargement of political skills of the public in Western societies in terms of a shift from 'elite-directed' to 'elite-challenging' politics.

been fascinated by the opposite phenomenon, namely the probable and dangerous enlargement of the ability of modern social institutions, especially various state institutions but also the economy to more ruthlessly impose its will on its citizens. Thus, social theorists have been concerned with discovering the conditions that produce and reproduce domination and repression rather than greater autonomy, freedom and independence. Modern science and technology have often been viewed, in the context of such analyses, as the handmaidens of regressive civilizational developments.

Concentration and regulation

Among the master metaphors which repeatedly and for long have informed the work of social theorists are those which in one way or another assert that certain (iron law-like) developments, for example, profound contradictions, excessive functional differentiation[2] and social divisions deny or even destroy the individual or corporate actor's capacity to take part in the craft of constructing his or her world, form her own opinion and protect his privacy. Contemporary social theorists are no exception to the rule, although some of the traditional threats to self-determination and moral neutralization appear to have vanished. For example, references to elite conspiratorial motives, such as the calculated aspiration to defend vested interests, or the conflictual division into opposing social classes are rarely advanced today. The reiteration of such threats to human agency have declined, though not disappeared, with considerable justification. However, allusions to these restrictive and oppressive structures have been replaced by allusions to much more ambiguous, at times even invisible threats and risks, for example, the threat of a decomposition of privacy.[3] At least responsible agents and sources for such threats and dangers as well as their rationales remain hidden or as ambiguous as are the irresistible coercions themselves. Reference more frequently now is made to largely self-evolving and self-propelled processes. In the end, such processes are

[2] In one of his early essays on the social consequences of technical developments, Helmut Schelsky (1954:26–27) for example blames not only the nature of modern technology but excessive functional differentiation for a serious decline or even disappearance of human agency. He describes the process as follows: 'The minimization in the ethical regulation is, in addition, related to another process dependent on technology, namely the extensive division of labor in productive and administrative relations as well as planning and decision-making processes. Inasmuch as these processes are made up of numerous interrelated individual acts, the meaning of the entire process and therefore the responsibility for it are divided among the contributing individuals. The ability to attribute meaning to one's own contribution is only possible in relation to the whole and therefore one's ethical responsibility also is dependent on the ethics of all participants.'

[3] Only by misunderstanding, as Narr ([1979] 1985:37) for example underlines, the 'logic of performance and regulation within production and bureaucracy could one assume that private spheres, free time, and autonomous personalities might be left to themselves. What is left to itself is only what is left over, what is no longer needed.'

even more dangerous because they deny and deflect human beings from experiencing and achieving opportunities, in self-regulated spheres of autonomy, considered essentially human.

Among prominent contemporary manifestations of such self-propelled processes and risks are the notions of an indifferent concentration of social activities, the threat of extremely efficacious surveillance and the widespread enforcement of a growing set of regulations of human conduct. In an effort to substantiate the threat of an increasing social regulation and concentration of life in contemporary society, observers, implicitly at least, dissent from predominant theoretical prescriptions which stress differentiation, division and fragmentation; for such outcomes would appear to be enigmas of effective and centralized social control. The outline of the argument is quite straightforward. Social, economic and political relations and technical means in modern society have become much more organized, regulated and systematized. The imperatives of performance in production and bureaucracy require discipline and adaptability. The pursuit of regulated integration and diminishing spheres of self-governed contexts of autonomy has been orchestrated by state and corporate groups in order to extend and solidify their power. Thus,

> drawing in and extending into once exempted activities, corporate capitalism and state agencies typically have achieved a greater management of social relationships, have increasingly 'scripted' roles and encounters, at the same time as they have advanced their criteria as those most appropriate for conducting affairs. This process should be seen as the rationalization of control in pursuit of particular interests (Robins and Webster, 1989:34).

The result is 'insufficient participation, insufficient integration, and unattainable, abstract requirements' (Narr, [1979] 1985:41). But what exactly has enabled state agencies and corporations to effectively rationalize and extend their control over ordinary and not-so ordinary everyday activities? How is it possible to translate the technological innovations in the 'information sector' with apparent ease into a repressive apparatus? Finally, how is one to escape from the iron grip of the manipulation, concentration and regulation that issue from these devices in order to expose their dangers?

Robins and Webster (1989) assign special responsibility to the ability of the state and corporations to gather, store, scrutinize and disseminate information requisite for systematic control. Successful surveillance with the help of new information-communication technologies is the crucial ingredient for disciplining workers and citizens. In the end, these technologies reinvent and reinforce conditions akin to a panopticon advocated by Bentham in 1791 as a control device (cf. Foucault, 1977).[4] Technological

---

[4] As Webster and Robins (1986:346) therefore suggest, what information technologies control is the 'same dissemination of power and control, but freed from the architectural constraints of Bentham's stone and brick prototype. On the basis of the "information revolution", not just the prison or the factory, but the social totality, comes to function as the hierarchical and disciplinary panoptic machine.'

innovation is seen to be driven by the need of corporate and state agencies, operating hand in hand, to manage and regulate their immensely enlarged domains of control and profitability.[5]

Although the precise reasons for the ability of the state and large corporations to collaborate efficiently and to fully subdue the development of technical knowledge under their control are somewhat clouded or mere assertions that need to be investigated thoroughly, there appears to be little doubt about the actual social and cultural consequences of these developments for modern society. Despite the unprecedented growth of the volume of information and the channels of communication, in the end, they diminish the individual's ability to participate, they intensify isolation, they threaten individual privacy, heighten the sense of helplessness and erode the differentiation between private and public spheres of life.

More specifically, society may, for example, at least in America for it is awash with tests, evolve into, if it has not already done so, a *test society*. It can be argued, therefore, that the increased use of tests in modern society primarily provides mechanisms 'for defining or producing the concept of the person in contemporary society' and for maintaining 'the person under surveillance and domination' (Hanson, 1993:3). In a similar sense, Gernot Böhme (1984:15) expresses the fear that modern society is on the way to evolving into a *registration society* empowering those who are legitimized to register, store and combine extensive quantities of information about individual citizens. In a more general sense, he argues that, in analogy to the notion of technical reality as socially appropriated nature, whereby the use of nature presupposes the isolation, purification and separation of 'natural objects' that limits the spontaneity of nature and fits it to socially determined functions, the social or self-appropriation of society requires similar preconditions. Society becomes controllable *once it is organized in terms of knowledge*: 'Social processes must be differentiated according to functions and arranged according to models, and social actors must be disciplined in a way which makes their behavior amenable to data collection or makes their social role and activities relevant only insofar as they produce data' (Böhme, 1992:42). If one wants to describe, from this perspective, modern society as a knowledge society it is necessary to stress that it involves reference to knowledge about a society that is already organized in terms of its knowability. Assuming that society is already pre-organized, a census, for example, becomes a duplication of society onto data bases for the purposes of control and simulation.

Anthony Giddens (1990b) advances what would appear to be an even more universal assertion in the form of a basic reservation about the nature of contemporary modern societies and what for him constitutes the essence

---

[5] As Wolf-Dieter Narr ([1979] 1985:43) for example stresses, 'the direction and the driving force determining the development of information, of the media, and of the various forms of communication . . . are based not on the individual's needs, potentials, or social organization but on the imperatives of a logic of capital realization (*ökonomische Verwertungslogik*).'

of *modernity*. According to Giddens, modernity involves four interrelated institutional dimensions: capitalism, industrialism, military power and administrative power.[6] The latter, given Giddens' (1990b:21) theoretical explication of the process of modernity, is of particular interest here. Administrative power is based on the control of information, and 'modernity has not just recently become an "information society": it was such from the very beginnings.' Printing, for example, was one of the early instruments which both facilitated the control and dissemination of information and represented one of the conditions for the rise of modernity: 'Administrative power is focused through *surveillance*: the use of information routinely to monitor the activities of subject populations, whether in the state, business organization, schools or prisons.' Evidently, and Giddens (1990b:22) agrees, the function of surveillance today is a much improved one since the development of new information technologies 'yield possibilities of centralized control far beyond those available in pre-modern social orders'. But whether such a scenario, a drift towards perfectly regulated authoritarianism, is the outcome, or whether the overall trend is more towards utopian and radical democratization, Giddens leaves, in skeptical mood, open as alternative future possibilities.[7]

Even for social theorists who display a sensible skepticism toward any built-in logic of technological development and choices, there is the tendency to voice the fear that new technological regimes inherently are instruments of repression, centralization and regulation. A case in point is the position advanced by Alain Touraine ([1984] 1988:107–108). Touraine is actually not a proponent of the idea that technologies prescribe choices and that some of the new technologies assuredly constitute instruments of power. On the contrary, he emphasizes that technologies have never ordered society; 'technological choices are first and foremost political ones' which implies that the conventional distinction between forces and relations of production is today obsolete. Nevertheless, Touraine expresses the conviction that it is

> certain that the elaboration of information producing and managing apparatuses results in most areas in a concentration of power. Such a concentration has been under way for quite some time in the industrial realm; it has advanced even further now, but the concentration of decision-making power has become even more pronounced in areas where it had limited importance until recently.

It is not immediately evident whether Touraine's statements are compatible. They could, of course, be compatible if his expressed doubt about the

[6] According to Giddens, this dimension is largely neglected in traditional debates among social theorists, in particular on the left. But Weber and Michels certainly offered their perspective on this problematic.

[7] Compare, however, Giddens' (1981:112) critique of Foucault; in this instance, his critique may apply to his own reasoning because Giddens critically asks of Foucault whether his portrait of the power to control and discipline by state agencies in fact underestimates the extent to which those who are the subject of these control efforts are themselves 'knowledgeable agents' that might end up resisting.

sensibility to assign any inherent positive or negative capabilities to technology itself is in the nature of a theoretical observation, while his comments about the concentration-enhancing effects of information technology are intended to be an empirical statement. After all, as Touraine stresses, the social effects of technology primarily display the state of relations among social forces. In other words, particular care should be taken not to fall into the trap of defining the evolving social structure as a technological society or to link its name to a specific technical instrument (cf. Touraine, [1984] 1988:115).[8]

The powerful images of moral neutralization of modern life envisioned in many of these warnings and the minimization of human agency or the ability of corporate actors to effectively intervene on their own behalf is linked in a potent manner to a specific conception of science and technology because regulation, surveillance and concentration are the direct outcome of scientific–technical developments. The inner and forceful logic of these developments creates a self-propelled superstructure within and outside science.[9] Science itself as well as its application becomes a technical process. It would appear that resignation or resentment are about the only appropriate responses in the face of the overwhelming and irresistible force of these developments.

However, if one, in the first instance, limits the analysis of the state apparatus – as a major player among modern control agencies – to the function of surveillance, registration and that of a collector of information, one invariably arrives at a reductionist perspective that collapses all state activity into a single ahistorical purpose. Of course, the role of the state and other modern institutions in terms of surveillance activities is not unimportant. But the state and other organizations do not merely only

---

[8] By the same token, the time, the clock and the schedule should not simply be seen as disciplinary devices but also as diversifying instruments that 'permit us to synchronize and coordinate a broad range of activities and relationships in dense and pluralistic social networks, and that can expand the possibilities for individual and organization flexibility within them' (Sirianni, 1991:241).

[9] While not all proponents of the possibility and the dangers of centralized control and regulation in modern society might subscribe to the images of the development and application of science developed by Arnold Gehlen (1949:12), his views none the less capture the 'flavor' of the intellectual prerequisites for such a conception, namely a particular epistemological view of the almost limitless powers of science and technology quite well. Natural science research interdicts the scientist, 'because he does not "pose" the problems, nor does he "decide", to apply the discoveries, as the laymen imagines. The determination of problems follows from what already has been discovered and it follows from the logic of the experiment that the control of outcomes already is part of experimental knowledge. The decision to apply the discovery is not required, is unnecessary, it is taken for the scientist by the object itself. The process of knowing already is a technical process. The relation between science, technical application and industrial exploitation already constitutes an automated and ethically indifferent superstructure. A radical departure can only be imagined if it commences at the extremes of the process, that is, at the starting point, the desire to know or, the desire to consume, the completion of the process. In each case, asceticism, if it should be observed at all, would be the signal of a new epoch.'

collect and monopolize information (or knowledge). This would be to both overestimate the practical efficacy of the state and underestimate the functions it performs. The state also functions as a producer of knowledge and information (cf. Schiller, 1993).

Fragile social structures

In the light of the potential climate change to come, one is well advised to not only keep the congenital frailty of human beings when compared to the immense forces of nature in mind (cf. Braudel, [1979] 1992:50) but also the essential fragility of social structures, especially when judged against the background of the widely imagined and promised stability of our designs directed toward maximizing prediction and control.

The degree of the fragility of social structures and human constructs in knowledge societies generally increases. This already follows from the observation that knowledge societies are increasingly human constructs. For example, there is now an immense stock of objectified knowledge which mediates our relation to nature and to ourselves. Nature is and can scarcely be experienced other than as a human product or within human products, and social relations are mediated by an increasing stock of arrangements of an administrative, legal or technical kind. The material appropriation of nature means that nature as a whole has gradually been transformed into a human product by superimposing on it a social structure. This structure is in essence objectified knowledge, namely, an explication and realization of what we know to be the laws of nature extended by engineering design and construction. The self-appropriation of society occurs through an analogous process, namely, by way of the social production and construction of data which are social facts and which constitute the social and political reality, the enforcement of rules which govern social conduct and the bureaucratization of community life.

One of the first characterizations one is able to give of our contemporary societal condition is a mere quantitative diagnosis: the superstructure of society and nature is now so immense that the greater part of the overall social activity is not production but reproduction; in particular, repro-duction of knowledge itself, and that means of the conditions which make specific effects and processes possible in the first place. At the same time, the overall level of knowledgeability of each and every individual in society is elevated while the distribution of knowledge is far less concentrated. Thus, one of the better images symbolizing and summing up the nature of the change from industrial to knowledge society would be to refer to the former as a community organized and controlled in a pyramid-like fashion, while the latter type of society more closely resembles delicate mosaics without definite centers.

But first, and for the purpose of contrast, I would like to look back to the design and texture of post-industrial societies as sketched by Daniel Bell.

That is, Daniel Bell's *The Coming of Post-industrial Society* (1973a) still stands, in many ways, for an intellectual and political era animated by enthusiastic support for and expectation of the benefits which will accrue from planning utopias. It will be possible, Bell (1973a:344) asserts, for example, 'to plot alternative futures in different courses, thus greatly increasing the extent to which we can choose and *control* matters that affect our lives'. If this proposition has a ring of truth at all, it might be accurate (but even in this instance only to a limited degree) at the individual or micro-social level, but that is not necessarily what Bell has in mind. The thesis of the ability to realize planning efforts points much more at the social realities of the collective level. At this level, the assertion about more efficacious planning and, therefore, control over alternative courses of action – take, for example, the goal to significantly alter the structure of inequality in society, or the desire to reduce and perhaps even eliminate certain patterns of conduct – is likely mistaken. But most of all, one gets a strong sense of optimism about our ability to construct, plan and control social relations from above, by governmental and administrative agencies at all levels, and by business or other major social institutions.

That this might well be a proposition with dubious assumptions becomes evident even from Bell's own account of the design of post-industrial society. For Bell (1973a:159) underlines, for example, that social life in post-industrial societies is that of a 'communal society' rather than a 'market society'. This means that the share of goods and services allocated by public mechanisms or public choice, rather than the market or individual preferences, grows significantly. A communal society is also one in which the number and range of 'rights' multiplies as does concern and public responsibility for the externalities of the market place. But, as a game between persons, social exchanges become much more difficult since 'political claims and social rights multiply, the rapidity of social change and shifting cultural fashion bewilders the old, and the orientation to the future erodes the traditional guides and moralities of the past' (Bell, 1973a:123). In addition, as Bell underlines in the same context, in post-industrial society increased public participation of individuals and groups is likely; however, 'the very increase in participation leads to a paradox: the greater the number of groups, each seeking diverse or competing ends, the more likelihood that these groups will veto one another's interests, with the consequent sense of frustration and powerlessness as such stalemates incur.' In other words, any design to plan and control social conduct becomes rather difficult under these circumstances. Moreover, the conditions Bell anticipates in this instance are likely to be a more realistic description of the essential fragility of future social structures and conduct.

None the less, Bell's account of post-industrial society is also animated by expectations of much better and effective 'management of organized complexity' in advanced society. Since the notion of complexity of the nature of social reality and the difficulty in intellectually reconstructing such reality is effectively one which has been a pervasive thesis for decades in social scientific discourse (cf. Stehr, 1992), it is not surprising to see Bell assert that social science and its kindred disciplines are about to conquer what many have felt has held them back in the past, namely, the difficulties of manipulating a greater bundle of 'variables'. In fact, Bell explicitly talks about the progress made in science since the eighteenth and nineteenth centuries as advances made in terms of the number of *variables* which can be handled simultaneously. The move is from two-variable problems, to a small number of interdependent variables and, finally, reflecting the very intellectual and sociological problems of post-industrial society, to a large number of interacting variables. Bell stresses approvingly (1973a:29) that 'It is the *hubris* of the modern systems theorist that the techniques for managing these systems are now available.'

The cognitive techniques designed to manipulate a large bundle of variables at one time represents the emergence of an *intellectual technology*. Intellectual technologies are defined as the substitution of algorithms for intuitive judgments. Problem-solving rules may be embodied, Bell (1973a:29–30) explains, in 'an automatic machine or a computer program or a set of instructions based on some statistical or mathematical formula'. Intuitive judgments are replaced by formalized decisions. The computer is particularly suited to implement and execute efficiently such problem-solving rules. In short, what is distinctive about intellectual technology, as far as Bell is concerned, is the clear separation of means and ends in social action and therefore the calculation of the risks and costs associated with alternative means, and, ultimately the pre-situational assignment of particular means to pre-set goals. In all situations, the desirable action would be a strategy that ensures the 'best' solution. What Bell therefore has in mind, with his notion of intellectual technology, is merely a re-statement of long-standing ambitions (or fears) to 'automate' decisions for which means (more or less independent of goals) and ends are known in advance. In other words, Bell's metaphor of an intellectual technology amounts to a heightened 'rationalization' process in and of modern society as we know it from Max Weber's extensive discussion, except that the computer now enters the equation as a *tool* of such 'technology' which presumably multiplies its efficiency.

In a distinctive contrast and in opposition to these images, knowledge societies are societies characterized, to an unprecedented degree, by self-made social relations and a self-produced future including, of course, the capacity to destroy themselves. But this does not imply that such capacities, in whatever fashion one might depict such cumulative or additive outcomes, add up to the ability to control and manipulate social conduct to a greater extent and in a more efficient manner. On the contrary, the greater capacity to act has the inverse consequence in that it reduces the ability of administrative bodies for example to plan and repress or, from the perspective of the potential targets of planning and manipulation, it heightens the capacity to resist these very efforts.

Knowledge is both a constant source of change and a principle of social organization. Knowledge societies offer unprecedented means to empower social actors to add to the self-transforming capacity of society.[10] The capacity of society to intervene and act upon itself is exceptional. As political entities, too, knowledge societies appear to be rather fragile. They are politically fragile, not because they are liberal democracies, as some might argue, but because they are knowledge societies. Knowledge societies potentially enhance the democratic character of liberal democracies. But as the potential for meaningful political participation is enlarged, some traditional attributes associated with the political system, especially its ability to 'get(s) things done' or, to impose its will, is increasingly diminished.

This thesis of the uneven promotion of the capacity to act and its consequences for society needs to be explicated and explored in more detail for a number of reasons. It is a thesis central to the present analysis, but it is also a thesis which can be easily misconstrued. In order to avoid any misconceptions, first, it does not follow from the general thesis of the increased contingency of social reality that there is a coalescence of social relations toward some center. On the contrary, social conflicts, for example, are generalized, which means that they lose their previous identity as primarily economic conflicts.

Secondly, this malleability and tenuousness of social relations should not be seen to result invariably in greater social inequality, even more effective forms of social control, and more demands for social discipline, which then may be enforced even more efficiently compared to societies in which the powerful have fewer and less effective means to impose their will and exploit others for their own ends.

Thirdly, the prevailing fears, at least among those who have examined critically the spread of technology and technical rationality, has been that what we have called the increased contingency of social reality will in fact be employed for the most part in the partial interests of then even more powerful groups and will increase immeasurably the social, cultural and political cleavages in modern society. Symptomatic and representative of this view is, perhaps, the conclusion that advanced technological institutions are agencies of highly centralized and intensive social control, that their logic defies and drives out any other values, that technology creates, therefore, its own politics, is resistant to intervention on other terms, imposes its own roles and values, and serves, in the final instance, the interests of a ruling elite (who appear to be capable of defying its constraints; e.g. McDermott, 1969). I have already considered one more sophisticated account of the self-propelled and then irresistible transformation of society through technical rationality. These accounts of the dawning of the 'technical state' are compatible with conservative and more liberal political philosophies. Both Helmut Schelsky and Herbert Marcuse

---

[10] Alain Touraine ([1984] 1988:11) denotes these changes as a heightened 'historicity' of society and assumes that actors increasingly will assert the 'importance, and the rights, of conscience and consciousness'.

have, as indicated, each in their own terms of course, developed theories of the victorious and apparently almost irreversible spread of the imperatives of technical rationality. However, the inevitable allegiance between technological rationality and domination in advanced industrial societies, in Schelsky's theory of scientific civilization or Marcuse's treatment of the one-dimensional man, is at best one-sided. At worst, it fails to capture the crucial features of advanced society.

Fourthly, the increased contingency of social reality is, perhaps paradoxically, associated with a strong sense of a lack of malleability or even of helplessness and impotence, rather than emancipatory possibilities in the face of existing societal arrangements. As Johannes Berger (1986:91) describes the association in question, for example:

> everything is highly contingent in modern societies but, at the same time, embedded in interest-laden 'systematic' contexts, it appears, therefore, nothing goes anymore . . . What can possibly be changed: the automobile traffic, the distribution of income or, at least, the laws governing the closing hours of stores? The experience of a resilience of social conditions is in a confusing sense linked to the consciousness of contingency.

However, the relevant issue is not merely or even mainly the question of the self-centered operation of societal subsystems, for example, of the neglect of the economy of goals other than economic interests. Even within subsystems, though there may be an increase in the range of options available, in the capacity to mobilize resources for action and in the ability to anticipate outcomes, there may well be a much greater autonomy. Such changes are accompanied by a decrease in the control over and manipulation of relevant dimensions of action. The expansion in autonomy goes hand in hand with a decline in the capacity to exercise control over innumerable dimensions of social action.

The degree and the consequences to which social action has become malleable in the consciousness of many citizens is an outflow of the availability of reflexive knowledge about the nature of social reality and the nature of nature and how to re-make both for ends which are socially constructed and known to be man-made. However, the effects this has are quite opposite to those anticipated by scholars who have warned about the dawn of the technical state or similar iron cages for social relations brought about by the social impact of science and technology. Of course, science and technology are creating cages but they are of a very different sort than the theories of society produced in the 1960s. The dissemination of such knowledge means that the capacity of traditional institutions to enforce discipline or compliance declines. Or, what is but the same, resources increase to effectively resist central agencies of social coercion.

Lübbe's (1987:95) observation about our ability to anticipate future conditions is therefore quite precise. That is, the inaccuracy of predictions has manifoldly increased as the result of increased knowledge: 'Every earlier period of history enjoyed, in relation to its future, the culturally significant advantage to be able to offer much more accurate pronouncements about the future than we today are capable to do.' The reasons for our inability to anticipate future conditions, and for the increase in the fragility of social conditions in this sense, are attributed by Lübbe directly to the increase in the quantity of knowledge. Although Lübbe focuses mainly on technical knowledge, he asserts for this realm that the volume of events which change the structural conditions of life grows directly with the quantity of available knowledge. The probability of anticipating and controlling the future declines, rather than improving with the growth of knowledge. But the thesis of the fragility of social structure in the sense of the unpredictability of future conditions is more than merely a restatement of the Popperian theorem that one cannot know what we will know in the future.[11]

None the less, the extension of the capacity to act in the case of individuals and small groups is considerable, especially since the enlargement of options to act can be quite small and still have a major impact, for example, in situations of conflict with corporate actors. As Dorothy Nelkin (1975:53–54) has shown in her study of the competitive use of technical expertise in two major controversial political decisions to extend a large airport and to site and develop a power plant in the United States, 'those opposing a decision need not muster equal evidence'. That is to say, 'it is sufficient to raise questions that will undermine the expertise of a developer whose power and legitimacy rests on his monopoly of knowledge claims or claims of special expertise.' In much the same spirit, Lowe (1971:576) describes that what is at issue is that growing affluence, cumulative technology, government interventions and, most of all, a widening and deepening knowledge of social reality has imparted a new 'freedom' to the elements that make up the social system – that is, a capacity to determine for themselves what shall be their patterns of behavior, their reactions to stimuli, their goals.

Losses of fear – especially in relation to the state, the state administrative apparatus and other positions of authority and power – coincide with considerable gains in fear, in particular, in relation to environmental problems, the fallout of technological artifacts, the realization that not all action can be subjected to rational planning and control, and the element of unanticipated consequences of social action initiated by fellow human beings. However, such gains in fear and concerns can, at times, lead to a heightened resolve to employ one's gains in capacity for social action to influence the balance of risks and gains favorably.

The gain many individuals experience in their capacity to act does not mean that the social distribution of knowledge in knowledge societies is equal or displays a greater degree of equality than was the case in industrial society. The distribution of knowledge is reason for and the result of social inequalities. Those who are powerful have fewer difficulties gaining access

---

[11] However, it is a comment on the sensibility of claims made on behalf of 'future studies' as relevant to future conduct.

to knowledge; at the same time, access to knowledge conveys influence, even power, in knowledge societies. None the less, what is of particular interest here is that in recent years knowledge, perhaps in the role of knowledge-based occupations or experts, has

> increasingly come to the assistance of grassroots pressure groups and other elements of the general public and local communities. And it is equally true that the grassroots have learned how to deploy expertise, and have exploited it with some success in furthering their interests and in embarrassing the establishment (Barnes, 1985:111).

In short, the rise in the general level of knowledge accessible and available to larger segments of the population than ever before contributes simultaneously to an enlargement of the fragility of modern social structures.

Governing knowledge societies

Not too long ago, social scientists were almost singularly preoccupied with chronicling the immense growth of certain functions of the state. These developments saw modern governments control around half (or even more) of the national product and profoundly affect the context within which modern politics occurs and societies are governed.[12] The fascination was with social, economic and cultural forces that appeared to rationalize, concentrate, consolidate and centralize. In the end, the portrait resembled the structure of the technical state sketched by Marcuse and Schelsky. However, such a singular focus naturally deflects attention away from structures and processes that sustain cleavages, diversity, traditional norms and plurality. In addition, the center of much of social science discourse concerned with the issue of governing modern societies was not only skewed to a remarkable extent to factors and forces that concentrate but also preoccupied with economic transformations and their impact on political developments. As Herbert Marcuse (1964:48) feared, the 'decline of freedom and opposition is not a matter of moral and intellectual deterioration or corruption. It is rather an objective societal process insofar as the production and distribution of an increasing quantity of goods and services make compliance a rational technologic attitude.'

Any discussion of the political system, political participation and realities generally, especially within the framework of knowledge societies, must be cognizant, in contrast to these views, of the profound transformation of the modern economy, the widespread affluence it has produced, the general decline in the fortune of purely economic matters and extent to

---

[12] Whether the proportion of the national product itself is a good indication of the exact role of the state in society, for instance, the modes of intervention and redistribution, is justifiably subject to considerable doubt.

which not only work has become a knowledge-based activity, last but not least among the politically active social strata in society.

Many observers of the contemporary political scene indeed have recognized the importance of many of these changes and focus their analysis on the proliferation of 'new' social movements for example. The challenge of the emerging social movements is not a 'revolutionary attack against the system, but a call for democracies to change and adapt' (Dalton et al., 1990:3). The task the new social movements have often set for themselves is to demand a more open political process. My discussion of the politics and the 'governability'[13] of knowledge societies will initially concentrate on what are perhaps old-fashioned politics and traditional criteria of efficacy today, namely the politics of the nation-state. I will take up the question of the internationalization, even 'globalization', of politics in the following section.

What may well appear to some to be a basic flaw of theories of post-industrial society, which after all offer rather sweeping generalizations with respect to most other trends in social life, is that it appears to be rather difficult, if not impossible, to infer from such theories much about the appropriate form of government and its efficacy. Daniel Bell's theory of post-industrial society is deliberately silent on the political and administrative consequences of the transition of the modern *economy* to a post-industrial economy, though he does refer to a number of political changes and desirable administrative responses. His projections and advice can, however, best be summed up in the phrase 'political business as usual'. Among them is the likely shift of the center of gravity in political influence in the 'communal society' – as the result of the growing influence of technical decision-making – from legislative and parliamentary bodies to the executive branch of government and even a charismatic leader, the necessity to find the appropriate size and scope of government units, the need to design, in the non profit-sector in particular, non-bureaucratic

---

[13] In the first part of the 1970s, as nervous pessimism about the ability of the state to govern became a prominent perception, more conservatively inclined social theorists took up the question of the reasons for manifest crisis tendencies in industrial societies under the general heading of the governability of modern society (cf. Crozier et al., 1975; Greven et al., 1975; King, 1975, 1976). Crisis tendencies within capitalism had always been a central topic within Marxist analyses. Equally evident were the reasons for such inherent conflicts within Marxist discourse, namely socio-structural tensions and contradictions. The rather neglected ideological or cultural sources of tensions within Marxist perspectives came to the forefront in analyses concerned with the governability of advanced industrial societies (cf. Heidorn, 1982) but in this instance, too, interesting parallels between neo-conservative and socialist critiques of Western industrial societies emerge as well (cf. Offe, [1979] 1984; Habermas, [1982] 1983:76). Habermas ([1982] 1983:76) concludes, after reviewing a number of political diagnoses of American society of the 1970s, that 'the formerly liberal neoconservatives are concerned with the alleged loss of authority of the central institutions, especially the political system. This phenomenon is presented suggestively with key terms like governability, decline of credibility, the loss of legitimacy, etc.' But the lack of consent is also diagnosed as a legitimacy crisis of modern society.

organizational structures[14] more adaptive to the requirements of more flexible and fluid environments and the benefits of devising a system of social accounts[15] as a planning tool.

The enumeration of these changes and tools generally affirms Daniel Bell's tempered confidence in the traditional sentiment of the possibility of improving social and political planning, prediction and control. In this sense, Bell's diagnosis and prescriptions are a somewhat skeptical augmentation of the existing ways of doing political business in industrial society and the benefits politics has typically promised in such a society. Bell's extension of the premises of the political frame of industrial society includes also the implicit reference to the nation-state as a most suitable point of reference for a discussion of the contingencies of governing modern society. I will return to these points below.

The lack of a more specific diagnosis of the politics of post-industrial society, especially the question of the changes in the nature of the relation between the economy and the state and the impact of economic transformations on the limits of what is possible politically, may not constitute a fundamental shortcoming of the theory of post-industrial society because such restraint may merely be self-exemplifying, signaling in effect that post-industrial societies are unlikely to have any unitary form of government or structure of political life and that its prediction, control and planning will actually become an even more precarious undertaking. A great variety of political forms and institutions may not only be compatible with the economic and cultural developments characteristic of knowledge societies but could be forced upon the political life of knowledge societies. Unpredictability, uncertainty and fragility are much more likely to be salient features of knowledge rather than industrial societies.

In discussing the politics of knowledge societies, I will try to focus on two aspects of their political life. First, the broader social and economic conditions within which and to which the political system has to respond.

---

[14] Fred Block, in a more general way, calls for a basic change in the way in which the state exercises its power in post-industrial society, that is, for a de-bureaucratization of the state. Post-bureaucratic state organizations would emulate efforts of corporations designed to achieve greater flexibility in organizational patterns. Such organizations are characterized by 'fewer levels of supervision, diminished deference to hierarchical authority, greater reliance on teamwork, and expanded decision making responsibilities for lower-level employees' (Block, 1987:29). For Block, various measures and initiatives, including a renewal of political participation grouped under the heading of de-bureaucratization of the state, represent the optimal response of the state to post-industrial developments that cannot be accommodated within the present framework of relations between state, society and economy.

[15] As Bell (1973a:326) specifies, such a system of social accounts 'would begin with a series of social indicators that would give us a broader and more balanced reckoning of the meaning of economic progress as we know it. This effort to set up a System of Social Accounts would move us toward measurement of the utilization of human resources in our society in four areas: (1) the measurement of social costs and net returns of innovations; (2) the measurement of social ills (e.g. crime, family disruption); (3) the creation of "performance budgets" in areas of defined social needs (e.g. housing, education); and (4) indicators of economic opportunity and social mobility.'

The conditions and circumstances for political action prescribe, to a large extent, the impact politics will have on society and what is possible politically. Secondly, the extent to which knowledge becomes a component of politics and the ways in which political actors define and comprehend reality; that is, as Haas (1990:11) describes it with required care, 'science becomes a component of politics because the scientific way of grasping reality is used to define the interests that political actors articulate and defend.' The explication of and efforts to enact the interests of a great variety of political actors to a considerable extent is informed by and oriented toward conceptions of society and nature as articulated in the scientific community. Knowledge-based politics also becomes knowledge-based resistance to political action. And since modern scientific discourse does not have a monolithic quality, it becomes a resource of political action for individuals and groups who may pursue rather diverse interests. Scientific discourse generally is, within practical contexts, often a source of uncertainty. Thus, a much more cautious conception of the interrelation between politics and science than found in the portrait of the technical state, for instance, is warranted as well as required. Such a perspective of science and politics that emphasizes the contingent nature of the relations does not advance the erroneous image of a science of politics and the pretense that science is consensual knowledge which holds the key for lasting well-being, the eradication of most problems and social harmony. Nor is knowledge only disinterested and politics only partisan. Knowledge *adds* to the capacity for action. But so does knowledge available to opponents of the regime and the administrative apparatus in power.

Daniel Bell (1973a:160) asks whether or not business has a disproportionate influence in post-industrial society. His answer is that

> one has to distinguish between the underlying *system* of society, which is still capitalist, and the actual 'ecology of games' wherein, on different issues, there are different coalitions, and even the sizable disagreements within the business community on specific political issues.

More generally, Bell anticipates a shift in the societal hierarchy of decision-making in modern society. In post-industrial society he detects a transfer of societal power toward government. He briefly specifies the circumstances that lead to such a shift as follows:

> In post-industrial society, production and business decisions will be subordinated to, or will derive from, other forces in society, the crucial decisions regarding the growth of the economy and its balance will come from government, but they will be based on the government's sponsorship of research and development, of cost-effectiveness and cost-benefit analysis; the making of decisions, because of the intricately linked nature of consequences, will have an increasingly technical character (Bell, 1973a:344).

In other words, Bell appears to reiterate a significant premise of many theories of modern society as industrial societies, namely the notion that modern social, political and economic life is, or at least can be, given the political will for example, be increasingly subject to *planning and rationalization* and that such efficacious instruments in the hand of the state lead to a concentration of power in modern society. Social life becomes more transparent and in that respect it becomes much easier to generate political options and execute governmental decisions. This, of course, implies that it becomes easier to administratively control individuals and groups. I am convinced that these expectations are seriously flawed even though they express sentiments within social science and politics that dominated their respective agendas for decades.

While it remains to be seen whose analysis is closer to the socio-political trends as they develop, assertions about a *narrowing* of the distribution of economic as well as political power in post-industrial society, as some critics of the theory of post-industrial society also anticipate (e.g. Birnbaum, 1971a:397), compete with assumptions and concerns, perhaps even fears, about a progressive decomposition of political power in advanced society. In some instances, these concerns easily give way to calls for ways of strengthening the role of the state.[16] However, at least until the early 1970s, the fears of classic discourse about a rapid and more or less *inevitable* concentration of power in capitalist society were not widely questioned or seen as invalidated. On the contrary, they represented operative theoretical analyses of the distribution of power in modern society.

But as Norbert Birnbaum (1971a:405) also observed at the time, 'a number of phenomena in many societies have recently pointed to a widespread conviction, on the part of even those in relatively well situated positions in the social structure, that they are powerless to alter the major political direction of their societies.'[17]

[16] A systems-theoretical perspective that stresses, above all, the reality of incessant functional differentiation and specialization in advanced society would come to the conclusion that aside from the persistence and relevance of asymmetrical power relations in modern society, modern societies importantly are entities in which co-existence, co-ordination and compatibility among subsystems constitute the paramount problem; that is, 'all subsystems find themselves under continual pressure to relate to other spheres of social action; as well, each subsystem needs to invest a portion of the growing options to act available to it toward the stabilization of these relations. In other words, in "modern" societies, subsystems can afford to behave in a recklessly selfish manner and demand to be the primary and superior agent for all forms of social action' (Offe, 1986:102). But how can co-ordination of the co-existence of subsystems be arranged, and by whom – by heroic or charismatic individuals at the helm of political and economic institutions (Max Weber), free-floating intellectuals (Karl Mannheim) or symbolic media of interchange (Talcott Parsons)?

[17] Claus Offe (1986:104) summarizes the relevant experiences of elites in Western societies as follows: 'On the one hand, virtually all relevant matters of social, economic and political existence are contingent, may be chosen and are changing . . . on the other hand, the institutional and structural frames that mediate all contingency are at the same time beyond political, perhaps even intellectual disposition. The perfected ability of subsystems to continually generate new options clashes with their inability to control or responsibly alter the newly created and difficult interrelations that also are generated at the macro-level.' One could summarize the argument by observing that the extension of the capacity of subsystems

Indeed, the assertion that social relations are increasingly difficult to design from above, or that the *governability* of society decreases, began to be more widely discussed in the 1970s, especially among neo-conservative social scientists.[18] Concern, in the context of the thesis of the lack of governability of modern society, is not with the departure of politics and politicians in the wake of the efficiency of instrumental rationality, but the disappearance of the ability of politicians to carry out their mandate as the result of a heightened 'irrationality' of politics.[19] And as the choice of terms already signals, the thesis about the loss of governability tends to be a state-centered approach. The specific diagnosis usually involves reference to (a) an overload of the political system with claims, expectations and objectives; and (b) the disparity between the 'inflation' in claims and ability of the state apparatus to deliver, or the state's steering and performance capacity.

The plausibility of such ungovernability appears to be – despite the absence of systematic and persuasive empirical analyses – widely shared. Claus Offe ([1979] 1984:75), for example, refers to the 'highly descriptive value of the ungovernability thesis', that is, the 'two components of the diagnosis fully and correctly circumscribe the functional problems that now confront the capitalist welfare and intervention state.' Moreover, the empirical evidence of a wealth of symptoms manifest, for example, in new social movements, is persuasive.[20] More recent political events, it would seem, this time add to the perception of the impotence especially of multinational political organizations. For the purposes of this discussion, I

---

goes hand in hand with the increasing rigidity of the macro-system itself or with an increasing backwardness of capacities to act at the collective level. And therefore, as Offe (1986:106) concludes, 'one of the flip sides and paradoxical outcomes of modernization processes is the preference for the status quo and immobility of modern society at large. Such a rigidity fails to resonate with the basic motive of modernity, namely the extension in abilities to act and select.'

[18] John Keane (1988:6–11) examines the apparent contradiction in neo-conservative discourse about the role of the state in modern society which, on the one hand, favors policies to roll back the state and, on the other hand, is concerned about the loss of its political authority.

[19] As a result, there is a fundamental contradiction between concerns voiced over the growing ungovernability of modern society and renewed warnings about the 'dangers of societal rationalization' in a post-modern age, especially the promotion of a 'deep and progressive disempowerment' of the clients of the modern welfare state and the subjects of corporate capitalism (White, 1991:7–8).

[20] Few, if any, social scientists implicate the social sciences themselves in these developments, especially in the story of the genesis of the overload of expectations that the state is capable in principle of solving many of the problems social scientists identify as in need of solution, in the first instance. One observer who does not hesitate to indict the social sciences is Friedrich Tenbruck (1977:144). He points to the central role of social sciences in conceptualizing problems as social problems and in offering solutions based on social science constructs. According to Tenbruck, the social sciences therefore ought to be credited with a long list of practical failures. At least indirectly, the social sciences are held responsible for a growing gap between performance and expectations.

also accept the premise that it is much more difficult for the state to govern under contemporary conditions.

But it is necessary to emphasize that the thesis of a loss of governability in modern society often turns into a lament about the deprivations the state appears to have to suffer and the need to increase state authority and power. My own concern, however, is not in any way devoted to a lament about the decline in the political authority of the modern state. Nor is my concern with therapies, especially in the sense of uttering profound doubts about the foundations of the liberal state, particularly the 'absolute' constitutional guarantees of freedom and equality because such rights are seen to undermine, deter or subvert from the required 'discipline' citizens ought to demonstrate in order to ease the immense difficulties the state faces in coping with growing problems.[21] I do not propose to abridge, finally, the question of politics in the knowledge society to a technocratic matter asserting, for instance, that one of the most urgent requirements is to effectively reduce the backwardness of the social sciences in order to more effectively generate 'healing', that is, practical social science knowledge.

The thesis of the decrease in governability of modern society would appear to imply, on the surface at least, that those groups and individuals harboring feelings of powerlessness, who either still recall the former extensive unassailable power of the state or who have effectively resisted, deflected, delayed and altered governmental decisions, now experience a greater sense of power. Those in power may well experience their inability to effectively cope with the problems at hand as a loss of authority, for example, as the result of a withdrawal of normative consent by the public.[22] Since the matter of governability was mainly examined from the perspective of the state, namely the agency of the state and its loss of

---

[21] The following warning by Wilhelm Hennis (1977:16) is perhaps representative of views that then may be interpreted as a strong justification for a dismantling of constitutional rights in an attempt to improve the capacity of the state to impose its will: 'Since all conduct, our entire existence is based on our opinions, it is self-evident how difficult it must be to govern or, at least could be, in communities based on absolute freedom and equality of all opinions . . . It is self-evident that the huge challenges humanity and individual political systems face or, are about to confront, can only be met with an unusual degree of *discipline, energy and morale (Zucht)*' (emphasis added). In the end, therefore, *systemic* attributes of the liberal state form are held responsible for its practical impotence. Thus, 'what Marxists erroneously ascribe to the capitalist economy is in reality a result of the democratic political process' (Huntington, 1975:73). The historian Ernst Nolte (1993) shares such a diagnosis and calls it merely a realistic appraisal of the state of modern liberal politics. As Offe ([1979] 1984:81) therefore has stressed 'in the conservative world-view the crisis of governability is a disturbance in the face of which the false path of political modernization must be abandoned and nonpolitical principles of order, such as family, property, achievement, and science, must again be given their due.' A return to the past, especially the early modern or even pre-modern world that derived its coherence from the adherence to centralized, hierarchical and patriarchal religious sanctions of course is an absurd demand.

[22] As Rose (1979:31) for example asserts, 'consent and effectiveness are inter-related, for the success of any public policy requires the co-operation of affected citizens.'

political authority, most diagnoses first and foremost made reference to a crisis brought about by the *disappearing* legitimacy[23] of governments.[24] Such diagnoses not only neglect to contemplate the gains and benefits of 'ungovernability' but also often fail to examine reasons, other than alleged withdrawal of consent, as responsible forces for the decline in the efficacy of the state. Such a set of symptoms also assumes that the *status quo ante* was characterized by extensive political authority enjoyed by the state but also that ineffectiveness gives rise to a loss of consent rather than the reverse.[25] Efficacy is about the ability to get things done. And to get things done means to be more or less in control of the circumstances (*Rahmenbedingungen*) of situations within which objectives actually have to be achieved.[26] Thus, a decline in the degree of governability primarily occurs as a result of a loss in control over conditions and circumstances of political action. Not only are government objectives extended in modern society but the range of circumstances to which they apply are enlarged as well. In addition, the circumstances, of course including the subjects themselves, within which political objectives are realized are changing. And these varied circumstances are not necessarily, at least not to the same degree as may have been the case in the past, subject to the control of state agencies. The unmanageability of circumstances has generally risen. The relative loss of sovereignty or territoriality of the nation-state is one element in the equation that produces a heightened recalcitrance of conditions of political action.[27] Fundamentally, however, the experience and perception of 'ungovernability' is linked to political conduct and administrative procedures that continue to attempt to realize objectives based on the premise that changes in the unmanageability of circumstances

[23] The change in the foundations of the legitimacy granted to the modern state includes, as some critics have stressed with particular force, an uncoupling from transcendental conceptions (cf. Hennis, 1977:18–19).

[24] Theodor Schieder's (1977:40) definition of the lack of governability reflects this preoccupation quite well: 'Ungovernability . . . constitutes the paralysation and inability to act of the executive . . . because of a *lack of consensus* of the citizens of a state, due to a *loss of confidence* of the state among its citizens, a so-called *legitimation crisis* may result.'

[25] In addition, much of the literature tends to be silent about the 'concrete objects of conflict that constitute the substance of the demands and expectations as they do about the character of those matters requiring regulation' (Offe, [1979] 1984:79).

[26] The distinction between social integration and system integration, or between rules that are followed by individuals and regularities at the collective level that are self-implementing, is discussed by Offe ([1979] 1984:83), who offers the following description of the loss of efficacy of the state that takes both of these dimensions into consideration: 'Social systems may be said to be ungovernable if the rules their members follow violate their own underlying functional laws, or if they do not *act* in such a way that these laws can *function* at the same time' (Offe ([1979] 1984:313).

[27] More generally, the developments I have sketched have frequently been described as a rise in the complexity of the conditions of political action (e.g. Skolnikoff, 1976). Often included in this description is reference to the growing, frequently involuntary, importation of problems into nation-states and rising 'outer direction' of possible political responses (cf. Hennis, 1977).

can be neglected as irrelevant.[28] The accelerated, 'home-made' transformation of society generally has lowered the sensitivity toward evolving limits and barriers against further, especially radical transformations of society. The limits in question, that is, the growing recalcitrance of circumstances are the product of these transformations including their unanticipated and undesirable consequences.

Shifts in the balance of power in society do not necessarily have zero-sum qualities or are uni-directional. That is to say, the decline in the governability may well go hand in hand with a continued decline in aspirations for power, or a process of general depoliticization among the citizens of a particular society.[29] On the other hand, the amount of available power may actually increase.

As a result of decline in the immediate societal significance of the economy due to its success in tackling relative material scarcity, the nature of political conflict is changing as well. With the diminished relevance of the traditional social constructs of property and labor there should be not merely a shift in values in the sense of objectives pursued by political actors but even more importantly an enlargement of the resources at the disposal of actors. Politics, once viewed as a struggle between owners of the means of production and those who own labor power, gives way to much broader political and social conflicts involving, generally speaking, life-style factors but also a repositioning in the agendas of political parties and the spectrum of parties.[30] Ronald Inglehart (1977, 1987) has described such a shift in *values* that govern political preferences and class-based politics in advanced societies as a modification in beliefs toward a post-materialistic outlook. The overall speed of the transformation of values in society as a whole is tempered by the persistence of beliefs during an individual's lifetime. The shift, therefore, follows very much along the lines Karl Mannheim described in his pioneering essay on the social fact of generations and generational differences in world-views. The emergence of a post-materialist world-view commences with those generations in the post-war era who spent their formative years in conditions of relative economic and physical security. The trend toward post-materialist values implies new political priorities, especially with regard to communal values and life-style

[28] Friedrich Tenbruck (1977:135) is correct when he speaks of the limited consciousness of the extent to which the conditions of actions can be 'manipulated' because such limits have been declared to be obsolete in light of the growing ability to rationally plan and control political conduct, or because experiences with such limits have become increasingly scarce in everyday life.

[29] Such a response might be especially strong if the expectations (and their disappointment) toward government also proceed from the premise that the state ought to be the primary agent for effectively coping with a growing range of recalcitrant problems.

[30] A repositioning of the platform or the spectrum of political parties takes place depending on the legal basis that either enables or discourages the formation of new political organizations.

issues,[31] and leads to a gradual neutralization of political polarization based on traditional class-based loyalties. The result is that overall class-linked voting, for instance, 'in most democracies is less than half as strong as it was a generation ago' (Inglehart, 1987:1298).

At the same time, the volume and quality of the resources available to political actors in modern society have risen considerably. But the increase in the resources available to the political actor is not the outcome of a redistribution of existing capacities of action. It is the result of an extension of capacities of action from which mainly 'ordinary' citizens have benefited. That is to say, the extension of the state paradoxically has empowered its citizens by extending the sphere of the private and personal and by producing numerous structural indeterminacies. The very 'success' of the state, its original autonomy and differentiation, the enlargement of the range, scope and intensity of its functions has meant that individuals and non-state groups have gained access to resources which have aided them in their ability to approach, entice, demand, resist, deflect etc. efforts of state agencies. And in the course of these developments, the state has lost its status as a monolithic entity.[32]

In short, the lament about the loss of authority of the state has to be augmented by the story of the rapid expansion of education, especially tertiary education (see Table 9.1), the enfranchisement and extension of citizenship to previously marginal groups in modern society, the defusion of class conflict, the growth of wealth and entitlements, the expansion of and easier access to communication networks, the enlargement of the mass media, the rapid growth of knowledge-based occupations and therefore of knowledge and skills that can be utilized as a resource not only on the job but in a variety of social and political contexts and, finally, the exceptional growth of professionals in many fields in search of extending their tasks. The devolution of state, if any, is much more likely the result of its own success than any other singular factor.[33]

---

[31] More specifically, Inglehart (1987:1297) enumerates issues that reflect some of the recent political discussions about environmental risks, disarmament and alternative energy sources as exemplary post-materialist political issues.

[32] And as Cerny (1990:197) observes, 'the actions of non-state agents and other structures in relation to the state have increasingly tended to involve approaching it in a partial way, creating pressure groups, policy demands, issue networks, and political allocation processes on single issues or limited clusters of issues.'

[33] At the level of intellectual culture and politics, the shift that may be observed toward a celebration of the local and the reassertion of traditional individual values perhaps resonates with the more general societal developments I have described and may also represent, at least in the self-consciousness of those active in such movements, a 'protest against homogenization of state-bureaucratic capitalism – against creeping mediocrity, mass-culture, unisex society' (Friedman, 1989:54). However, such a diagnosis simultaneously perpetuates the myth of the efficacy of the power of the state in the past and underestimates the importance of fundamental transformations in the structure of society as a precursor of important cultural shifts.

Table 9.1   *Education at tertiary level[1] in selected countries, 1950–1989 (number of students per 100,000 inhabitants)*

	1950	1965	1975	1980	1985	1989
Chad	–	–	14	–	34	69[2]
Kenya	–	32	65	78	108	135
Mexico	136	312	908	1321	1522	1515
United States	1508	2840	5179	5311	5118	5596
Canada	593	1857	3600	4040	5100	5034
Japan	471	1110	2017	2065	1943	2184
Austria	338	680	1286	1811	2292	2638
France	334	1269	1971	1998	2318	2842
Germany (FRG)	256	632	1684	1987	2540	2843
Spain	19	41	1518	1859	2422	2655[2]
Sweden	241	888	1985	2062	2200	2196
United Kingdom	242	579	1304	1468	1824	1954[2]

[1] Tertiary education requires, as a minimum condition of admission, the successful completion of education at the secondary level (e.g. high school or *Gymnasium*).
[2] 1988.

Sources: UNESCO, *Statistical Yearbook 1970* (Table 2.12); UNESCO, *Statistical Yearbook 1991* (Table 3.10)

Fragmentation and homogenization of social life

During the past fifty years, there has been no scarcity of serious and not so serious reflections advancing the suggestion that contemporary society already is or is in danger of becoming a *mass society* (e.g. Adorno and Horkheimer, [1947] 1987:140–196). Some of these observations are credible efforts to come to grips with what makes the contemporary cultural epoch special, but many other writings that come to the same conclusions are at best superficial cultural critiques which proclaim to have witnessed the destruction of culture itself. In many cases, these reflections are manifestations of the phenomenon they claim to have discovered (cf. König, [1956] 1965). In recent years, the mass society thesis has lost much of the appeal it had during and after the war when it was associated with totalitarianism.

In any case, the well-entrenched standard view of much of modern society, more recently, of modernization on a global scale, or even more generally of 'modernity' itself, is, it seems to me, the simple notion that we are witnessing greater and greater *homogeneity* (generalization) in virtually all important aspects of social and cultural life. As a matter of fact, that modern society is embarking on an apparently irreversible course toward homogenization accompanies the description of the development of modern society from its beginning. Each major technological innovation in turn is feared as a further serious threat to individuality, and is seen as instrumental in heightening the monotony of social life. The most recent threat, of course, is the advent of information technology, while the previous phase on the road to a mass society was the evolution of the mass media and its monotonous message.

In the meantime, it seems, the argument, which sees such an unavoidable trend toward a generalization of life styles and life chances in society, has become somewhat more sophisticated and differentiated. Some critics observe that improvements in technology make it now possible, for example in the area of advertising, to reach the individual as an individual or, better, as a member of a segment of the total market. In the past, individuals had to be homogenized in order to be reached in large numbers. Initially, while the main threat of mass society is to individuality, the additional novel danger, posed by the new techniques of control and advertising, is the emergence of a form of social equality which is reduced to natural inequalities. Curtis (1988:104), for example, sees recent developments as a 'powerful reinforcement of social stratification that could be hereditary' and therefore as a peril that modern society will become almost caste-like since advertisers also succeed in their aim to 'socialize' *new* cohorts in each market segment into similar values and life styles and, in the end, help to perpetuate structures of inequality. One wonders, of course, whether the repeatedly recited warnings are not really the hopes and desires only of the alleged masters of these techniques and their main clients. The state, corporations and multinational political organizations, for example, invest enormous energy and resources to achieve the very influence that some observers ascribe to these techniques or even describe as actual outcomes of such public relations efforts. But perhaps the only victims of this alleged massive influence are the clients and critical observers who take the claims for the excessive efficacy of the new instruments of social control and influence seriously.

The mass society thesis and its more recent variants perhaps also exemplify the much more complex thesis that decreasing variation through time is one of the crucial and predictable features of stabilizing systems and social evolution. This thesis, in turn, has surfaced more recently within the context of discussions about the *globalization* of social action. The concept of globalization, in a number of theoretical works, appears to have become the substitute for what was at one time primarily conceived as the increasing rationalization (or homogenization) of social relations. While it may well be *theoretically* true that decreasing variation is associated with or even brings about stable systems, the premise ought to be examined rather carefully in order to determine whether our age actually is an age of decreasing variation. It could well be that knowledge, to state it merely in these terms, in practice, increases variation and therefore operates in exactly the opposite direction by maintaining or even increasing the extent of the variety of life-styles and living conditions. In short, the specific questions which one needs to raise in this context are whether knowledge societies not only are increasingly politically contingent societies but whether such contingency is even more general[34] and associated with increased immobility, rigidity *and* generalization; that is, contingency and extension may well be attributes of essentially the same developmental process pointing to persistent stretching of social action and acting as catalysts of greater homogeneity and this time not merely on the national but a global scale.

Since the second half of the 1980s, there has been a widely asserted notion of a globalization of environmental risks, economic processes and cultural practices as a new phase in world history. While I will limit my discussion to the recent past (and immediate future) and to the possible social rather than natural (physical or biological) coherence of the world,[35] it is quite plausible to assert that the processes under increasing scrutiny by contemporary social scientists are not of recent origin, let alone modern phenomena (cf. Robertson, 1990), nor have theoretical assertions about global economic markets and the emergence of a world culture necessarily been constructed for the first time in recent years.[36] In addition, it might be equally reasonable to assert that genuine global processes are unusual if not exceptional events and processes. Global processes tend to be quite exceptional if one applies a conception of global that requires that such processes lose both any relevance of the location of their origin[37] and any

---

[34] Witness, for example, observations which pertain to the relation between state authority, the legal system and modern technology: 'The legal system as the foundation and stabilizing force of state authority will lose in importance to the extent to which modern information and communication technologies displace traditional means of administrative authority in the form of dossiers' (Wolf, 1988:170).

[35] Fernand Braudel ([1979] 1992:49) refers to the possibility of the physical coherence of the world and the possibility that it and a 'generalization of a certain biological history common to all mankind suggests one way in which the globe could be said to be unified, long before the voyages of discovery, the industrial revolution or the interdependence of economies.'

[36] Perhaps it is somewhat unusual to do so now but I like to quote from the *Communist Manifesto* (Marx and Engels, [1848] 1971:93) to illustrate the point about the long-standing assertion of material as well as cultural movement toward globalization: 'The need of a constantly expanding market for its products chases the bourgeoisie over the whole surface of the globe. It must nestle everywhere, settle everywhere, establish connections everywhere. The bourgeoisie has through its exploitation of the world-market given a cosmopolitan character to production and consumption in every country . . . In place of the old local and national seclusion and self-sufficiency, we have intercourse in every direction, universal interdependence of nations. And as in material, so also in intellectual production. The intellectual creations of individual nations become common property. National one-sidedness and narrow-mindedness become more and more impossible, and from the numerous national and local literatures, there arises a world literature.' In short, Marx and Engels not only anticipated a world capitalist economy but a global superstructure but paid little if any attention to persisting or emerging collective economic inequalities resulting from globalization. Twentieth-century theories of imperialism, dependency theory or, more recently, world-system theory, in contrast, fill the void and would stress the pattern of inequality within the global economy.

[37] Such an assertion, for example, may well apply to the release of carbon dioxide (CO_2) and other gases released anywhere in the world that rapidly disperse into a kind of global

influence of the setting that they effect and in which they become established as they are dispersed and disseminated globally.[38]

One of the general dangers associated with the thesis of a global impact of social activities, as a result, is the treatment of the globalization process as an undifferentiated process, easily taking on as a theoretical category almost black box-like qualities.[39] The globe is a divided world, a fact often lost in the rush to assert globalization as the new master process of societal transformation. The world population is growing at a staggering rate. Virtually all of the increase occurs in the poorest nations of the world. Nationalism is a vital political, cultural and economic force in most countries of the world. Most so-called global companies or firms are correctly perceived as having a home base.[40] In this respect, the notion of global change could easily take the place vacated by the black box of 'scientific knowledge' or some other master concept simultaneously signifying relentless social change and its foundation and often its consequences.

There is also the danger that the analysis of globalization is merely driven by a functionalist perspective concerned only with the alleged world-wide consequences of social, political and economic change, for instance, in the sense of a growing interdependence of societies, or a rapidly escalating cultural homogeneity and generalization of cultural practices across national boundaries. Invoking globalization and its often only implicit counterpart, for example, local, national, embeddedness, permits a perpetuation of the preference of classic social science discourse for conceptual dichotomies or binary codes as strict antitheses (cf. Baldamus, 1976). In addition, although many other clichés abound in discussions of globalization, including such notions as 'late capitalism', the 'multinational corporation' or 'global environmental change', the primary assertion appears to be that these changes are effected by economic developments on all fronts. The outcome is often that a crude form of economic determinism is reintroduced into social science discourse as well

---

inventory of gas concentration through global circulation patterns of air and water. In such a case, the location of origin of the gases makes no difference.

[38] For example, any country that decides to mitigate the process of global warming with the help of an energetic program of energy conservation and/or energy conversion and does so without an international agreement of cost sharing or some other form of compensation arrangement will alone bear the *costs* while the *benefits* are dispersed globally. By the same token, any country that aggressively industrializes and in the process raises its conventional energy consumption will reap certain benefits, for example, in terms of higher employment and a growing domestic product while the costs in terms of higher fossil fuel emissions are distributed more equally across nations (cf. Schelling, 1990).

[39] Another potential 'danger' or referent associated with discussions about globalization in social science concerns the role of the term and whatever it signifies in continuing political struggles, for example, between corporations and the state, corporations and labor unions, the state and labor unions, political regions and the national government or, finally, between different states in trade negotiations, for example.

[40] According to an article in *The Economist* (February 6–12, 1993, p. 69), 'in 1991 only 2% of the board members of big American companies were foreigners. In Japanese companies, foreign directors are as rare as British sumo wrestlers.'

as a conflation of structural and cultural transformations. But the range of theorizing and research about global processes is fairly diverse signifying perhaps that any global transformation of the world has yet to impose anything resembling cognitive closure on social science discourse.

The now almost taken for granted and widely discussed assumption about the nature of dominant trends in the social, cultural and economic relations of advanced societies is that the internationalization of the economy, that is, the extent to which national boundaries become irrelevant to economic affairs or the extent to which cultural products and economic commodities become international rather than local objects, implies, in an almost linear cause and effect relationship, that forms of social life, taken in its broadest sense possible, will also invariably converge into more unitary patterns and structures. And in this expansive sense at least, contemporary theories of globalization manage to reiterate assumptions of classic nineteenth-century social science that also anticipated a conjunction of modern life toward dominant evolutionary societal features.[41]

More specifically, the global shifts in economic activity effect the emergence of a global culture *and* 'the potential demise of national, regional, local and ethnic cultures in the face of the globalization of many aspects of life' (Dicken, 1992:422). As master processes, fragmentation and differentiation, it would appear, give way to homogenization and possibly create the foundations for building the 'planet's first global civilization' (Perlmutter, 1991:898). The motor of these transformations is always the economy. Generalization and fragmentation are rarely seen as concurrent trends of global shifts. However, even if fragmentation and homogenization are considered as concurrent outcomes of global trends, an essential asymmetry between both shifts remains because the trend toward correspondence is understood to represent the much more powerful economic forces while fragmentation 'merely' applies to cultural practices and only further undermines the effectiveness of the 'superstructure'. As a result, cultural artifacts and processes remain subordinate to material processes.[42] I would like to criticize these perspectives as hasty and imprecise generalizations.

---

[41] In the light of these assumptions about irreversible and powerful modern societal trends, prominent social scientists conclude that the time has come to advocate and develop 'a single sociology' (cf. Archer, 1991:131) because the 'key change over the last few decades has been Globalisation – a multi-faceted process entailing *a growing interconnectedness of structure, culture and agency*, and a parallel *de-differentiation of traditional boundaries* . . . In short, as we begin to live in One World, this new social reality supplies us with good reasons for overhauling our theoretical assumptions and frameworks' (Archer, 1991:133; emphasis added).

[42] Purely economic processes are not always identified as the only or even primary motor for the current convergence or fragmentation of cultural practices on a global scale. Greater monotony and homogeneity, in particular, are attributed to other processes as well, for example, cultural monism is expected to be the outcome of the revolution in mass communication, computer technology, global travel and so on (e.g. Sartori, 1971:64).

First of all, from a theoretical point of view, the terms homogenization and fragmentation are ill suited to capture trends which may extend to some institutions in some societies but not to a range of others in the same society in which such shifts may encounter severe intentional and unintended opposition. The terms, at least as typically employed, do not do justice to more complicated outcomes of global shifts since they tend to demand, almost by definition, that social processes are mutually exclusive, consistent and universal. Some care has to be taken in choosing the terms which best capture the persistent *enlargement* of modern life for it is by no means self-evident that the forces of the market, for example, can easily, if at all, conquer and displace existing cultural processes.

Secondly, from an empirical point of view, widespread manifestations of an

> implosive loss of faith in the progress of civilization and a corresponding explosion of new cultural movements, from cults and religious revival to primitivism, a new traditionalism, a striving for the re-establishment of a new culturally defined identity . . . [which] is accompanied by an increasing 'national' and ethnic fragmentation . . . and an exponential increase in culturally-based political movements' (Friedman, 1989:51)

would appear to have the first claim to represent a truly global phenomenon.

One of the notable formal attributes of the crude globalization thesis is the implicit assumption that a cohesive foundation for social solidarity and co-operation requires distinct limits to what is socially sanctioned and possible.[43] The globalization thesis, in this respect certainly, represents an extension of the persistent attractiveness to social scientists of theorizing about a reduction in the enormous variety of existing cultural practices and political contexts of societies toward more unitary formations as a deterrent to social disorder. Concern with the threat of social disorganization, anomie, even chaos as the result of the break-up of traditional forms of life have been a part of social science discourse from its inception. The birth of modern, industrialized society also represents the dawn of the destruction of the basis of traditional forms of social solidarity and a persistent threat to social solidarity unless a new solid foundation is somehow located. It is possible therefore that the preoccupation with the extent to which globalization has the function of leveling social diversity represents a continuation of the classic search for new forms of social cement, solidarity and co-operation in the form of fewer legitimate manifestations of social and cultural conduct.

The theoretical attention paid to the phenomena of generalization and fragmentation was not always identical and the meaning of the terms was not necessarily symmetric. For a long time, the term 'fragmentation' conveyed the greater threat to the foundations of society. In general,

---

[43] Another significant example of the priority of such a concern, and for the agreement often found with respect to this issue in social science discourse, is the debate surrounding the alleged threats of relativism (see Meja and Stehr, 1992).

however, it would appear that a preoccupation with forces which may overcome, if not fragmentation *per se*, then at least bitter diversities and cleavages among groups and classes, has not really lessened very much since it first become a central focus of classic social science discourse. The thrust of the explicit or implicit normative assessments of the rise of fragmentation or the rapid upsurge of homogenization has shifted somewhat in recent years. It has shifted from a broadly affirmative stance, still an essential part of the modernization approach, to a more skeptical attitude about global shifts that are assumed to induce much greater homogeneity of forms of life. But the displacement of once predominant and affirmative expectations and assessments of forces diminishing social fragmentation has not been completely reversed.

If not quite explicit, at least implicit in Bell's theory of post-industrial society, for example, is the idea that all industrial societies will sooner or later be moving along 'America Road' (Floud, 1971:31) and that forms of life in post-industrial society therefore converge toward patterns anticipated in societies that first experience these transformations. But what exactly is being diffused and at what rate? What aspects resist diffusion? What images diffuse rapidly and by what means, for example, oral, visual or written images? How homogeneous is the process of global change and how much alike are its consequences? Are there still national technologies? And, does an internationalization of the economy imply a disappearance of the imbalances of wealth? Is this process somehow subject to the control of identifiable agents and mainly for the benefit of some and not others? It would seem that these and many other issues simply lose significance and relevance in any theoretical effort preoccupied with manifestations of a decline in the fragmentation of societies and the rise of social coherence within societies.

But before I attempt to sketch some of the characteristics of globalization as a form of extension or 'stretching process' (Giddens, 1990c:64), especially in the area of economic and political activity, I will add critically to the list of some of the typical shortcomings of an overly enthusiastic and radically affirmative endorsement of the notion of globalization.

The essential shortcoming of the thesis of an increasing cultural, social and economic globalization which will result in a growing generalization of local, regional and national forms of life involves, first, the dubious assertion, that local contexts are (a) virtually identical; (b) condemned to be mere passive recipients of a dominant system; and (c) have few if any choices in the face of the overwhelming supremacy, attractiveness, excellence and superiority of the conquering social facts. The assumption that there is a threat to local, regional and national cultural practices is based on the questionable premise that the recipients, the audience, the consumers of what may otherwise well be globally distributed commodities, trends in fashion and cultural practices have little if any means to adjust or even combat or liberate themselves from the influence of these forces. Such a thesis actually tells us more about the desires of the forces attempting to colonize than about their chances of succeeding in simply replacing local cultures, for instance with imports. Generalizations about homogenization are premature and even misleading.[44] Dominant civilizations in the past were not able to easily achieve dominance, nor do current developments warrant the conclusion that local cultures and identities are simply displaced or even destroyed by so-called global trends. The probability that such leveling developments occur should actually decline in the context of knowledge societies since the availability of potentially effective resources to comprehend and resist homogenization increases.[45]

For it is one of the striking features of the present dissolution, perhaps even decline of Western hegemony, assuming such an image was ever adequate, that new and more forceful cultural movements, novel local identities, regional and national identities have appeared undermining and resisting any existential homogenization on a world scale. As a matter of fact, such developments are by no means novel since similar processes can be observed in earlier civilizational systems (Friedman, 1992:364).[46] Whether the (re-)emergence of renewed but transformed and more assertive local identities and culture is possible only in the face of a weakness in the center and a loss of identity, or whether the rise and strong assertion of local identities is concomitant with and accentuated by efforts to colonize local contexts remains an open question.[47]

In any event, the limits to cultural homogenization on a world scale or within the confines of an ancient civilization have to do, as Ralf Dahrendorf (1980:753), for example, also observes, with the fact that 'every culture has assimilated the symbols of modernity in its own traditions; every individual converts these symbols into part of his own and only his own life.' Local contexts cannot be apprehended as entirely passive and openly receptive

---

[44] In much the same sense, Manuel Castells (1989:2) underlines that new information technologies obviously do have 'a fundamental impact on societies, and therefore on cities and regions, but their effect varies according to the interaction with the economic, social, political, and cultural processes that shape the production and use of technological medium.'

[45] A similar assertion, though without much elaboration, can be found in Niklas Luhmann's (1988:170) discussion of the modern economy: 'A simultaneous increase in regional differences and global interdependencies perhaps is the most remarkable fact [about modern societies committed to growth]. Global society more and more becomes a unitary system and, at the same time, a system that produces and has to cope with enormous discrepancies.' And such a development precludes, as Luhmann finally assumes, 'a political unification without offering a functional equivalent'.

[46] Friedman (1992:365) primarily refers to the populations affected by the conquest of the Greeks and integrated into the Hellenistic empire. For example, there appears to have been during a specific phase of Hellenism, an 'explosive increase in ethnic identification and religious mysticism'.

[47] Friedman (1992:366) favors a model which assumes a loss of traditional cultural identity as an initial response to an outside conquest followed by a re-emergence and ultimately revival of cultural identity in the phase of the decline. In other words, there may be an inverse relation between the formation and spread of an imperial system and the constitution and maintenance of cultural identities. But it is in periods of declining hegemony that local cultural identities acquire space to re-assert themselves.

situations to outside influences. Local contexts not only offer resistance but means of transforming (actively 'assimilating') cultural practices which are not native to the context in question. Moreover, local and regional contexts do not necessarily constitute identical circumstances but are as collectivities, in relation to each other, for example, stratified in some sense. In addition, a variety of local contexts display, each in its own way, different patterns of internal stratification affecting the impact of practices and products produced elsewhere but now consumed locally and made sensitive to contingent local circumstances. In short, cultural products and practices are not put to use and enacted independent of the context-in-use.

The assertion of an incessant globalization of life involves, secondly, the dubious proposition that generalization and fragmentation are radically opposed processes. However, a more reasonable assertion views the intensification of world-wide social relations, which often rapidly links local with distant events, as processes concomitant with an intensification of local sentiments and practices as a response to the former. As Anthony Giddens (1990c:65), for example, illustrates, 'globalised social relations probably serve to diminish some aspects of nationalist feeling linked to nation-states (or some states) but may be causally involved with the intensifying of more localised nationalist sentiments.' The forward extension of social conduct in terms of time and distance also generates pressures to extend conduct backwards in terms of time and location.

There are, on the other hand, some positive entries in the ledger of the thesis of globalization. The reason why the notion of globalization is so readily endorsed with respect to economic activities, that is, with respect to trade patterns, financial transactions, consumption preferences, the organization of production, labor market constraints, capital movements, economic cycles etc., is based, to a large extent, on the concurrent assumption that economic activities are increasingly market driven. And as long as they are freed from the constraints and chains of local, regional, national and transnational government regulation and intervention, economic activities have an almost natural tendency to expand across the disappearing boundaries to form a global market and, due to workings of the invisible hand of the market, economic transactions become context insensitive. In the end, the actual functioning of the now global market comes closer and closer to the economic model of a perfect market.

Such a representation of economic processes of course is inaccurate. Not only is it probable that completely unregulated markets are utopian and self-destructive, but to date every political system has employed political means to support and shield economic actors within its sphere of influence from unemployment, for example, and every political regime has utilized political instruments to redistribute market outcomes and thereby affect subsequent market processes. Pressures to extend self-regulated economic markets will always be tempered by different kinds of social movements which champion redistributive interests as well as non-economic goals. These concerns will be translated into regulations and constraints on the market by government and ultimately affect the competition in international trade and its reciprocal impact on national economies.[48] In general, economic activities continue to be mediated, though in a stratified pattern, by a broad range of non-economic factors including a wide scope of national (compare the trade imbalance between the US and Japan) and multinational government (compare the difficulties in concluding a GATT agreement) regulation.

Commodities are losing their national identities though they may still carry, for sentimental, image-enhancing, legal, trade-policy driven or other reasons, labels which identify a product as 'Made in Germany' for example. But a close examination of the composition of many consumer goods will show that they are made up of parts from many continents and many nations.[49]

What is new about social, economic and cultural processes subsumed under the label of globalization, the global system or the emergence of transnational institutions then is that these developments constitute a further intensification, stretching and expansion of transactions, co-ordination, interconnection and fusion of conduct. These processes are sustained and mediated by the emergence of the knowledge society; however, they have to be seen as developments that intensify world-wide social relations and nurture local transformations. The outcome is not, as Giddens (1990c:64) reminds us, 'a generalized set of changes acting in a uniform direction, but consists of mutually opposed tendencies'.

The social control of knowledge

In the course of the development of industrial society, liberal democracies successively institute increasingly elaborate legal frames pertaining to the social status and use of property and labor. Thus the freedom of economic actors to exercise power and authority by virtue of their individual or collective ownership over labor power or the means of production is increasingly constrained and circumscribed by a host of legal norms. Ownership is restrained not only spontaneously, for example, by the market but by the state. Deliberate and anticipatory legal constraints on the use of property and labor are not neutral. Legal norms convey, from the point of view of certain actors, especially for those who feel impotent in acquiring ownership and in affecting the legal rules pertaining to their disposition, privileges while they signal (natural) rights to those who control property and labor. Unequal access to ownership and therefore any

---

[48] However, it is inaccurate to conclude that markets relatively free of government regulation, for example, in the United States in the field of health care, are necessarily more competitive internationally (cf. Block, 1987:179–184).

[49] At the end of the 1980s, the car 'Golf' produced, or better assembled, by the Volkswagen company in Germany was an aggregate of parts from four continents and twenty-one different countries (cf. *Der Spiegel*, January 11, 1993, p. 107).

stratification of effective influence on the construction of the legal restraints and rights, in turn, is often, but not always exclusively, based on an unequal distribution of labor and property in industrial society, elements that are constitutive of its social and economic existence.

It is almost self-evident that *legal* efforts and legislation in knowledge societies will more and more be directed toward the ways of controlling both the development and employment of knowledge. I emphasize legislative efforts to control scientific knowledge rather then more tenuous forms of informal or spontaneous social control because the latter simply is part and parcel of the conventional state of affairs of science and its relation to society, namely the standard selectivity with which knowledge develops and is utilized. Vigorous opposition to political ventures to limit the considerable autonomy of the modern scientific community and to control knowledge will be as common as was opposition to efforts to control the use of property or the ways in which labor power might be utilized by the owners of the means of production.

While the legal constructs pertaining to labour and property evolved at a time when the 'distance' to the empirical manifestations of these constructs for those who demanded, enacted and sanctioned legal rules was hardly a major concern, today, however, the 'loss of contact' (Holton, 1986:92) itself between science, the public and its representatives is a salient attribute in the dynamics of the interrelation between knowledge and society. That it to say, large segments of the public could be said to have become disenfranchised, at least this is at times the view of the scientific community. The loss of contact is by no means limited to a growing cognitive distance between science and everyday knowledge but is associated with the speed with which knowledge expands and is deployed as a productive capacity. The loss of cognitive proximity extends the political distance to science, for example by limiting public involvement in reflecting on the expected and unanticipated transformations knowledge is capable of producing.[50] The lack of intellectual proximity is an attribute for which the scientific community itself has to share responsibility since the preferred image of science, for example, as a consensual, even monolithic and monologic enterprise is increasingly in conflict both with its actual, contentious public role and its internal struggles over science-in-progress, namely the logic-in-use with respect to defining research priorities, generating data and their interpretation. However, on political and moral grounds and independent of the cognitive distance to science and technology, many groups and institutions will be at the table when decisions are made about issues that affect the development of science and technology. It would be a misleading historical analogy, it seems to me, to think that

[50] At least in the late 1970s, the confidence the public displayed in 'disinterested' scientists to be best qualified to resolve public issues in the area of space exploration, nuclear power or food additive regulation, for example, was still considerable and exceeded that of other groups or agencies by a significant margin (cf. Miller, 1983:90–93; Jasanoff, 1990:12).

the distance, the loss of contact with science, or the considerable scientific illiteracy in modern societies is somehow a 'potentially fatal flaw in the self-conception of the people today' (Holton, 1992:105) and/or signals the possibility of a dramatic collapse in public support for science and a return to the dark ages, whatever that may mean. It would be more accurate to speak of a precarious balance in the dependence and the autonomy of science in modern society. As well, a loss of intellectual contact between science and the public is not incompatible with an equally diffuse support for science in modern society.

From the point of view of the scientific community, the lack of cognitive proximity to the public has its assets and its downside. In another sense, however, the loss of cognitive contact is almost irrelevant. It is rather irrelevant if one means by contact close cognitive proximity, especially as a demand or as a meaningful prerequisite for public participation in issues that have a high science and technology content. Such a suggestion becomes almost meaningless because it would require that the public engages in science-in-progress which is, as we know, highly controversial (cf. Collins, 1987:691).

The loss of contact between science and its public perhaps points, on the other hand, to a partial answer to the question of how the scientific community, in the light of its attractiveness and usefulness for corporations, the military and the state, has been able to maintain its relative intellectual autonomy (cf. Gilbert and Mulkay, 1984). Such autonomy of course is not without its limits and is contingent on a host of factors within and external to the scientific community. The loss of contact is a resource to the scientific community. At least symbolically, it can signal detachment and independence. And detachment and independence can be translated into an asset to the state and other societal agencies that value apparent autonomy. Science becomes an authoritative voice in policy matters or it serves to symbolize, in an ideological and material struggle with different political systems, the openness of the society (cf. Mukerji, 1989:190–203). But the cognitive distance limits, at the same time, the immediate effectiveness of the 'voice of science' in policy matters.[51] From the point of view of the extra-scientific institutions, any extensive autonomy and independence from science results in an excessive celebration of 'normal' scientific activity and a lack of innovativeness. Efforts from the outside to initiate and promote new research programmes may be seen as a counter-vailing force (cf. Krohn and Küppers, 1989:89–95) short of instituting legally binding social control mechanisms.

---

[51] Chandra Mukerji (1989:197) describes the trade-off in this respect well: 'What reassures scientists the most when they face the power of the voice of science and their powerlessness to use the voice in the public arena is the idea of their autonomy. Scientists are not, in the end, politicians, and they suffer political defeats better than the loss of face among their peers. As long as they can conduct research with which they can advance science (both science itself and their positions in it), they can feel potent. But the cost is that scientists cultivate an expertise that empowers someone else.'

It is possible, in fact in some controversies already manifested, that discussions, demands and efforts to legislate selectivity in the ways in which knowledge is developed and employed are linked to strong disaffections with science and will be branded as part of an anti-science crusade. The term 'anti-science' is vague and potentially lumps together a broad range of things that perhaps 'have in common only that they tend to annoy or threaten those who regard themselves as more enlightened' (Holton, 1992:104). Moreover, disaffection with science and technology has always accompanied its development.

The social control of science and technology that has successfully moved from the stage of being-in-progress to some form of completion is already extensive. In all modern societies, we now find elaborate drug regulation agencies that register, test, control or permit pharmaceutical substances to enter the market as drugs. Only a few decades ago, decisions about the production and marketing of chemicals as drugs was in the hands of corporations, individual pharmacists or physicians (cf. Bodewitz et al., 1987). As scientific knowledge is 'applied', it becomes embedded in social contexts external to science. As a part of such embeddedness, knowledge is subject to the kinds of control mechanisms found in these contexts. It simply cannot escape the selectivity that issues from such external contexts, be it only in efforts designed to generate trust toward a certain artifact or solution offered by novel knowledge.

The whole area of national and international intellectual property and copyright protection is another arena in which legislation to control the deployment of scientific and technical knowledge is already extensive. In many ways, such controls date back to at least the 1883 Paris Convention for patents and related industrial matters and the 1886 Berne Convention for copyrights. The acceleration in speed with which inventions reach the market, their shortened economic life span and the extent to which recent inventions, for example, in the field of microelectronics, the organization of production, medical treatments and biotechnology are difficult to protect from copying efforts, will increase pressures to enact further protective legislation (cf. Vaitsos, 1989).

But to legislate and attempt to closely control science-in-progress is a most difficult if not impossible enterprise. In addition, efforts to do so would have the unintended consequence of reducing the authority of science as an asset to politics. Perhaps the most significant barrier to extensive measures to impose external social control mechanisms on science-in-progress is the size and organization of the scientific enterprise today as well as its competitive and international character.[52]

The politics of science should not be conflated with the politics of society. The politics of knowledge are not or cannot merely be reduced to

[52] The enlargement of the scientific community into a genuine international or even global community is beginning to become a focus of reflection and research in science studies (e.g. Schott, 1988, 1993).

the politics of societal power, nor does science only generate knowledge that is essentially political and therefore perhaps eminently practical.

The institution generating knowledge and the institution contemplating and executing political action were once seen to be completely detached domains. At the beginning of this century, the dilemmas of the indispensable separation of science and politics found one of its most appealing expressions in Max Weber's ([1921] 1948:77–128; [1922] 1948:129–156) essays on science and politics as a vocation. Today, the intellectual foundations which allowed Weber to legitimize the fundamental division between the practice of knowledge and politics have fallen into disrepute. While the scientific community and polity still have professional roles and vocations with ideals and career patterns which are at odds, any remaining confidence in the neutral, purely instrumental and apolitical character of science has eroded significantly.

At the present time, therefore, any reference to the politics of knowledge does not any longer constitute a profound break or violation of precious norms of scientific action and essential attributes of scientific knowledge. Science is deeply implicated in social action and political agendas hold sway over science. Precisely how dependent or interdependent science and politics are is a matter of genuine debate and continued empirical analysis. But the widespread disenchantment with science and the extensive material dependence of the scientific community on the state should not give rise to the equally unrealistic proposition that the boundaries between politics and science have vanished without a trace. Science is embedded in particular political realities, and as long as it is situated and implanted in a specific form of civil and political society, in particular one free of totalitarian strains, scientific activity benefits. By the same token, as long as the traffic across the boundaries of science and the rules which govern such transactions remain open in principle and negotiable, both science and society stand to gain.

In as much as knowledge becomes the constitutive principle of modern society, the production and distribution of knowledge can no longer escape, if it ever could, explicit political struggles and conflicts. The production and distribution of knowledge will increasingly also become a domain of more explicit legislation and generally become the target of political and economic decisions. On the one hand, such a development is inevitable because 'as the institutions of knowledge lay claim to public resources, some public claim on these institutions is unavoidable' (Bell, 1968: 238). But in addition, and in some ways perhaps more consequential, as the importance of knowledge as a central resource in modern society increases, its social, economic and political consequences for social relations generally grow rapidly and so will demands to regulate the production, the utilization and access to knowledge.

A significant part of a politics of knowledge will have to be concerned with the consequences of the social distribution of knowledge, especially the stratified access to knowledge. To what extent any dispossession of knowledge, for example, may generate social conflicts and in what ways such struggles may manifest themselves, is an open question. However Daniel Bell (1964:49) warned as early as twenty years ago that right-wing extremism may 'benefit' from any exclusion of social groups from access to and acquisition of technical expertise.

Emancipation through knowledge

A peculiar feature of the heterogeneous discussion of the role of knowledge, information and skills in modern society is how slanted it happens to be; that is, reflections are very often skewed toward and preoccupied with concerns about the repressive potential of growing human knowledge, especially as it enters the 'employ' of powerful aggregate agents, be it a social class, the state, a multinational corporation, the intellectuals, the military-industrial complex, the professions, the estate of science, the Mafia, political parties, the managerial class and so on. Similarly, at the opposite end of the spectrum, discussions about the social distribution of knowledge in modern society often tend to be concerned with the dispossession of the individual from access to expertise and technical competence reducing him or her to playing the role of helpless victim, exploited consumer, alienated tourist, colonized viewer, bored student, de-skilled worker and manipulated voter.

Not only have predictions about the impending assent to almost monolithic power and authority of any of these large social formations so far proved to be illusions, discussions about the social role of knowledge have been, for the most part, state-centered, class-centered, profession-centered, science-centered and so on. Reflections about the social role of knowledge therefore have rarely invoked that tradition of the Enlightenment that saw knowledge as a strong and peculiar force in the liberation of individuals, citizens, workers, women and men. Obviously, if it is the case, as Hans Morgenthau (1970:38) for example observes that people have the feeling that they now live in 'something approaching a Kafkaesque world, insignificant and at the mercy of unchangeable and invisible forces . . . a world of make-believe, a gigantic hoax', then the Enlightenment project that attributed liberating qualities to knowledge has failed miserably to date and, at best, is a utopian promise that may hardly be closer to realization than in the distant past.

A realistic appraisal, an assessment without illusions, however, has to accept that on balance the enlargement of our capacity to act for some has produced not only elements of liberation but also threatening and risk-rich attributes for the same individuals as well as others, as the critics of the growing role of science and technology have long been able to enumerate.[53] The main barrier to a realistic assessment of the impact of

---

[53] Even Karl Popper ([1961] 1992:141) expresses a skeptical judgment about overall benefits for mankind as the result of the advancement of science: 'The progress of science –

knowledge in modern society has been its taken-for-granted image as an instrument that 'naturally' centralizes power, that has virtually uncontested features suppressing any chance of launching effective resistance and that sieves off local knowledge and easily succeeds to fill the vacuum.

As I have tried to argue with respect to a range of issues, such an image is not deserving. This image of knowledge underestimates the influence of various factors on the production of knowledge and the difficulties knowledge encounters as it travels across social and cultural contexts. But such difficulties are opportunities for actors encountering authoritative knowledge or 'expertise' (cf. Smith and Wynne, 1989). That is to say, the need to continually reappropriate knowledge alone leaves its mark on knowledge and the agents engaged in reappropriation. As actors acquire more and more skills in reappropriating knowledge, they also acquire a greater capacity to act. Setting specific pressures and interests further heightens the possibilities of critically 'deconstructing' and reassembling knowledge claims. The social distribution of knowledge is not a zero-sum game. The extension of aggregate knowledge actually may lead, in comparative terms, to an explosion in the capacity of individuals and groups to reappropriate knowledge for their ends, and therefore represent a movement from a situation in which a *few* control circumstances of action to a condition in which *many* exercise some influence.

All this does not mean that ordinary citizens, students, voters and consumers acquire a strong sense of control over either the circumstances of their day-to-day existence or any secure feeling of comprehension of the events beyond local contexts (cf. Giddens, 1990c:146). In short, the general extension of the capacity to act should not be mistaken to mean an abolition of anxiety, risk, luck and, especially, conditions of conduct over which only limited control is exercised. However, such is a far cry from virtual individual impotence in the face of conditions of action controlled by a powerful few.

Knowledge, uncertainty and contingency

The growth of knowledge and the growing societal importance of knowledge forces society to confront at least dual contingencies directly linked to the enlargement of modern knowledge. There is (a) the contingency of knowledge itself; and (b) the heightened contingency of social relations as the result of the growing penetration of knowledge into society. For these reasons, the future, more than ever, is much harder to visualize. It is more difficult to imagine than even Daniel Bell reckoned in his important treatise on post-industrial societies in the mid-1970s. Social, economic and

---

itself partly a consequence of the ideal of self-emancipation through knowledge – is contributing to the lengthening and to the enrichment of our lives; yet it has led us to spend those lives under the threat of an atomic war, and it is doubtful whether it has on balance contributed to the happiness and contentment of man.'

intellectual strains that undoubtedly will attend the dual contingency are not resolved by reverting to the now largely discredited deference for a scientific politics, a return to whatever 'foundations', the image of 'progress' or technocratic solutions of societal problems. However, setting specific opportunities, strains, ambitions, pressures and traditions will lead to very different forms of knowledge societies.

The image of the logic of science from which all individuals and groups associated with the production and dissemination of scientific knowledge directly or indirectly have benefited in the past has been dismantled and replaced by a perspective which comprehends the construction of scientific knowledge as a social and intellectual endeavor and not as a meta-social enterprise progressively approximating a recalcitrant objective reality. The social construction of scientific claims to knowledge or scientific facts and theories, as examined by ethnographic studies of laboratories, public controversies involving scientific expertise and the socio-historical recon-struction of the emergence, establishment and decline of scientific theories (e.g. Mulkay, 1979; Knorr-Cetina and Mulkay, 1983; Stehr and Meja, 1984b; Zuckerman, 1988) strongly attribute a contingency to knowledge. In the past, the eradication of contingency (or disagreement) was seen as the hallmark of the scientific enterprise.

As a result, the harnessing of knowledge will be accompanied not only by continuing concerns about past threats that are persistent fears, for example, the horror of global destruction through nuclear weapons or a major environmental catastrophe, but by a decline in the authority of experts and growing skepticism toward the possibility of disinterested expertise. None the less, reliance on knowledge will increase, and the ways in which scientists, experts and knowledge-based occupations in general are able to maintain cognitive authority in the face of uncertainty, political conflict and skepticism toward expertise represent one of the main challenges for these occupations in knowledge societies (cf. Gieryn, 1983; Jasanoff, 1990).

But despite such misgivings and any sustained demystification of knowl-edge, the alternative cannot be to randomly invoke any odd belief as an equivalent. The challenge is to cope with contingency, not labor under the illusion that it is merely a temporary aberration.

Conclusion

Not only Western industrial societies but industrial societies in other parts of the world have been quite successful in enlarging the material well-being of their citizens. The same economic transformation allows for the possibility of the expansion of modern science and technology, education, occupational skills, social security provisions or the welfare state (and with it, a reduction in long economic insecurity), political participation, the increase of other state activities as well as cultural shifts that often invert meanings and orientations associated with what appear to be entrenched political platforms. In the process of 'solving' its problems, which industrial society both inherited and saw as its own peculiar agenda, industrial society not only produced new problems and conflicts but exhausted the sources as well as the organizational frames that were crucial for the resolution of old problems; at the same time, industrial society reached the limits of enlarging its capacities in the same direction and in the same fashion. The economy of industrial society is undergoing a mutation. The sources of its wealth or added value have been exhausted and a new force of production takes the place of the productive factors, labor and property, that had dominated industrial society.

These transformations propel industrial society on its way to form a knowledge society. However, these changes do not occur as revolutionary transformations. They evolve gradually and re-write what is constitutive of society. New phenomena require new perspectives, as I have argued. Knowledge *societies* as highly self-transformative social constructs differ in important ways from industrial societies. The core of classic social discourse is directed to the analysis of industrial society. Within such analysis, as it were, there is, as Alain Touraine ([1984] 1988:4) has argued convincingly,

> scant room left for the idea of social action. The more one speaks of society, the less one talks of social actors, since the latter can be conceived only as the bearers of the attributes that are proper to the place they occupy in the social system: whether they are at the center or at the periphery, at the top or at the bottom, they take part, to a greater or lesser extent, in the values of modernity.

The agency and intentionality of actors and intermediate social groups are subservient to the logic of social collectivities and institutions that dispense with the often repressive cement of social life, insuring that social order prevails despite the many pressures to the contrary. Whether or not such a perspective ever accurately portrayed social reality, or was primarily an ideological conviction, this conception is now disqualified. In a knowledge society, the capacity of individuals to disengage themselves from the pressures of institutions and collectivities grows immeasurably. But the rise in the level of knowledge as a whole 'does not mean by any means . . . a general leveling, but rather the opposite' (Simmel ([1907] 1978:440). New forms of social inequality based on knowledge emerge and are firmly institutionalized, creating and extending advantages as well as forms of deprivation. The unity of collectivities now derives from the fact that they are arenas of contests of knowledgeable actors. However, knowledge does have some of the crude and cruel qualities of those factors (of production) that are constitutive of industrial societies. Just as 'industrialization transformed societies in a fashion that empowered subordinate classes and made it difficult to politically exclude them' (Rueschemeyer et al., 1992:vii), the core of the economic transformation of knowledge societies further empowers those groups and individuals in democratic societies still marginalized even in the face of universal suffrage.

But the transition from industrial to knowledge society is not without serious problems. The likelihood that the loss of full employment will in the future also be associated with economic growth is one of the salient features of an economy in which the major source of added value is knowledge and in which more production will be possible with less labour.

As the proportion of the gross national product that is appropriated and distributed by governments, for example, reaches well above 50 percent, there would appear to be no further room for a continuation of enlarging state activities. Further growth of state activities not only reaches a point of diminishing returns but effectively curbs those sources of economic expansion taking the place of forces of production that prevailed in industrial society.

The promise, challenge and dilemma knowledge societies pose for every individual derives from the need to cope with and even welcome greater transience and volatility, the recognition that uncertainty is a necessary by-product of the search for any elimination of disagreements and the need to accept the transitoriness of virtually all social constructs. Efforts to arrest, cure or reverse these predicaments are likely to result in conditions worse than the alleged disease.

Bibliography

Under each author's name the more recent works are listed first. In the case of translations or revised editions, the original date of publication is also shown, within square brackets.

Adorno, Theodor W. (1969) 'Spätkapitalismus oder Industriegesellschaft', pp. 12–26 in Theodor W. Adorno (ed.), *Spätkapitalismus oder Industriegesellschaft*. Verhandlungen des 16. Deutschen Soziologentages. Stuttgart: Ferdinand Enke.

Adorno, Theodor W. ([1966] 1973) *Negative Dialectics*. London: Routledge and Kegan Paul.

Adorno, Theodor W. and Max Horkheimer ([1947] 1987) *Dialektik der Aufklärung*, pp. 13–290 in Max Horkheimer, *Gesammelte Schriften*, vol. 5. Frankfurt am Main: Fischer.

Alestalo, Matti, Sven Bislev and Bengt Furåker (1991) 'Welfare state employment in Scandinavia', pp. 36–58 in Jon E. Kolberg (ed.), *The Welfare State as Employer*. Armonk, NY: Sharpe.

Alexander, Jeffrey C. (1992a) 'Durkheim's problem and differentiation theory today', pp. 179–204 in Hans Haferkamp and Neil J. Smelser (eds), *Social Change and Modernity*. Berkeley: University of California Press.

Alexander, Jeffrey C. (1992b) 'The promise of a cultural sociology: technological discourse and the sacred and profane information machine', pp. 293–323 in Richard Münch and Neil Smelser (eds), *Theory as Culture*. Berkeley: University of California Press.

Alexander, Jeffrey C. (1990) 'Differentiation theory: problems and prospects', pp. 1–15 in Jeffrey C. Alexander and Paul Colomy (eds), *Differentiation Theory and Social Change. Comparative and Historical Perspectives*. New York: Columbia University Press.

Alexander, Jeffrey C. and Paul Colomy (eds) (1990) *Differentiation Theory and Social Change: Comparative and Historical Perspectives*. New York: Columbia University Press.

Anders, Günther ([1956] 1980) *Die Antiquiertheit des Menschen*. Munich: Beck.

Anderson, Allen R. and Omar K. Moore (1969) 'Some principles of the design of clarifying educational environments', pp. 571–613 in David A. Goslin (ed.), *Handbook of Socialization Theory and Research*. Chicago: Rand McNally.

Archer, Margaret S. (1991) 'Sociology for one world: unity and diversity', *International Sociology*, 6: 131–147.

Arendt, Hannah ([1960] 1981) *Vita activa, oder vom tätigen Leben*. Munich: Piper.

Arendt, Hannah (1958) *The Human Condition*. Chicago: University of Chicago Press.

Aron, Raymond ([1983] 1990) *Memoirs: Fifty Years of Political Reflection*. New York: Holmes & Meier.

Aron, Raymond ([1966] 1968) *The Industrial Society: Three Essays on Ideology and Development*. New York: Praeger.

Aron, Raymond (1964a) *La lutte de classes*. Paris: Gallimard.

Aron, Raymond (1964b) *Eighteen Lectures on Industrial Society*. New York: Free Press.

Badham, Richard (1986) *Theories of Industrial Society*. London: Croom Helm.

Baldamus, Wilhelm (1976) *The Structure of Sociological Inference*. London: Martin Robertson.

Barker, Jane and Cynthia Downing (1985) 'Word processing and the transformation of patriarchal relations of control in the office', pp. 147–164 in Donald MacKenzie and Judy Wacjman (eds), *The Social Shaping of Technology*. Milton Keynes: Open University Press.

Barnes, Barry (1985) *About Science*. Oxford: Blackwell.

Basiuk, Victor (1977) *Technology, World Politics and American Policy*. New York: Columbia University Press.

Bates, Benjamin J. (1988) 'Information as an economic good: sources of individual and social value', pp. 76–94 in Vincent Mosco and Janet Wasko (eds), *The Political Economy of Information*. Madison, Wis.: University of Wisconsin Press.

Bauman, Zygmunt (1992) *Intimations of Postmodernity*. London: Routledge.

Bauman, Zygmunt (1991) *Modernity and Ambivalence*. Ithaca, NY: Cornell University Press.

Bauman, Zygmunt (1987) *Legislators and Interpreters: on Modernity, Post-modernity and Intellectuals*. Ithaca, NY: Cornell University Press.

Baumol, William J. (1967) 'The macroeconomics of unbalanced growth: the anatomy of urban crisis', *American Economic Review* 57:415–426.

Baumol, William J., Sue Anne Batey Blackman and Edward N. Wolff (1985) 'Unbalanced growth revisited: asymptotic stagnancy and new evidence', *American Economic Review* 75:806–817.

Bean, Charles (1990) *European Unemployment: a Survey*. Centre for Economic Performance Working Paper No. 35. London: London School of Economics.

Bell, Daniel ([1979] 1991) 'Liberalism in the postindustrial society', pp. 228–244 in Daniel Bell, *The Winding Passage: Sociological Essays and Journeys*. New Brunswick, NJ: Transaction Books.

Bell, Daniel (1987) 'The world and the United States in 2013', *Daedalus* 116:1–31.

Bell, Daniel ([1979, 1980] 1982) *Social Science since the Second World War*. New Brunswick, NJ: Transactions Books.

Bell, Daniel ([1975] 1980) 'Technology, nature, and society: the vicissitudes of three world views and the confusion of realms', pp. 3–33 in Daniel Bell, *The Winding Passage: Essays and Sociological Journeys 1960–1980*. Cambridge, Mass.: Abt Books.

Bell, Daniel (1979a) 'The social framework of the information society', pp. 163–211 in Michael L. Dertouzos and Joel Moses (eds), *The Computer Age: Twenty-Year View*. Cambridge, Mass.: MIT Press.

Bell, Daniel (1979b) 'The new class: a muddled concept', pp. 169–190 in B. Bruce-Biggs (ed.), *The New Class?* New Brunswick, NJ: Transaction Books.

Bell, Daniel (1976) *The Cultural Contradictions of Capitalism*. New York: Basic Books.

Bell, Daniel (1974) 'A reply to Peter N. Stearns', *Society* 11:23–24.

Bell, Daniel (1973a) *The Coming of Post-industrial Society: a Venture in Social Forecasting*. New York: Basic Books.

Bell, Daniel (1973b) 'A rejoinder to Timothy A. Tilton', *Social Research* 40:745–752.

Bell, Daniel (1973c) 'Technology, nature and society: the vicissitudes of three worlds views and the confusion of realms', *The American Scholar* 42:385–404.

Bell, Daniel (1972) 'Labour in the post-industrial society', *Dissent* 19:163–189.

Bell, Daniel (1971) 'Technocracy and politics', *Survey* 16:1–24.

Bell, Daniel (1968) 'The measurement of knowledge and technology', pp. 145–246 in Eleanor B. Sheldon and Wilbert E. Moore (eds), *Indicators of Social Change: Concepts and Measurements*. Hartford, Conn.: Russell Sage Foundation.

Bell, Daniel (1967a) 'Notes on the post-industrial society', *The Public Interest* 7:24–35.

Bell, Daniel (1967b) 'Notes on the post-industrial society', *The Public Interest* 7:102–118.

Bell, Daniel (1964) 'The post-industrial society', pp. 44–59 in Eli Ginzberg (ed.), *Technology and Social Change*. New York: Columbia University Press.

Bell, Daniel (1960) *The End of Ideology*. Glencoe, Ill.: Free Press.

Bennis, Warren G. and Philip E. Slater (1969) *The Temporary Society*. New York: Harper & Row.

Benveniste, Guy (1972) *The Policy of Expertise*. Berkeley: Glendessary Press.

Berger, Johannes (1986) 'Gibt es ein nachmodernes Gesellschaftsstadium? Marxismus und Modernisierungstheorie im Widerstreit', pp. 79–96 in Johannes Berger (ed.), *Die Moderne: Kontinuitäten und Zäsuren*. Special issue no. 4, *Soziale Welt*. Göttingen: Schwartz and Co.

Berger, Peter (1987) *The Capitalist Revolution: Fifty Propositions about Prosperity, Equality, and Liberty*. New York: Basic Books.

Berger, Peter and Thomas Luckmann (1967) *The Social Construction of Reality: a Treatise in the Sociology of Knowledge*. New York: Doubleday.

Bernal, John D. (1954) *Science in History*. London: Watts.

Bijker, Wiebe E., Thomas P. Hughes and Trevor J. Pinch (eds) (1987) *The Social Construction of Technological Systems: New Directions in the Sociology and History of Technology*. Cambridge, Mass: MIT Press.

Birch, Anthony H. (1984) 'Overload, ungovernability and delegitimation: the theories and the British case', *British Journal of Political Science* 14:135–160.

Birnbaum, Norman (1971a) 'Is there a post-industrial revolution?', pp. 393–415 in Norman Birnbaum, *Toward a Critical Sociology*. New York: Oxford University Press.

Birnbaum, Norman (1971b) 'Is there a knowledge elite?', pp. 416–441 in Norman Birnbaum, *Toward a Critical Sociology*. New York: Oxford University Press.

Bledstein, Burton J. (1976) *The Culture of Professionalism: the Middle Class and the Development of Higher Education in America*. New York: W.W. Norton.

Block, Fred (1990) *Postindustrial Possibilities: a Critique of Economic Discourse*. Berkeley: University of California Press.

Block, Fred (1987) *Revising State Theory: Essays in Politics and the Contradictions of Contemporary Capitalism*. Philadelphia: Temple University Press.

Block, Fred (1985) 'Postindustrial development and the obsolescence of economic categories', *Politics and Society* 14:71–104; 416–441.

Block, Fred and Larry Hirschhorn (1979) 'New productive forces and the contradictions of contemporary capitalism', *Theory and Society* 17:363–395.

Bluestone, Barry and Harrison, Bennett (1982) *The Deindustrialization of America*. New York: Basic Books.

Bodewitz, Henk J.H.W., Henk Buurma and Gerard H. de Vries (1987) 'Regulatory science and the social management of trust in medicine', pp. 243–259 in Wiebe E. Bijker, Thomas P. Hughes and Trevor Pinch (eds), *The Social Construction of Technological Systems: New Directions in the Sociology and History of Technology*. Cambridge, Mass: MIT Press.

Böhme, Gernot (1992) 'The techno-structures of society', pp. 39–50 in Nico Stehr and Richard V. Ericson (eds), *The Culture and Power of Knowledge: Inquiries into Contemporary Societies*. Berlin and New York: de Gruyter.

Böhme, Gernot (1988) 'Coping with science', *Graduate Faculty Philosophy Journal* 12:1–47.

Böhme, Gernot (1984) 'The knowledge-structure of society', pp. 5–17 in Gunnar Bergendal (ed.), *Knowledge Policies and the Traditions of Higher Education*. Stockholm: Almquist & Wiksell.

Böhme, Gernot and Nico Stehr (eds) (1986) *The Knowledge Society*. Dordrecht: Reidel.

Böhme, Gernot, Wolfgang van den Daele and Wolfgang Krohn (1978) 'The "scientification" of technology', pp. 173–205 in Wolfgang Krohn, Edwin T. Layton, jr and Peter Weingart (eds), *The Dynamics of Science and Technology*. Dordrecht: Reidel.

Bogner, Artur (1992) 'The theory of the civilizing process – an ideographic theory of modernization?', *Theory, Culture and Society* 9:23–53

Bon, Frédéric and M. Antoine Burnier (1966) *Les nouveaux intellectuels*. Paris: Editions du Seuil.

Borgmann, Albert (1992) *Crossing the Postmodern Divide*. Chicago: University of Chicago Press.

Bottomore, Tom B. (1960) 'The ideas of the founding fathers', *European Journal of Sociology* 1:33–49.

Boulding, Kenneth (1967) 'The "two cultures" ', pp. 686–695 in Melvin Kranzberg and Carroll W. Pursell, jr (eds), *Technology in Western Civilization*, vol. 2. New York: Oxford University Press.

Boulding, Kenneth (1966) 'The economics of knowledge and the knowledge of economics', *American Economic Review* 56:1–13.

Boulding, Kenneth (1965) *The Meaning of the Twentieth Century: the Great Transition*. New York: Harper & Row.

Bourdieu, Pierre (1986) 'The forms of capital', pp. 241–258 in John G. Richardson (ed.), *Handbook of Theory and Research for the Sociology of Education*. New York: Greenwood Press.

Bourdieu, Pierre ([1979] 1984) *The Distinction: a Social Critique of the Judgement of Taste*. Cambridge, Mass.: Harvard University Press.

Bourdieu, Pierre (1983) 'Ökonomisches Kapital, kulturelles Kapital, soziales Kapital', pp. 183–198 in Reinhard Kreckel (ed.), *Soziale Ungleichheiten*. Special issue no. 2, *Soziale Welt*. Göttingen: Verlag Otto Schwartz & Co.

Bourdieu, Pierre (1979) 'Les trois états du capital culturel', *Actes de la recherche en sciences sociales* 30:3–6.

Braudel, Fernand ([1979] 1992) *The Structures of Everyday Life: the Limits of the Possible*, vol. 1: *Civilization and Capitalism 15th – 18th Century*. Berkeley: University of California Press.

Braverman, Harry (1974) *Labor and Monopoly Capital: the Degradation of Work in the Twentieth Century*. New York: Monthly Review Press.

Bray, Dennis, Nico Stehr and Guy C. Germain (1994) 'The interaction between climate and society: assessing temporal and spatial dimensions from a historical perspective' (unpublished manuscript).

Brick, Howard (1986) *Daniel Bell and the Decline of Intellectual Radicalism: Social Theory and Political Reconciliation in the 1940s*. Madison: University of Wisconsin Press.

Britton, Stephen (1990) 'The role of services in production', *Progress in Human Geography* 14:529–546.

Bruyn, Severyn T. (1991) *A Future for the American Economy: the Social Market*. Stanford: Stanford University Press.

Brzezinski, Zbignew (1970) *Between the Ages: America's Role in the Technotronic Age*. New York: Viking Press.

Brzezinski, Zbignew (1968) 'America in the technotronic age: new questions of our time', *Encounter* 30:16–26.

Bucher, Rue and Anselm Strauss (1961) 'Professions in process', *American Journal of Sociology* 66:325–334.

Buchner, Bradley J. (1988) 'Social control and the diffusion of modern telecommunications technologies: a cross-national study', *American Sociological Review* 53:446–453.

Calhoun, Craig (1993) 'Postmodernism as pseudohistory', *Theory, Culture and Society* 10:75–96.

Calhoun, Craig (1992) 'The infrastructure of modernity: indirect social relationships, information technology, and social integration', pp. 205–236 in Hans Haferkamp and Neil J. Smelser (eds), *Social Change and Modernity*. Berkeley: University of California Press.

Carr-Saunders, Alexander M. and P.A. Wilson (1933) *The Professions*. Oxford: Oxford University Press.

Castells, Manuel (1989) *The Informational City: Information Technology, Economic Restructuring, and the Urban-Regional Process*. Oxford: Basil Blackwell.

Cavestro, William (1989) 'Automation, new technology and work content', pp. 219–234 in Stephen Wood (ed.), *The Transformation of Work?* London: Unwin Hyman.

Cerny, Philip G. (1990) *The Changing Architecture of Politics: Structure, Agency and the Future of the State*. London: Sage.

Channell, David F. (1982) 'The harmony of theory and practice: the engineering science of W.J.M. Rankine', *Technology and Culture* 23:39–52.

Clark, Colin (1940) *The Conditions of Economic Progress*. London: Macmillan.

Clegg, Stewart (1992) 'French bread, Italian fashion and Asian enterprises: modern passions and postmodern prognoses', pp. 55–94 in Jane Marceau (ed.), *Reworking the World: Organisations, Technologies, and Cultures in Comparative Perspective*. Berlin and New York: de Gruyter.

Clegg, Stewart, Paul Boreham and Geoff Dow (1986) *Class, Politics and the Economy*. London: Routledge & Kegan Paul.

Cohen, Stephen S. and John Zysman (1987) *Manufacturing Matters: the Myth of the Post-industrial Economy*. New York: Basic Books.

Collingridge, David and Colin Reeve (1986) *Science Speaks to Power: the Role of Experts in Policy Making*. London: Frances Pinter.

Collins, Harry M. (1993) 'The structures of knowledge', *Social Research* 60:95–116.

Collins, Harry M. (1987) 'Certainty and the public understanding of science: science on TV', *Social Studies of Science* 17:689–713.

Collins, Harry M. (1982) 'The replication of experiments in physics', pp. 94–116 in Barry Barnes and David Edge (eds), *Science in Context: Readings in the Sociology of Science*. Cambridge, Mass.: MIT Press.

Colomy, Paul (1990) 'Revisions and progress in differentation theory', pp. 465–495 in Jeffrey C. Alexander and Paul Colomy (eds), *Differentiation Theory and Social Change: Comparative and Historical Perspectives*. New York: Columbia University Press.

Constant, Edward W. II (1987) 'The social locus of technological practice: community, system or organization?', pp. 223–242 in Wiebe E. Bijker, Thomas P. Hughes and Trevor J. Pinch (eds), *The Social Constructions of Technological Systems: New Directions in the Sociology and History of Technology*. Cambridge, Mass.: MIT Press.

Coser, Lewis A. (1970) *Men of Ideas: a Sociologist's View*. New York: Free Press.

Crozier, Michel, Samuel P. Huntington and Joji Watanuki (eds) (1975) *The Crisis of Democracy*. New York: New York University Press.

Curtis, Terry (1988) 'The information society: a computer-generated caste system?', pp. 95–107 in Vincent Mosco and Janet Wasko (eds), *The Political Economy of Information*. Madison, Wis.: University of Wisconsin Press.

Cutler, Tony, Karel Williams and John Williams (1986) *Keynes, Beveridge and Beyond*. London: Routledge and Kegan Paul.

Dahme, Heinz-Jürgen (1988) 'Der Verlust des Fortschrittglaubens und die Verwissenschaftlichung der Soziologie: ein Vergleich von Georg Simmel, Ferdinand Tönnies und Max Weber', pp. 222–274 in Otthein Rammstedt (ed.), *Simmel und die frühen Soziologen. Nähe und Distanz zu Durkheim, Tönnies und Max Weber*. Frankfurt am Main: Suhrkamp.

Dahrendorf, Ralf (1988) *The Modern Social Conflict: an Essay on the Politics of Liberty*. Berkeley: University of California Press.

Dahrendorf, Ralf (1987) 'Changing perceptions of the role of government', pp. 110–122 in Organization for Economic Co-operation and Development, *Interdependence and Co-Operation in Tomorrow's World*. Paris: OECD.

Dahrendorf, Ralf (1980) 'Im Entschwinden der Arbeitsgesellschaft: Wandlungen in der sozialen Konstruktion des menschlichen Lebens', *Merkur* 34:749–760.

Dahrendorf, Ralf (1977) 'Observations on science and technology in a changing socio-economic climate', pp. 73–82 in Ralf Dahrendorf (ed.), *Scientific-Technological Revolution*. London: Sage.

Dahrendorf, Ralf ([1967] 1974) 'Soziologie und industrielle Gesellschaft', pp. 64–73 in Ralf Dahrendorf (ed.), *Pfade aus Utopia: Arbeiten zur Theorie und Methode der Soziologie*. Munich: Piper.

Dahrendorf, Ralf (1969) 'The intellectual and society: the social function of the "fool" in the twentieth century', pp. 53–56 in Phillip Rieff (ed.), *On Intellectuals*. New York: Anchor Books.

Dahrendorf, Ralf ([1957] 1959) *Class and Class Conflict in Industrialized Society*. Stanford: Stanford University Press.

Dalton, Russel J., Manfred Kuechler and Wilhelm Bürklin (1990) 'The challenge of new movements', pp. 3–20 in Russel J. Dalton, and Manfred Kuechler (eds), *Challenging the Political Order: New Social and Political Movements in Western Democracies*. New York: Oxford University Press.

Daniels, Peter W. (1989) 'Some perspectives on the geography of services', *Progress in Human Geography* 13:427–433.

Daniels, Peter W. (1985) *Service Industries: a Geographical Appraisal*. London: Methuen.

Dasgupta, Partha (1987) 'The economic theory of technology policy', pp. 7–23 in Partha Dasgupta and Paul Stoneman (eds), *Economic Policy and Technological Performance*. Cambridge: Cambridge University Press.

Dasgupta, Partha and Paul Stoneman (1987) 'Introduction', pp.1–6 in Partha Dasgupta and

Paul Stoneman (eds), *Economic Policy and Technological Performance*. Cambridge: Cambridge University Press.

Denison, Edward (1979) *Accounting for Slower Economic Growth*. Washington, DC: Brookings Institution.

Dennett, Daniel C. (1986) 'Information, technology, and the virtues of ignorance', *Daedalus* 115:135–153.

Derber, Charles (1982) 'Toward a new theory of professionals as workers: advanced capitalism and postindustrial labour', pp. 193–208 in Charles Derber (ed.), *Professionals as Workers: Mental Labour in Advanced Capitalism*. Boston: Hall.

Derber, Charles, William A. Schwartz and Yale Magrass (1990) *Power in the Highest Degree: Professionals and the Rise of a New Mandarin Order*. New York: Oxford University Press.

Dicken, Peter (1992) *Global Shift: the Internationalization of Economic Activity*, 2nd edn. New York and London: Guilford Press.

Dickson, David (1984) *The New Politics of Science*. New York: Pantheon Books.

DiMaggio, Paul J. and Walter W. Powell (1983) 'The iron cage revisited: institutional isomorphism and collective rationality in organization fields', *American Sociological Review* 48:147–160.

Dosi, Giovanni (1984) *Technical Change and Industrial Transformation: the Theory and an Application to the Semiconductor Industry*. London: Macmillan.

Dosi, Giovanni (1982) 'Technological paradigms and technological trajectories: a suggested interpretation of the determinants and directions of technical change', *Research Policy* 11:147–162.

Dosi, Giovanni, Christopher Freeman, Richard Nelson, Gerald Silverberg and Luc Soethe (eds) (1988) *Technical Change and Economic Theory*. London: Pinter.

Drucker, Peter F. (1989) *The New Realities: in Government and Politics / in Economics and Business / in Society and World View*. New York: Harper & Row.

Drucker, Peter F. (1986) 'The changed world economy', *Foreign Affairs* 64:768–791.

Drucker, Peter F. (1969) *The Age of Discontinuity: Guidelines to our Changing Society*. New York: Harper & Row.

Drucker, Peter F. (1967) 'Technological trends in the twentieth century', pp. 10–33 in Melvin Kranzberg and Carroll W. Pursell, jr (eds), *Technology in Western Civilization*, vol. 2. New York: Oxford University Press.

Drucker, Peter F. (1965) *The Future of Industrial Man*. New York: John Day.

Dubin, Robert (1956) 'Industrial workers' worlds: a study of the "central life interests" of industrial workers', *Social Problems* 3:131–142.

Dunning, John H. (1989) 'Transnational corporations and the growth of services: some conceptual and theoretical issues', *United Nations Centre on Transnational Corporations*. Current Studies Series A, No. 9. New York: United Nations.

Durkheim, Emile ([1950] 1992) *Professional Ethics and Civic Morals*. London: Routledge.

Durkheim, Emile ([1912] 1965) *The Elementary Forms of Religious Life*. New York: Free Press.

Durkheim, Emile ([1893] 1964) *The Division of Labor in Society*. New York: Free Press.

Durkheim, Emile ([1950] 1957) *Professional Ethics and Civic Morals*. London: Routledge & Kegan Paul.

Eder, Klaus (1992) 'Contradictions and social evolution: a theory of the social evolution of modernity', pp. 320–349 in Hans Haferkamp and Neil J. Smelser (eds), *Social Change and Modernity*. Berkeley: University of California Press.

Elias, Norbert ([1987] 1991) *The Society of Individuals*. Oxford: Blackwell.

Elias, Norbert (1987) 'The retreat of sociologists into the present', pp. 150–172 in Volker Meja, Dieter Misgeld and Nico Stehr (eds), *Modern German Sociology*. New York: Columbia University Press.

Elkins, Paul (ed.) (1986) *The Living Economy: a New Economics in the Making*. London: Routledge & Kegan Paul.

Ellul, Jacques (1954) *The Technological Society*. New York: Vintage.

Esping-Andersen, Gosta (1992) 'Three postindustrial employment regimes', pp. 149–188 in Jon E. Kolberg (ed.), *The Welfare State as Employer*. Armonk, NY: Sharpe.

Esquith, Stephen L. (1987) 'Professional authority and state power', *Theory and Society* 16:237–262.

Eulau, Heinz (1973) 'Skill revolution and consultative commonwealth', *American Political Science Review* 62:169–191.

Fagerberg, Jan (1991) 'Innovation, catching-up and growth', pp. 37–46 in Organization for Economic Co-operation and Development, *Technology and Productivity: the Challenge for Economic Policy*. Paris: OECD.

Fagerberg, Jan (1988) 'Why growth rates differ?', pp. 432–457 in Giovanni Dosi, Christopher Freeman, Richard Nelson, Gerald Silverberg, and Luc Soethe (eds), *Technical Change and Economic Theory*. London: Pinter.

Feigenbaum, Edward A. and Pamela McCorduck (1983) *The Fifth Generation: Artificial Intelligence and Japan's Computer Challenge to the World*. Reading, MA: Addison-Wesley.

Feller, Irwin (1987) 'The economics of technological change filtered through a social knowledge system framework', *Knowledge* 9:233–253.

Ferkiss, Victor (1979) 'Daniel Bell's concept of post-industrial society: theory, myth and ideology', *The Political Science Reviewer* 9:61–99.

Feuer, Lewis S. (1976) 'What is an intellectual', pp. 47–58 in A. Gella (ed.), *The Intelligentsia and the Intellectuals*. Beverly Hills, Calif.: Sage.

Fisher, A. (1939) 'Production – primary, secondary and tertiary', *The Economic Record* 15:24–38.

Florence, P. Sargent (with W. Baldamus) (1948) *Investment, Location, and Size of Plant*. Cambridge: Cambridge University Press.

Floud, Jean (1971) 'A critique of Bell', *Survey* 16:25–37.

Forstner, Helmut and Robert Ballance (1990) *Competing in a Global Economy: an Empirical Study of Specialization and Trade in Manufactures*. Prepared for the United Nations Industrial Development Organization. London: Unwin Hyman.

Foucault, Michel (1977) *Discipline and Punish*. New York: Random House.

Foucault, Michel (1970) *L'Ordre du Discours*. Paris: Gallimard.

Fourastié, Jean ([1951] 1960) *The Causes of Wealth*. Glencoe, Ill.: Free Press.

Fourastié, Jean (1950) *Le Grand Espoir du XX siècle*. Paris: PUF.

Fox, Renee C. (1967) 'Training for uncertainty', pp. 20–24 in Mark Abrahamson (ed.), *The Professional in the Organization*. Chicago: Rand McNally.

Frankel, Boris (1987) *The Post-industrial Utopians*. Madison, Wis.: University of Wisconsin Press.

Freeman, Christopher (1979) 'The Kondratiev long waves, technical change and unemployment', in OEDC, *Structural Determinants of Employment and Unemployment*. Paris: OECD.

Freeman, Christopher, John Clark, and Luc Soethe (1982) *Unemployment and Technical Change: a Study of Long Waves and Economic Development*. Westport, Conn.: Greenwood Press.

Freidson, Eliot (1986) *Professional Powers: a Study of the Institutionalization of Formal Knowledge*. Chicago: University of Chicago Press.

Freidson, Eliot (1984) 'Are professions necessary?', pp. 3–27 in Thomas L. Haskell (ed.), *The Authority of Experts*. Bloomington, Ind.: Indiana University Press.

Freyer, Hans (1987) *Herrschaft, Planung und Technik*. Weinheim: VCH, Acta Humaniora.

Freyer, Hans (1960) *Über das Dominantwerden technischer Kategorien in der Lebenswelt der industriellen Gesellschaft*. Mainz: Academie der Wissenschaften.

Freyer, Hans (1955) *Theorie des gegenwärtigen Zeitalters*. Stuttgart: Deutsche Verlagsanstalt.

Friedman, Jonathan (1992) 'General historical and culturally specified properties of global systems', *Review* 15:335–372.

Friedman, Jonathan (1989) 'Culture, identity, and world process', *Review* 12:51–69.

Friedmann, George ([1956] 1992) *The Anatomy of Work: Labor, Leisure and the Implications of Automation*. New Brunswick, NJ: Transaction Books.

Fuchs, Victor (1968) *The Service Economy*. New York: Columbia University Press.

Galbraith, John K. (1973) *Economics and the Public Interest*. Boston: Houghton Mifflin.

Galbraith, John K. (1967) *The New Industrial State*. New York: Houghton Mifflin.

Geertz, Clifford (1973) *The Interpretation of Cultures*. New York: Basic Books.

Gehlen, Arnold ([1940] 1988) *Man: his Nature and Place in the World*. New York: Columbia University Press.

Gehlen, Arnold ([1957] 1980) *Man in the Age of Technology*. New York: Columbia University Press.

Gehlen, Arnold (1949) *Sozialpsychologische Probleme der industriellen Gesellschaft*. Tübingen: J.C.B. Mohr (Paul Siebeck).

Gellner, Ernest (1983) *Nations and Nationalism*. Oxford: Basil Blackwell.

Gellner, Ernest (1964) *Thought and Change*. London: Weidenfeld & Nicolson.

Gershuny, Jonathan I. (1988) *The Social Economics of Post-industrial Societies*. A Report to the Joseph Rowntree Memorial Trust. Bath: University of Bath.

Gershuny, Jonathan I. and Ian D. Miles (1983) *The New Service Economy: the Transformation of Employment in Industrial Societies*. London: Frances Pinter.

Giddens, Anthony (1991) *Modernity and Self-identity: Self and Society in the Late Modern Age*. Stanford: Stanford University Press.

Giddens, Anthony (1990a) 'R.K. Merton on structural analysis', pp. 97–110 in Jon Clark, Celia Modgill and Sohan Modgill (eds) *Robert K. Merton: Consensus and Controversy*. London: Falmer Press.

Giddens, Anthony (1990b) 'Sociology, modernity and utopia', *New Statesman and Society* 3(125):20–22.

Giddens, Anthony (1990c) *The Consequences of Modernity*. Stanford: Stanford University Press.

Giddens, Anthony (1984) *The Constitution of Society: Outline of the Theory of Structuration*. Cambridge: Polity Press.

Giddens, Anthony (1981) *A Contemporary Critique of Historical Materialism*, vol. 1. London: Macmillan.

Giddens, Anthony ([1973] 1980) *The Class Structure of the Advanced Societies*. London: Hutchinson.

Gieryn, Thomas F. (1983) 'Boundary-work and the demarcation of science from non-science: strains and interests in professional ideologies of scientists', *American Sociological Review* 48:781–795.

Gilbert, Nigel G. and Michael Mulkay (1984) *Opening Pandora's Box*. Cambridge: Cambridge University Press.

Gipsen, C.W.R. (1988) 'German engineers and American social theory: historical perspectives on professionalization', *Comparative Studies in Society and History* 30:550–574.

Glaser, Barney G. (1964) *Organizational Scientists: their Professional Careers*. Indianapolis: Bobbs-Merrill.

Glasmeier, Amy (1990) 'High-tech policy, high-tech realities: the spatial distribution of high-tech industry in America', pp. 67–96 in Jürgen Schmandt and Robert Wilson (eds), *Growth Policy in the Age of High Technology: the Role of Regions and States*. Boston: Unwin Hyman.

Godelier, Maurice (1984) *L'idéel et le matériel*. Paris: Fayard.

Goldhamer, Herbert (1978) *The Adviser*. New York: Elsevier.

Goldthorpe, John H. (1982) 'On the service class, its formation and future', pp. 162–185 in Anthony Giddens and G. Mackenzie (eds), *Social Class and the Division of Labor: Essays in Honour of Ilja Neustadt*. Cambridge: Cambridge University Press.

Goldthorpe, John H. (1971) 'Theories of industrial society: reflections on the recrudescence of historicism and the future of futurology', *European Journal of Sociology* 12:263–288.

Goode, William J. (1969) 'The theoretical limits of professionalization', pp. 266–313 in Amitai Etzioni (ed.), *The Semi-professions and their Organization: Teachers, Nurses, Social Workers*. New York: Free Press.

Goode, William J. (1957) 'Community within a community: the professions', *American Sociological Review* 22:194–200.

Gorz, André ([1971] 1976) 'Technology, technicians and class struggle', pp. 160–189 in André Gorz (ed.), *The Division of Labour: the Labour Process and Class Struggle in Modern Capitalism*. Hassocks: Harvester.

Gouldner, Alvin W. (1979) *The Future of Intellectuals and the Rise of the New Class*. New York: Seabury Press.

Gouldner, Alvin W. (1976) *The Dialectic of Ideology and Technology. The Origins, Grammar, and Future of Ideology*. New York: Seabury Press.

Granovetter, Mark (1990) 'The old and the new economic sociology: a history and an agenda', pp. 89–112 in Roger Friedland and A. F. Robertson (eds), *Beyond the Marketplace: Rethinking Economy and Society*. New York: Aldine de Gruyter.

Gray, Jon (1988) 'Hayek, the Scottish school, and contemporary economics', pp. 53–70 in Gordon C. Winston and Richard F. Teichgraeber III (eds), *The Boundaries of Economics*. Cambridge: Cambridge University Press.

Greven, Michael T., Bernd Guggenberger and Johano Strasser (eds) (1975) *Krise des Staates? Zur Funktionsbestimmung des Staates im Spätkapitalismus*. Darmstadt: Luchterhand.

Grilli, Enzo R. and Maw Cheng Yang (1988) 'Primary commodity prices, manufactured good prices, and the terms of trade of developing countries: what the long run shows', *World Bank Economic Review* 2:1–47.

Gross, Bertram M. (1971) 'Planning in an era of social revolution', *Public Administration Review* 31:259–296.

Haas, Ernst B. (1990) *When Knowledge is Power: Three Models of Change in International Organizations*. Berkeley: University of California Press.

Habermas, Jürgen ([1981] 1984) *The Theory of Communicative Action*, vol. 1: *Reason and the Rationalization of Society*. Boston: Beacon Press.

Habermas, Jürgen ([1982] 1983) 'Neoconservative culture criticism in the United States and West Germany: an intellectual movement in two political cultures', *Telos* 56:75–89.

Habermas, Jürgen (1982) 'A reply to my critics', pp. 219–283 in John B. Thompson and David Held (eds), *Habermas: Critical Debates*. Cambridge, Mass.: MIT Press.

Habermas, Jürgen ([1980] 1981a) 'Modernity versus postmodernity', *New German Critique* 22:3–14.

Habermas, Jürgen ([1980] 1981b) 'Die Moderne – ein unvollendetes Projekt', pp. 444–464 in Jürgen Habermas, *Kleine Politische Schriften* I–IV. Frankfurt am Main: Suhrkamp.

Habermas, Jürgen ([1968] 1978) 'Praktische Folgen des wissenschaftlich-technischen Fortschritts', pp. 336–358 in Jürgen Habermas, *Theorie und Praxis: Sozialphilosophische Studien*. Frankfurt am Main: Suhrkamp.

Habermas, Jürgen ([1963] 1974) *Theory and Practice*. London: Heinemann [*Sozialphilosophische Studien*. Frankfurt am Main: Suhrkamp].

Habermas, Jürgen ([1968] 1971) *Knowledge and Human Interests*. Boston: Beacon Press.

Habermas, Jürgen ([1968–69] 1970) *Toward a Rational Society: Student Protest, Science and Politics*. Boston: Beacon Press.

Hacker, Andrew (1991) *Two Nations: Black and White, Separate, Hostile, Unequal*. New York: Scribner's.

Halliday, Terence C. (1987) *Beyond Monopoly: Lawyers, State Crises and Professional Empowerment*. Chicago: University of Chicago Press.

Hamlin, Christopher (1992) 'Reflexivity in technology studies: toward a technology of technology (and science)?', *Social Studies of Science* 22:511–544.

Hanson, F. Allan (1993) *Testing Testing: Social Consequences of the Examined Life*. Berkeley: University of California Press.

Hartwell, Ronald M. (1973) 'The service revolution: the growth of services in the modern economy', pp. 358–395 in Carlo M. Cipolla (ed.), *The Economic History of Europe*. London: Collins-Fontana.

Haskell, Thomas L. (ed.) (1984) 'Professionalism *versus* capitalism: R.H. Tawney, Emile Durkheim, and C.S. Peirce on the disinterestedness of professional communities', pp. 180–

225 in Thomas L. Haskell (ed.), *The Authority of Experts*. Bloomington, Ind.: Indiana University Press.

Haug, Marie R. (1975) 'The deprofessionalization of everyone?', *Sociological Focus* 8:197–213.

Haug, Marie R. and Marvin B. Sussman (1969) 'Professional autonomy and the revolt of the client', *Social Problems* 17:153–161.

Hayek, Friedrich A. von ([1945] 1948) 'The use of knowledge in society', pp. 77–91 in Friedrich A. Hayek, *Individualism and Economic Order*. Chicago: University of Chicago Press.

Heertje, Arnold (1977) *Economics and Technical Change*. London: Weidenfeld & Nicolson.

Heidegger, Martin (1978) *Vorträge und Aufsätze*. Pfullingen: Neske.

Heidegger, Martin (1977) *Gelassenheit*. Pfullingen: Neske.

Heidorn, Joachim (1982) *Legitimität und Regierbarkeit: Studien zu den Legitimitätstheorien von Max Weber, Niklas Luhmann und Jürgen Habermas und der Ungleichheitsforschung*. Berlin: Duncker & Humblot.

Heilbroner, Robert L. (1973) 'Economic problems of a post-industrial society', *Dissent* 20:163–176.

Held, David (1991) 'Democracy, the nation-state and the global system', *Economy and Society* 20:138–171.

Henderson, Jeffrey and Manual Castells (eds) (1987) *Global Restructuring and Territorial Development*. London: Sage.

Hennis, Wilhelm (1977) 'Zur Begründung der Fragestellung', pp. 9–21 in Wilhelm Hennis, Peter Graf Kielmansegg and Ulrich Matz (eds), *Regierbarkeit: Studien zu ihrer Problematisierung*, vol. 1. Stuttgart: Klett-Cotta.

Hennis, Wilhelm ([1971] 1977) 'Ende der Politik?', pp. 176–197 in Wilhelm Hennis, *Politik und praktische Philosophie*. Stuttgart: Klett-Cotta.

Hepworth, Mark (1986) 'The geography of technical change in the information economy', *Regional Studies* 20:407–424.

Heyden, Günter (1969) 'Industriegesellschaft', p. 520 in Georg Klaus and Manfred Buhr (eds), *Philosophisches Wörterbuch*, 6th edn. Leipzig: VEB Bibliographisches Institut.

Hinrichs, Karl (1991) 'Working-time development in West Germany: departure to a new state', pp. 27–59 in Karl Hinrichs, William Roche and Carmen Sirianni (eds), *Working Time in Transition: the Political Economy of Working Hours in Industrial Nations*. Philadelphia: Temple University Press.

Hinrichs, Karl, Claus Offe and Helmut Wiesenthal (1988) 'Time, money, and welfare-state capitalism', pp. 221–243 in John Keane (ed.), *Civil Society and the State: New European Perspectives*. London and New York: Verso.

Hirst, Paul and Jonathan Zeitlin (1991) 'Flexible specialization versus post-Fordism: theory, evidence and policy implications', *Economy and Society* 20:1–56.

Hobson, John A. (1910) *The Industrial System: an Inquiry into Earned and Unearned Income*. London: Green.

Hollinger, David A. (1984) 'Inquiry and uplift: Late nineteenth-century American academics and the moral efficacy of scientific practice', pp. 142–156 in Thomas L. Haskell (ed.), *The Authority of Experts: Studies in History and Theory*. Bloomington, Ind.: Indiana University Press.

Holton, Gerald (1992) 'How to think about the 'anti-science' phenomenon', *Public Understanding of Science* 1:103–128.

Holton, Gerald (1986) 'The advancement of science and its burdens', *Daedalus* 115:77–104.

Holzner, Burkart, William N. Dunn and Muhammad Shahidullah (1987) 'An accounting scheme for designing science impact indicators', *Knowledge* 9:173–204.

Holzner, Burkart and John H. Marx (1979) *Knowledge Application: The Knowledge System in Society*. Boston: Allyn and Bacon.

Hübner, Kurt ([1978] 1983) *Critique of Scientific Reason*. Chicago: University of Chicago Press.

Hughes, Everett C. (1958) *Men and their Work*. New York: Free Press.

Hunter, Alfred A. (1988) 'Formal education and initial employment', *American Sociological Review* 53:753–765.

Huntington, Samuel P. (1975) 'The United States', pp. 59–118 in Michel Crozier, Samuel P. Huntington and Joji Watanuki (eds), *The Crisis of Democracy*. New York: New York University Press.

Illich, Ivan (1980) *Toward a History of Needs*. New York: Bantam.

Illich, Ivan (1977) *Disabling Professions*. London: Marion Boyars.

Inglehart, Ronald (1990) *Culture Shift in Advanced Industrial Society*. Princeton, NJ: Princeton University Press.

Inglehart, Ronald (1987) 'Value change in industrial society', *American Political Science Review* 81:1289–1303.

Inglehart, Ronald (1977) *The Silent Revolution*. Princeton, NJ: Princeton University Press.

Innis, Harold A. (1951) *The Bias of Communication*. Toronto: University of Toronto Press.

International Monetary Fund (1992) *World Economic Outlook*. Washington, DC: IMF.

Jackman, Richard and S. Roper (1987) 'Structural unemployment', *Oxford Bulletin of Economic and Statistics* 49:9–36.

Jacoby, Russell (1987) *The Last Intellectuals: American Culture in the Age of Academe*. New York: Basic Books.

Jasanoff, Sheila (1990) *The Fifth Branch: Science Advisors as Policymakers*. Cambridge, Mass: Harvard University Press.

Jaynes, Gerald D. and Robin M. Williams, jr (eds) (1989) *A Common Destiny: Blacks and American Society*. Washington, DC: National Academy Press.

Joas, Hans (1992) *Die Kreativität des Handelns*. Frankfurt am Main: Suhrkamp.

Johnson, Harry G. (1965) *The World Economy at the Crossroads: a Survey of Current Problems of Money, Trade, and Economic Development*. Oxford: Clarendon Press.

Johnson, Terrance J. (1972) *Professions and Power*. London: Macmillan.

Jones, Bryn (1990) 'New production technology and work roles: a paradox of flexibility versus strategic control', pp. 293–309 in Ray Loveridge and Martyn Pitt (eds), *The Strategic Management of Technological Innovation*. New York: Wiley and Son.

Jünger, Friedrich Georg (1946) *Die Perfektion der Technik*. Frankfurt am Main: Vittorio Klostermann.

Kalmbach, Peter (1988) 'Der Dienstleistungssektor: noch immer die grosse Hoffnung des 20. Jahrhunderts?', pp. 166–181 in Werner Süss and Klaus Schroeder (eds), *Technik und Zukunft: neue Technologien und ihre Bedeutung für die Gesellschaft*. Opladen: Westdeutscher Verlag.

Keane, John (1988) *Democracy and Civil Society: on the Predicaments of European Socialism, the Prospects for Democracy, and the Problem of Controlling Social and Political Power*. London: Verso.

Kellner, Douglas (1984) *Herbert Marcuse and the Crisis of Marxism*. Berkeley: University of California Press.

Kern, Horst and Michael Schumann (1983) 'Arbeit und Sozialcharakter: alte und neue Konturen', pp. 353–365 in Joachim Mattges (ed.), *Krise der Arbeitsgesellschaft*. Verhandlungen des 21. Deutschen Soziologentages in Bamberg 1982. Frankfurt am Main: Campus.

Kettler, David, Volker Meja and Nico Stehr (1984) *Karl Mannheim*. London: Tavistock.

Keynes, John M. (1936) *The General Theory of Employment, Interest and Money*. London: Macmillan.

King, Anthony (1975) 'Overload: problems of governing in the 1970s', *Political Studies* 23:284–296.

King, Anthony (ed.) (1976) *Why is Britain Harder to Govern?* London: BBC.

King, Lauriston R. and Philip H. Melanson (1972) 'Knowledge and politics: some experiences from the 1960s', *Public Policy* 20:83–101.

Klaw, Spencer (1968) *The New Brahmans: Scientific Life in America*. New York: Morrow.

Klotz, Hans and Klaus Rum (1963) 'Über die Produktivkraft Wissenschaft', *Einheit* 2:25–31.

Knorr-Cetina, Karin and Michael Mulkay (eds) (1983) *Science Observed: Perspectives on the Social Study of Science*. Newbury Park, Calif.: Sage.

Koch, Claus and Dieter Senghaas (eds) (1970) *Texte zur Technokratiediskussion*. Stuttgart: Europäische Verlagsanstalt.

Köhnke, Klaus C. (1986) *Entstehung und Aufstieg des Neukantianismus: die deutsche Universitätsphilosophie zwischen Idealismus und Positivismus*. Frankfurt am Main: Suhrkamp.

König, René (1987) 'Kontinuität oder Unterbrechung: ein neuer Blick auf ein altes Problem', pp. 388–440 in René König, *Soziologie in Deutschland: Begründer, Verächter, Verfechter*. Munich: Hanser.

König, René ([1984] 1987) 'Vom vermeintlichen Ende der deutschen Soziologie vor der Machtergreifung des Nationalsozialismus', pp. 343–387 in René König, *Soziologie in Deutschland. Begründer, Verächter, Verfechter*. Munich: Hanser.

König, René (1979) 'Gesellschaftliches Bewußtsein und Soziologie: eine spekulative Überlegung', pp. 358–370 in Günther Lüschen (ed.), *Deutsche Soziologie seit 1945*. Special issue no. 21, *Kölner Zeitschrift für Soziologie und Sozialpsychologie*. Opladen: West-deutscher Verlag.

König, René ([1956] 1965) 'Masse und Vermassung', pp. 479–493 in René König, *Soziologische Orientierungen: Vorträge und Aufsätze*. Cologne: Kiepenheuer & Witsch.

Kolberg, Jon E. and Gosta Esping-Andersen (1992) 'Welfare states and employment regimes', pp. 3–35 in Jon E. Kolberg (ed.), *Between Work and Citizenship*. Armonk, NY: Sharpe.

Kolberg, Jon E. and Arne Kolstad (1992) 'Unemployment regimes', pp. 171–192 in Jon E. Kolberg (ed.), *Between Work and Citizenship*. Armonk, NY: Sharpe.

Konrád, Gyoergy and Ivan Szelényi (1979) *The Intellectuals on the Road to Class Power: a Sociological Study of the Role of the Intelligentsia in Socialism*. Brighton: Harvester.

Kornhauser, William (1962) *Scientists in Industry: Conflict and Accommodation*. Berkeley: University of California Press.

Krämer, Sybille (1982) *Technik, Gesellschaft und Natur: Versuch über ihren Zusammenhang*. Frankfurt am Main: Campus.

Kreibich, Rolf (1986) *Die Wissenschaftsgesellschaft: von Galilei zur High-Tech Revolution*. Frankfurt am Main: Suhrkamp.

Krohn, Wolfgang und Günter Küppers (1989) *Die Selbstorganisation der Wissenschaft*. Frankfurt am Main: Suhrkamp.

Krohn, Wolfgang and Werner Rammert (1985) 'Technologieentwicklung: Autonomer Prozess und industrielle Strategie', pp. 411–433 in Burkart Lutz (ed.), *Soziologie und gesellschaftliche Entwicklung*. Verhandlungen des 22. Deutschen Soziologentages. Frankfurt am Main: Campus.

Krugman, Paul (1991) *Geography and Trade*. Cambridge, Mass.: MIT Press.

Küng, Emil (1976) *Steuerung und Bremsung des technischen Fortschritts*. Tübingen: J.C.B. Mohr.

Kumar, Krishnan (1989) 'The limits and divisions of industrial capitalism', pp. 16–43 in Richard Scase (ed.), *Industrial Societies: Crisis and Division in Western Capitalism and State Socialism*. London: Unwin Hyman.

Kumar, Krishnan (1978) *Prophecy and Progress: the Sociology of Industrial and Post-industrial Society*. Harmondsworth: Penguin.

Ladd, Everett C., jr (1970) *American Political Parties: Social Change and Political Response*. New York: Norton.

Landes, David (1980) 'The creation of knowledge and technique: today's task and yesterday's experience', *Daedalus* 109:111–120.

Lane, Robert E. (1966) 'The decline of politics and ideology in a knowledgeable society', *American Sociological Review* 31:649–662.

Lapp, Ralph E. (1965) *The New Priesthood: the Scientific Elite and the Uses of Power*. New York: Harper & Row.

Larson, Magali Sarfatti (1990) 'In the matter of experts and professionals, or how impossible it is to leave nothing unsaid', pp. 24–50 in Rolf Torstendahl and Michael Burrage (eds), *The Formation of Professions: Knowledge, State and Strategy*. London: Sage.

Larson, Magali Sarfatti (1984) 'The production of expertise and the constitution of expert authority', pp. 28–80 in Thomas L. Haskell (ed.), *The Authority of Experts*. Bloomington, Ind.: Indiana University Press.

Larson, Magali Sarfatti (1977) *The Rise of Professionalism*. Berkeley: University of California Press.

Lasch, Christopher (1972) 'Toward a theory of post-industrial society', pp. 36–50 in M. Donald Hancock and Gideon Sjoberg (eds), *Politics in the Post-welfare State: Responses to the New Individualism*. New York: Columbia University Press.

Lash, Scott and John Urry (1987) *The End of Organized Capitalism*. Madison, Wis.: University of Wisconsin Press.

Lassow, Ekkhard (1967) 'Problem der Produktivkrafttheorie in der Periode des umfassenden Aufbaus des Sozialismus und der technisch-wissenschaftlichen Revolution', *Deutsche Zeitschrift für Philosophie* 15:373–398.

Layard, Richard and Stephen Nickell (1985) *The Causes of British Unemployment*. London: National Institute of Economic and Social Research.

Layard, Richard, Stephen Nickell and Richard Jackman (1991) *Unemployment: Macroeconomic Performance and the Labour Market*. Oxford: Oxford University Press.

Layton, Edwin T. (1976) 'American ideologies of science and technology', *Technology and Culture* 17:688–701.

Lazega, Emmanual (1992) *Micropolitics of Knowledge. Communication and Indirect Control in Workgroups*. New York: Aldine de Gruyter.

Lazonick, William (1979) 'Industrial relations and technical change: the case of the self-acting mule', *Cambridge Journal of Economics* 3:231–262.

Lederer, Emil ([1931] 1938) *Technical Progress and Unemployment: an Inquiry into the Obstacles of Economic Expansion*. London: P.S. King & Son.

Lenk, Hans (1987) *Zwischen Sozialpsychologie und Sozialphilosophie*. Frankfurt am Main: Suhrkamp.

Leontief, Wassily (1985) 'The choice of technology', *Scientific American* 252:37–45.

Leontief, Wassily (1977) *The Future of the World Economy*. New York: Oxford University Press.

Lerner, Allan W. (1976) *The Politics of Decision-making: Strategy, Cooperation, and Conflict*. Beverly Hills, CA: Sage.

Levy, Marion (1966) *Modernization and the Structure of Societies*. Princeton, NJ: Princeton University Press.

Lieberman, Jethro K. (1970) *The Tyranny of Experts: How Professionals are Closing the Open Society*. New York: Walker.

Lipset, Seymour M. (1981) 'Whatever happened to the proletariat? An historic mission unfulfilled', *Encounter* 56:18–34.

Lipset, Seymour M. (1960) *Political Man: the Social Basis of Politics*. Garden City, NY: Doubleday.

Lipsey, Richard G. (1992) 'Global change and economic policy', pp. 279–299 in Nico Stehr and Richard V. Ericson (eds), *The Culture and Power of Knowledge: Inquiries into Contemporary Societies*. Berlin and New York: de Gruyter.

Lopata, Helena Z. (1976) 'Expertization of everyone and the revolt of the client', *The Sociological Quarterly* 17:435–447.

Lowe, Adolph (1986) 'The specter of technological unemployment', Working Papers: Forschungsgruppe 'Technologischer Wandel und Beschäftigung', Universität Bremen.

Lowe, Adolph (1971) 'Is present-day higher learning "relevant"?', *Social Research* 38:563–580.

Lübbe, Hermann (1987) 'Der kulturelle Geltungsschwund der Wissenschaften', pp. 89–108 in Helmut de Rudder and Heinz Sahner (eds), *Wissenschaft und gesellschaftliche Verantwortung*. Berlin: Arno Pitz.

Luhmann, Niklas (1988) *Die Wirtschaft der Gesellschaft*. Frankfurt am Main: Suhrkamp.

Luhmann, Niklas (1981) 'Gesellschaftsstrukturelle Bedingungen und Folgerungen des naturwissenschaftlich-technischen Fortschritts', pp. 113–134 in Reinhard Löw, Peter Koslowski and Philipp Kreuzer (eds), *Fortschritt ohne Mass?* Munich: Piper.

Lyon, David (1986) 'From "post-industrialism" to "information society": a new social transformation?', *Sociology* 20:577–588.

Lyotard, Jean-François ([1979] 1984) *The Postmodern Condition: a Report on Knowledge.* Minnesota: University of Minnesota Press.

Machlup, Fritz (1984) *The Economics of Information and Human Capital.* Princeton, NJ: Princeton University Press.

Machlup, Fritz (1981) *Knowledge and Knowledge Production.* Princeton, NJ: Princeton University Press.

Machlup, Fritz (1979) 'Uses, value, and benefits of knowledge', *Knowledge* 1:62–81.

Machlup, Fritz (1962) *The Production and Distribution of Knowledge in the United States.* Princeton, NJ: Princeton University Press.

Machlup, Fritz and Trude Kronwinkler (1975) 'Workers who produce knowledge: a steady increase 1900 to 1970', *Weltwirtschaftliches Archiv* 3:752–759.

MacKenzie, Donald and Judy Wajcman (eds) (1985) *The Social Shaping of Technology: how the Refrigerator Got its Hum.* Milton Keynes: Open University Press.

Malinowski, Bronislaw (1955) *Magic, Science and Religion.* Garden City, NY: Doubleday Anchor.

Mannheim, Karl ([1980] 1982) *Structures of Thinking*, edited and introduced by David Kettler, Volker Meja and Nico Stehr. London: Routledge & Kegan Paul.

Mannheim, Karl ([1935] 1940) *Man and Society in an Age of Reconstruction: Studies in Modern Social Structure.* London: Routledge & Kegan Paul.

Mannheim, Karl ([1929] 1936) *Ideology and Utopia: an Introduction to the Sociology of Knowledge.* London: Kegan Paul.

Marcuse, Herbert (1964) *One-dimensional Man: Studies in the Ideology of Advanced Industrial Society.* Boston: Beacon Press.

Marcuse, Herbert (1941) 'Some social implications of modern technology', *Studies in Philosophy and Social Science* 9:414–439.

Marshall, Thomas H. (1939) 'The recent history of professionalization in relation to social structure and social policy', *Canadian Journal of Economics and Political Science* 5:128–155.

Marx, Karl ([1939–1941] 1973) *Grundrisse: Introduction to the Critique of Political Economy.* New York: Vintage Books.

Marx, Karl ([1867] 1967) *Capital*, vol. 1. New York: International Publishers.

Marx, Karl and Friedrich Engels ([1848] 1971) *Birth of the Communist Manifesto, with Full Text of the Manifesto.* New York: International Publishers.

Marx, Karl and Friedrich Engels ([1932] 1960) *Die deutsche Ideologie.* Berlin: Dietz.

Marx, Karl and Friedrich Engels ([1848] 1954) *Manifest der kommunistischen Partei.* Berlin: Dietz.

McDermott, John (1969) 'Technology: the opiate of the intellectuals', *New York Review of Books* 13(2):25–35.

McKinley, John B. (1982) 'Toward the proletarianization of physicians', pp. 37–62 in Charles Derber (ed.), *Professionals as Workers: Mental Labor in Advanced Capitalism.* Boston: Hall.

Meadows, Donella H., Dennis L. Meadows, Jørgen Randers and William W. Behrens III (1972) *The Limits to Growth.* New York: Universe Books.

Meja, Volker and Nico Stehr (1992) 'Social scientific and epistemological discourse: the problem of relativism', pp. 1–13 in Diederick Raven, Lieteke van Vucht Tijssen and Jan de Wolf (eds), *Cognitive Relativism and Social Science.* New Brunswick, NJ: Transaction Books.

Meja, Volker and Nico Stehr (1988) 'Social science, epistemology, and the problem of relativism', *Social Epistemology* 2:263–271.

Merton, Robert K. (1975) 'The uses of institutionalized altruism', pp. 105–113 in *Seminar Reports: Program of General and Continuing Education in the Humanities.* New York: Columbia University.

Merton, Robert K. (1973) *The Sociology of Science: Theoretical and Empirical Investigations*. Chicago: University of Chicago Press.

Merton, Robert K. ([1942] 1973) 'The normative structure of science', pp. 267–278 in Robert K. Merton, *The Sociology of Science: Theoretical and Empirical Investigations*. Chicago: University of Chicago Press.

Merton, Robert K. ([1945] 1957) 'Role of the intellectual in public bureaucracy', pp. 207–224 in Robert K. Merton, *Social Theory and Social Structure*, rev. edn. New York: Free Press.

Merton, Robert K. (1947) 'The machine, the worker and the engineer', *Science* 105:79–84.

Merton, Robert K. (1936) 'The unanticipated consequences of purposive social action', *American Sociological Review* 1:894–904.

Meyer, Alfred G. (1970) 'Theories of convergence', pp. 313–341 in Chalmers Johnson (ed.), *Change in Communist Systems*. Stanford: Stanford University Press.

Miller, Jon D. (1983) *The American People and Science Policy*. New York: Pergamon.

Miller, S. Michael (1975) 'Notes on neo-capitalism', *Theory and Society* 2:1–35.

Mills, C. Wright ([1955] 1967) 'On knowledge and power', pp. 599–613 in Irving L. Horowitz (ed.), *Power, Politics and People: the Collected Essays of C. Wright Mills*. New York: Oxford University Press.

Mills, C. Wright (1958) *The Causes of World War Three*. New York: Simon & Schuster.

Mingione, Enzo (1991) *Fragmented Societies: a Sociology of Economic Life beyond the Market Paradigm*. Oxford: Basil Blackwell.

Mises, Ludwig von (1922) *Die Gemeinwirtschaft: Untersuchungen über den Sozialismus*. Jena: Gustav Fischer.

Montgomery, David (1979) *Worker's Control in America: Studies in the History of Work, Technology and Labour Struggles*. Cambridge: Cambridge University Press.

Morgenthau, Hans (1970) 'Reflections on the end of the republic', *New York Review of Books* 15:38–41.

Mukerji, Chandra (1989) *A Fragile Power: Scientists and the State*. Princeton, NJ: Princeton University Press.

Mulkay, Michael (1979) *Science and the Sociology of Knowledge*. London: Allen & Unwin.

Mumford, Lewis (1970) *The Myth of the Machine: the Pentagon of Power*. New York: Harcourt Brace Jovanovich.

Mumford, Lewis (1962) *Technics and Civilization*. New York: Harcourt Brace Jovanovich.

Myles, John (1990) 'States, labor markets, and life cycles', pp. 271–298 in Roger Friedland and A.F. Robertson (eds), *Beyond the Marketplace: Rethinking Economy and Society*. New York: Aldine de Gruyter.

Myles, John and Gail Fawcett (1990) *Job Skills and the Service Economy*. Working Paper No. 4. Ottawa: Economic Council of Canada.

Narr, Wolf-Dieter ([1979] 1985) 'Toward a society of conditioned reflexes', pp. 31–66 in Jürgen Habermas (ed.), *Observations on 'The Spiritual Situation of the Age'*. Cambridge, Mass: MIT Press.

Nelkin, Dorothy (1975) 'The political impact of technical expertise', *Social Studies of Science* 5:35–54.

Nelson, Richard R. (1981) 'Research on productivity growth and productivity differentials: dead ends and new departures', *Journal of Economic Literature* 19:1029–1064.

Nelson, Richard R. and Sidney G. Winter (1982) *An Evolutionary Theory of Economic Change*. Cambridge, Mass: Harvard University Press.

Nettl, J. Peter and Roland Robertson (1968) *International Systems and the Modernization of Societies: the Formation of National Goals and Attitudes*. New York: Basic Books.

Neurath, Otto (1944) *Foundations of the Social Sciences*. Chicago: University of Chicago Press.

Newman, Rhona and Julian Newman (1985) 'Information work: the new divorce?', *British Journal of Sociology* 34:497–515.

Nicol, Lionel (1985) 'Communications technology: economic and spatial impacts', pp. 191–209 in Manuel Castells (ed.), *High Technology, Space and Society*. Beverly Hills, Calif.: Sage.

Niethammer, Lutz ([1989] 1992) *Posthistory: Has History Come to an End?* London: Verso.
Nietzsche, Friedrich ([1878] 1984) *Human, All-Too-Human*. Lincoln: University of Nebraska Press.
Noble, David F. (1984) *Forces of Production: a Social History of Industrial Automation*. New York: Knopf.
Nolte, Ernst (1993) 'Die Fragilität des Triumphs: zur Lage des liberalen Systems nach der neuen Weltordnung', *Frankfurter Allgemeine Zeitung* (151), July 3.
Nora, Simon and Alain Minc (1980) *The Computerisation of Society*. Cambridge, Mass.: MIT Press.
Nowotny, Helga (1979) *Kernenergie: Gefahr oder Notwendigkeit? Anatomie eines Konflikts*. Frankfurt am Main: Suhrkamp.
Offe, Claus (1986) 'Die Utopie der Null-Option: Modernität und Modernisierung als politische Gütekriterien', pp. 97–117 in Johannes Berger (ed.), *Die Moderne: Kontinuitäten und Zäsuren*. Special issue no. 4. *Soziale Welt*. Göttingen: Schwartz & Co.
Offe, Claus (1984) *Arbeitsgesellschaft: Strukturprobleme und Zukunftsperspektiven*. Frankfurt am Main: Campus Verlag.
Offe, Claus ([1979] 1984) 'Ungovernability: on the renaissance of conservative theories of crisis', pp. 67–88 in Jürgen Habermas (ed.), *Observations on 'The Spiritual Situation of the Age'*. Cambridge, Mass.: MIT Press.
Oppenheimer, Martin (1973) 'The proletarianization of the professional', pp. 213–227 in Paul Halmos (ed.), *Professionalization and Social Change*. Sociological Review Monograph 20. Keele: University of Keele.
Organization for Economic Co-operation and Development (1992a) *Economic Outlook: Historical Statistics, 1960–1990*. Paris: OECD.
Organization for Economic Co-operation and Development (1992b) *Employment Outlook*. Paris: OECD.
Organization for Economic Co-operation and Development (1992c) *National Accounts: Detailed Tables, 1978–1990*, vol. 2. Paris: OECD.
Organization for Economic Co-operation and Development (1992d) *Quarterly Labour Force Statistics*, no. 3. Paris: OECD.
Organization for Economic Co-Operation and Development (1992e) *Structural Change and Industrial Performance: a Seven Country Growth Decomposition Study*. Paris: OECD.
Organization for Economic Co-operation and Development (1991a) *Employment Outlook*. Paris: OECD.
Organization for Economic Co-operation and Development (1991b) *Labour Force Statistics, 1969–1989*. Paris: OECD.
Organization for Economic Co-operation and Development (1990) *Main Economic Indicators: Historical Statistics, 1969–1988*. Paris: OECD.
Organization for Economic Co-operation and Development (1987) *Historical Statistics 1960–1985*. Paris: OECD.
Organization for Economic Co-operation and Development (1985) *Labour Force Statistics, 1963–1983*. Paris: OECD.
Pacey, Arnold (1983) *The Culture of Technology*. Cambridge, Mass.: MIT Press.
Parkin, Frank (1979) *Marxism and Class Theory: a Bourgeois Critique*. London: Tavistock.
Parsons, Talcott (1970) 'The impact of technology on culture and emerging new modes of behavior', *International Social Science Journal* 22:607–627.
Parsons, Talcott (1968) 'Professions', pp. 536–547 in David Sills (ed.), *International Encyclopedia of the Social Sciences*, vol. 12. New York: Macmillan.
Parsons, Talcott (1939) 'The professions and social structure', *Social Forces* 17:457–467.
Parsons, Talcott (1937) *The Structure of Social Action*. New York: McGraw-Hill.
Penty, Arthur J. (1917) *Old World for New: a Study of the Post-industrial State*. London: Allen & Unwin.
Perl, Martin L. (1971) 'The scientific advisory system: some observations', *Science* 173:1211–1215.

Perlmutter, Howard V. (1991) 'On the rocky road to the first global civilization', *Human Relations* 44:897–920.

Perrole, Judith A. (1986) 'Intellectual assembly lines: the rationalization of managerial, professional, and technical work', *Computers and the Social Sciences* 2:111–121.

Perrow, Charles (1984) *Normal Accidents*. New York: Basic Books.

Pfaffenberger, Bryan (1992) 'Technological dramas', *Science, Technology, and Human Values* 17:282–312.

Pinch, Trevor and Wiebe J. Bijker (1987) 'The social construction of facts and artifacts, or how the sociology of science and technology might aid each other', pp. 17–49 in Wiebe E. Bijker, Thomas P. Hughes and Trevor J. Pinch (eds), *The Social Construction of Technological Systems: New Directions in the Sociology and History of Technology*. Cambridge, Mass.: MIT Press.

Piore, Michael J. and Charles F. Sabel (1984) *The Second Industrial Divide*. New York: Basic Books.

Polanyi, Michael (1962) 'The republic of science, its political and economic theory', unpublished lecture at Roosevelt University, Chicago.

Popitz, Heinrich (1986) *Phänomene der Macht: Autorität-Herrschaft-Gewalt-Technik*. Tübingen: J.C.B. Mohr.

Popper, Karl ([1961] 1992) 'Emancipation through knowledge', pp. 137–150 in Karl Popper, *In Search of a Better World: Lectures and Essays from Thirty Years*. London: Routledge.

Price, Derek J. de Solla (1963) *Big Science, Little Science*. New York: Columbia University Press.

Price, Derek J. de Solla (1961) *Science since Babylon*. New Haven: Yale University Press.

Price, Don K. (1965) *The Scientific Estate*. New York: Oxford University Press.

Radder, Hans (1986) 'Experiment, technology and the intrinsic connection between knowledge and power', *Social Studies of Science* 16:663–683.

Rahman, Syed S. and Surendra Gera (1990) *Long-term Unemployment: the Canadian Experience*. Working Paper No. 12. Ottawa: Economic Council of Canada.

Ravetz, Jerome R. (1987) 'Usable knowledge, usable ignorance', *Knowledge* 9:87–116.

Richta, Radovan (1977) 'The scientific and technological revolution and the prospects of social development', pp. 25–72 in Ralf Dahrendorf (ed.), *Scientific-Technological Revolution*. London: Sage.

Richta, Radovan et al. (1969) *Civilization at the Crossroads: Social and Human Implications of the Scientific and Technological Revolution*. White Plains, NY: International Arts and Sciences Press.

Riesman, David ([1958] 1964) 'Leisure and work in postindustrial society', pp. 162–183 in David Riesman, *Abundance for What? and Other Essays*. Garden City, NY: Doubleday.

Riesman, David (1953/1954) 'Some relationships between technical progress and social progress', *Explorations in Entrepreneurial History* 6:131–145.

Riesman, David (1950) *The Lonely Crowd: a Study of the Changing American Character*. New Haven: Yale University Press.

Roach, Stephen S. (1991) 'Pitfalls on the "new" assembly line: can services learn from manufacturing?', pp. 119–129 in Organization for Economic Co-operation and Development, *Technology and Productivity: the Challenge for Economic Policy*. Paris: OECD.

Robertson, Roland (1990) 'Mapping the global condition: globalization as the central concept', pp. 15–30 in Mike Featherstone (ed.), *Global Culture. Nationalism, Globalization and Modernity*. London: Sage.

Robins, Kevin and Frank Webster (1989) *The Technical Fix: Education, Computer and Industry*. New York: St Martin's Press.

Rose, Günther (1971) *'Industriegesellschaft' und Konvergenztheorie. Genesis, Strukturen, Funktionen*. Berlin: VEB Deutscher Verlag der Wissenschaften.

Rose, Richard (1979) 'Pervasive problems of governing: an analytic framework', pp. 29–54 in Joachim Matthes (ed.), *Sozialer Wandel in Westeuropa*. Verhandlungen des 19. Deutschen Soziologentages, Berlin 1979. Frankfurt: Campus.

Rosenberg, Nathan (1974) 'Science, invention and economic growth', *The Economic Journal* 84:90–108.

Rouse, Joseph (1987) *Knowledge and Power: Toward a Political Philosophy of Science.* Ithaca, NY: Cornell University Press.

Rubin, Michael R. and Mary Taylor Huber (1986) *The Knowledge Industry in the United States, 1960–1980.* Princeton, NJ: Princeton University Press.

Rueschemeyer, Dietrich (1986) *Power and the Division of Labor.* Stanford: Stanford University Press.

Rueschemeyer, Dietrich, Evelyne Huber Stephens and John D. Stephens (1992) *Capitalist Development and Democracy.* Chicago: University of Chicago Press.

Sabel, Charles F. (1991) 'Moebius-strip organizations and open labor markets: some consequences of the reintegration of conception and execution in a volatile economy', pp. 23–54 in Pierre Bourdieu and James S. Coleman (eds), *Social Theory for a Changing Society.* Boulder, Colorado: Westview Press.

Salomon, Jean-Jacques (1973) *Science and Politics.* Cambridge: Cambridge University Press.

Salz, Arthur (1932) 'Die Kontrolle des technischen Fortschritts: Technischer Fortschritt und Arbeitslosigkeit', *Der Deutsche Volkswirt* 6:1607–1609.

Sartori, Giovanni (1971) 'Technological forecasting and politics', *Survey* 16:60–68.

Scharpf, Fritz W. (1988) 'Strukturen der post-industriellen Gesellschaft oder: Verschwindet die Massenarbeitslosigkeit in der Dienstleistungs- und Informations-Ökonomie?', *Soziale Welt* 38:3–24.

Scheler, Max ([1926] 1980) *Problems of a Sociology of Knowledge.* London: Routledge & Kegan Paul.

Scheler, Max ([1925] 1960) 'The forms of knowledge and culture', pp. 13–49 in Max Scheler, *Philosophical Perspectives.* Boston: Beacon Press.

Schelling, Thomas C. (1990) 'Global environmental forces', *Technological Forecasting and Social Change* 38:257–264.

Schelsky, Helmut (1975) *Die Arbeit tun die anderen: Klassenkampf und Priesterherrschaft der Intellektuellen*, 2nd edn. Opladen: Westdeutscher Verlag.

Schelsky, Helmut ([1961] 1965) 'Der Mensch in der wissenschaftlichen Zivilisation', pp. 439–480 in Helmut Schelsky, *Auf der Suche nach der Wirklichkeit: Gesammelte Aufsätze.* Düsseldorf: Diederichs.

Schelsky, Helmut (1961) *Der Mensch in der wissenschaftlichen Zivilisation.* Cologne/Opladen: Westdeutscher Verlag.

Schelsky, Helmut (1956) 'Gesellschaftlicher Wandel', *Offene Welt* 41.

Schelsky, Helmut (1954) 'Zukunftsaspekte der industriellen Gesellschaft', *Merkur* 8:13–28.

Schieder, Theodor (1977) 'Einmaligkeit oder Wiederkehr: Historische Dimensionen der heutigen Krise', pp. 22–42 in Wilhelm Hennis, Peter Graf Kielmansegg and Ulrich Matz (eds), *Regierbarkeit: Studien zu ihrer Problematisierung*, vol. 1. Stuttgart: Klett-Cotta.

Schiller, Dan (1993) 'Capitalism, information, and uneven development', pp. 386–406 in Stanley A. Deetz (ed.), *Communication Yearbook*, vol. 16. Newbury Park, CA: Sage.

Schiller, Herbert I. (1981) *Who Knows: Information in the Age of the Fortune 500.* Norwood, NJ: Ablex.

Schimank, Uwe (1985) 'Der mangelnde Akteurbezug systemtheoretischer Erklärungen gesellschaftlicher Differenzierung – ein Diskussionsvorschlag', *Zeitschrift für Soziologie* 14:421–437.

Schmookler, Jakob (1966) *Invention and Economic Growth.* Cambridge, Mass.: Harvard University Press.

Schott, Thomas (1993) 'World science: globalization of institutions and participation', *Science, Technology, Human Values* 18:196–208.

Schott, Thomas (1988) 'International influence in science: beyond center and periphery', *Social Science Research* 17:219–238.

Schroyer, Trent (1974) 'Review of Daniel Bell, *The Coming of Post-industrial Society*', *Telos* 19:162–176.

Schumpeter, Joseph A. ([1942] 1950) *Capitalism, Socialism and Democracy*. New York: Harper Torchbooks.

Shearing, Clifford and Richard V. Ericson (1991) 'Culture as figurative action', *British Journal of Sociology* 42:481–506.

Shils, Edward (1968) 'Intellectuals', pp. 399–415 in Edward Shils (ed.), *International Encyclopedia of the Social Sciences*, vol. 7. New York: Macmillan.

Sibley, Mulford Q. (1973) 'Utopian thought and technology', *American Journal of Political Science* 17:255–281.

Simmel, Georg ([1908] 1992) *Soziologie: Untersuchungen über die Formen der Vergesellschaftung*. Gesamtausgabe Band 11. Frankfurt am Main: Suhrkamp.

Simmel, Georg ([1890] 1989) 'Über sociale Differenzierung', pp. 109–295 in Georg Simmel, *Aufsätze 1987–1980: Über sociale Differenzierung: die Probleme der Geschichtsphilosophie (1892)*. Frankfurt am Main: Suhrkamp.

Simmel, Georg ([1909] 1984) 'Die Zukunft unserer Kultur', pp. 92–93 in Georg Simmel, *Das Individuum und die Freiheit: Essais*. Berlin: Wagenbach.

Simmel, Georg ([1907] 1978) *The Philosophy of Money*. London: Routledge & Kegan Paul.

Simmel, Georg ([1919] 1968) *The Conflict in Modern Culture and Other Essays*. Trans. K. Peter Etzkorn. New York: Teachers College Press.

Simmel Georg ([1911] 1968) 'On the concept and the tragedy of culture', pp. 27–46 in Georg Simmel, *The Conflict in Modern Culture and Other Essays*. New York: Teachers College Press.

Simonis, Udo E. (1989) 'Ecological modernization of industrial society: three strategic elements', *International Social Science Journal* 41:347–361.

Singelmann, Joachim (1978) *From Agriculture to Services: the Transformation of Industrial Employment*. Beverly Hills, Calif.: Sage.

Sirianni, Carmen (1991) 'The self-management of time in postindustrial society', pp. 231–274 in Karl Hinrichs, William Roche and Carmen Sirianni (eds), *Working Time in Transition: the Political Economy of Working Hours in Industrial Nations*. Philadelphia: Temple University Press.

Skolnikoff, Eugene B. (1976) 'The governability of complexity', pp. 75–88 in Chester L. Cooper (ed.), *Growth in America*. Westport, Conn.: Woodrow Wilson International Center for Scholars.

Smart, Barry (1992) *Modern Conditions, Postmodern Controversies*. London: Routledge.

Smith, Anthony (1986) 'Technology, identity, and the information machine', *Daedalus* 115:155–169.

Smith, Roger and Brian Wynne (eds) (1989) *Expert Evidence: Interpreting Science in the Law*. London: Routledge.

So, Alvin Y. (1990) *Social Change and Development: Modernization, Dependency, and World-System Theories*. Newbury Park, Calif.: Sage.

Sohn-Rethel, Alfred (1978) *Intellectual and Manual Labour: A Critique of Epistemology*. Atlantic Highlands, NJ: Humanities Press.

Sola Pool, Ithiel de (1990) *Technologies without Boundaries: on Telecommunications in a Global Age*. Cambridge, Mass.: Harvard University Press.

Solow, Robert (1957) 'Technical change and the aggregate production function', *Review of Economics and Statistics* 39:312–320.

Spittler, Gerd (1980) 'Abstraktes Wissen als Herrschaftsbasis: zur Entstehungsgeschichte bürokratischer Herrschaft im Bauernstaat Preussen', *Kölner Zeitschrift für Soziologie und Sozialpsychologie* 32:574–604.

Stark, David (1980) 'Class struggle and the transformation of the labour process', *Theory and Society* 9:89–130.

Stearns, Peter N. (1974) 'Comment on Daniel Bell's *The Coming of Post-industrial Society*', *Transaction* 11:10–22.

Stehr, Nico (1992) *Practical Knowledge: Applying the Social Sciences*. London: Sage.

Stehr, Nico (1978) 'Man and the environment: a general perspective', *Archives for Philosophy of Law and Social Philosophy* 74:1–17.

Stehr, Nico and Volker Meja (1990) 'Relativism and the sociology of knowledge', pp. 285–306 in Volker Meja and Nico Stehr (eds), *Knowledge and Politics: the Sociology of Knowledge Dispute*. London and New York: Routledge.

Stehr, Nico and Volker Meja (1984a) 'The development of the sociology of knowledge', pp. 1–18 in Nico Stehr and Volker Meja (eds), *Society and Knowledge: Contemporary Perspectives on the Sociology of Knowledge*. New Brunswick, NJ: Transaction Books.

Stehr, Nico and Volker Meja (eds) (1984b) *Society and Knowledge: Contemporary Perspectives on the Sociology of Knowledge*. New Brunswick, NJ: Transaction Books.

Stich, Stephen P. and Richard E. Nisbett (1984) 'Expertise, justification, and the psychology of inductive reasoning', pp. 226–241 in Thomas L. Haskell (ed.), *The Authority of Experts*. Bloomington, Ind.: Indiana University Press.

Stigler, George J. (1961) 'The economics of information', *Journal of Political Economy* 69:213–225.

Stigler, George J. (1947) *Trends in Output and Employment*. New York: National Bureau of Economic Research.

Stoljarow, Vitali (1963) 'Die Entwicklung der Wissenschaft zur unmittelbaren Produktivkraft und die materialistische Geschichtsauffassung', *Deutsche Zeitschrift für Philosophie* 11:826–837.

Storper, Michael and Richard Walker (1983) 'The theory of labour and the theory of location', *International Journal of Urban and Regional Research* 7:1–41.

Swedberg, Richard (1987) 'Economic sociology: past and present', *Current Sociology* 35:1–221.

Tawney, Richard H. (1920) *The Acquisitive Society*. New York: Harcourt Brace.

Tenbruck, Friedrich H. (1977) 'Grenzen der staatlichen Planung', pp. 134–149 in Wilhelm Hennis, Peter Graf Kielmansegg and Ulrich Matz (eds), *Regierbarkeit: Studien zu ihrer Problematisierung*, vol. 1. Stuttgart: Klett-Cotta.

Therborn, Göran (1986) *Why some People are More Unemployed than Others: the Strange Paradox of Growth and Unemployment*. London: Verso.

Thompson, Victor A. (1969) *Bureaucracy and Innovation*. Alabama: University of Alabama Press.

Tilly, Charles (1984) *Big Structures, Large Processes, Huge Comparisons*. New York: Russell Sage Foundation.

Tilton, Timothy A. (1973) 'The next stage of history? A discussion of Daniel Bell's *The Coming of Post-Industrial Society*', *Social Research* 40:728–745.

Tinbergen, Jan (1961) 'Do communist and free economics show a converging pattern?', *Soviet Studies* 12:333–341.

Tondl, Ladislav ([1968] 1972) 'Stellung und Aufgabe der Wissenschaft in der wissenschaftlich-technischen Revolution', pp. 120–145 in Radovan Richta et al., *Technischer Fortschritt und die industrielle Gesellschaft*. Frankfurt am Main: Makol Verlag.

Touraine, Alain ([1984] 1988) *Return of the Actor: Social Theory in Postindustrial Society*. Minneapolis: University of Minnesota Press.

Touraine, Alain (1986) 'Krise und Wandel des sozialen Denkens', pp. 15–39 in Johannes Berger (ed.), *Die Moderne: Kontinuitäten und Zäsuren*. Special issue no. 4. *Soziale Welt*. Göttingen: Schwartz & Co.

Touraine, Alain (1977) 'Science, intellectuals and politics', pp. 109–130 in Ralf Dahrendorf (ed.), *Scientific-Technological Revolution*. London: Sage.

Touraine, Alain ([1969] 1971) *Post-industrial Society: Tomorrow's Social History*. New York: Random House.

Turner, Bryan S. (ed.) (1990) *Theories of Modernity and Postmodernity*. London: Sage.

Ulrich, Peter (1987) *Transformation der ökonomischen Vernunft: Fortschrittsperspektiven der modernen Industriegesellschaft*. Berne and Stuttgart: Paul Haupt.

United Nations (1992) *Economic Survey of Europe in 1991–1992*. New York: United Nations Publications.

United Nations (1991) *Economic Survey of Europe in 1990–1991*. New York: United Nations Publications.

United Nations Educational, Scientific and Cultural Organization (1991) *Statistical Yearbook*. Paris: Unesco.
United Nations Educational, Scientific and Cultural Organization (1990) *Statistical Yearbook*. Paris: Unesco.
United Nations Educational, Scientific and Cultural Organization (1970) *Statistical Yearbook*. Paris: Unesco.
United States Department of Labor (1984) *Technological Change and its Labor Impact in Four Industries*. Washington, DC: US Department of Labor.
United States National Commission on Technology, Automation and Economic Progress (1966) *Technology and the American Economy*. Washington, DC: United States Government Printing Office.
Vaitsos, Constantine V. (1989) 'Radical technological changes and the new "order" in the world-economy', *Review* 12:157–189.
van den Belt, Henk and Arie Rip (1987) 'The Nelson-Winter-Dosi model and synthetic dye chemistry', pp. 135–158 in Wiebe E. Bijker, Thomas P. Hughes and Trevor J. Pinch (eds), *The Social Construction of Technological Systems: New Directions in the Sociology and History of Technology*. Cambridge, Mass.: MIT Press.
van den Daele, Wolfgang and Wolfgang Krohn (1982) 'Anmerkungen zur Legitimität der Naturwissenschaften', pp. 416–429 in Klaus Michael Meyer-Abich (ed.), *Physik, Philosophie und Politik: Festschrift für Carl Friedrich von Weizsäcker*. Munich: Hanser.
Vidich, Arthur J. and Stanford M. Lyman (1985) *American Sociology: Worldly Rejections of Religion and their Directions*. New Haven: Yale University Press.
Vogel, Ezra (1980) *Japan as Number One*. New York: Harper.
Walker, Richard A. (1985) 'Is there a service economy: the changing capitalist division of labor', *Science and Society* 69:42–83.
Walsh, Kenneth (1987) *Long-term Unemployment: an International Perspective*. London: Macmillan.
Weber, Max ([1920] 1978) *Gesammelte Aufsätze zur Religionssoziologie*, vol. 1. Tübingen: J.C.B. Mohr.
Weber, Max ([1922] 1968) *Economy and Society*. New York: Bedminster Press.
Weber, Max ([1922] 1964) *The Theory of Social and Economic Organization*, edited by Talcott Parsons. New York: Free Press.
Weber, Max ([1922] 1948) 'Science as a vocation', pp. 129–156 in Hans H. Gerth and C. Wright Mills (eds), *From Max Weber*. London: Routledge & Kegan Paul.
Weber, Max ([1921] 1948) 'Politics as a vocation', pp. 77–128 in Hans H. Gerth and C. Wright Mills (eds), *From Max Weber*. London: Routledge & Kegan Paul.
Webster, Frank and Kevin Robins (1986) *Information Technology: a Luddite Analysis*. Norwood, NJ: Ablex.
Weingart, Peter (1979) 'Das 'Harrisburg-Syndrom oder die De-Professionalisierung der Experten', pp. 9–17 in Helga Nowotny (ed.), *Kernenergie: Gefahr oder Notwendigkeit?* Frankfurt am Main: Suhrkamp.
White, Stephen K. (1991) *Political Theory and Postmodernism*. Cambridge: Cambridge University Press.
Whitehead, Alfred North (1926) *Science and the Modern World*. Lowell Lectures, 1925. Cambridge: Cambridge University Press.
Whitley, Richard (1988) 'The transformation of expertise by new knowledge: contingencies and limits to skill scientification', *Social Science Information* 27:391–420.
Wiio, Osmo A. (1985) 'The information society: is it really like this?' *Intermedia* 13:12–14.
Wilensky, Harold L. (1971) *Organizational Intelligence: Knowledge and Policy in Government and Industry*. New York: Basic Books.
Wilensky, Harold L. (1964) 'The professionalization of everyone', *American Journal of Sociology* 70:137–158.
Wilensky, Harold L. (1956) *Intellectuals in Labor Unions: Organizational Pressures on Professional Roles*. Glencoe, Ill.: Free Press.
Wiles, Peter (1971) 'A comment on Bell', *Survey* 16:37–43.

Willis, Evan (1983) *Medical Dominance: the Division of Labour in Australian Health Care*. London: Allen & Unwin.

Winner, Langdon (1980) 'Do artefacts have politics?', *Daedalus* 109:121–133.

Wolf, Rainer (1988) '"Herrschaft kraft Wissen" in der Risikogesellschaft', *Soziale Welt* 39:164–187.

Wolfe, Alan (ed.) (1991) *America at Century's End*. Berkeley, Calif.: University of California Press.

Wolff, Edward N. and William J. Baumol (1989) 'Sources of postwar growth of information acitivity in the United States', pp. 17–46 in Lars Osberg, Edward N. Wolff and William J. Baumol, *The Information Economy: the Implications of Unbalanced Growth*. Halifax: The Institute for Research on Public Policy.

Wolkow, G.N. (1969) 'Der Wandel in der sozialen Orientierung der Wissenschaft', *Sowjetwissenschaft* 7:709–720.

World Bank (1992) *World Development Report 1992: Development and the Environment*. New York: Oxford University Press.

Wuthnow, Robert and Wesley Shrum (1983) 'Knowledge workers as a "new class": structural and ideological convergences among professional-technical workers and managers', *Work and Occupations* 10:471–487.

Wynne, Brian (1988) 'Unruly technology: practical rules, impractical discourse and public understanding', *Social Studies of Science* 18:147–167.

Yuchtman-Yaar, Ephraim (1987) 'Economic culture in post-industrial society: orientation toward growth, work and technology', *International Sociology* 2:77–101.

Zghal, Abdelkader (1973) 'The reactivation of tradition in a post-traditional society', *Daedalus* 102:225–237.

Znaniecki, Florian (1940) *The Social Role of the Man of Knowledge*. New York: Columbia University Press.

Zuckerman, Harriet (1988) 'The sociology of science', pp. 511–574 in Neil J. Smelser (ed.), *Handbook of Sociology*. Newbury Park, Calif.: Sage.

zur Nedden, F. (1930) 'Technischer Fortschritt und Weltwirtschaftskrise', *Die Hilfe* 36:899–903.

Author Index

Subject Index